Sharia Tribunals, Rabbinical Courts, and Christian Panels

Sharia Tribunals, Rabbinical Courts, and Christian Panels

Religious Arbitration in America and the West

Michael J. Broyde

OXFORD
UNIVERSITY PRESS

OXFORD
UNIVERSITY PRESS

Oxford University Press is a department of the University of Oxford. It furthers the University's objective of excellence in research, scholarship, and education by publishing worldwide. Oxford is a registered trademark of Oxford University Press in the UK and certain other countries.

Published in the United States of America by Oxford University Press
198 Madison Avenue, New York, NY 10016, United States of America.

Library of Congress Cataloging-in-Publication Data

Names: Broyde, Michael J., author.
Title: Sharia tribunals, rabbinical courts, and christian panels : religious arbitration in America and the West / Michael J. Broyde.
Description: New York : Oxford University Press, 2017. | Includes bibliographical references and index.
Identifiers: LCCN 2016055690 | ISBN 9780190640286 ((hardback) : alk. paper)
Subjects: LCSH: Ecclesiastical courts—United States. | Dispute resolution (Law)—United States. | Church and state—United States. | Islamic courts—United States. | Rabbinical courts—United States.
Classification: LCC KF4868.R43 B76 2017 | DDC 347/.09—dc23
LC record available at https://lccn.loc.gov/2016055690

Note to Readers

This publication is designed to provide accurate and authoritative information in regard to the subject matter covered. It is based upon sources believed to be accurate and reliable and is intended to be current as of the time it was written. It is sold with the understanding that the publisher is not engaged in rendering legal, accounting, or other professional services. If legal advice or other expert assistance is required, the services of a competent professional person should be sought. Also, to confirm that the information has not been affected or changed by recent developments, traditional legal research techniques should be used, including checking primary sources where appropriate.

(Based on the Declaration of Principles jointly adopted by a Committee of the American Bar Association and a Committee of Publishers and Associations.)

This book is dedicated to those who offered their support
when I needed it most.

Family, colleagues, friends
and even a few people who were strangers to me until my time of need.
They are my true community.

Thank you all.

CONTENTS

PREFACE: WHY A BOOK ABOUT RELIGIOUS ARBITRATION

This book is being written to explain the rise in religious arbitration in America.

This rise is a result of three phenomena that are jointly changing aspects of American society. The first—not the focus of this book, but touched on many times in a variety of ways—is the rise in arbitration generally. Increasingly, companies and individuals are agreeing to leave the court system and its laws and opting for private resolution of a variety of disputes. Second, some important religious communities are feeling more and more that they are at the margins of American law, and are seeking to opt-out where possible from vast amounts of civil law, particularly family law. A third phenomenon is now occurring because of the first two—almost otherwise unrelated—trends: many religious communities are forming arbitration tribunals to resolve disputes within their communities. This work explores the rise of such tribunals.

Although most of this work is theoretical in nature, I was not originally a theoretician of this field. I served as the director and a member of a Jewish court—the Beth Din of America—for many years, hearing countless matters as a rabbinical arbitrator. I saw the many ways in which religious arbitration works within the traditional Jewish community, sometimes complementing secular state law, sometimes conflicting with it, and sometimes dealing with issues in an entirely oblique and independent way. Eventually, I developed some theories about the relationship between civil law and religious law and the importance of arbitration law, which I began to share.

Over the last five years, two factors have dramatically renewed interest in this field. The first is renewed interest in the question of whether expanded arbitration law is generally good in areas as diverse as class actions or securities law, with both family law and religious law widely discussed as well.[1] Many people are discussing the values and virtues of allowing members of secular societies and subjects of secular legal systems to choose both different forums and different legal systems to resolve their civil disputes. Equally important, the rise of Islamic law courts—both perceived and real—within the United States has generated much discussion over whether religious arbitration in particular is a good idea, and even if it is a good idea in the abstract; whether it is a good one in practice, given the ways in which religions will use it; and how it will or should be implemented.

This book explores the rise of private arbitration in religious and other values-oriented communities, and argues that secular societies should use secular legal frameworks to facilitate, enforce—and also regulate—religious arbitration. In doing so, it covers the history of religious arbitration, the kinds of faith-based dispute resolution models currently in use, how the law should look at them, and what the role of religious arbitration in the United States should be.

This book first explains why religious communities and individuals are increasingly turning to private, faith-based dispute resolution rather than traditional courts in order to resolve litigious disputes over commercial, property, familial, consumer, and other non-religious matters. Next, it moves on to explain how it is that American law came to permit litigants to opt-out of secular law and instead choose to resolve their disputes through faith-based arbitration, which embraces norms and values that are quite different from those expressed through ordinary American law and policy. Given the law's allowance of religious arbitration, this book turns to consider the limits that American law imposes on all forms of arbitration in order to ensure that peoples' basic rights and fundamental interests are protected in the context of private dispute resolution processes. Finally, this book turns to the important policy question of whether U.S. law and policy should permit religious individuals and communities to avoid the standards of generally applicable state and federal laws by facilitating and enforcing private faith-based arbitration. This work believes that the answer to this question is yes. Although religious dispute resolution does pose some risks and challenges, rigorous application of existing statutory limitations on private arbitration to religious dispute resolution will largely ameliorate these concerns. If religious communities, seeking to provide effective and legally enforceable faith-based dispute resolution to their

1. Indeed, the New York Times ran a series of three front-page articles about arbitration, one of which focused on religious arbitration; *see* Jessica Silver-Greenberg & Robert Gebeloff, *Arbitration Everywhere, Stacking the Deck of Justice*, N.Y. TIMES DEALBOOK, http://www.nytimes.com/2015/11/01/business/dealbook/arbitration-everywhere-stacking-the-deck-of-justice.html.

constituents, dedicate themselves to developing professional, legally compliant, and expert arbitration processes, the existence of robust and legally binding faith-based dispute resolution alternatives serves the interests of religious communities as well as secular society.

At the outset, it is also important to understand what this book is *not* about. This is not a book about how or why religious tribunals resolve internal ecumenical questions about the faith, doctrinal disputes between congregations, or conflicts between religious individuals over matters of faith. Nor is this a book about how American courts deal with or should deal with such matters when those kinds of cases are brought to state or federal judges for resolution. The latter issue is the concern of a rich body of judicial precedents and scholarly analyses concerning the scope and applicability of free exercise, non-establishment, and religious question doctrines. The former concern is an internal religious matter that constitutional and prudential commitments of American law maintain outside the purview of ordinary secular courts. Both these issues are briefly discussed later in this book in order to show that American courts are barred from addressing certain kinds of disputes between religious individuals, leaving such litigants with no practical choice but to adjudicate such matters through private arbitration.

The conduct of ecumenical courts dealing with strictly religious questions and the relationship between such tribunals and American law and courts is, however, largely tangential to the central focus of this book. This work does not address the issue of religious courts resolving ecumenical conflicts. Instead, it focuses on what happens when religiously observant individuals seek to resolve ordinary secular disputes over mundane property, contract, employment, consumer, finance, or family matters in religious courts and in accordance with religious norms and values. Such cases are the daily trade of state and federal courts throughout the United States, and could be resolved through traditional adjudication. Many religiously observant parties, however, do not want their basically secular disputes resolved by American courts in accordance with American law. Their religious commitments obligate them to order their material lives and relationships as well as their beliefs in accordance with faith-based norms and values. To fulfill these commitments, such litigants may choose to avoid the secular justice system and have their disputes resolved by religious arbitrators in accordance with substantive and procedural standards set by religious texts and traditions.

It is this kind of religious dispute resolution that is the central focus of this book. How should American courts generally relate to the use of faith-based arbitration to decide essentially secular disputes using standards, values, and policies that at times differ significantly from those embraced by general secular society?

ACKNOWLEDGMENTS

Many people contributed to the writing of this work, either directly or indirectly. First and most important, the Emory University Law School and the Emory University Center for the Study of Law and Religion have been my intellectual home for more than twenty years, and it is there that I have spent countless hours studying the interplay of law and religion. My friend, colleague, and Center Director John Witte, Jr. has always provided insight, leadership, and vision in the field, and he has never ceased encouraging me to write this and many other books. Thank you for your encouragement. Our Associate Director, Silas Allard, has provided much administrative support and without him, our Center would be less.

Dr. Shlomo Pill, a post-doctoral Fellow in the Center, provided me with much assistance in writing this book, as did Andrew Bolender, a recent Emory Law graduate. Parts of the material in the book were previously published in an article Dr. Pill, Dr. Ira Bedzow, and I co-authored, entitled "The Pillars of Successful Religious Arbitration: Models for American Islamic Arbitration Based on the Beth Din of America and Muslim Arbitration Tribunal Experience," which was published in the *Harvard Journal of Racial and Ethnic Justice,* and I thank them for letting me use that material. Liza D. Schwartzwald also provide some research and writing assistance. **Many people contributed to this work by reading various versions and I thank them all deeply. All errors remain my own.**

I was privileged to be a member of the Beth Din of America for many years, and I am grateful to Rabbis Gedalia Dov Schwartz, Mordechai Willig, Jonathan Reiss, and Shlomo Weissmann for the platform that that valuable organization provided me to ponder matters of religious arbitration, as well as to each of them personally for thinking about these many matters with me. I thank as well the late Rabbi Sheldon Rudoff (deceased now for almost seven years), who was the president of the Beth Din of America for many years, and who wisely pondered these issues with me.

Emory University School of Law provided research funding for the writing of this book, and The Tam Institute of Jewish Studies has always provided assistance for many different projects, including this one. Dr. David Blumenthal has been a source of constant conversation about this matter over many years and I am grateful to him for his many contributions.

INTRODUCTION

Changing Values and Laws

Recent polls indicate that the U.S. population is becoming less religious and more secular.[1] This seems to mirror the nation's movement—a movement reflected in its laws—away from certain traditional Judeo-Christian values. Government, law, and policy have slowly but surely aligned themselves with the sociological shift away from traditional religious values, and the pleas of the religious to keep their principles interlaced with the laws that govern the country have fallen on deaf ears. This movement has left some members of the religious population in a precarious situation, surrounded by a society whose values are changing before their eyes. One common response to the secularization of general society has been for religious individuals and communities to cling more tightly to their respective faiths and become more entrenched in the faith-based norms and values they profess.[2] Instead of proselytizing to recruit new followers and continuing to look to the government to continue weaving religion into society, religions and their faithful have begun to look inward for ways to bridge the gap between what they believe and what society believes.

Over the last sixty years, the substance of American law has come to reflect secular principles, as opposed to the religious values upon which it was historically based. This new secular law has a sharper focus on the religiously neutral principles of equality and fairness, rather than the historical commitment to traditional values.[3] This development coincides with important sociological

1. *See, e.g.*, *America's Changing Religious Landscape*, PEW RES. CTR. (May 12, 2015), http://www.pewforum.org/2015/05/12/americas-changing-religious-landscape/; ROBERT P. JONES, THE END OF WHITE CHRISTIAN AMERICA (2016) (confirming the trends found in the Pew Report).

2. For more on this, see FUNDAMENTALISMS COMPREHENDED (Martin Marty & R. Scott Appleby eds., 1995).

3. *See* Michael J. Broyde, Ira Bedzow & Shlomo Pill, *The Pillars of Successful Religious Arbitration: Models for American Islamic Arbitration Based on the Beth Din of America and Muslim Arbitration Tribunal Experience*, 30 HARV. J. RACIAL & ETHNIC JUST. 33, 33–76 (2014); *see also* David Aikman, *America's Religious Past Fades in a Secular Age*, WALL ST.

changes. Perhaps most important, there is no longer a majority religion in the United States. Although most Americans still identify as Christians, no denomination or sect predominates, and most Christians or Jews no longer look to their faith for their basic values.[4] Moreover, since the mid-twentieth century, the United States has become more of a multicultural society. It is increasingly comfortable with multiple expressions of individual and subgroup identity coexisting in the public sphere. In sociological terms, the metaphor of the "melting pot" has been replaced by that of the "salad bowl."[5]

So although the culture wars still sometimes flare, religious communities have begun to realize that they are all minority groups. Secular law is no longer broadly reflective of traditional values, nor will this change in the foreseeable future. Whether this has become apparent to everyone or not, it is motivating religious communities to step outside the framework of secular law and into the realm of private dispute resolution in order to preserve their communities.[6]

The common social fabric in America has shifted to a secular model. Secular interests and mores predominate in every value-driven public discussion, leaving traditional religious communities feeling less and less comfortable with general social norms and values and, at the same time, increasingly disconnected from common public discourse and law.[7] Debates

J., Oct. 25, 2012, *available at* http://online.wsj.com/news/articles/SB1000142405297 0203630604578073171838000416.

4. Aikman, *supra* note 3. Pew Research Center data from 2007 indicated "that the United States is on the verge of becoming a minority Protestant country; the number of Americans who report that they are members of Protestant denominations now stands at barely 51 percent." *Religious Landscape Study*, Pew Res. Ctr. (Feb. 2008), http://religions.pewforum.org/pdf/reportreligious-landscape-study-full.pdf. By 2012, this prediction had come true. *"Nones" on the Rise: One-in-Five Adults Have No Religious Affiliation*, Pew Res. Ctr. (Oct. 9, 2012), http://www.pewforum.org/2012/10/09/nones-on-the-rise/ ("In surveys conducted in the first half of 2012, fewer than half of American adults say they are Protestant (48%). This marks the first time in Pew Research Center surveys that the Protestant share of the population has dipped significantly below 50%.").

5. Carl N. Degler, Out of Our Past: The Forces That Shaped Modern America 296 (1970) ("[T]he metaphor of the melting pot is unfortunate and misleading. A more accurate analogy would be a salad bowl, for, though the salad is an entity, the lettuce can still be distinguished from the chicory, the tomatoes from the cabbage.").

6. Some religious communities even welcome this, as they see a greater threat from alternative religious values than from secular ones. *See* Michael J. Broyde, *Jewish Law and American Public Policy: A Principled Jewish Law View and Some Practical Jewish Observations*, *in* Religion as a Public Good: Jews and Other Americans on Religion in the Public Square 161 (Alan Mittleman ed., 2003).

7. For just the most recent example of this, see Michael Paulson, *Colleges and Evangelicals Collide on Bias Policy*, N.Y. Times, June 9, 2014, *available at* http://www.nytimes.com/2014/06/10/us/colleges-and-evangelicals-collide-on-bias-policy.html (discussing how many institutions are forcing off campus religious student organizations whose values discriminate against homosexual conduct).

surrounding same-sex marriage are some of the public criers of this change, and the religious-secular battlefield is shifting now to address transgender rights. Religious groups may not be able to influence secular law as much as they once did, but they have responded to their new place in society by changing their approach to these concerns. Many religious individuals and groups are choosing to opt out of general societal norms grounded in secular mores by developing internal legal bodies that provide members of faith communities with opportunities to order even their secular affairs, such as business relationships, property transactions, and family matters, in accordance with their own religious commitments.

The rise of faith-based arbitration courts follows key developments in the ways American law deals with private dispute resolution generally. Over the course of the twentieth century, U.S. law has evolved from offering only one venue and method for dispute resolution to permitting numerous options from which parties can choose. Today, the traditional court system run by state and federal governments is not the only avenue for binding dispute resolution in the United States. Alongside government-run public courts, there exist a variety of private modes of resolving disputes that have collectively come to be known as Alternative Dispute Resolution, or ADR. ADR is made up of several branches that, as this book will later discuss, have characteristics that make them distinct from one another, and it is markedly different from litigating disputes in court in a traditional sense. ADR developed for numerous reasons, but the one on which this work will focus here is that ADR enables litigating parties to customize the adjudicatory process in the ways that best suit their particular needs and interests while enabling them to gauge their expectations for dispute resolution either at the outset of their relationship or later on. ADR's customization is notable, but the effectiveness of private, party-centered dispute resolution is hampered if these processes lack the teeth necessary to render ADR dispute resolutions legally binding and enforceable. This problem was solved through the development of arbitration.

Arbitration is a form of ADR that is typically binding. This allows parties to take advantage of the expediency, cost efficiency, and customizability of ADR while still benefiting from the legally binding character of a traditional court decree. Realizing the value of arbitration, many groups—labor unions, employers, and various industries—took notice and began to implement arbitration agreements, which led to more fully developed systems of arbitration.

The customizability of arbitration does not stop at the ability of parties to set up the procedure by which they settle disputes; it also extends to their ability to choose experts in their industries to resolve these cases, and permits them to develop their own bodies of regulations for said arbitrators to follow. Although the court system in the United States was not quick to give arbitration the green light, it eventually embraced the practice, recognizing that individuals and organizations involved in an industry or practice are likely best suited to understand and resolve disputes arising therein. This justification is bolstered by the right of individuals to contract freely with one another so long as they are not contracting for an illegal purpose.

As discussed in Chapter Four, religious courts have existed and functioned within secular Western societies for a long time. However, until the advent of legally enforceable ADR processes in the early twentieth century, religious groups in the United States had never attempted vigorous and successful religious arbitration that was legally binding and enforceable in state and federal courts. Religious individuals and institutions seeking to resolve ecclesiastical questions either had such matters dealt with by religious tribunals within their respective religious orders whose rulings had no secular legal effect, or sought to have such cases adjudicated by state or federal courts who would resolve them subject to the limits of constitutional free exercise and non-establishment doctrines. The advent of legal frameworks for enforceable religious arbitration created new possibilities for religious individuals to resolve private disputes in accordance with religious norms in a manner that would be enforced by the courts. However, even after legal hurdles had been leveled and various organizations and industries began utilizing arbitration, barriers—some more imagined than real—still stood in the way of various other groups, especially religious groups, creating their own effective ADR processes. In particular, many of the early faith-based arbitration tribunals and organizations were made up of first- or second-generation immigrants who were unsure of the law and unfamiliar with the culture.

Even in those early stages of arbitration in the United States, secular law was moving further and further away from serving as a vehicle for religious laws and values. The country as a whole, in fact, was slowly becoming less religious and more secular. At the same time, those who remained religious became more deeply entrenched in their religious values. Such entrenchment gave rise to religious communities, where such individuals could live and interact with like-minded ones. Like-minded, however, does not mean dispute-free. Members of religious communities, like anyone else, have all manner of commercial, employment, property, and family disputes with each other. As religious groups' understandings of and relationships with the rest of society evolved, they took notice of the ways in which other organizations were implementing arbitration. They saw how other organizations, trade groups, and industries used arbitration to effectively manage internal disputes over typical litigious matters in ways that preserved the expectations of the parties in a manner that courts applying American law could not. Many religious people wanted the same opportunities. Religious arbitration was born from this desire.

Religious groups soon began taking advantage of America's legal arbitration regime by creating mechanisms that would allow religious practitioners to settle disputes with their co-religionists under the norms of their faith ("choice of law") and in tribunals staffed by religious functionaries serving as arbitrators ("choice of forum").

The fact that religious arbitration is historically explainable, however, does not mean that it is necessarily desirable. Arbitration can result in the underhanded waiver of rights. The ability of parties to faith-based arbitration to use the legal arbitration framework to choose the applicable law and adjudicatory forum that will resolve their disputes can lead to injustice.

The recent case of *Hayes v. Delbert Services Corporation* is illustrative.[8] In that case, the defendant was a payday loan company engaged in extending extremely high-interest loans to debtors against their future earnings, a practice widely considered ethically debatable, and one that is illegal in many states. The company loaned James Hayes $2,600 and charged him an annual interest rate of nearly 140 percent, in violation of both state and federal law. To avoid state and federal restrictions on usurious interest, the company inserted a simple provision into its loan agreement:

> This Loan Agreement is subject solely to the exclusive laws and jurisdiction of the Cheyenne River Sioux Tribe, Cheyenne River Indian Reservation.[9]

As you may have already guessed, the Cheyenne River Sioux Tribe has no usury limitations. By using this choice-of-law provision, the company intended to get around usury laws. Instead of the borrow-lender relationship being governed by federal and state laws, under this provision, both parties agreed to opt out of the burdens and benefits of the law's usury limits and abide by Cheyenne Sioux law instead. As another provision of the agreement stated:

> Neither this Agreement nor Lender is subject to the laws of any state of the United States of America. By executing this Agreement, you hereby expressly

8. 811 F.3d 666 (4th Cir. 2016).
9. *Id.*

> agree that this Agreement is executed and performed solely within the exterior boundaries of the Cheyenne River Indian Reservation, a sovereign Native American Tribal Nation. You also expressly agree that this Agreement shall be subject to and construed in accordance only with the provisions of the laws of the Cheyenne River Sioux Tribe, and that no United States state or federal law applies to this Agreement.[10]

The agreement repeated this yet again in still another form:

> GOVERNING LAW. This Agreement is governed by . . . the laws of the Cheyenne River Sioux Tribe. We do not have a presence in South Dakota or any other states of the United States. Neither this Agreement nor lender is subject to the laws of any state of the United States of America. . . . You also expressly agree that this Agreement shall be subject to and construed in accordance only with the provisions of the laws of the Cheyenne River Sioux Tribe, and that no United States state or federal law applies to this Agreement.[11]

Thus, the company selected, and the borrower agreed to be bound by, a legal system that has no usury laws. Both parties also contracted to have any disputes arising out of the loan resolved by the tribal court, which recognizes and enforces the usury-free standards of Cheyenne Sioux law. Does this mean that this intentional avoidance of state and federal usury restrictions is now permitted? Not in *Hayes*, at least.

The U.S. Court of Appeals refused to enforce the agreement because, according to the court,

> the [Cheyenne River Sioux] Tribe has no authorized representatives who conduct arbitrations, and . . . the Tribe does not even possess a method through which it might select and appoint such a person. In fact, one official from the Tribe has acknowledged that the tribal "governing authority does not authorize Arbitration" and the tribal court "does not involve itself in the hiring of an arbitrator."[12]

More to the point, the court ruled that "a party may not underhandedly convert a choice-of-law clause into a choice-of-no-law clause—it may not flatly and categorically renounce the authority of the federal statutes to which it is and must remain subject."[13] The fact that the Cheyenne Sioux

10. *Id.*
11. *Id.*
12. *Id.*
13. *Id.*

tribe did not have any functioning mechanisms in place for arbitration suggested that the defendant sought to use its choice-of-law and choice-of-forum clauses as means of deceptively avoiding ordinary legal duties.

To the extent the court viewed the company's choice-of-law provision as underhanded, and because the tribe in question did not even have arbitrations, the opinion makes perfect sense. The first step to waiving one's rights—in this case the borrower's right to pay only a reasonable interest rate on the loan—is to be aware of those rights. A deceptive or "underhanded" waiver is certainly bad. But, in truth, all private agreements to arbitrate involve parties waiving their rights under state law, and choosing instead to be subject to a different legal system with alternative standards upheld and enforced not by traditional judges, but by private arbitrators. Given such outcomes, perhaps all arbitration is undesirable, full stop.

But, consider whether invalidating the choice-of-law and choice-of-forum agreements would have been the right result if the parties had engaged in an overt and knowing waiver of their civil law rights in favor of arbitration in a legal system that was fully functional but simply lacked any usury prohibition. For example, a standard provision of the most common Jewish prenuptial agreement states simply and directly that it does not accept no-fault divorce as a principle relevant to the adjudication of end of marriage property distribution and financial obligations. The prenuptial agreement states among its choices that the parties agree to authorize the Beth Din of America to decide all monetary disputes consistently with either equitable distribution or community property, as the parties direct. However, the standard agreement then adds the following clause: "The Beth Din of America may consider the respective responsibilities of either or both of the parties for the end of the marriage, as an additional, but not exclusive, factor in determining the distribution of marital property and maintenance . . ."[14]

The Beth Din of America is doing exactly what Jewish law directs it to do—considering marital fault in the distribution of assets.[15] But in doing so it directly contravenes the law and intent of the "no fault" divorce regime currently dominant throughout the United States.

On the one hand, why shouldn't parties be able to structure their marriage rules in a way that reflects the values that they both agree to at the time of their marriage? Is it truly objectionable to have a clause in a prenuptial agreement stating that one who commits adultery shall receive less

14. http://theprenup.org/pdf/Prenup_Standard.pdf (last visited Jan. 17, 2017).
15. *See, e.g.*, Ketubot 72a for a discussion in the Talmud of fault-based adjudication of the financial aspects of divorce.

money due to the adultery, even if many states do not have such a clause as part of their default law? Unlike in the *Hayes* case above, where the agreement nefariously required arbitration in front of a non-existent tribunal with no clear waiver of rights, this instance has a clear waiver of rights and submission to a highly reputable panel.

Then again, the Beth Din of America's relationship to "no fault divorce" might be no different from the Cheyenne River Sioux Tribe's relationship to usury law. The parties in the Beth Din of America example authorized fault-based communal property or fault-based equitable distribution, even though no American state has fault-based community property.

When all is said and done, the central question remains: Is allowing this type of wholesale contractual revision of basic law through arbitration a good idea?

This book will address this question by discussing the four different issues, each of which will be considered in a Part composed of several chapters.

The first Part will explore why religious individuals and communities are increasingly turning to private faith-based dispute resolution to arbitrate their litigious disputes. Part I will also focus on why religious communities feel disenfranchised from secular law, and particularly secular family law. It will begin in Chapter One by focusing on the rise of arbitration in Jewish, Islamic, and Christian communities in America. Chapter Two will discuss a host of cultural changes that have not only increased the gap between the secular and religious, but also increased the sense in religious communities that they have lost the war over family law and need to retreat into their own little fortress communities with their own laws and courts. Chapter Three addresses a more pragmatic cause for the rise of faith-based arbitration as an increasingly popular way for religious individuals to choose to resolve private disputes: the fact that religious arbitration tends to resolve cases about commerce between religious individuals better than do secular courts unfamiliar with the expectations and understandings of religious parties.

The second Part will look at why American law is so comfortable with faith-based arbitration, given its penchant for enabling parties to order their relationships and resolve their disputes using norms and values that are often different from and sometimes opposed to secular standards. Chapter Four surveys the historical roots of contemporary faith-based arbitration in premodern ecclesiastical tribunals that operated within European and Anglo-American societies. Chapter Five discusses contemporary faith-based dispute resolution in the United States. Premodern religious courts were primarily concerned with resolving ecclesiastical disputes between feuding congregations and between religious communities and their members. Interactions between these religious processes and state courts was—and still is—filtered through the framework of constitutional free exercise and non-establishment principles. Today, however, faith-based dispute resolution operates principally in the realm of ordinary secular disputes—contract, property, family, consumer, employment, and finance matters—that religiously observant litigants wish to resolve in accordance with religious norms and values. In other words, contemporary religious arbitration in America is more a choice-of-law and choice-of-forum matter than a free exercise or non-establishment issue. This kind of faith-based dispute resolution became possible when, during the twentieth century, American law moved from generally prohibiting private arbitration to permitting parties in a dispute to choose both the law they want to apply to their dispute and the venue for resolving such a dispute. In the last thirty years, it has become clear that when people have a dispute, they can agree to choose both the law that applies to them and the arbitration panel that will determine the result. This is true in commercial law and family law, and has revolutionized all aspects of private law in the United States. Having permitted such agreements in many different areas of commercial law, the general establishment clause jurisprudence of the U.S. would be loath to prohibit the same to religious tribunals, and such is actually the law of the land. This section will also review criticism of this transformation, which reflects Justice Cardozo's approach of almost a century ago, and respond to it.

Part III weighs the proper procedural, jurisdictional, and contractual limits of arbitration generally, and of religious arbitration in particular. It identifies and explains the reasonable limitations on religious arbitration. Chapter Six explores the current legal limitations, including judicial policing of the contractual viability of arbitration agreements, procedural requirements in arbitration processes, and concerns of duress and unconscionability in the use of private dispute resolution as an alternative to traditional courts. Chapter Seven explores how Jewish arbitration in the United States has embraced these secular legal requirements, and gone further to add additional features that have contributed to the legal viability and pragmatic effectiveness of contemporary Jewish arbitration processes. Chapter Eight looks at the ways in which this Jewish model of effective, legally enforceable arbitration has been utilized by some Muslim communities in the United Kingdom to create their own viable faith-based dispute resolution processes, and how it can be—and to some extent has been—adopted by Muslim and Christian groups in the United States.

Part IV looks to whether secular societies should seek to facilitate effective, legally enforceable religious dispute resolution, and argues that religious arbitration is not only good for the religious community itself, but that having many different avenues for faith-based arbitration (as long as they are properly limited) is good for any vibrant pluralistic democracy inhabited by diverse faith groups. Chapter Nine explains that there are good reasons to be concerned about religious tribunals from a secular perspective. Chapter Ten, however, argues that properly regulated and judicially policed faith-based dispute resolution enhances both the religious and the civil side of a society. As to enhancing religion, there are three key benefits. First, religious arbitration fosters domestic tranquility in religious communities. Second, it allows people to organize their consensual affairs as they deem proper. Third, it encourages civil society to see value in religious communities governing their own affairs in a fair and efficient way that reduces tension, particularly with the rest of society. Religious arbitration also advances two major goals of civil society that significantly reduce the tension present between secular and religious members. It allows religious communities to be moderately self-governing in those areas of law where secular adjudication of religious values and expectations is very hard. Equally important, it creates a framework for resolution of the problems that occur when people want to unexpectedly enter or exit religious communities. These problems, called "exit problems," plague all religious communities (and thus their civil counterparts), particularly in divorce settings, by insisting that exit disputes be treated no differently than any other contract dispute. This book concludes that, on the whole, regulated religious arbitration is a positive contribution to liberal western democracies.

PART ONE

CHAPTER 1

The Rise of Religious Arbitration

This chapter surveys the contemporary landscape of religious arbitration in the United States by exploring how different religious communities utilize arbitration, how these processes differ from each other, and where various faith-based dispute resolution models fall on the broader ADR spectrum. In particular, this chapter will explore developments in Jewish, Christian, and Islamic arbitration in America over the last several decades, and discuss what internal concerns and external stimuli have spurred these changes. In this context, this chapter will also reflect on why American Catholics have not moved in the same direction as some other religious groups, which have been eager to embrace the use of religious arbitration as a means of enabling their adherents to resolve ordinary secular conflicts in accordance with religious norms and values. Finally, this chapter will discuss the historical limitations of utilizing religious arbitration in many faiths and how some have evolved to embrace the practice.

Although controversial,[1] religious arbitration has grown immensely since its inception. In fact, almost every religion in the United States has its own system for settling disputes, each of which functions as an alternative to the civil courts. While these vary in detail, with different religious groups utilizing different methods of ADR and some developing more intricate, sophisticated, and successful systems than others, they all share the same goal: creating a system for settling disputes outside the realm of the secular court system.

1. Michael Corkery & Jessica Silver-Greenberg, *In Religious Arbitration, Scripture is the Rule of Law*, N.Y. TIMES, Nov. 2, 2015.

A. CUSTOMIZING LAW: THE DEVELOPMENT OF RELIGIOUS ARBITRATION

Law is defined by Black's Law Dictionary as "[t]he aggregate of legislation, judicial precedents, and accepted legal principles; the body of authoritative grounds of judicial and administrative action; esp., the body of rules, standards, and principles that the courts of a particular jurisdiction apply in deciding controversies brought before them."[2] This definition, among other things, highlights the importance many practitioners of the law place on the so-called "rule of law," or law as a rules-based system. For some time, law was viewed solely as a vehicle for setting standards of accepted behavior and managing said behavior. However, as the law has developed, it has turned into something different altogether—a structure that allows parties to set and meet their own expectations. These expectations could be those of employment for a certain period of time or for the purchase of a particular piece of property. No matter what the expectation is, however, the law has morphed into a vehicle that enables individuals to drive their dealings.

At one point in U.S. history, the only way parties could settle legal disputes was through the court system. As discussed later in Chapter Five, for various reasons, no arbitration—or anything similar—existed. Courts did not trust arbitrators to handle disputes in a manner consistent with the law. Moreover, they believed that arbitration interfered with the right of individuals to petition the court system for redress of their grievances. In the early twentieth century, however, the courts came to accept the idea of parties' right to agree to settle disputes by arbitration. Arbitration at that point, however, bore little resemblance to what it has become today. Parties had no ability to add choice-of-law provisions to their arbitration agreements, and were thus governed by federal, state, and local rules. Once this changed, however, and choice-of-law provisions were allowed, arbitration became a different tool altogether. Individuals and organizations could craft the rules by which they wanted their disputes to be governed. This led them to further embrace arbitration.

The better developed the system of arbitration became in the United States, the more comfortable judges, practitioners, and, most important, parties were with utilizing it. Although the rise of arbitration in general in the United States will be discussed in further detail later, it is helpful to

2. Black's Law Dictionary 962 (9th ed. 2009).

give a short summary here in order to situate the development of religious arbitration in particular.

B. A BRIEF HISTORY OF ARBITRATION'S RISE IN THE UNITED STATES

For a long time, courts in the United States were viewed as experts in everything. Almost any dispute could be settled in a courtroom. In fact, courts were viewed as the only arena where legal disputes between parties *could* be settled. Over time, however, the ability of courts to settle disputes efficiently and effectively came into question. Courts got backed up, and volumes of codified law piled up. Litigation progressively became more expensive and draconian. Parties sought viable alternatives. Out of this frustration, alternative dispute resolution (ADR)—and arbitration in particular—was born.

Arbitration is "[a] method of dispute resolution involving one or more neutral third parties who are usually agreed to by the disputing parties and whose decision is binding."[3] Although arbitration is now widely accepted by the U.S. legal system, this was not always the case. In its infancy, arbitration was shunned as an inferior method of settling disputes. Initially, in fact, the practice was entirely banned.

Judges shunned arbitration for a number of reasons. The most often cited factors were that arbitrators lack as robust an understanding of the law as judges, the lack of adequate judicial oversight of the arbitration process, and the lack of a binding effect. As time went on, however, and the body of American contract law developed, courts became satisfied that individuals could contract with one another to make their future disputes subject to arbitration. However, this freedom-of-contract theory only went so far.

Those who decided on arbitration were forced to remain subject to American law, thus moving the dispute out of the courtroom while maintaining the somewhat fixed variable of the U.S. rule of law. This method of regulating individual agreements came into question as individuals were progressively given more freedom to craft their agreements to meet their individual needs and expectations. Eventually, the rule requiring arbitrations to apply American law gave way to one giving individual contracting parties the ability to choose the applicable law. Although there have certainly been bumps in the road for arbitration, it has weathered the storms

3. *Id.* at 119.

and gained a significant amount of respect from almost the entire legal community, including judges whose dockets have become quite a bit more manageable because of the practice.

In short, arbitration allows parties to agree to settle disputes that arise from their dealing outside of the traditional court system and beyond the realm of the traditional rule of law, opting instead for a venue and law they find mutually agreeable. Therefore, the rule of law, at least in the customizable realm of arbitration, has become less of a fixed structure and more adaptive to individual needs and desires. This development has shifted the law from being viewed as a science from which a singular correct answer can be found, to a search for more contextual answers dictated by the parties' agreement to arbitrate. Stemming almost entirely from the contract setting, this newly discovered malleability of the law at most highlighted the fact that courts are not experts in all things and often do a poor job of settling disputes to the satisfaction of either—if any—of the parties, and at least justified allowing another avenue for parties to take in settling their disputes.

By analogy, it is helpful to think of arbitration and litigation as separate houses, with each arbitral specialization as a room within the arbitration house. At first, religious groups stood by and watched the construction of what would become the house of arbitration. Labor unions were one of the first groups to move in, quickly embracing it and testing its structural soundness. They soon found that arbitration was an excellent outlet for resolving disputes governed by collective bargaining agreements. Other groups then started occupying other parts of the house, each decorating its own room. As the number of individuals embracing arbitration increased, so did the number of arbitrators who focused solely on one type of dispute or one type of arbitrating party.

This specialization added new strength and beauty to the house of arbitration, and resolved an initial discrepancy between it and the litigation house—the latter of which initially had a vast knowledge and understanding of the law and, in turn, how disputes should be decided. By contrast, arbitrators were at first asked to balance the law on one hand and the wishes of the disputing parties on the other. Early critics of arbitration cited this as one of the reasons litigation was superior. But as arbitrators specialized, groups of prospective arbitral parties were able to build de facto court systems within which to settle their disputes, wherein they could have their legal issues decided, but with a slant toward their own internal policy preferences. As the class of arbitrable disputes grew, so did the groups who embraced the practice. Merchants, employers, and banks all began implementing it in some form or another.

Meanwhile, religious groups saw the litigation house tossing out the furniture of the values and beliefs that had, for a long time, gone hand in hand with religion. Too skeptical to move into arbitration at first, religious groups bided their time. In addition to the general concerns about arbitration's durability—especially its ability to stand up to the wrecking balls of judicial review and expectations for arbitration awards to be consistent with state and federal law—religion was faced with the very real concern that church and state should remain separate. In the eyes of many, cohabitation of legal and religious principles in arbitration set up religious arbitration to be judicially walled off. Courts were always wary of quasi-judicial bodies, and were prone to be especially so when religious groups were involved.

C. THE BIRTH OF RELIGIOUS ARBITRATION

Although there are still arguments against arbitration—particularly the fear that certain parties invoke it in a coercive manner—the practice is continuing to grow, and will only be hampered inasmuch as certain government regulatory bodies allow it to be. To a great extent, as this book will explain, religious groups entered the arbitration universe later than other groups, mostly due to a lack of comfort with the skills needed to produce binding arbitration. Now, however, religious groups step over the threshold regularly.

The fact that religious groups settle disputes through quasi-arbitral bodies is nothing new. The Catholic Church has long utilized some manner of arbitration to settle matters of canon law. However, this method of dispute resolution has not been a matter of major concern because Catholic religious courts do not typically come in direct conflict with American law or draw judicial challenges from American courts for one very important reason: although there is a system of Catholic religious law, the Church distinguishes between the canon law and secular law jurisdictions. Canon law never moved into what would now be called arbitration because modern arbitration in the United States handles matters that fall under the scope of ordinary secular law—matters such as private property disputes, employer-employee conflicts, regular commercial and contractual matters, and so on. Canon law, by contrast, was historically concerned with the internal governance of the Church and its functionaries, as well as sacerdotal and ritual matters. Ordinary property disputes, employment matters, or other decidedly secular contract disputes between Catholic parishioners simply did not fall within the scope of canon law or Church court jurisdictions. So, from a religious perspective, there was no need to resolve such issues based on religious principles. With respect to those kinds of secular disputes, at least, good Catholics could litigate cases in state courts without concern, rendering unto Caesar what is Caesar's.

Various Protestant groups have, until recently, also largely avoided the clash between faith-based dispute resolution and secular law. In the case of Protestant denominations, however, the tension was not diffused by the kind of strict jurisdictional separation between ecclesiastical and secular matters and law embraced by Catholicism, but by the confluence of two other factors. First, Protestantism in general lacks the kinds of nomoscentric characteristics of some other faiths, such as Judaism, Islam, and to some extent Catholicism. Consequently, the notion that disputes between Protestant practitioners had to be resolved in accordance with religious norms rather than secular laws was not particularly pronounced. Indeed, there was not much "Protestant law" to speak of to provide an alternative system of behavioral and relational norms that Protestants might be expected to utilize in structuring their ordinary material relations. Moreover, for much of American history, Protestants have made up a substantial majority of the population, and Protestant values and sensibilities have featured prominently in American law and policy. As a result, even deeply religious Protestant Americans often found little issue in adjudicating their litigious disputes in state federal courts. There was no relevant body of specific religious precepts that had to be observed and, in any case, the American law results issuing from traditional courts largely reflected their religious sensibilities.

But religious arbitration has taken on a much more sweeping public significance recently because of shifts in American social and legal values. The last half of the twentieth century saw the erosion of cultural foundations built upon religious values and their gradual replacement with more secular ones. Religious groups were keenly aware of the chasm that had developed between cultural values held by the general U.S. population and those held by them and their parishioners. They began to build upon the inroads made by the Catholic Church years earlier, slowly but surely wading deeper into the waters to see what limits courts would place on their use of arbitration. Judaism pioneered and perfected this practice, developing its own intricate system for settling disputes arising between individual members of the religion, even those that went beyond the pale of religious issues and into the realm of contract and family law. This went relatively unnoticed, however, because even though it has the largest number of followers of any non-Christian religion, as of 2007, only 1.9 percent of the U.S. population identified as Jewish.[4] The attention drawn by religious arbitration as a viable option for settling religious disputes would only increase with time, as the cultural mores of the country strayed even further from Judeo-Christian values.

For some time, law in the United States was in very close alignment with Judeo-Christian values on many issues (race being the huge area of tension). The reason for this was obvious: most people in the United States identified as followers of a Judeo-Christian religion. As of 2007, 80.1 percent of the population identified as such.[5] Although this number fell to 72.5 percent in 2014, Judeo-Christians still make up a staggering majority of the population.[6] Even with this majority, however, there is no doubt that the U.S. population is progressively becoming less religious. Those individuals identifying as "Unaffiliated" with a religion—including atheists, agnostics, and those identifying as "Nothing In Particular"—have seen a notable increase in the past decade and a half, going from 16.1 percent of the population to 22.8 percent, a 6.7 percent increase in just seven years.[7] This group also has had the largest gains over the seven-year period from 2007 to 2014.[8] As the laws and principles of Americans have continued to develop in a more secular direction, these religious groups—especially Evangelical and mainline Protestant communities—whose religious beliefs were once perfectly reflected in the law—have realized they are now falling into the minority. They have essentially lost control of the law. This is evident in the decision to legalize same-sex marriage in the United States. Attempting to retake control of the law, and equipped with the history of Judaism's success with arbitration, newly-minority religious groups have started building arbitral bodies of their own. More than anything, these groups have lost the ability to participate in—and in most cases actually dictate—family law, the area of the law where cultural values are manifested most directly.

As secular law loses its Judeo-Christian roots, a trend that is likely to continue in the coming years, the people still rooted in Judeo-Christian values and traditions will continue to find other means for settling their disputes outside of the court system, whose values increasingly differ markedly from their own. Even non-Judeo-Christian religious groups, most notably Muslims, have followed suit in beginning to build their own arbitral bodies. They do so because arbitration gives them an opportunity

4. *America's Changing Religious Landscape*, Pew Research Ctr. (May 12, 2015), http://www.pewforum.org/2015/05/12/americas-changing-religious-landscape/.

5. *Id.*

6. *Id.*

7. *Id.*

8. *Id.*

to decide matters through a lens that considers both the secular and the religious laws to which they are subject.

The movement by religious groups to create their own internal arbitral bodies has proven extremely controversial. Perhaps the skepticism toward religious arbitration stems from the secretive nature of certain churches, our own general lack of understanding of different religions, or even the deeply ingrained American principle that church and state should remain separate, and that allowing "religious courts" to exist pushes parties into an inherently unconstitutional forum. Nevertheless, religious groups have become arbitration specialists. In turn, the arbitral bodies developed by religious groups are intricately built and likely here to stay for the foreseeable future.

D. VARIANTS OF RELIGIOUS ARBITRATION IN PRACTICE

Religious arbitration is a "process in which arbitrators apply religious principles to resolve disputes."[9] Although generally true, this simplistic definition does not do justice to what has become a widely implemented system of dispute resolution in the United States. In fact, even the definition of arbitration fails to fully summarize religious arbitration. In a sense, religious arbitration can run the gamut of dispute resolution practices. Some religious arbitral bodies utilize relaxed methods of ADR, such as negotiation, conciliation, and mediation, whereas others have implemented very strict, litigation-like procedures.

The advent of religious arbitration comes at an extremely interesting time in the United States. Many religiously observant Americans view the secularization of American laws and policies as repugnant to their own beliefs and principles, and have become further entrenched in their traditional beliefs. They also favor having their religious beliefs govern their everyday lives in all respects, including the way in which they settle disputes. Religious arbitration presents a perfect outlet for this by allowing religious individuals to agree to arbitrate all manner of basically secular disputes with their co-religionists in arbitral forums established and governed by their religion.[10]

9. Caryn Litt Wolfe, *Faith-Based Arbitration: Friend or Foe? An Evaluation of Religious Arbitration Systems and Their Interaction with Secular Courts*, 75 FORDHAM L. REV. 427 (2006).

10. Indeed, in recent years there has been a considerable increase in articles addressing religious arbitration. *See, e.g.*, Farrah Ahmed & Senwung Luk, *How Religious Arbitration Could Enhance Personal Autonomy*, 1 OXFORD J.L. & RELIGION 424 (2012); Amanda M. Baker, *A Higher Authority: Judicial Review of Religious Arbitration*,

It can be a bit difficult to understand why it is important for religious individuals to be governed by the law of their religion.

To illustrate the *why* of religious arbitration and the problems that why can cause, let us consider a recent case of religious arbitration that was enjoined by a bankruptcy court as violative of the automatic stay, a provision designed to force all parties to adhere to bankruptcy rules:[11] *In re Congregation Birchos Yosef*.[12] In this case, an Orthodox Jewish creditor sought to have an Orthodox Jewish debtor or his proxy summoned to an Orthodox Jewish religious tribunal to adjudicate the propriety (and even perhaps the validity) of the debtor's bankruptcy filing as a matter of Jewish law. In the absence of the debtor's agreeing to appear before the rabbinical court for such adjudication, the creditor wished the rabbinical court to issue a writ of contempt, or *seruv*, against the debtor as being in violation of Jewish law. The debtor filed a motion in bankruptcy court seeking to enjoin the creditor and the rabbinical court in question from considering whether bankruptcy is a valid option under Jewish law, whether the creditor owed the debtor money, and whether the rabbinical court may issue a contempt citation under Jewish law.

The bankruptcy court held that the automatic stay applies to the proceedings of the rabbinical court no differently than to any other court. It stated simply:

> The automatic stay is clearly neutral on its face and is also neutral and generally applicable, as far as religious exercise is concerned, in practice. It applies to anyone who falls within the ambit of 11 U.S.C. § 362(a) (here, to anyone who commences a proceeding or takes another action covered by either 11 U.S.C. § 362(a)(1) or (3)). It prohibits the invocation of all covered proceedings, whether in state or federal court, a foreign court, **or a *beis din*.** (emphasis added)[13]

37 VT. L. REV. 157 (2012); Michael A. Helfand, *Religious Arbitration and the New Multiculturalism: Negotiating Conflicting Legal Orders*, 86 N.Y.U. L. REV. 1231 (2011); Nicholas Walter, *Religious Arbitration in the United States and Canada*, 52 SANTA CLARA L. REV. 501 (2012); Michael J. Broyde, *Faith-Based Private Arbitration as a Model for Preserving Rights and Values in a Pluralistic Society*, 90 CHI.-KENT L. REV. 111 (2015); Michael A. Helfand, *Arbitration's Counter-Narrative: The Religious Arbitration Paradigm*, 124 YALE L.J. 2994 (2015).

11. The Bankruptcy Code's automatic stay prohibits a wide array of actions that attempt to collect prepetition claims or that otherwise interfere with property of the estate. *See* 11 U.S.C. § 362 (1982).

12. *In re* Congregation Birchos Yosef, 535 B.R. 629 (Bankr. S.D.N.Y. 2015).

13. *Id.* at 637.

It is worth understanding what was *not* under consideration in this case. All parties agreed to the following:

- The rabbinical court cannot issue a legally binding order, even with an arbitration agreement signed by both parties, if it contradicts the directive of the bankruptcy court.
- The debtor's assets cannot be used to repay the debt upon the directive of the rabbinical court, as the assets are under the control of the bankruptcy court.

By noting that the automatic stay applies directly to the rabbinical court in question, the bankruptcy court not only precluded the creditor and debtor from submitting to rabbinic court arbitration (which is an easy matter to preclude under bankruptcy law), but also used its authority to stay the rabbinical court's religious pronouncements concerning the correctness under Jewish law of the debtor's decision to file bankruptcy to begin with. Even if it could not have reached any meaningful decision on the merits of the case itself, the rabbinical court may have wished to issue the *seruv*, or writ of contempt, against the debtor in order to signal to both the parties and the wider Jewish community that the debtor had violated Jewish religious law by filing for bankruptcy in order to avoid paying his debts.[14] Although such religious pronouncements lack any real legal authority or implications, they are important from a religious perspective. The bankruptcy court, however, made it clear that such religious pronouncements must cease.[15]

This type of case is symptomatic of problems that secular courts and liberal society can encounter by allowing religious arbitration. Religious systems sometimes impede—from the secular view—the reasonable and orderly operation of the justice system by operating a religious arbitration system that perceives itself as morally and legally free from the constraints of the law. In particular, four problems arise, and these types of cases highlight all four of them.

14. For more on this, see Michael J. Broyde, *Forming Religious Communities and Respecting Dissenters' Rights*, *in* HUMAN RIGHTS IN JUDAISM: CULTURAL, RELIGIOUS, AND POLITICAL PERSPECTIVES 35 (Michael J. Broyde & John Witte, Jr. eds., 1998).

15. The bankruptcy court states directly: "Based on the record of the hearing, while the full extent of the effect of a *sirov*, if issued, is somewhat unclear, the mere threat of the issuance of a *sirov*, and, in fact, the commencement of the *beis din* proceeding itself, has already adversely affected the Debtor, through its principals, and made it more difficult to conduct this case by exerting significant pressure to cease pursuing the Debtor's claims against those who invoked the *beis din*." Birchos Yosef, 535 B.R. at 631–32.

First, a religious system could be attempting to govern disputes between parties that did not actually consent to the religious legal system's authority. This concern is particularly present in the area of bankruptcy as (when a debtor is insolvent) money to pay creditors is very limited, and directions to pay Peter are also always about how much Paul will receive. Although this is sometimes a slippery slope (and money is frequently limited), it is particularly the case with bankruptcy that adjudication of any part of the estate impacts on all of the estate.

Second, a religious system could be attempting to adjudicate a case in which the secular legal authorities are expecting exclusive secular court jurisdiction. Criminal law is an example, as is bankruptcy, particularly commercial bankruptcy. Almost by definition, all attempts at arbitration violate society's legal sense that certain types of cases can and should be adjudicated only by a court of the government. Of course, religious communities might very well object to that policy, based on their faith's ideas of proper dispute resolution.[16]

Third, a religious legal system could be making an ecclesiastical point—that one party is a sinner—even though the underlying claim is financial and ought to be resolved in secular court. Ecclesiastical pronouncements in commercial matters—such as debtor and creditor rights—are easily understood (or misunderstood) by the courts to be attempts to coerce one of the parties out of his or her right to use the secular court system, and to generate a false consent to arbitration by labeling certain lawful conduct to be sinful.

Finally, a religious legal system could be attempting to impose a choice-of-law rule on a dispute in which all the parties did not wish or expect religious law to govern. This is related, but not identical, to the first objection, as a party does have the secular right to file for bankruptcy even if that party had a "religious law" choice-of-law clause, regardless of whether the religious law has provisions for bankruptcy. But such a choice-of-law provision—particularly when used in some commercial contracts and not others—gives rise to the possibility that this adjudication is prejudicial to some of the creditors in a way that is inconsistent with secular law.

On the other hand, this case is important to religious ADR because people in religious communities do not wish to be considered "sinners" by their communities. Allowing a functioning alternative religious court system creates the distinct possibility that religious communities will seek even greater autonomy from the general norms of secular law and life—in

16. Such as the Jewish ideal of disputes between Jews being resolved in rabbinical court or the Islamic ideal of the same.

this case, those of bankruptcy law. So, as one considers religious arbitration abstractly, one must consider both its impact in any given case as well as the systemic impact of an alternative legal system—almost a shadow law—on society as a whole. Even when lacking enforceable authority, the rabbinical court in this case had religious authority, and that is what it was enjoined against exercising.

The next section will outline the various arbitral bodies and procedures utilized by three of the different religions of the Abrahamic faith—Judaism, Christianity, and Islam—and explain how likely problems of the type the court encountered in *Birchos Yosef* can be endemic to religious arbitration. The greater the *Birchos Yosef* problem, the less compatible religious arbitration might be with Western democratic law.

Jewish Arbitration

As previously noted, those who identify as Jewish make up about 1.9 percent of the U.S. population.[17] Although small in terms of the number of adherents—at least relative to other religions—Judaism has been a trailblazer in the area of religious arbitration in the United States.[18] Today, it enjoys the most sophisticated and formal systems of religious arbitration in the country.[19] It takes a pseudo-litigation or pseudo-adjudication approach similar to that of the secular court system. Highly specialized by area of law and well-versed in the historical foundations of Judaism and the Jewish people—including the Bible, *Talmud*, writings of Jewish scholars, and *halakha* (Jewish law)—Jewish law courts work to implement these religious principles and "preserve Jewish culture and religious law through Judaism-based dispute resolution."[20]

Pivoting around the principle of peace, in Jewish ADR, adversarial dispute resolution takes a back seat to conciliatory proceedings. This preference is a reflection of Judaism's central texts. The Talmud "highlights the advantages

17. Pew Research Ctr., *supra* note 4.

18. *See generally* Michael J. Broyde, *Jewish Law Courts in America: Lessons Offered to Sharia Courts by the Beth Din of America Precedent*, 57 N.Y.L. Sch. L. Rev. 287 (2012–2013).

19. *Id.*

20. R. Seth Shippee, *"Blessed Are the Peacemakers": Faith-Based Approaches to Dispute Resolution*, 9 ILSA J. Int'l & Comp. L. 237, 249 (2002); *see also* Nicholas Walter, *Religious Arbitration in the United States and Canada*, 52 Santa Clara L. Rev. 501 (2012); Michael C. Grossman, *Is This Arbitration?: Religious Tribunals, Judicial Review, and Due Process*, 107 Colum. L. Rev. 169 (2007); Michael A. Helfand, *Litigating Religion*, 93 B.U. L. Rev. 493 (2013).

of mediation and compromise over a legal decision finding for one party or the other,"[21] and the *Shulchan Aruch*, the authoritative code of Jewish law, counsels adherents to work at settling disputes in a mutually beneficial manner as opposed to one in which the winner takes all.[22] However, realizing that disputes must be settled with some finality, Judaism-based dispute resolution leaves room for parties to move from conciliation to mediation and, if necessary, from mediation to arbitration. Therefore, Jewish ADR runs the gamut of ADR—from informal, to formal and non-binding, to formal and binding.

Most commonly, Jewish dispute resolution begins with an informal mediation or arbitration-like process referred to as a *bitzua* or *p'sharah*.[23] These proceedings can be presided over by a panel of two to three individuals, which can include a rabbi or simply individuals agreed to by the parties and familiar with the law.[24] The panel hears arguments from both sides and renders a decision, which can be either binding or non-binding, depending on the wishes of the parties.[25] If a non-binding decision issues and the parties are unsuccessful at settling their dispute, the parties may submit the matter to a Jewish court, or *beth din*.

These rabbinical courts are the flagship bodies in the Jewish dispute resolution arena. *Beth dins* are responsible for many things, from constructing internal rules of procedure to providing "a forum for arbitrating disputes through the *din torah* process, obtaining Jewish divorces, and confirming Jewish personal status issues."[26] Although cases heard by *beth dins* often involve issues of secular law, and *beth dins* rely primarily on Jewish law in reaching their decisions, their success has depended significantly on their ability to utilize "erudite rabbinic judges . . . capable of addressing *halachic* issues in areas of financial and family law through the prism of contemporary commercial practice and secular law."[27] *Beth dins'* ability to interweave religious and secular law is their key to success and, perhaps more importantly, why "their rulings are usually binding and enforceable in the secular court system."[28]

21. Shippee, *supra* note 20, at 249–50.
22. *Id.*
23. *Id.* at 251.
24. *Id.* at 249, 250.
25. *Id.* at 252.
26. *About Us*, BETH DIN OF AM., https://bethdin.org/about/ (last visited Jan. 15, 2016).
27. Shippee, *supra* note 20, at 253; *see also* Ginnine Fried, *The Collision of Church and State: A Primer to Beth Din Arbitration and the New York Secular Courts*, 31 FORDHAM URB. L.J. 633 (2004); Linda S. Kahan, *Jewish Divorce and Secular Courts: The Promise of Avitzur*, 73 GEO. L.J. 193 (1984); Aviva Vogelstein, *Is ADR the Solution? How ADR Gets Around the Get Controversy in Jewish Divorce*, 14 CARDOZO J. CONFLICT RESOL. 999 (2013).
28. Shippee, *supra* note 27.

It is worth referring back to the case of *In re Congregation Birchos Yosef* to understand how common such cases are in the Jewish tradition. Because the Jewish tradition recognizes that Jewish law is a complete legal code, it *does not* recognize that secular law is even needed to resolve any dispute between Jews. It does have a vibrant concept of "the law of the land is the law,"[29] but there are no disputes in Jewish law that cannot be resolved exclusively through reference to Jewish law. So, cases such as this are complex—the debtor's assets are finite, and allowing the rabbinical court to resolve any disputes related to them removes them from the bankruptcy estate. On the other hand, enjoining a religious tribunal from voicing its religious view on a matter is not a simple issue. Furthermore, the question of whether Jewish law even recognizes the validity of secular bankruptcy law remains an open one about which scholars do not agree.[30] The more "modern" in orientation the rabbinical court is, the more likely it is to work very hard to prevent the *Birchos Yosef* problem in all its four forms. For this reason, the rules of the Beth Din of America speak regularly about the civil law of the jurisdiction in which it is conducting arbitrations, and seek mightily to adhere to the law of the land.[31] Other rabbinical courts in the United States are less deferential to secular law and therefore more likely to encounter a *Birchos Yosef* problem.[32]

Protestant Christian Arbitration

Those who identify as Christian make up about 70 percent of the U.S. population.[33] Although Judaism may be considered the trailblazer in religious arbitration, Christianity has developed its own successful, albeit less formal, system of settling disputes through ADR. Recognizing that Christianity has

29. For an explanation of the various theories relating to secular and Jewish law, see Michael J. Broyde, *Public and Private International Law from the Perspective of Jewish law*, *in* The Oxford Handbook of Judaism and Economics 363 (Aaron Levine ed., 2010).

30. *See, e.g.*, Steven H. Resnicoff, *Bankruptcy—A Viable Halachic Option?*, 24 J. Halacha & Contemp. Soc'y 5 (1992); Rabbi Yona Reiss, *Establishing a Rabbinical Court Hearing in the Case Where the Plaintiff Has Filed for Bankruptcy*, 15 Sharai Tzedek 139 (5775/2014).

31. *See, e.g.*, Resnicoff, *supra* note 30; Reiss, *supra* note 30 (this article is written by a member of the Beth Din of America and seeks exactly the accommodation noted in the text).

32. *See, e.g.*, Michael A. Helfand, *Fighting for the Debtor's Soul: Regulating Religious Commercial Conduct*, 19 Geo. Mason L. Rev. 157 (2011) for a discussion of this issue.

33. Pew Research Ctr., *supra* note 4.

almost countless denominations, which cannot realistically be discussed here, it will suffice to discuss Christian ADR in a general sense.

Unlike Judaism's more formal, litigation-like arbitral process, Christian ADR looks significantly more like negotiation or mediation,[34] and is the least formal method of dispute resolution that will be discussed here. This less formal method of settling disputes has deep roots in Christian religious doctrine.

Christian ADR is based on teachings of the Bible, and particularly those of Jesus Christ from the New Testament,[35] which encourage Christians to settle disputes in a peaceful manner.[36] For this reason, Christian ADR focuses more on negotiation and mediation than arbitration.[37]

Although many Christian ADR tribunals exist, the industry's leader is Peacemaker Ministries.[38] Peacemaker Ministries has grown tremendously since its inception in 1982, and now counts as members "over three hundred churches, ministries, and organizations."[39] This makes Peacemaker "the largest, multi-denominational Christian dispute resolution service in the country."[40] Along with growing in size and membership, Peacemaker has gained experience and sophistication, and has developed a streamlined process for settling disputes efficiently and effectively.

Peacemaker Ministries' method of settling disputes begins with giving the parties an opportunity to reflect on whether they were perhaps partially to blame. If reflection does not settle the dispute, the parties are required to negotiate with one another. In the case that private negotiations are unsuccessful, the parties are asked to look to a "spiritually mature" person in the church to coach them in their negotiations.[41] If one of these conciliators is not enough, it is suggested that the parties turn to two respected individuals in the church to assist in settling the dispute through mediation and, if necessary, arbitration.[42] If even these individuals fail and the parties cannot reach a mutually agreeable resolution, the disputants may request

34. Shippee, *supra* note 20, at 241; *see also* Glenn G. Waddell & Judith M. Keegan, *Christian Conciliation: An Alternative to "Ordinary" ADR*, 29 CUMB. L. REV. 583 (1998/1999); Joseph Allegretti, *Dialogue and the Practice of Law and Spiritual Values: A Christian Perspective on Alternative Dispute Resolution*, 28 FORDHAM URB. L.J. 997 (2001).

35. Shippee, *supra* note 34.

36. *Id.*

37. *Id.* at 242.

38. *Frequently Asked Questions*, PEACEMAKER MINISTRIES, http://peacemaker.net/icc-frequently-asked-questions/ (last visited Jan. 15, 2016).

39. Shippee, *supra* note 20, at 242.

40. *Id.* at 243.

41. *Id.*

42. *Id.*

that a trained peacemaker from the Institute of Christian Conciliation get involved.[43] Although peacemakers charge to hear a dispute, they are arguably better trained and equipped to settle it, and the parties are encouraged to settle more quickly with the weight of a fee looming.

Christian ADR, like Jewish ADR, touches almost every method of ADR, from conciliation to arbitration, allowing adherents a wide variety of ways in which to settle disputes. As with Jewish arbitration, when disputants turn to arbitration and work through to an arbitration award, courts uphold it more often than not. However, in contrast to Judaism, there seem to be vast areas of secular law that have no direct Christian counterpart, vastly reducing the likelihood of the type of conflict found in *In re Congregation Birchos Yosef*, where the basic issue is what legal system ought to actually govern a substantive area of commercial law between two co-religionists. In a faith in which there is no substantive religious law governing commercial matters independently of secular law, Peacemaker Ministries serves as a "choice of forum," rather than a "choice of law." No matter what forum is chosen, secular bankruptcy law will govern—and, as secular bankruptcy law does not allow any forum other than bankruptcy court without leave of the court itself, the conflict is greatly diminished.[44]

Catholic Christian Arbitration

Outside of Protestant Christianity, which has embraced ADR, there are Christian denominations that have very robust bodies of law, yet have distanced themselves from it. The most notable of these is the Catholic Church.

About 20 percent of Americans identify as Catholic.[45] It is worth focusing on the Catholic Church directly, as it is the exception to the rule of religious groups adopting methods for ADR. This is not to say that Catholics do not have laws governing their churches and parishioners. In fact, canon law, the body of ecclesiastical laws and regulations created to internally govern the Catholic Church, is one of the most ancient and robust legal systems in the world.[46] Even with its robust ecclesiastical law, however, the Catholic

43. *Id.* at 244.

44. *See* Bankruptcy Code, 11 U.S.C. §§ 105(a), 362(d) (1978) (permitting modification of the automatic stay with permission of the court).

45. Pew Research Ctr., *supra* note 4.

46. For the most recent and complete code of Canon Law, see *Code of Canon Law*, Holy See, http://www.vatican.va/archive/ENG1104/_INDEX.HTM (last visited Jan. 19, 2017).

Church has not embraced ADR. Although there are likely many reasons for this reluctance, it is mainly due to the fact that canon law is used mostly for church governance issues. Although canon law is "the law of the Catholic church by which all Catholics are bound,"[47] it is not easily accessible to—or often used by—individual members of the Catholic Church. It also extends to issues of marriage and divorce between Catholics, but it does not extend as far as general private disputes between co-religious parties—it neither professes to be a "choice of law" nor a "choice of forum" available for commercial disputes between members of the Catholic Church.

Because Catholic Church ecclesiastical law has no private ADR mechanism to resolve disputes between private parties, cases such as *In re Congregation Birchos Yosef* cannot appear or be settled under canon law. An exception exists when one of the adjudicants is a Catholic church itself, but even in such a case, canon law might simply send the matter to secular court, as it lacks civilly binding force in most such tribunals.

Islamic Arbitration

Only about 1 percent of the U.S. population identifies as Muslim;[48] however, Islam has become the fastest-growing religious group in the United States.[49] With this growing population has come an interest, as in Jewish and Christian communities, in preserving its own culture. One way Muslims have done this is through settling disputes outside of the secular court system using Islamic principles of law. The procedures used by Muslim arbitral bodies fall somewhere between Christian and Jewish ones—between mediation and arbitration.[50]

The *Qur'an*, Islam's holiest book, like the Bible and Talmud, encourages settling disputes in a peaceful and conciliatory manner. Because of this emphasis, "the Islamic tradition has developed specialized intermediaries known as *qadis* who interpret and apply Islamic law (*Shari'a*), often in an

47. Everson v. Bd. of Educ., 330 U.S. 1 (1947).

48. PEW RESEARCH CTR., *supra* note 4.

49. Shippee, *supra* note 20, at 245.

50. *See generally* Eugene Volokh, *Religious Law (Especially Islamic law) in American Courts*, 66 OKLA. L. REV. 431 (2014); Mohammad H. Fadel, *Shari'a and Halakha in North America: Religious Law, Family Law and Arbitration: Shari'a and Halakha in America*, 90 CHI.-KENT L. REV. 163 (2015); Michael J. Broyde, *Shari'a and Halakha in North America: Faith-Based Private Arbitration as a Model for Preserving Rights and Values in a Pluralistic Society*, 90 CHI.-KENT L. REV. 111 (2015); Cristina Puglia, *Will Parties Take to Tahkim?: The Use of Islamic law and Arbitration in the United States*, 13 CHI.-KENT J. INT'L & COMP. L. 151 (2013).

attempt to preserve social harmony by reaching a negotiated solution to a dispute."[51] *Qadis* work in the areas of conciliation, mediation, and arbitration, although conciliation and mediation are "the preferred dispute resolution approaches of the Prophet Mohammed."[52]

Disputing couples are the likeliest parties to become involved in Islamic ADR. Typically, a couple will name an older family member or some other individual to mediate their dispute. Commonly, one of the arbitrators is the couple's *imam*, or religious leader.[53] Following the *Qur'an*, the mediator's job is to give both parties an opportunity to hear one another's side of the story and identify the underlying issues causing the dispute.[54] Facilitating negotiation between the parties, the mediator's end goal is to help them find a mutually satisfactory resolution to the dispute. Muslim mediation is more often enforced in secular courts than its arbitration counterpart, as arbitration agreements stemming from *Shari'a* are often incompatible with local laws.[55]

Whether due to the fact that arbitration agreements stemming from *Shari'a* will not be enforced, or for some other reason, Muslims in the United States rarely use arbitration, at least currently.[56] However, many Islamic legal scholars feel that arbitration needs to be utilized more frequently, as arbitral decisions provide more finality than their less binding ADR counterparts, since they do not need additional court approval, but simply serve as stand-alone judgments.[57] Muslim arbitration can likely find enforceability in the same way Jewish and Christian arbitration have—through the development of a sophisticated arbitration board or multiple boards with specialized experts familiar with both Islamic and secular law. In this way, trained Muslim arbitrators could help Muslims settle their disputes through a religious lens, while ensuring that the principles being enforced run parallel to—and do not interfere with—secular laws.[58]

Much like Jewish and Christian ADR, Islamic dispute resolution has seen significant developments since its inception, and looks to continue to evolve by following in the footsteps of its predecessors. However, Muslim arbitration is likely to face many hurdles with which its predecessors were not forced to deal. Unlike Jewish law, Islamic law has a very weak doctrine of "the law of the land is the law," and this is likely to create significant ongoing

51. Shippee, *supra* note 20, at 246.
52. *Id.*
53. *Id.* at 247.
54. *Id.*
55. *Id.*
56. *Id.* at 248.
57. *Id.*
58. *Id.*

tension between it and secular law over the content of the laws used in adjudication. Cases such as *In re Congregation Birchos Yosef* will thus be much more common in Islamic tribunals because the basic validity of American bankruptcy law can be questioned from the rubric of Islamic law, whereas a significant strain of Jewish law validates secular bankruptcy law.[59]

E. THE FUTURE OF RELIGIOUS ARBITRATION

Religious arbitration's viability rests on its ability to maintain the respect of secular courts and on the number of participants it can attract.

Religious groups have maintained success in the field of arbitration law particularly by following in the footsteps and procedural methods of their predecessors, building on a foundation of secular contract law and solid procedural foundations commensurate with secular procedural rules. With these foundations in place, religious arbitral bodies take secular courts to the outer limits of constitutionally permitted review, leaving them no choice but to uphold awards. Courts allowing such awards to stand, in turn, give parties faith in the religious arbitral process and make them more likely to view religious arbitration as a viable alternative to secular methods of dispute resolution.

So long as potential participants in religious arbitration view religious dispute resolution as a method that will be respected and upheld by courts, there is not likely to be a shortage of individuals who wish to settle their disputes through the lenses of their religious beliefs. This is especially true in light of recent developments in American religious culture, namely in the movement of secular Americans away from traditional, conservative values.

History shows that a strong system of arbitration may allow a religion to meet this desire by implementing its own law in settling disputes, but there are certain steps each successful religious arbitral body has taken in developing into a viable alternative to the secular court system, and in ensuring that its decisions will be enforceable in, and respected by, secular courts.

F. CRAFTING A FRAMEWORK FOR ENFORCEABLE ARBITRATION DECISIONS

The legal system in America will not honor religious arbitration of family or any other matters unless lawmakers and judges can be confident that

59. *See* Resnicoff, *supra* note 30; MICHAEL BROYDE, THE PURSUIT OF JUSTICE AND JEWISH LAW ch. 3, 4, 5 (2d ed. 2007).

religious arbitration is just and proper as understood by secular law and society. At the same time, faith-based arbitration, like any other form of ADR, is built upon the Federal Arbitration Act (FAA),[60] which is deeply rooted in the contractual approach to private dispute resolution. Under the FAA, courts defer to binding arbitration agreements and subject them only to procedural review for matters such as voluntariness and procedural fairness. Arbitration clauses that include both choice-of-law and choice-of-forum provisions are an especially powerful means of adopting alternative legal models, even when the chosen forum is an arbitration court and the chosen law is religious. Indeed, courts will defer even to decisions of panels that operate under principles that are dramatically different from the existing laws of any state, such as Jewish law, *Shari'a*, or even a non-law structure such as Christian conciliation, provided the parties' selection of the forum and decisional norms is voluntary and the arbitration procedures used are clear and reasonably fair.

As explained in greater detail in Chapter Seven, experience shows that there are six basic principles of procedural regularity that religious arbitration panels must incorporate to ensure that their decisions are honored by secular courts.[61]

First, the arbitration panel must develop and promulgate detailed, standardized rules of procedure. Uniform rules and procedures set clear expectations for the proceedings and protect vulnerable parties. More importantly, procedural safeguards are crucial to the viability of private arbitration, as courts generally review arbitration decisions for procedural, rather than substantive, fairness.

Second, any organization providing arbitration services should also develop an internal appellate process. This reduces the likelihood of errors, increases trust, and helps prevent decisions from being routinely overturned by courts.

Third, the governing rules should spell out choice-of-law provisions to facilitate the accommodation of religious traditions and principles, where possible.

Fourth, in addition to religious authorities, the arbitration panel should employ skilled lawyers and professionals who are also members of the

60. Federal Arbitration Act, 9 U.S.C. §§ 1–16 (1947). Before Congress enacted the FAA, courts were often hostile to alternative dispute resolution, including arbitration. *See* Meacham v. Jamestown, 105 N.E. 653, 655 (N.Y. 1914).

61. Michael Broyde, *Jewish Law Courts in America: Lessons Offered to Sharia Courts by the Beth Din of America*, 57 N.Y.L. Sch. L. Rev. 287 (2012/2013).

panel's constituent religious community and who can provide expertise in secular law and contemporary commercial practices.

Fifth, to ensure the effective resolution of commercial arbitrations, the organization should recognize and, to the greatest extent possible, incorporate into its rulings the realities of conduct in the public arena—even in family law. This is crucial to understanding the actions and intent of the parties in common transactions, but perhaps more important, it will inspire confidence in potential disputants. After all, a dispute resolution system that reflects grand abstract ideals but has little notion of business realities is unlikely to attract voluntary participants.

Finally, the tribunal should recognize that an aggregate of individual arbitrations will likely give rise to an active role in communal leadership. By dint of having organizations that a particular faith group recognizes as "dispensing justice," boundary line disputes within faith-based organizations can be settled judicially, rather than politically. This is particularly true among adherents, but it is to be more broadly expected as well.[62]

These six rules are based on a fundamental reality of religious arbitration: other than in child custody disputes,[63] American arbitration law pays little attention to notions of substantive due process. Neither the government nor the courts has a preconceived notion of the "right" substantive resolution of most any dispute, if the parties contractually choose to opt for a different resolution or a process that produces a different resolution from what state or federal law might. Rather, the FAA and the myriad state laws that derive from it have a strong notion of *procedural* due process.[64]

62. This basic idea is the focus of three recent articles of mine. *See* Michael J. Broyde, *Shari'a and Halakha in North America: Faith-Based Private Arbitration as a Model for Preserving Rights and Values in a Pluralistic Society*, 90 CHI.-KENT L. REV. 111 (2015); Michael J. Broyde, Ira Bedzow & Shlomo C. Pill, *The Pillars of Successful Religious Arbitration: Models for American Islamic Arbitration Based on the Beth Din of America and Muslim Arbitration Tribunal Experience*, 30 HARV. J. RACIAL & ETHNIC JUST. 33 (2014); Michael Broyde, *Jewish Law Courts in America: Lessons Offered to Sharia Courts by the Beth Din of America*, 57 N.Y.L. SCH. L. REV. 287 (2012/2013).

63. *See* Broyde, *supra* note 62, at page 115.

64. There are certain things arbitration panels may and may not do in the course of making decisions: They may not call a hearing at 4:00 AM on a federal holiday; they must provide litigants with a reasonable amount of notice; they must conduct hearings in a language that the parties understand; arbitrators may not have a financial interest in the resolution of the case or financial involvement with the parties, and they must honor other basic ideas of procedural fair play. *See, e.g.*, *JAMS Policy on Employment Arbitration: Minimum Standards of Procedural Fairness*, JAMS, http://www.jamsadr.com/employment-minimum-standards/ (last visited Oct. 1, 2016). Of course, the JAMS policy is only binding when it is incorporated by contract, and the minimal obligations of the arbitrator under state law are considerably lower.)

Religious tribunals recognize that, in order for secular courts to honor their decisions, they must follow only procedural, rather than substantive, due process. The Beth Din of America has promulgated legally sophisticated rules and procedures that are published on its website.[65] The Institute for Christian Conciliation[66] and the Muslim Arbitration Tribunal have done likewise.[67] These rules set out requirements such as the number of days between filing and response. They describe matters such as discovery, motion practice, transcription, and the appropriate place to file. They also establish the proper language for hearings, the procedure for compiling a record, waiver doctrines, notice provisions, and other rules of procedure.

Religious groups and their adherents have slowly realized that, so long as these foundations are in place, religious arbitration can be used to settle almost any dispute between any groups of disputants—be they individuals or business entities. The latter group are the most recent adopters of religious arbitration, having implemented the practice to settle disputes arising out of what has been dubbed "co-religionist commerce."

G. RELIGIOUS ARBITRATION'S BIGGEST CHALLENGES MOVING FORWARD: MOLDING ANCIENT LAWS TO FIT A MODERN PARADIGM, AND EQUAL ACCESS OF ALL RELIGIONS TO RELIGIOUS ARBITRATION

Religious arbitration's proliferation still faces difficult issues, especially as new religions embrace the practice. The two biggest issues are apparent in the fledgling branch of Islamic religious arbitration in the United States. First, Islamic arbitrators, much like those of other religions, must mold ancient laws to fit a modern paradigm. This is indeed a challenge for any nomos-centric faith tradition that wishes to use its religious norms and values to effectively and convincingly resolve modern conflicts. Although doing so can often be challenging in practice, it is something that religious leaders and scholars of many faiths have done before and have within their power to do again. The second challenge is more difficult to overcome. Contemporary American Muslims face serious Islamophobia

65. *Rules and Procedures*, BETH DIN OF AM., http://bethdin.org/wp-content/uploads/2015/07/Rules.pdf (last visited Jan. 15, 2016).

66. PEACEMAKER MINISTRIES, http://www.peacemaker.net/site/c.nuIWL7MOJtE/b.5394441/k.BD56/Home.htm (last visited Jan. 15, 2016).

67. MUSLIM ARBITRATION TRIBUNAL, http://www.matribunal.com/ (last visited Jan. 15, 2016).

that is specifically directed at concerns over Islamic religious norms and practices—precisely the standards that Islamic arbitration would seek to uphold among Muslim disputants. Although this problem is particularly acute for Muslims—thus far, no states have attempted to ban the application of Jewish law or Christian values—it is in many ways part of a broader tension between contemporary societal values and traditional religious mores and practices.

As with Christian denominations, Islam is composed of numerous sects, some more conservative—strict in their adherence to the laws of their faith—than others. These subsets also have different interpretations of the *Qur'an* and its teachings. Different subsets will thus be more readily able to implement religious arbitration acceptable to American secular courts than will others. As with every other branch of dispute resolution, the enforceability of arbitration proceedings applying religious norms is limited by the bounds of public policy. Some groups' interpretations of the *Qur'an* breach or run contrary to public policy and thus will not be enforceable even in consented-to arbitration.

That said, with the growth of Islamic arbitral bodies has come the type of sophistication developed by other religions in their utilization of arbitration. Islamic arbitral bodies have gotten better at ensuring that they keep their decisions, arbitral awards, and arbitral procedures within the bounds of public policy, and they continue to work at perfecting this skill.

But instead of being met with increasing acceptance, Islamic religious arbitration has been framed as a different practice altogether. Muslims' arbitral bodies are often characterized as full-blown courts. This sort of characterization can be found in the following passage, taken from the less-than-mainstream Breitbart News, but which captures well the popular sentiment:

> An Islamic Tribunal using Sharia law in Texas has been confirmed by *Breitbart Texas*. The tribunal is operating as a non-profit organization in Dallas. One of the attorneys for the tribunal said participation and acceptance of the tribunal's decisions are "voluntary."[68]

68. Bob Price, *Islamic Tribunal Confirmed in Texas; Attorney Claims "It's Voluntary"*, BREITBART.COM (Jan. 27, 2015), http://www.breitbart.com/texas/2015/01/27/hold-islamic-tribunal-confirmed-in-texas-its-voluntary-says-attorney/ (last visited Oct. 1, 2016). Of course, as Snopes.com notes (see http://www.snopes.com/politics/religion/shariatexas.asp, last accessed January 17, 2017), this Breitbart story is hyperbolistic, exaggerated, and not reliable in its details. It is quoted here exactly because this type of story emphasizes how Islamic tribunals—acting not much differently than

> *Breitbart Texas* spoke with one of the "judges," Dr. Taher El-badawi. He said the tribunal operates under Sharia law as a form of "non-binding dispute resolution." El-badawi said their organization is "a tribunal, not arbitration." A tribunal is defined by Merriam-Webster's Dictionary as "a court or forum of justice." The four Islamic attorneys call themselves "judges" not "arbitrators."
>
> El-badawi said the tribunal follows Sharia law to resolve civil disputes in family and business matters. He said they also resolve workplace disputes.

Upon review, the tribunal's website indicates a practice directly in line with other religious arbitral bodies.[69] Even if the tribunal were to decide issues not in accordance with the laws of the United States, such decisions could be challenged in the secular court system. Nevertheless, the fear of such tribunals captured by the tone of the above excerpt persists. For example, "[i]n 2006, the province of Ontario banned arbitration of family law disputes under any body of laws except Ontario law, in part to prohibit arbitration under religious laws."[70] Moreover, within the United States, seven states have passed their own laws banning courts from considering *Shari'a*.[71] Because bans on consideration of *Shari'a* in particular will likely be found unconstitutional in the United States, states that pass such laws will need to draft them broadly in order for them to pass constitutional muster. The unintended consequences can be significant:

> [T]he bans can have unintended consequences like disrupting marital prenuptial agreements or invalidating court decisions in other states. Especially in divorce and contract law, religious beliefs (like Sharia, orthodox Jewish or Catholic canon) can factor into how judges or arbitrators preside over a dispute. For example, a couple may sign a prenuptial agreement that requires them to go to an imam and that a religious leader must conduct the mediation. Alabama's [ban on consideration of *Shari'a*] nullifies that requirement.[72]

rabbinical courts—are treated differently by the public. *See also* Eric Celeste, "Anti-Muslim Sentiment in Irving (and the Imam Who Has To Tolerate It)," http://www.dmagazine.com/frontburner/2015/03/anti-muslim-sentiment-bubbles-up-in-irving-and-the-imam-who-has-to-tolerate-it/, last accessed Jan. 17, 2017).

69. *About Us*, Islamic Tribunal, http://www.islamictribunal.org (last visited Oct. 1, 2016).

70. Bilal M. Choksi, Comment, *Religious Arbitration in Ontario—Making the Case Based on the British Example of the Muslim Arbitration Tribunal*, 33 U. Pa. J. Int'l L. 791, 791 (2012).

71. Liz Farmer, *Alabama Joins Wave of States Banning Foreign Laws*, Governing (Nov. 4, 2014), http://www.governing.com/topics/elections/gov-alabama-foreign-law-courts-amendment.html (last visited Aug. 28, 2016).

72. *Id.*

Religious leaders fear such effects—as reflected in their willingness to stand united against such laws.[73] This trend must continue for universal acceptance of religious arbitration to continue. If bans are passed and awards from religious arbitral bodies consistently struck down, the practice will be less likely to be selected as a method for settling disputes between parties. Such nullification is unlikely, however, as it would disregard contract law.

H. CONCLUSION

This chapter has provided a brief survey of contemporary faith-based dispute resolution in the United States and, in doing so, has set the stage for the following sections of this book. Religious arbitration serves an important function for religious individuals and communities in the United States. It provides a legally recognized mechanism whereby people can choose to bring their ordinary legal disputes over mundane matters such as property, employment, and commercial transactions to religious courts, staffed by religious functionaries who will resolve such conflicts in accordance with the parties' religious commitments. Although adjudications by religious courts have always existed in this country, it is only in recent decades that the presence and practice of faith-based dispute resolution has become both more urgent for religious individuals and communities, as well as more troublesome for some in the broader American political and legal landscape. In response, different major faith traditions, including Protestant, Jewish, and Muslim communities, have developed different models of dispute resolution. As was briefly alluded to above, the rise of various models of religious arbitration in recent decades is in part due to the gradually growing distance between the traditionally religious—especially Protestant Christian—bases for American law and policy, and contemporary societal norms and attitudes that embrace a different set of values. It is to this important catalyst for the development of faith-based arbitration as a serious alterative to American courts and American law that this book now turns.

73. *See, e.g.*, Tara Culp-Ressler, *Christians Blast Ballot Initiative Banning Sharia Law in Alabama*, ThinkProgress (Nov. 2, 2014), https://thinkprogress.org/christians-blast-ballot-initiative-banning-sharia-law-in-alabama-7166c97ae507#.qejhnbffj (last visited Aug. 28, 2016).

CHAPTER 2

The Movement Away from Secular Values in the Religious Community

One of the major causes for religious individuals' and communities' increased interest in faith based arbitration in recent decades is the ever-widening gap between traditional values and societal law and policy in the United States. As the norms and values embraced by American law and enforced by state and federal courts have moved away from their historically-grounded religious roots, people of faith have become increasingly less comfortable with ordering their lives based on such secular commitments. One solution has been to use America's legal arbitration framework to opt out of being bound by current legal norms, and to instead choose to resolve disputes in accordance with religious commitments. This chapter explores one of the most acute areas of tension between traditional and secular values within evolving standards of American law and policy: the realm of family law. This chapter will review the family law culture wars that have raged in American society over the last half century or so, focusing on the deeply changing values of general society in the areas of same-sex marriage, adultery, and premarital sex. It will trace both this revolution and religious responses to it, which are important cultural battlegrounds that contribute substantially to the belief by many in religious communities that private religious alternatives to American law are needed.

Sharia Tribunals, Rabbinical Courts, and Christian Panels. Michael J. Broyde.

A. THE SETTLING DUST OF THE CULTURE WARS

Differences between the ways in which religious groups and secular individuals think about and approach family law and family issues have fueled what have been referred to as "The Culture Wars."[1] The term "Culture Wars" refers to a conflict between those values considered traditionalist or conservative and those considered progressive or liberal. When culture war-like disputes began to arise in the 1920s, they tended to stem from the urban and rural divide that existed between Americans, as well as the Progressive Movement. The idea was re-introduced in the early 1990s by James Davidson Hunter in his book, *Culture Wars: The Struggle to Define America*. Unlike Hunter, who defined the culture wars as between warring factions not separated by religion or class, but rather by impulse, I will discuss the family culture wars of the 1990s through the scope of the religious divide that existed between religious and secular society.

B. CULTURAL AND MORAL SHIFTS IN THE UNITED STATES

The United States has changed significantly throughout its existence, from its geographic makeup to its legal climate. In the last sixty years or so, the United States has seen the biggest shift in its cultural and moral foundations. This change was dubbed the "culture wars,"[2] and it has slowly but increasingly changed the way a majority of Americans think about various social issues.

The so-called culture wars started in the 1960s and continue today. Although the issues have changed, their divisive nature has not. They encompass everything from whether the United States should be governed by a large or small federal government to whether individuals of the same sex should be able to marry. However, family law issues have gained more traction and could be considered the central battleground.[3] Family is one of the central issues in the culture wars because it helps define America's identity and has shaped the country's moral principles.[4]

1. *See* James Davison Hunter, Culture Wars: The Struggle to Define America (1992).
2. *Id.*
3. Jamie Alan Aycock, *Contracting Out of the Culture Wars: How the Law Should Enforce and Communities of Faith Should Encourage More Enduring Marital Commitments*, 30 Harv. J. L. & Pub. Pol'y 231, 232 (2006).
4. *See generally* Susan Milligan, *The New Culture Wars*, U.S. News (Sept. 25, 2015).

Standing by and watching the country's principles change has been disconcerting for many. One author notes:

> [This comes] from a sense—especially among older, white male voters—that the country they knew when they were younger is vanishing, taken over by racial, ethnic and religious minorities. Add to that social changes, such as the prevalence of women working outside the home and the expansion of rights for gay, lesbian, bisexual and transgender people, and older white men naturally wonder what happened to the cultural identity of their youth.[5]

It is highly unlikely that these culture wars will ever end—they will simply shift from one issue to the next. One author summarizes it as such: "In the 1960s, it was abortion, amnesty and acid. In the early part of the 21st century, it was God, guns and gays."[6] But there has been real and pervasive change in the way America views "moral" issues, especially in the arena of family law. As one commentator notes, "[i]n relation to marriage, divorce, and cohabitation, two trends are especially significant: (1) the liberalization of moral values (or rise of moral relativism); and (2) the shift in family law toward focusing on individuals rather than groups."[7] This shift has emphasized the ability of individuals to make their own decisions.

Changes in popular opinion have translated to changes in the law. Particularly, "[i]n response to this waning of traditional moral values, the law has dropped statements of moral aspiration."[8] In the family law context, this means the law is "desert[ing] its function of prescribing and describing norms of conduct whose purpose is to maintain families as places for interdependent, collective living and the nurture of children."[9] Instead of shifting from one set of moral values to another, Jamie Alan Aycock argues that "the law has 'relinquish[ed] most of its overt attempts to promote any particular set of ideas about family life,' reflecting instead modern legal values of pragmatism, anti-formalism, and neutrality."[10] Individuals have come to view alternative lifestyles as morally acceptable and thus are "less likely to believe that the law should enforce or even encourage particular

5. *Id.*
6. *Id.*
7. Aycock, *supra* note 3, at 237.
8. *Id.* at 238.
9. *Id.* at 238–39 (quoting Barbara Bennett Woodhouse, *Towards a Revitalization of Family Law*, 69 Tex. L. Rev. 245, 247 (1990) (reviewing Mary Ann Glendon, The Transformation of Family Law: State, Law and Family in the United States and Western Europe (1989))).
10. *Id.* at 239 (quoting Glendon, *supra* note 9, at 297).

lifestyles."[11] The law, in turn, "has moved away from its traditional emphasis on group values such as interdependence and attachment in favor of individual values such as equality and individuality,"[12] and now "protects the family because it serves individual fulfillment rather than because it serves society."[13]

One group has been alienated from this movement more than others: the religious in the United States.

C. MOVEMENT AWAY FROM RELIGION AND RELIGIOUS MORES IN THE UNITED STATES

Recent polls indicate that the United States population, generally speaking, is getting less religious and more secular.[14] This seems to mirror the country's—and its laws'—movements away from certain traditional values. These movements have left the religious population in a precarious situation—surrounded by a society whose values are changing before their eyes—and have also caused many within the religious community to become even more invested and devoted to their respective faiths as sources of all-encompassing personal values.

As the government more clearly aligns itself with the shift away from traditional religious values, the religious communities' attempts to keep their principles as the foundational principles of secular law and life have failed: from marriage law to blue laws, religion is a less dominant force. Realizing that this is the new normal, religions are much more inclined to incrementally withdraw from aspects of society. Many faithful individuals and groups have looked inward for justice, law, ethics, love, and many other values where the bridge between secular and religious is narrower than ever.

That so many religious communities are coming to embrace this view reflects another change in our legal system: the substance of American law is dominantly secular in principles rather than religious (as it was historically). Religiously neutral principles of equality and fairness, rather than

11. *Id.*
12. *Id.*
13. *Id.*
14. *America's Changing Religious Landscape*, Pew Research Ctr. (May 12, 2015), http://www.pewforum.org/2015/05/12/americas-changing-religious-landscape/; *Study: More Americans than Ever Spurning Religion*, CBS News (May 12, 2015), http://www.cbsnews.com/news/study-number-of-americans-who-spurn-religion-hits-record-high/ (last visited Oct. 1, 2016).

the historical commitment to traditional values, have become the major cultural and political currency, and the principles of no specific religion or even those of religion generally are given any privilege.[15] As noted above, this change is part of the most significant demographic one of the last century: there is no longer a majority religion in the United States. Although most Americans still identify as Christians, no denomination or sect predominates, and most Christians or Jews no longer look to their faith for their basic values.[16] Moreover, since the mid-twentieth century, the United States has become more of a multicultural society. It is increasingly comfortable with multiple expressions of individual and subgroup identity coexisting in the public sphere. In sociological terms, the metaphor of the melting pot has been replaced by a salad bowl.[17]

So, although the culture wars still flare, religious communities have begun to realize that they are all minority groups. They understand that secular law is no longer broadly reflective of traditional values, and this will not change in the foreseeable future. Whether this has become apparent to everyone or not, it is motivating religious communities to step outside the framework of secular law into the realm of private dispute resolution in order to preserve their communities.[18] Even more important, the common social fabric has shifted to a secular model—gay marriage is just the most public crier of this change—which predominates in every value-driven public discussion, leaving traditional religious communities feeling less

15. *See, e.g.*, David Aikman, *America's Religious Past Fades in a Secular Age*, WALL ST. J., Oct. 25, 2012, *available at* http://online.wsj.com/news/articles/SB100014240529702036306045780731718380004 16 (last visited Oct. 1, 2016).

16. Pew Research Center data from 2007 indicated "that the United States is on the verge of becoming a minority Protestant country; the number of Americans who report that they are members of Protestant denominations now stands at barely 51 percent." *Religious Landscape Study*, PEW RESEARCH CTR., http://religions.pewforum.org/pdf/reportreligious-landscape-study-full.pdf (last visited Oct. 1, 2016). By 2012, the prediction had come true. *"Nones" on the Rise*, PEW RESEARCH CTR. (Oct. 9, 2012), *available at* http://www.pewforum.org/2012/10/09/nones-on-the-rise/ (last visited Oct. 1, 2016) ("In surveys conducted in the first half of 2012, fewer than half of American adults say they are Protestant (48%). This marks the first time in Pew Research Center surveys that the Protestant share of the population has dipped significantly below 50%.").

17. CARL N. DEGLER, OUT OF OUR PAST: THE FORCES THAT SHAPED MODERN AMERICA 296 (1970) ("[T]he metaphor of the melting pot is unfortunate and misleading. A more accurate analogy would be a salad bowl, for, though the salad is an entity, the lettuce can still be distinguished from the chicory, the tomatoes from the cabbage.").

18. Some religious communities even welcome this, as they see a greater threat from alternative religious values than secular ones. *See* Michael J. Broyde, *Jewish Law and American Public Policy: A Principled Jewish Law View and Some Practical Jewish Observations*, *in* RELIGION AS A PUBLIC GOOD: JEWS AND OTHER AMERICANS ON RELIGION IN THE PUBLIC SQUARE 161 (Alan Mittleman ed., 2003).

and less comfortable with general social mores and increasingly disconnected from common public discourse or law.[19]

D. EXAMPLES OF CHANGING VALUES

The gap between public opinion and the opinions held by religious groups has widened, especially with regard to social issues. The topics that make this most clear are wide-ranging, but include abortion, premarital sex, marriage, same-sex marriage, divorce, and the use of contraceptives.

Many religious groups oppose abortion[20] and same-sex marriage,[21] while secular society has gone the other way. For example, in 2004, 60 percent of the population opposed legalizing same-sex marriage, while 31 percent favored it. Eleven years later, in 2015, 55 percent favored legalizing same-sex marriage, while 39 percent were opposed. On abortion, the numbers are less clear, with 50 percent of people considering themselves pro-choice and 44 percent considering themselves pro-life, as opposed to 1996, when 56 percent of people considered themselves pro-choice and 33 percent of respondents considered themselves to be pro-life.[22] Even on less sensitive topics, Americans have moved away from the views historically held by mainline churches. On the subject of premarital sex, 68 percent found it morally acceptable in 2015, while 29 percent found it morally wrong. This as opposed to 2001, when only 53 percent of respondents found premarital sex to be morally acceptable, while 42 percent found it to be morally wrong.[23] In contrast to these issues, which the Church has relatively little control over, the issues of marriage and divorce have been embraced by the Church as a place where they can draw a line between their principles and those of the general population.

19. For just the most recent example of this, see Michael Paulson, *Colleges and Evangelicals Collide on Bias Policy*, N.Y. TIMES, June 9, 2014, *available at* http://www.nytimes.com/2014/06/10/us/colleges-and-evangelicals-collide-on-bias-policy.html (discussing how many institutions are forcing off campus religious student organizations whose values discriminate against homosexual conduct).

20. *Religious Groups' Official Positions on Abortion*, PEW RESEARCH CTR. (Jan. 16, 2013), http://www.pewforum.org/2013/01/16/religious-groups-official-positions-on-abortion/ (last visited Oct. 1, 2016).

21. *Religious Groups' Official Positions on Same-Sex Marriage*, PEW RESEARCH CTR. (Dec. 7, 2012), http://www.pewforum.org/2012/12/07/religious-groups-official-positions-on-same-sex-marriage/ (last visited Oct. 1, 2016).

22. *Abortion*, GALLUP.COM, http://www.gallup.com/poll/1576/abortion.aspx (last visited Oct. 1, 2016).

23. *Marriage*, GALLUP.COM, http://www.gallup.com/poll/117328/marriage.aspx (last visited Oct. 1, 2016).

On divorce, in 2015, 71 percent of respondents found it morally acceptable, while 20 percent found it morally wrong. This is strikingly different from the survey taken in 2001, which indicated that 59 percent of respondents found divorce to be morally acceptable, while 28 percent found it to be morally wrong. As the secular population's opinion became more favorable on the subject of divorce, the court system has streamlined the divorce process. Although this has made it easier for individuals to procure a divorce, it has shifted the focus away from traditional means of doing so. In particular, many religious individuals are required to get both a legal divorce in the court system and a religious one under the dictates of their Church. This allows Churches to impose their beliefs upon their followers by giving them some control over the institution of marriage, at least in its religious sense.

E. RELIGIOUS GROUPS TAKING BACK CONTROL OVER MARRIAGE

Although religious groups may have lost control over how the state defines marriage, they still have control over how they define the institution, are free to either accept or reject various forms of it, and can create various hurdles for getting married in conformity with their religious principles. In particular, some religious communities have embraced an alternative form of marriage called "covenant marriage." This form of marriage has been fostered by conservative states desperate to allow religious groups to maintain some sovereignty over religious marriage.

Covenant marriage is "[a] special type of marriage in which the parties agree to more stringent requirements for marriage and divorce than are otherwise imposed by state law for ordinary marriages."[24] Although requirements vary by state, "most . . . require couples who opt for covenant marriage to undergo premarital counseling. A divorce will be granted only after the couple has undergone marital counseling and has been separated for a specified period . . . ."[25] In opting into covenant marriage, couples are in essence entering back into the fault-based divorce system that has been nullified in most states in favor of a no-fault system.[26] In Arizona,

24. Black's Law Dictionary 1060 (9th ed. 2009).

25. Katherine S. Spaht, *Louisiana's Covenant Marriage: Social Commentary and Legal Implications*, 59 La. L. Rev. 63 (1998), *available at* http://faculty.law.lsu.edu/katherine-spaht/covenantmarriage.htm.

26. Mark Baer, *The Problem with Covenant Marriages and Fault-Based Divorce*, The Huffington Post Blog (Nov. 6, 2014, 6:05 PM), http://www.huffingtonpost.com/mark-baer/the-problem-with-covenant_b_6110600.html.

Arkansas, and Louisiana, after entering into a covenant marriage, a couple may obtain a divorce for only three reasons: (1) adultery by the other spouse, (2) commission of a felony or other infamous crime by the other spouse, or (3) physical or sexual abuse of the spouse or of a child of either spouse.[27] In addition to these three grounds for immediate divorce, couples may divorce following a period of separation if: (1) the spouses have been living separate and apart continuously without reconciliation for two years; or (2) if there are minor children involved, the couple must have been living separate and apart for two years and six months from the date the judgment for judicial separation was signed. If abuse of a child was the basis for judicial separation, the couple must live separate and apart for only one year from the date the judgment was signed.[28]

Although some argue that these restrictions will reduce the instances of divorce in the states where implemented, others believe it is detrimental to the individuals who enter into such covenant marriages.[29]

Laws allowing for covenant marriage were passed in Arizona, Arkansas, and Louisiana in the late 1990s.[30] Its supporters hope that these will create a lower divorce rate while keeping divorce disputes in the secular courts and out of religious venues. Covenant marriage allows religious groups to develop their own system of marriage that runs parallel with state law—another obstacle marrying couples must overcome in order to have their unions recognized. Although seemingly unrelated to religious arbitration, covenant marriage provides religious groups with a similar mechanism to engage secular law while instituting their religious beliefs. It is a separate but equal system of regulating relationships between religious individuals.

Of course, this example is not perfect. Only three states actually adopted covenant marriage as a legal alternative to regular marriage, and even in those jurisdictions secular covenant marriage has failed to attract many adherents. Moreover, for many people of faith, the covenant marriage frameworks offered by state law do not really satisfy religious needs. As the United States maintains a separation of church and state, these legally-sanctioned covenant marriages are really just alternative models of formal secular marriage contracts rather than religiously meaningful

27. *Covenant Marriage License*, THE CENTER FOR HEALTHY RELATIONSHIPS, http://liferelationships.com/resources/covenant-marriage-license/ (last visited Oct. 1, 2016).
28. *Id.*
29. *See* Spaht, *supra* note 25.
30. *See* Baer, *supra* note 26.

sacraments.[31] Precisely because a secular institution cannot successfully develop or encompass the passion, flavor, and fervor of a religious model, religious marriage is simply not well imitated by secular society, even when state laws appear to mimic religious forms.

Family law, however, is not the only area in which religious individuals are drawing lines in the sand to separate themselves from the values and modes of conduct embraced by the wider secular society. Religious individuals have taken to developing fully functioning religious communities within regular society, complete with their own generally observed standards of behavior reinforced through networks of religious schools, houses of worship, charitable organizations, and dispute resolution forums. In this way, religious communities have worked to insulate themselves from the secular world and secular values by creating functional alternatives more in line with religious norms and values.

F. THE RISE OF RELIGIOUS COMMUNITIES AS A CENTERPIECE

As the number of religious individuals in the United States shrinks, religious individuals cling more tightly to their religious beliefs and principles. In so doing, these individuals tend to seek to surround themselves with other like-minded individuals. As these individual connections multiply, small groups of religious individuals grow into religious communities. In this way, religious individuals are re-establishing themselves as a central feature, where religion is still at the centerpiece of the community. These communities create a different set of norms and seek to engage in cultural, but not economic withdrawal from the secular community. This, notably, is where the new religious communities differ from the Amish, for example, who withdrew both culturally and economically a century ago.

Religious communities allow religious individuals not only to live among individuals sharing their own religious beliefs, but also to live their lives in a way that is fully commensurate with their religious beliefs, a way that reinforces such beliefs throughout the surrounding community and, in many ways, also accommodates their lifestyle.

31. Less than 2 percent; *see* Steven L. Nock, Laura A. Sanchez & James D. Wright, Covenant Marriage: The Movement to Reclaim Tradition in America 3, Appx. A (2008); Spaht, *supra* note 25.

Religious communities are, in essence, groups of religious individuals abandoning the secular community. Although certainly in the minority of communities in the United States, religious communities have maintained their strength over time, the strength of such communities is at its peak when the religious group comprising a religious community is not the majority religion in the country. The reason for this is simple: building a religious community allows religious groups to concentrate their power in a specific area. In these communities, religious groups can uphold their own rules and live through the lens of their religious values.

Being surrounded by like-minded individuals, in turn, allows religious individuals to enter into agreements with one another, and to add a clause in such agreement establishing religious arbitration as the method to be used to settle any disputes arising from the transaction. This highlights the point where religious arbitration is at its strongest—when it is utilized by two members of a religious community. If a religious community makes up the population at large, their values go beyond religious values and constitute cultural values. In sum, when a religious community is strong and shaping society, it is less culture and more popular culture. This leaves arbitration agreements in such environments reeking of coercion, or at least hinting at it. On the contrary, if a religious community is composed of a minority religion, and two like-minded individuals agree to arbitrate their disputes through a religious lens, such an agreement acquires a hint of validity, and it is less likely that either of the parties to the agreement was coerced into religious arbitration.

Religious individuals in more insular religious communities are able to develop reasonable expectations in their dealings with other individuals in their community. Therefore, they are able to enter into contractual relationships governed by their religious beliefs, essentially allowing them to inject their religious beliefs into their everyday lives. This goes beyond the realm of what is typically thought of as the religious realm, into secular life. These individuals are able to agree with fellow religious individuals on how their food will be prepared, how their roof will be fixed, how their hardwood flooring will be installed, and beyond. Professors Michael Helfand and Barak Richman have dubbed such commerce between religious individuals "co-religionist commerce." Religious communities allow for this commerce to develop. This commerce, in turn, creates a ripe situation for religious arbitration—where two individuals who share the same religious beliefs and principles agree to arbitrate any disputes arising from their relationship.

G. CONCLUSION

This chapter has explained part of the rise of religious arbitration in America in connection to the twentieth and early twenty-first century culture wars between religious and secular values in the realm of family law. As societal laws and policies have moved away from their traditional foundations in broad religious principles, religiously observant Americans have found that their adherence to state and federal legal systems fails to adequately satisfy their deep religious commitments. People of faith have responded to these developments in a variety of ways. Some have sought to avoid ordering their lives in accordance with secular norms in discrete areas, such as family law. In other cases, religious communities have gone further and sought to withdraw to a greater or lesser degree from secular society and instead form relatively insular communities wherein religiously like-minded individuals and institutions can associate, work, educate, worship together, and order their relationships in accordance with shared religious beliefs and practices.

CHAPTER 3

Co-religionist Commerce Is Better Adjudicated in Arbitration

The formation of insular religious communities and associations described at the end of the last chapter does not in and of itself solve the problems that many religiously observant Americans have with fully participating in the normative value systems of general secular society. Although the creation of insular associational communities of co-religionists enables religious people to order their affairs in accordance with their respective faith commitments, it brings to the fore the issue of dispute resolution. Members of religious communities, like anyone else, are engaged in all kinds of commerce with each other. They buy and sell homes, hire and fire employees, purchase cars and groceries, have slip-and-fall accidents on each other's sidewalks, get married and divorced, get treated by doctors, give gifts and inherit estates, and send their children to school. Depending on the nature of any particular individual or community, more or less of this commerce may take place between co-religionists who all want to govern their affairs based on religious rather than secular legal principles. Also, like anyone else, these religious parties often get embroiled in disputes over their mundane interpersonal dealings, and need ways of resolving such conflicts fairly and effectively.

Of course, state and federal courts are available to resolve disputes between co-religionist parties the same way that they are available to all Americans. Religious parties, however, are increasingly choosing to avoid resolving co-religionist conflicts of this kind in traditional courts, instead opting for private dispute resolution methods based on religious principles. This chapter explores this phenomenon by focusing on an argument put forth by Professors Michael A. Helfand and Barak D. Richman that state and federal courts can and should be more willing to engage in resolving co-religionist disputes. This chapter argues that one of the reasons for the increased demand for and importance of religious arbitration is that secular courts are simply poorly equipped to address such cases in ways that effectively uphold the understandings and expectations of religious parties engaged in co-religionist commercial conflicts.

A. CO-RELIGIONIST COMMERCE AND CONTEXTUAL ADJUDICATION

Co-religionist commerce is defined by Professors Michael A. Helfand and Barak D. Richman as "commerce between co-religionists who intend their transactions to adhere to religious principles or to pursue religious objectives."[1] As was noted in Chapter Two, the United States has generally become less religious, yet those who have stayed religious have become even more entrenched in their religions. This religiously entrenched population counts co-religionist commerce as a characteristic activity. Importantly, "[i]n recent years, American religious communities have become increasingly sophisticated players in commercial markets, developing legal instruments that comply with the demands of religious dictates while engineering substantial business transactions."[2] Although the concentration of religious individuals into religious communities allows them to govern themselves from within, their religious foundations place them in the precarious—yet unavoidable—position of facing major hurdles in the secular court system. Perhaps the biggest challenge is that the secular court system is not sufficiently equipped to deal with highly specialized disputes involving co-religionist parties.

Although similar to typical commerce, co-religionist commerce—like all specialized commerce—has numerous inherent perspectives and flavors. Its ecclesiastical qualities frequently bleed into the general aspects of its culture. This includes remedies that vary from tradition to tradition. Although seemingly benign, the ecclesiastical qualities inherent in co-religionist commerce present a number of problems for courts. As examples, Helfand

1. Michael A. Helfand & Barak D. Richman, *The Challenge of Co-Religionist Commerce*, 64 Duke Law Journal 769-822 (2015) at 771.
2. *Id.* at 771–72.

and Richman point to the fact that courts often "shy away from adjudicating co-religionist commercial disputes, fearing that intervention would impermissibly contravene prevailing interpretations of the Establishment Clause" due to the fact that settling such disputes involves "interpret[ing] religious terminology, standards, . . . practices," and common commercial customs.[3] Even when no establishment clause bar exists, the correct resolution of disputes between co-religionist parties still involves interpreting religion, which courts find difficult. This is due in part to the fact that "[c]onstitutional doctrine . . . has instructed courts, when confronted with disputes that are imbued with ecclesiastical circumstances, to adjudicate on the basis of 'neutral principles of law'—that is, to issue rulings based 'on objective, well-established concepts of [] law familiar to lawyers and judges.'"[4] This cuts two ways—it keeps courts from becoming entangled in religious doctrine and practice, and takes away the right of parties to settle their disputes through a lens reflective of their religious principles, thus undermining the religious purpose and significance of agreements between co-religionist parties.

Helfand and Richman point to a number of issues with secular courts interpreting religious doctrine and settling disputes between co-religionist parties, including that the movement toward favoring textual interpretations of contracts takes away the option to invoke contextual evidence to interpret religious terminology. There is also the aforementioned growing wariness of courts to adjudicate disputes involving ecclesiastical interests—culminating in a tendency to interpret the establishment clause expansively to preclude adjudication of co-religionist disputes. These two trends, Helfand and Richman argue, converge to place co-religionist parties in an untenable position wherein their agreements will be judged by the explicit language contained therein. If such language draws too much on religious doctrine, courts will refuse to adjudicate.

Helfand and Richman thus suggest that courts take a contextualist approach to settling disputes between co-religionists. This approach would ask judges to attempt to understand and uphold the intent and understandings of transacting parties given their religious contexts. To use Helfand and Richman's examples, rather than try to understand the correct textual meaning of the word "kosher" in a consumer contract—or the meaning and applicability of traditional, ritual terminology in religious marriage and divorce agreements—courts should look to enforce

3. *Id.* at 773.
4. *Id.* at 774.

the parties' subjective understandings of these terms and the ways in which they expected these terms to structure their contractual relationship. Judicial attempts to definitively determine whether some food item or practice qualifies as "kosher" would almost certainly run headlong into serious establishment clause and religious question doctrine concerns.[5] The same would be true if a court set out to decide what qualifies as "cause" for firing a religious functionary under the rules and principles of that particular faith tradition. Helfand and Richman argue that courts can avoid such problems by resolving such cases contextually. Instead of trying to determine what the doctrines and teachings of the relevant religion say on the matter, judges should merely seek to uphold the intentions and expectations of the parties, which can be done on a neutral basis as a matter of secular contract law.

I agree that a contextualist stance is a reasonable solution, but would note that Helfand and Richman's suggestion is not the most efficient or effective way of resolving co-religionist disputes. Adopting a contextualist approach is principally an internal, subjective process. It asks judges to realize that agreements between co-religionists are no different than agreements between completely secular parties, and to adjudicate these cases according to the religious principles that the parties incorporated into their agreements. Moreover, this approach forces courts to step outside of their areas of expertise and resolve disputes they are inherently incapable of solving. I would thus argue that taking a contextualist approach is inferior to establishing a more robust system of private arbitration between co-religionist parties. Such a system provides co-religionists with a better venue for reasonably addressing and resolving their disputes in accordance with their own beliefs and faith commitments.

B. THE STRENGTH OF INDUSTRY AND CO-RELIGIONIST ARBITRATION

As in the case of industry arbitration, parties to co-religionist arbitration are united by a common field and the common social interests of their respective communities. They also have a common language and common rules for doing business with one another. These rules allow such parties to develop reasonable expectations regarding the manner in which they will settle any disputes, and the laws and rules that will be applied in doing

5. *See id.* at 785.

so. In communities that have embraced ADR, all disputing—or potentially disputing—parties mutually agree to, and are benefitted by, the rules that will govern their disputes. This gives rules an underpinning of mutuality, and they are thus more likely to lead to a satisfactory outcome for both parties. In the case of co-religionists in particular, arbitration thus allows for personalization.

Arbitration also gives co-religionists the freedom to utilize religious language in their agreements with one another. Instead of presenting their dispute to generalist judges, parties using arbitration can place their disputes before decision-makers of their own choosing, who are experts in the area of the dispute and understand what the terms utilized by the parties in the principal agreement actually mean. Submitting a matter to private arbitration—as long as there are robust arbitral rules and sophisticated tribunals in place—places two sophisticated parties in a pleasant position.

Of course, religious arbitration is not a novel idea, and it can be understood as a form of specialized arbitration. Specialized industries have developed and utilized very robust arbitral rules and bodies to govern their disputes for years. Industries that have their own systems of arbitration include the construction industry, diamond merchants, and professional sports leagues. These groups share the belief that courts have a difficult time putting disputes between their members in the proper context, and settling such disputes efficiently and in a manner satisfactory to the parties involved. The unique common business culture and language, industry particulars, and transactional practices within such industries make specialized arbitration by neutral decision-makers with insider familiarity with these fields especially compelling. Judges living and working in a standard legal mindset often fail to appreciate the subtleties of these niche industries, whereas expert arbitrators can craft solutions that uphold the nuanced and intuitive expectations and understandings of parties working in these fields.

Co-religionists are no different. Religious communities have their own unique cultures and modes of thinking about and practicing their faiths. Oftentimes, these cultures are not readily knowable to outsiders; they are not written in official scriptures or important religious texts, but are subtle ways of being religious that inhere in the lives of the faithful. These common cultures, customs, understandings, and practices are often products of experience. They are the subtle ways in which faith traditions evolve and grow through their interactions with norms, values, and modes of being in the world beyond the strict confines of the doctrinal teachings of the faith. These subtle understandings inform the ways in which religious practitioners understand and practice their faiths as much as—if not more than—the formal teachings of the religion.[6] Upholding such understandings through the resolution of co-religionist conflict may be almost impossible if done by outsiders such as judges. Erudite and well-intentioned as they may be, it is difficult to fully appreciate such things without having lived them. Like specialized industries in the commercial world, therefore, religious groups should not be held back from resolving co-religionist disputes in specialized arbitration forums. In creating such a system, co-religionists will be able to combine a common law and a common culture to reach a common, foreseeable, and mutually agreeable resolution.

C. THE SPECIAL LANGUAGE OF INDUSTRIES AND THE SPECIAL LANGUAGE OF CO-RELIGIONIST COMMERCE

Like commercial and professional fields that have developed robust systems of private arbitration, co-religionist commerce is special in that it has fostered, through the course of business, a language that only members of the groups thoroughly understand. Whether it is words such as "*halakha*," "*Sharia*," "Christian love," or the many more specific terms of art that members of a faith use to convey religious ideas, or terms of art such as "kosher," "*halal*," or "Catholic lifestyle" that denote very specific ideas to the community of the faithful, understanding these words is needed to understand the agreement of the parties.

When members of these groups reach an agreement on how they will conduct business with one another, they utilize this specialized language. An agreement by members of these groups to privately arbitrate disputes arising from their business relationships with one another allows these individuals to submit their highly specialized disputes to a highly specialized court that speaks their highly specialized language. As mentioned earlier, this specialization is not something secular courts can offer. When confronted with disputes, courts apply their own general understanding of the law to settle them. Even if courts were to seek to uphold the understandings and expectations of religious parties, more often than not, their unfamiliarity with the special culture of the parties would likely result in judges falling short. Unfortunately, this often leaves parties in highly specialized groups feeling as if their dispute has not been fully settled, or

6. For a discussion of this phenomenon in the Islamic context, see Shahab Ahmed, What Is Islam: The Importance of Being Islamic (2015).

has been settled in an unsatisfactory or incorrect manner. As will be discussed below, this is quite common. Fortunately, arbitration provides a better venue.

Specialization between religious parties comes in the form of religious language and religious objectives. Helfand and Richman argue that such objectives "cannot be captured in alternative secular terminology . . . and resist translation"[7] by secular courts. Although they are correct in this assertion, their solution of courts taking a contextual approach is not the most expedient way to resolve disputes between co-religionist parties. A contextual approach demands that judges develop a robust understanding of the religious principles underpinning an agreement between co-religionists, which is difficult as such parties often "enter co-religionist commercial arrangements to purchase religious goods or secure religious performance . . . not susceptible to description in secular terminology."[8] Helfand and Richman correctly point out that "[i]n drafting . . . agreements [with one another], [co-religionist] parties aim to create commercial or financial arrangements that will comport with shared religious rules and values," and that "[r]eference to specific religious terms is essential to the agreement."[9] They point to contractual obligations of ministers and standards for supervising kosher products as examples of very specific agreements between co-religionists, and acknowledge that disputes arising out of these agreements cannot be satisfactorily settled by resorting to secular terminology.

However, I would go a step further and argue that they cannot be satisfactorily settled by secular courts, at least not to the same extent they would be if submitted to a highly specialized arbitral panel. Highly specialized arbitrators would not only be able to glean the parties' contractual expectations stemming from highly specific religious language, but could do so in a way that would not require parties to use what the authors refer to as "secular analogs" in place of religious language. Combined with the fact that specialized arbitral bodies could more expediently settle disputes arising between co-religionists, this benefit makes private arbitration superior to settling disputes in secular courts.

Beyond the fact that some religious language is not susceptible to secular interpretation, Helfand and Richman also acknowledge that "religious traditions and doctrines place formal restrictions on the structure and terms of the relevant documents."[10] Again, the authors suggest that

7. Co-religionist Commerce, *supra* note 1, at 782.
8. *Id.* at 782.
9. *Id.*
10. *Id.* at 783.

courts take a contextualist approach to interpreting agreements between co-religionists, and again this falls short of a more robust system of private religious arbitration, as the true intentions of the parties may be—and often are—deeply rooted in religious traditions or practices. Therefore, for courts to ably settle these disputes, they must develop their own robust understanding of religious underpinnings, principles, and norms. This takes a significant amount of time, which takes away any aspect of efficiency in settling highly specialized disputes. Moreover, it would be difficult to require courts to learn all the religious traditions and doctrines inherent in every potential agreement between co-religionists. Specialized arbitral bodies, on the other hand, are presided over by arbitrators who are deeply rooted in religious traditions and doctrines—as much as, or even more than, the parties to the dispute. This allows for the arbitrator to draw on his or her own understanding and implement the nuances inherent in a particular religion that are sometimes inaccessible to outsiders.

As noted above, Helfand and Richman are correct—courts *could* satisfactorily solve disputes between co-religionists without running afoul of the establishment clause. Moreover, I agree that it is not a religious impossibility for judges to settle disputes between co-religionist parties. Judges and courts, as sophisticated parties and bodies themselves, given sufficient time and experience, will be able to figure out a way to effectively interpret agreements between co-religionists and settle disputes that arise therefrom. The problem, however, is that this is an imperfect method of settling co-religionist disputes. It is also unlikely to be popular with co-religionists. As demonstrated below, experience has shown that different courts developing different levels of experience in addressing co-religionist disputes over different periods of time often reach inconsistent results. This leads to uncertainty on the part of parties, and so they will be less likely to submit their sophisticated disputes to courts of general jurisdiction.

These concerns are evidenced by the historical record. In the following sections, I will look at how courts have approached various disputes between sophisticated religious parties in the past, and why they have often failed to resolve them in a manner that is consistent, predictable, objective, and reflective of religious parties' understandings and expectations of the structure of their religio-legal relationships.

D. CO-RELIGIONIST DISPUTES IN SECULAR COURTS

Individuals recognize that courts have a difficult time interpreting religious doctrine. In fact, one proposed measure for the 2015 ballot in Texas "would have required judiciaries to refrain from involvement in religious doctrinal interpretation or application."[11] This type of measure arose from claims put forth by churches advocating for church autonomy, or "a claim to autonomous management of a religious organization's internal affairs."[12] Because churches and their parishioners are often governed by church doctrine that would be complicated for outsiders to interpret, and such interpretation by courts may have First Amendment implications, proponents of church autonomy believe that courts should stop short of interpreting religious doctrine.

First Amendment issues certainly present a problem for courts seeking to resolve some kinds of religious matters. Judicial determinations of correct religious teachings or practices in order to resolve cases arising from co-religionist commerce contexts can run afoul of constitutional and prudential doctrines that, due to free exercise and establishment concerns, bar courts from interpreting religious doctrines.

There are important limitations on this judicial principle. American courts have held that judges can resolve cases involving co-religionist disputes if they do so based on "neutral principles of law." An employment dispute between a church and its pastor, for example, may be adjudicated under ordinary principles of contractual interpretation, even if the employment agreement at issue includes religious terminology and imposes faith-based job requirements. Courts have been using the neutral principles of law approach for deciding religious disputes since *Jones v. Wolf*.[13] In *Jones*, the Supreme Court of the United States found that neutral principles, having been developed for use in all general disputes, "can be applied without [violating the establishment clause of the First Amendment]."[14] The Court called the state's interest in peacefully resolving disputes through such principles "obvious and legitimate."[15] Other courts have lauded this approach, as can be seen in the case of *In re Scholl*:

> The United States Supreme Court, in holding that a state may adopt any approach to resolving religious disputes which does not entail consideration of doctrinal matters, specifically approved the use of a "neutral principles of law"

11. http://ballotpedia.org/Texas_Judicial_Restraint_in_Religious_Doctrine_Interpretation_Amendment_(2015).
12. Douglas Laycock, *The Things That Are Not Caesar's: Religious Organizations as a Check on the Authoritarian Pretensions of the State*, 7 GEO. J.L. & PUB. POL'Y 253, 254 (2009).
13. 443 U.S. 595 (1979).
14. Jones v. Wolf, 443 U.S. 595 (1979).
15. *Id.*

> approach as consistent with constitutional limitations. This approach contemplates the application of objective, well-established principles of secular law to the dispute, thus permitting judicial involvement to the extent that it can be accomplished in purely secular terms.[16]

Although many cases arising from religious contexts do not present serious First Amendment concerns, judicial treatment of such cases raises another issue. The problem is that, in translating religious doctrine into established principles of secular law, courts must interpret religious doctrine—something courts are not well-equipped to do. This has led to inconsistent results, and does not allow individual parties to gauge their expectations. This is not a legal problem so much as a doctrinal one. Simply put, courts often interpret religious terms and doctrines incorrectly; they get co-religionist commerce cases wrong. As discussed above, there is no good way to avoid this; the nuanced practices and expectations of co-religionist commerce cannot be easily grasped by outsiders. When this happens, parties to such disputes are left feeling as if their conflict has not been satisfactorily settled.

Giving religious institutions total autonomy to resolve their own internal disputes is not the answer, however. As we have sometimes seen in the past, allowing churches to have carte blanche control over settling disputes between their parishioners can take away the right of individuals to settle their own disputes. The median between these two extremes is to allow individuals to contract to have their matters arbitrated by someone familiar with church doctrine. If given the opportunity, arbitrators who are religious insiders well-versed in religious doctrines, languages, and cultures could temper expectations and resolve disputes in ways that would be satisfactory to all parties.

Helfand and Richman's proposal that courts contextualize co-religionist disputes in order to resolve them properly faces another practical hurdle. The authors note that a contextual approach runs counter to the prevailing model of contractual interpretation, which they term the new formalism. According to Helfand and Richman, the new formalism maintains that courts must interpret contracts by looking at the language through the lens of well-established legal principles. Unfortunately, this limits the amount of parole evidence that can be utilized in settling contractual disputes, as the interpretation comes principally from the four corners of the original contract. This means that religious parties, when submitting contractual disputes to courts, often do not have an opportunity even to explain the foundational religious principles upon which the contract was

16. *In re* Scholl, 621 A.2d 808 (Family Court of Delaware, 1992).

constructed. If it is to have any hope of succeeding, contextual resolution of co-religionist disputes would require courts to abandon the new formalism and be far more flexible in the means they use to understand the intent and expectations of contracting parties. Although Helfand and Richman urge courts to reject the new formalism and adopt a more flexible contextual approach, at least when addressing co-religionist disputes, that is not how judges presently approach such cases. Thus, left to the courts, co-religionist commerce cases are not likely to be resolved contextually, and even if they were, experience suggests that judges who are religious outsiders often do a poor job at really understanding the religious contexts and implications of such disputes.

Co-religionist Family Law Disputes and the Secular Courts

The inability of courts to deal effectively and consistently with co-religionist disputes in ways that accurately reflect the understandings and expectations of religious parties is particularly evident in family law cases. Consider, for example, courts' treatment of the *ketubah*, or Jewish religious marriage contract. Courts have reached very different answers to the question of whether a *ketubah* is a legally enforceable contract, and if its stipulations ought to be upheld in divorce proceedings. In *Avitzur v. Avitzur*, for instance, a court decided to enforce an arbitration clause included in a *ketubah*, finding that the religious marriage agreement was a legally binding and enforceable contract.[17] Likewise, in *In re Marriage of Goldman*, a court enforced a *ketubah* as an ordinary contract. It went so far as to construe the Hebrew, and technical religious phrase "*k'daat Moshe v'yisrael*," in which the parties commit to entering into their marriage in accordance with rabbinic law, as requiring the husband to grant his wife a *get*, or ritual bill of divorce, as prescribed by Jewish law.[18] In one mid-twentieth-century case, a court took the extraordinary step of concluding that it could in theory order the specific performance of a promise made by a husband in a *ketubah* to give his wife a *get* in the event of a divorce because doing so would merely amount to the courts compelling the husband to fulfill his earlier promise, which could be done on a purely secular contract basis.[19]

Contrast these cases with other instances in which American courts have refused to consider the *ketubah* an enforceable secular contract, found

17. *See* Avitzur v. Avitzur, 446 N.E.2d 136 (1983).
18. *See In re* Marriage of Goldman, 54 N.E.2d 1016 (1990).
19. *See* Koeppel v. Koeppel, 138 N.Y.S. 2d 266 (1954).

its terms too vague to be interpreted or enforced, or found that adjudicating *ketubah* disputes would violate First Amendment concerns. In *Victor v. Victor*, for instance, a court ruled that the terms of a *ketubah* are not specific enough, and, because of vagueness, the agreement could not be enforced. The court further held that any attempts to interpret the *ketubah* in order to determine whether it really required a husband to grant his wife a *get* would overstep the court's authority by deciding a religious question.[20]

This, of course, is a very different outcome than the one reached in *Goldman*, where the court actually did interpret a relatively vague Jewish law term of art to find in the *ketubah* a legally enforceable contractual promise by the husband to give his wife a *get*. Moreover, in contrast to *Avitzur*, a state court in *Aflalo v. Aflalo* held that a *ketubah* cannot be enforced as an ordinary secular contract, and therefore rejected a woman's suit to compel her ex-husband to give her a *get*.[21] This case in particular highlights the court's poor understanding of religious realities. The court reasoned that the husband's refusal to grant his wife a *get* was not really a justiciable injury because her inability to remarry was due to her own choice to observe Jewish law. Although perhaps true in the abstract, that line of reasoning reflects a poor understanding of the complex realities and consequences faced by Jewish women raised, embedded, and closely tied with ritual, infrastructural, geographical, commercial, and educational aspects of Jewish communal living if they were to simply leave religious observance or attempt to remarry without a *get*. Religious arbitrators would most certainly recognize that, regardless of the wife's theoretical liberty to leave religious observance or disregard the Jewish law bar on remarriage without a *get*, she was not truly free to do so. Either course of action would have severe implications on numerous aspects of her life, including family associations and support, the future schooling for her children, relations with neighbors, and her ability to work and live comfortably within the community.

What is particularly glaring about the *ketubah* cases, aside from the inconsistency and unpredictability of court judgments on such matters, is the way in which many of these decisions reflect a poor grasp of the ways Jewish parties actually understand and relate to the *ketubah* in practice. The decisions in several of these cases reveal that the courts are wrestling with an issue they are ill-equipped to deal with effectively. In *Avitzur*, for instance, the court developed a theory that a court can parse a religious

20. *See* Victor v. Victor, 866 P.2d 899 (1993).
21. *See* Aflalo v. Aflalo, 685 A.2d 523 (1996).

agreement, separating language that is wholly religious and wholly secular, and hearing cases only based on that portion of the document that is secular. The counter-argument to this reasoning is that a document such as a *ketubah* should be viewed as principally religious, even where secular language is utilized. In this way, one can avoid the chance that courts hijack a case they have no business deciding. Moreover, documents that are principally religious often use language that appears to be secular, but is in fact religious. This goes back to the idea that religious parties and those familiar with said religion understand the underlying meaning of language particular to their agreement, and even inherent points that parties take for granted in entering an agreement with one another.

The *Avitzur* decision brings us full circle back to the point that religious arbitration is oftentimes a superior alternative to secular courts. That case features a court taking it upon itself to invalidate a religious contract in which the parties agreed to take their dispute before a *beit din*, to hold that the wife did, in fact, have a cause of action and to hold that courts can play a role in enforcing agreements to arbitrate disputes. In each aforementioned case involving co-religionist commerce, courts likewise went back and forth on the meaning of certain religious language, and even the enforceability of religious documents. Although matters of enforceability are within the court's domain, interpretation of religious language and religious doctrine fall squarely beyond the jurisdiction of courts. *Avitzur* was the ideal and correct approach in that it recognized that religious arbitration is the best method to resolve this dispute. Because of this, courts should recognize where their review may begin and end, and religious parties should realize that religious arbitration presents a better way to resolve disputes that may arise with fellow members of their religious group.

Indeed, a discussion of the Jewish *ketubah* provides as good an example as any for discussing the way courts can easily misunderstand religious law. Judges might make a decision that is not a completely wrong one, but merely a decision that is "no longer correct," even if it was the right decision at a different time and place. Consider the *ketubah*—the document traditional Jews sign prior to a wedding.[22] The Jewish tradition has required since time immemorial that couples marry with a *ketubah*, whose text mandates how much the husband should pay the wife if he divorces her without cause.[23] Among European Jews, this contractual tradition did not continue much beyond

22. *See* Michael Broyde & Jonathan Reiss, *The Ketubah in America: Its Value in Dollars, Its Significance in* Halacha *and Its Enforceability in American Law*, 47 J. HALACHA & CONTEMP. SOC. 101, 101 (2004).

23. As well as other things.

the end of the first millennium of the Common Era. Through the efforts of the luminous leader of tenth-century European Jewry, Rabbenu Gershom, a decree[24] was enacted that moved Jewish law toward a covenantal model of marriage and away from a contract model.[25] Rabbenu Gershom's view was that it was necessary to prohibit unilateral no-fault divorce by the husband.[26] Divorce was limited to cases of provable fault or mutual consent.[27] In only a few cases could the husband actually be forced to divorce his wife, or she him, and in such cases, the *ketubah* did not govern, as its provisions do not apply to faulted divorce.[28]

In those places where the decrees of Rabbenu Gershom were implemented, the basis for Jewish marriage changed. In Talmudic and Gaonic times, the parties pre-negotiated the amount the husband would have to pay his wife if he divorced her against her will—she could not prevent her husband from divorcing her, except by setting the payment level high enough that the husband was deterred from divorce by dint of its cost.[29] All this changed in light of the decrees of Rabbenu Gershom.[30] Couples would have to negotiate payments to facilitate divorce that one party wanted more than the other, and the *ketubah* stopped being a contract.[31] Rabbenu Gershom's ban against divorcing a woman without her consent or without a showing of hard fault[32] called into question the value of the marriage contract itself. Simply put, the Talmudic rabbis instituted the *ketubah*

24. The decree of Rabbenu Gershom was enacted under penalty of a ban of excommunication (*herem*). The collective decrees of Rabbenu Gershom are thus known as Herem deRabbenu Gershom. Michael J. Broyde, *New York's Regulation of Jewish Marriage: Covenant, Contract or Statute?*, *in* Marriage and Divorce in a Multicultural Context: Multi-Tiered Marriage and the Boundaries of Civil Law and Religion 142, n.16 (Joel A. Nichols ed., 2012) (internal citation omitted).

25. Michael J. Broyde, Marriage, Divorce, and the Abandoned Wife in Jewish Law: A Conceptual Understanding of the *Agunah* Problems in America 21 (2001).

26. *Id.*

27. *Id.*

28. *Id.*

29. *See supra* note 22.

30. This insight is generally ascribed to the twelfth-century Tosafist Rabbenu Tam in his view of the repugnancy claim (Heb.: *mais alay*). In fact, it flows logically from the view of Rabbenu Gershom, who not only had to prohibit polygamy in order to end coerced divorce, but even divorce for soft fault.

31. Absent the prohibition on polygamy, the decree restricting the right to divorce would not work, as the husband who could not divorce would simply remarry and abandon his first wife. This prevented that conduct.

32. In which case, the value of the *ketubah* need not be paid as a penalty for misconduct imposed on the woman. What exactly is hard fault remains a matter of dispute, but it generally includes adultery, spouse beating, insanity, and frigidity. *See* Rabbi Yosef Karo, Even HaEzer 154, in Shulchan Aruch (Version 22, Bar Ilan Responsa Project ed., 2013).

payments to deter the husband from rashly divorcing a wife. But now, as the husband could not divorce his wife without her consent, there seemed to be no further need for the *ketubah*.[33] As Rabbi Moses Isserles (Rama), the leading codifier of European Jewry, wrote at the beginning of his discussion of the laws of the *ketubah* nearly five hundred years ago: "Thus, nowadays, in our countries, where we do not divorce against the will of the wife because of the ban of Rabbenu Gershom . . . it is possible to be lenient and not write a *ketubah* at all [when getting married] . . . ."[34]

Of course, the *ketubah* did remain a fixture of Jewish weddings after the tenth century,[35] but it was transformed from a marriage contract that governed a contractual marriage to a ritual document whose transfer initiated a covenantal marriage. The *ketubah* held no economic or other value as a contract. Indeed, the contractual model of marriage ended for those Jews—all European Jews—who accepted the refinements of Rabbenu Gershom. Consider the observation of Rabbi Moses Feinstein, the leading American Jewish law authority of the last century, on this matter:

> The value of the *ketubah* is not known to rabbis and decisors of Jewish law, or rabbinical court judges; indeed we have not examined this matter intensely as for all matters of divorce it has no practical ramifications, since it is impossible for the man to divorce against the will of the woman, [the economics of] divorce are dependent on who desires to be divorced.[36]

Notwithstanding this fact, one still occasionally sees American courts actually looking at the *ketubah* as a valid Jewish marriage "contract" between the husband and wife and seeking to enforce its provisions.[37] To make this matter even more complex, the trend in modern rabbinical courts in

33. Thus, for example, Shulchan Aruch (Even HaEzer) states that "a man who rapes a woman . . . is obligated to marry her, so long as she . . . wishes to marry him, even if she is crippled or blind, and he is not permitted to divorce her forever, except with her consent, and thus he does not have to write her a ketubah." *Id.* at 177:3. The logic seems clear. As he cannot divorce her under any circumstances without her consent, the presence or absence of a *ketubah* seems to make no difference to her economic status or marital security. When they both want to get divorced, they will agree on financial terms independent of the *ketubah*, and until then, the *ketubah* sets no payment schedule. Should she insist that she only will consent to be divorced if he gives her $1,000,000 in buffalo nickels, they either reach an agreement or stay married.

34. *Id.* at 66:3.

35. Broyde & Reiss, *supra* note 22, at 118–19.

36. Moses Feinstein, Iggrot Moshe, Even Haezer 4:91. This responsum was written in 1980.

37. *See, e.g.*, Victor v. Victor, 866 P.2d 899, 901–02 (Ariz. 1993); *In re* Marriage of Goldman, 554 N.E.2d 1016, 1021–23 (Ill. App. Ct. 1990) (holding that the words "in accordance with the law of Moses and Israel" appearing in the *ketubah* created a

Israel is that the *ketubah* is the basis for divorce settlements and is in fact enforced, in accordance with the older Talmudic custom and the prevailing norm of Sephardic Jews,[38] which is distinctly different from the modern American practice (which is frequently to use secular law concepts such as equitable distribution to reflect the actual intent of the parties as to how they wish to govern their divorce).[39]

Similar inconsistencies and lack of judicial understanding of the mechanics of religious life have been demonstrated in American courts' consideration of Islamic marriage contracts. Islamic marriage agreements typically include a *mahr* provision, which includes a promise by the husband to pay the wife a certain sum of money or property in the event of a divorce or his death. In Islamic law, because divorce is in principle the unilateral prerogative of the husband, the *mahr* was used as a mechanism to both discourage frivolous divorces by the husband and to provide the wife with leverage in order to negotiate the granting of a divorce with her otherwise unwilling husband. In some cases, courts have treated *mahr* contracts as enforceable agreements, and have ordered divorcing husbands to pay the promised amounts as part of their divorce settlements. Other courts have refused to enforce *mahr* agreements for a variety of different reasons. In *Habibi-Fahnrich v. Fahnrich*, for example, the court declined to treat a *mahr* contract as legally enforceable because it found its religious formulations too vague.[40] The religiously observant Muslim parties to that agreement, however, likely knew exactly what the contract meant and implied; after all, such agreements are routine within Muslim communities. If a non-Muslim American judge could not construe the contract's meaning and implications, a Muslim religious arbitrator certainly could have, and the latter's disposition of the

contractual obligation to give a *get*); Avitzur v. Avitzur, 446 N.E.2d 136 (N.Y. 1983); Hurwitz v. Hurwitz, 216 A.D. 362, 364 (N.Y. App. Div. 1928); *In re* Estate of White, 356 N.Y.S.2d 208, 210 (N.Y. Sur. Ct. 1974); *but see* Aflalo v. Aflalo, 685 A.2d 523, 531 (N.J. Super. Ct. Ch. Div. 1996) (rejecting a similar argument); Morris v. Morris (1973), 42 D.L.R. 3d 550 (Can. Man. C.A.). For more on this, see Irving A. BREITOWITZ, BETWEEN CIVIL AND RELIGIOUS LAW: THE PLIGHT OF THE *AGUNAH* IN AMERICAN SOCIETY 50–55 (Greenwood Press: Westport, Connecticut, 1993) and Helfand & Richman, *supra* note 20, which calls for courts to distinguish between contract and ceremony, a very astute observation.

38. See Michael Broyde & Jonathan Reiss, Erkah shel Ha-Ketubah [*The Value of the* Ketubah], 25 TEHUMIN 180 (2005) (Isr.) (the editor of the journal noting in footnotes the contrary practice in Israel).

39. *See, e.g.*, the standard prenuptial agreement used in the Orthodox Jewish community, which gives two choices for how to divide assets in the case of divorce, each grounded in secular law. The Prenup, http://theprenup.org (last visited Nov. 25, 2014); see also Broyde, *supra* note 25, at 127–36.

40. *See* Hibibi-Fahnrich v. Fahnrich, no. 46186/93, WL 507388 (1995).

case would have better preserved the parties' expectation and understandings. Even more remarkably, in *In re Marriage of Dajani*, a California court refused to enforce a *mahr* agreement because it violated public policy.[41] The court reasoned that because *mahr* is only paid to the wife in the event of a divorce, the contract encouraged her to gratuitously dissolve the marriage in contradiction to public policy preferences favoring the maintenance of marriages. The court badly misunderstood the nature of *mahr* agreements, however. As religious arbitrators would have well known, *mahr* is designed to discourage frivolous unilateral divorce by a Muslim husband, and merely creates an avenue for wives to bargain for a divorce from their unwilling husbands by offering to waive their right to *mahr* payments.

The inability of secular courts to truly appreciate the implications of Islamic marriage agreements is further illustrated by a more recent case, *In re Marriage of Obaidi*.[42] The parties in *Obaidi*, a husband and wife, both children of Afghan immigrants, were married according to Afghan custom, signing a *mahr* agreement during an engagement ceremony. In the *mahr*, the husband agreed to pay a dowry to his wife. The ceremony was conducted in Farsi, which the husband did not speak, and the husband was only made aware that such an agreement would be included in the ceremony fifteen minutes prior to the signing of the document. More specifically, he was unaware of the terms of the *mahr* until they were explained to him by his uncle after the document had been signed.

The trial court held that the wife was entitled to the dowry payment established by the *mahr*. However, on appeal, the decision of the trial court was reversed. Without alluding to the historical significance of *mahr* agreements in Islamic law, the court deferred to the age-old principle in American law that a valid contract requires a meeting of the minds on the essential terms, and because the husband was placed at a disadvantage by his lack of knowledge of Farsi, and did not understand the terms to which he was agreeing, the agreement was invalid. In particular, the court's holding was that a prenuptial agreement lacks a meeting of the minds and is unenforceable if it was negotiated and drafted in a foreign language unknown to one of the parties and was unexpectedly presented to the party on short notice for the party's signature as a necessity of completing a traditional engagement ceremony already under way.[43]

The court in *Obaidi* equated the *mahr* agreement with a prenuptial agreement—something very familiar to the court. The problem with such

41. *See* In re Marriage of Dajani, 129 Cal. App. 2d 1387 (1988).
42. 226 P.3d 787, 789 (Wash. Ct. App. 2010).
43. *See In re* Marriage of Obaidi, 154 Wash. App. 609, 616 (Wash. Ct. App. 2010).

an approach, however, is that it ignores the religious underpinnings of a *mahr* agreement, and in essence secularizes it. At the same time, such an approach puts agreements such as *mahr* agreements at risk, and reduces the ability of parties to rely upon them to be enforced. This issue would not be as much of a burden if the dispute were submitted to religious arbitration. In such a case, an arbitrator trained in the area of *Shari'a* could weigh the facts—exactly the same way the court did in this case—and, utilizing the underpinnings of *Shari'a*, coupled with foundations of secular law, could be in a better position to judge the *mahr's* validity.

In a similar case out of Florida, *Akileh v. Elchahal*,[44] the court was faced with a *sadaq*, which is a postponed dowry that protects the wife in the event of a divorce under the Islamic religion. The parties and the appellant wife's father agreed to a *sadaq* prior to the parties' marriage. The parties' marriage ended rather quickly and, during the divorce proceedings, the husband contested the wife's claim to the *sadaq* on the basis that the wife was the one who filed for divorce. The trial court, like that in *Obaidi*, held that there was no meeting of the minds, and thus the contract was invalid. On appeal, however, the court concluded that the *sadaq* was enforceable as a contract.

The appellate court, perhaps unimportantly, noted that the agreement fell into the category of ante-nuptial agreement, as opposed to the prenuptial nature of the agreement in *Obaidi*. In the end, the court called the husband's intent that the *sadaq* be invalid should the wife file for divorce subjective and immaterial to the terms of the contract.[45] The emphasis the court placed on neutral principles of law is misleading. The husband argued that, traditionally speaking, *sadaqs* are based on the assumption of invalidity should the wife initiate divorce proceedings. To call this "subjective intent" is to ignore the religious underpinnings of such an agreement. If such a case had been submitted to an arbitrator well-versed in Islamic law, he or she would have been better equipped to parse what was and was not subjective intent, while also applying secular legal principles to settle the dispute.

Co-religionist Commercial Disputes and the Secular Courts

Secular courts have also reached inconsistent results in dealing with more mundane issues of commercial interactions between religious parties. In some such cases, judges, working as well-meaning but inadequately

44. Akileh v. Elchahal, 666 So. 2d 246 (Fla. Dist. Ct. App. 1996).
45. *Id.* at 249.

familiar outsiders to religious commerce mechanisms and traditions, have reached results that seem on their face to be formally correct but will actually frustrate the intent and understandings of religious parties. One notable illustration of this phenomenon can be found in judicial treatment of the Jewish *heter iska*, a document designed to circumvent the Biblical prohibition against lending money on interest.

In Jewish law, paying or receiving *ribis*, or any interest on a loan of money or goods, is prohibited by the Torah.[46] The exact parameters of this prohibition are complex, and are elaborated and marked out by the Talmud. The basic idea, however, is that it is prohibited for a borrower to provide, or for a lender to receive, any benefit beyond repayment of the actual loan in consideration for the loan's having been extended. For obvious reasons, the *halakhic* prohibition on *ribis* poses serious problems for the effective functioning of capital markets that rely heavily on credit. The concept may work in an agrarian society reliant on subsistence commerce, but even in the Roman world, rabbinic scholars recognized the need for the robust credit markets.

In order to circumvent the prohibition on *ribis*, the Talmudic rabbis came to accept the use of a business structure known as the *iska*. In essence, an *iska* is a means of structuring a partnership-like business relationship as a lending vehicle in order to avoid, at least in form, the creation of a loan. The *iska* works as follows: one party—really the borrower—has a business idea but no available capital to execute the plan. Another party—really the lender—has available capital to lend or invest. The two parties form a relationship in which the borrower is entrusted with a sum of money provided by the lender to execute the business venture. Half of the "borrowed" capital is formally characterized as an investment, while the other half is characterized as a loan. The loan portion of the capital must be repaid—without any added interest—regardless of whether the venture is successful. The investment portion of the capital, however, need not be repaid; both the profits and losses of that half of the capital are shared by the two parties. In this way, the loan is structured as a partial investment. The lender may see a return on his money, not in interest on the loan, but in capital gains on his investment, and is guaranteed to be paid back for at least half his outlay no matter how badly the venture turns out. The borrower, in turn, receives all the capital he needs for his venture, and avoids interest payments, but must share a portion of his profits with the lender while also remaining personally liable for only half the amount received.

46. *See* Exodus 22:24; Leviticus 25:36–37; Deuteronomy 23:20.

The obvious problem with the Talmudic *iska* is that it does not offer the lender a guaranteed profit on his "loan"; indeed, the lender risks losing half the capital return on his investment without enjoying any effective control over the venture. The borrower too is disadvantaged by having to share a portion of his profits with the lender rather than fixed interest percentage. In response to these deficiencies, medieval rabbis developed a structure known as the *heter iska* to provide the lender with a fixed interest-like return on his investment and assured repayment of the principal capital outlay.

The *heter iska* worked as follows: a "lender" would provide capital to a "borrower," and rather than this capital outlay being structured as a loan—which would have to be paid back without any added consideration—the funds were offered as an investment in the borrower's venture. As the relationship was structured as an investment rather than as a loan, this meant that in principle the lender would see a return on his money only if the venture succeeded, and would lose even his principal if the venture failed. However, the investment would be burdened with terms and conditions, which, if the borrower did not fulfill them, would trigger the borrower's obligation to pay back part of the principle as well as liquidated damages that took the place of a standard interest payment. Importantly, these conditions were written so that they were virtually impossible to fulfill. Thus, the borrower's liability for portions of the principle and liquidated damages at regular intervals throughout the life of the investment was virtually guaranteed. In this way, an "investor" was assured a regular return on his investment without the outlay being technically structured as a loan, thus avoiding the prohibition on *ribis*.

It is important to understand that the *heter iska* structure technically creates a legal partnership between the borrower and lender through the lender's "investment" in the business. On paper, it is not a debtor-creditor relationship; it cannot be, as that would prevent as interest the payment of any additional funds by the debtor to the creditor. However, regardless of the formalities, Jewish parties to a *heter iska* understand well that this is not an investment-based partnership. It is a loan, albeit a loan that has been technically arranged so as to avoid the application of standard *ribis* prohibitions and thus enable the lender to receive a guaranteed return on his capital outlay. Viewing the structure as a partnership and investment with attendant liability and control interest issues would substantially undermine the intent and understandings of the parties and functionally undo the entire purpose of the *heter iska* structure.

Not all secular courts that have encountered business relationships structured through a *heter iska* understand this reality of co-religionist commerce, however. In several cases, courts have considered the possibility that the existence of a *heter iska* arrangement may serve as a defense to suit for non-payment of a debt on the grounds that the relationship was actually an investment partnership rather than a loan. In *IDB v. Weiss & Wolf*, for instance, a New York court held that whether a *heter iska* could serve as a defense for a borrower-defendant was a triable issue of fact.[47] Even considering the possibility that the *heter iska* transformed a loan into a partnership investment reflected a deep misunderstanding of what the Jewish parties—in that case, a bank and private borrowers—understood themselves to be doing. Everyone who enters into a *heter iska* arrangement knows that what they are really doing is borrowing a sum of money that will be repaid with "interest." The formal structure of an investment and partnership arrangement is a legal fiction that effectively avoids the religious prohibition on interest-bearing loans, but that is not understood to materially change the terms of the parties' commercial relationship. In *IDB*, the court's misunderstanding had broader negative consequences for co-religionist commerce. Whereas previously Israeli banks had incorporated *heter iska* arrangements into their individual loans to observant Jews in compliance with Jewish law, they now became wary of doing so. Subsequently, these banks have scrupulously avoided signing any actual *heter iska* documents in connection to specific loans. Instead, lending institutions merely place framed copies of *heter iska* documents on the walls of rooms in which lending deals are negotiated and executed, under the theory that this creates an unspoken understanding that these loans will be *iska* and Jewish law compliant. In a real sense, however, this practice makes an already fictional legal formalism even less concrete, less substantial, and less legally genuine from a Jewish religious perspective.[48]

The results in *IDB* led to further muddying of the *heter iska* waters in American courtrooms. In 1986, another New York court considered a *heter iska* defense by a borrower who, following the results of *IDB*, had entered into a loan agreement with a bank while a *heter iska* was displayed on the wall. The court found that the defendant could not claim the *heter iska* as a defense to the debt because he did not in fact reasonably rely on the *iska* as a serious component of his relationship with the bank at the time the loan was made.[49] In another case, *Bollag v. Dresdner*, a plaintiff-lender tried to

47. IDB v. Weiss & Wolf, NYS Sp. Ct. 1984, NYLJ 2/4/85 at p. 14.

48. *See* Leonard Grunstein, "Interest, Ribit, and Riba: Must These Disparate Concepts be Integrated or is a More Nuanced Approach Appropriate for the Global Finance Community?", 130 BANKING L. J. 439, 537, 745 (2013).

49. *See* Bank Leumi Trust Co. of New York v. Morris Spitzer, NYS Sup. Ct. 9/18/86, no. 017734/1986.

use the *heter iska* to justify collecting an illegal usurious interest rate from the borrower. The lender argued that, due to the *heter iska*, the parties' relationship was not actually a loan, and thus not subject to the legal restrictions on usury charged on loans. The court again held that the substance of the parties' relationship was more important than the technical form. Again, the court found that the parties' relationship was a loan, and that the *heter iska* was not actually operable.[50] It seems that both courts reached the correct substantive results; it is hard to imagine that the explicit promissory notes drafted and signed by both parties should be superseded by an unsigned *heter iska* form that was neither read not even noted during the lending process, and about which the borrower was unaware. Nevertheless, the court's decision, in effect finding that the religiously-necessary *heter iska* was never a part of the parties' relationship, raised serious questions about the efficacy of the contracting parties' attempts to comply with their religious obligations.

Consider what may have happened had these cases been dealt with by a rabbinic arbitration tribunal. The substantive results would likely have been the same; consistent with Jewish law, the borrowers would have been held liable to repay the loans with "interest." The relationships would not have been treated as partnership investments, but not because the *heter iskas* were found inoperable. Instead, the defendants would have been obligated to repay the loan because the onerous terms of the traditional *heter iska* would not have been met, thus triggering the liquidated damages remedy. The difference is important. Whereas the courts' decisions undermined the religious effectiveness of the *heter iska* as a means of structuring loans in a religiously-compliant way, a rabbinic court would have reached the same result without doing damage to the bases for these or other parties' co-religionist commerce.

Importantly, the failure of secular courts to deal effectively with co-religionist commerce cases is not always a product of courts attempting to resolve disputes when they have a poor outsider's understanding of the expectations and understandings of the parties. Sometimes, courts avoid dealing with co-religionist commerce cases that could in fact be resolved with relative ease and clarity without special insider knowledge of the religious culture. Oftentimes, such courts demur because they wish to avoid wading into and attempting to resolve what they regard as "religious questions" without having recourse to neutral principles of law. Such hesitancy, however, is sometimes premised on misunderstandings of the religious

50. *See* Bollag v. Dresdner, 495 NYS 2d 560 (1985).

issues at play, which religious insiders would recognize to be far more clear-cut and susceptible to a neutral principles of law approach.

One area in which this issue seems to occur time and again is in litigation over the observance of kosher food requirements in connection with commercial agreements. The question was presented in *Wallace v. ConAgra Foods, Inc.*, in which consumers sued ConAgra, the owner of Hebrew National, on the basis that beef franks purchased from them were not up to minimum kosher standards.[51] More specifically, the case required the court to determine the meaning of the word "kosher." The court concluded that the customers lacked Article III standing to bring a claim based on allegedly false advertising of a product as using 100 percent kosher beef because the plaintiffs could not show that the specific products they purchased contained non-kosher beef.[52] In its decision, the court noted that "[t]he definition of the word 'kosher' is intrinsically religious in nature, and this Court may not entertain a lawsuit that will require it to evaluate the veracity of Defendant's representations that its Hebrew National products meet any such religious standard."[53] The court went on: "[b]ecause all of Plaintiffs' claims derive from Defendant's alleged misrepresentation that its Hebrew National products are '100 percent kosher,' all counts of the Amended Complaint are barred by the First Amendment."[54] The court found that it "lack[ed] the requisite subject matter jurisdiction to preside over th[e] dispute," and so dismissed the case.[55]

Although difficult to pinpoint explicitly from the text of the court's decision, in its reasoning, the court indicated that it was stuck between two extremes—on the one hand, the definition of kosher was "properly the subject of rabbinical debate and [has] evolved over the course of many centuries."[56] Even if objective standards for kosher existed, the court noted that the existence of such a standard would be immaterial, as more than one objective standard is present, and the court would have to determine the "correct" one.[57] On the other hand, the court acknowledged that its decision likely left "consumers without a remedy—save opting not to purchase or ingest Defendant's Hebrew National products."[58] Thus, the court opted to sidestep deciding the meaning of the word "kosher."

51. 920 F. Supp. 2d 995 (D. Minn. 2013),
52. Wallace v. ConAgra Foods, Inc., 747 F.3d 1025, 1030–31 (8th Cir. 2014).
53. http://ia601602.us.archive.org/13/items/gov.uscourts.mnd.126355/gov.uscourts.mnd.126355.59.0.pdf, at *10. (last visited Jan. 20, 2017).
54. *Id.*
55. *See id.*
56. *Id.* at 9.
57. *See id.* at 9–10.
58. *See id.* at 9.

Multiple decisions have criticized *Wallace's* standing ruling, with one noting that

> it would be a bizarre result if sellers advertising food as halal or kosher, diamonds as conflict-free, or products as union-made could knowingly mix compliant and non-compliant products with impunity so long as there was no way for a buyer to trace the specific item he or she purchased back to the source.[59]

That court went on to argue that "if a customer has paid a premium for an assurance that a product meets certain standards, and the assurance turns out to be meaningless, the premium that the customer has paid is an actual, personal, particularized injury that is cognizable under Article III."[60]

Frustrated by decisions such as those in *Wallace*, many state and local legislatures attempted to implement definitions of "kosher" that could give the word an objective meaning measurable by courts.[61] However, even these measures left courts thinking that litigation over compliance with kosher laws raised serious constitutional and practical problems.

One case brought under these kosher laws, *Barghout v. Bureau of Kosher Meat & Food Control*, involved an appeal from a lower court judgment convicting a food shop owner for violating a city kosher ordinance.[62] The law in question required purveyors who claimed to offer kosher food for sale to actually comply with traditional Orthodox Jewish kosher laws. In order to ensure compliance, the ordinance created an unpaid bureau, consisting of three Orthodox rabbis and three laymen selected from a list submitted by two local Orthodox rabbinical councils. The defendant in *Barghout* was charged, convicted, and fined for violating the city ordinance after members of the bureau caught him placing kosher hot dogs on the same rotisserie alongside non-kosher hot dogs, in violation of Orthodox kosher rules. Subsequently, Barghout sought a declaratory judgment on the basis that the ordinance violated the First and Fourteenth Amendments because it could find him in violation of the kosher laws even if he genuinely and sincerely believed that he was following those rules properly. The district

59. McCoy v. Nestle United States, Inc., 2016 U.S. Dist. LEXIS 41601, *24–25 (N.D. Cal. Mar. 29, 2016).

60. *Id.*

61. *See* Barghout v. Bur. of Kosher Meat & Food Control, 66 F.3d 1337, 1340 n.5 (4th Cir. 1995) (listing twenty-one states that have adopted such laws). For a discussion of the constitutionality of these laws, see Kent Greenawalt, *Religious and Civil Law: Using Secular Law to Assure Observance of Practices with Religious Significance*, 71 S. Cal. L. Rev. 781, 785–810 (1998).

62. 66 F.3d 1337, 1338 (4th Cir. 1995).

court sided with the deli owner, finding the ordinance unconstitutional and enjoining its enforcement. On appeal, the city argued that "the experts were advisory, held no real power, and that any unconstitutional portions of the ordinance could have been severed." The court did not buy it, holding: "(1) that the ordinance fostered obvious excessive entanglement between church and state, and (2) that the offending portions of the ordinance could not be severed from the standards of compliance that required adoption of the orthodox rules and regulations."[63]

Notably, twenty-one states have adopted laws protecting consumers from kosher fraud. Only one state has invalidated its consumer protection law, so decisions such as *Barghout* are in the minority.[64] What will prove interesting, however, is how the Supreme Court's traditional stance on kosher food consumer fraud statutes will be affected given the narrowing ability of legislatures to make laws dealing with religion.

The Supreme Court weighed in on statutes enforcing kosher standards more than three-quarters of a century ago, in the case of *Hygrade Provision Co. v. Sherman*.[65] In *Hygrade*, the Court "upheld New York's kosher food consumer fraud statute against a challenge launched by butchers who claimed the term "kosher" was unconstitutionally vague."[66] Although avoiding the question of whether the law was constitutional under the First Amendment's religion clauses, "because the Supreme Court had yet to determine that the First Amendment applied to the states,"[67] the Court did hold that the term "kosher" "was not so vague as to violate the Due Process Clause . . . ."[68] The foundation of this decision is shaky at best, and will likely be toppled by First Amendment issues, at least if judged through the lens of the Court's *Lemon* test. Such a strike to these kinds of laws leaves consumers without any way to seek recompense for injuries stemming from suppliers' false promises.

The core problem with courts' hesitance to address kosher law cases is that, although courts dismiss the meaning of a word such as "kosher" as having a sort of floating definition, it is, in fact, relatively well-defined by Jewish law. Jewish law "dictate[s] methods of slaughtering animals and meat preparation," while also "forbid[ding] the consumption of meat

63. *Barghout*, 66 F.3d at 1338.

64. Only one state has struck down its kosher food law as in violation of the United States Constitution; the New Jersey Supreme Court invalidated its kosher food consumer fraud law in *Ran-Dav's*, 608 A.2d at 1353.

65. 266 U.S. 497 (1925).

66. *Barghout*, 66 F.3d at 1338.

67. *Id.*

68. *Id.*

and dairy products together."[69] If courts were more attuned to the insider understandings of co-religionist commerce parties, they would recognize that an objective, neutral principles of law approach could be used to address many of these kosher-related disputes. An objective standard can be ably gleaned from existing Jewish law, but this is not attainable through the *Lemon* standard as it requires too much entanglement in religious law, other than for the simplest of cases, such as the claim that pig's feet are kosher, or the like.

As Helfand and Richman point out, cases such as *Wallace* "significantly endanger co-religionist commerce because they so severely limit the flexibility of important ecclesiastical terms."[70] However, if courts take a contextualist approach, as Helfand and Richman recommend, the danger is that society gets varying decisions grounded in some theoretical distinction of religious law that the court has fixated on, but which is lacking any connection to the religious "facts on the ground." Without a fixed point and definition to rely upon, consumers are not protected and have no way to gauge the chance that they might be successful. Religious arbitration is a better way to resolve issues such as these. It not only allows arbitrators well-versed in the field to decide issues specific to their religious specialization, but does so in a way that allows for small variations on the basis of particular subgroups of religious groups. Admittedly, cases dealing with sometimes-large groups of customers are more difficult settings in which to utilize religious arbitration. In family law, however, religious arbitration proves a viable and sometimes superior alternative to the secular court system for religious parties, since the religious arbitrators well understand the family norms. So too, words such as "kosher" have either a clear or a much clearer meaning to co-religionists within a common community than they might to a person with no familiarity with the faith. Allowing people to select religious arbitration as an option to resolve the meaning of these many terms seems reasonable and efficient. The complexity and difficulty is clear: once religious individuals seek to avoid the secular norms and values of society's laws by engaging in co-religionist commerce that they agree will be governed by religious principles, there is no reliable way to have disputes arising from such relationships resolved by state and federal courts consistent with party expectations. Understanding a foreign legal system is hard, and courts that are forced to adjudicate co-religionist commence frequently do not understand the law that they are adjudicating.

69. *Id.* (quoting 6 Encyclopedia Judaica 28 (1971)).
70. Co-religionist Commerce, *supra* note 1, at 795.

Co-religionist commerce is best adjudicated in co-religionist courts, just like Georgia law is best resolved in Georgia courts. This is not an argument that secular courts cannot do such adjudication. And it certainly is not an argument that courts should not do so when no arbitration court can be agreed on by the parties. But it is clear that when courts engage in adjudication of co-religionist commerce, they are adjudicating foreign law and culture, and that it is easy to err.

For this and other reasons, religious individuals and communities have sought greater opportunities to resolve co-religionist commercial conflicts privately through faith-based arbitration. This model of ADR gives religious litigants the opportunity to choose to have religious norms and values be treated as the applicable law by decision- makers. Perhaps more important, however, religious arbitration also permits parties to bring such cases to dispute resolution forums staffed by arbitrators with an intimate understanding of the parties' religiously-grounded expectations and understanding of their relationships. Such religious arbitrators, rather than non-religious—albeit highly professional—state and federal judges, are really the ones best positioned to decide co-religionist disputes most effectively.

PART TWO

CHAPTER 4

A History of Religious Arbitration

The second Part of this book steps back from explaining the rise of religious arbitration in the United States to take a broader historical view of the development of private arbitration in general and of faith-based arbitration in particular. In order to assess the best ways for American society to approach religious arbitration as it stands today, it is important to understand where it came from. In this regard, contemporary faith-based arbitration has two distinct roots. On the one hand, modern religious dispute resolution is a continuation of a long tradition of Western societies recognizing both legally and socially the important roles played by various kinds of religious courts in governing religious individuals and institutions. However, modern faith-based arbitration tribunals in the United States are not direct descendants of these earlier ecclesiastical courts. One of the main distinguishing features of premodern religious tribunals was that they operated within a legal space that was ceded to them by nonreligious political authorities. Religious matters were largely left to ecclesiastical courts to resolve, whereas secular matters—the kinds of property, contract, employment, and tort matters that regularly clog the judicial dockets—were the province of traditional state-run courts.

Contemporary religious arbitration does not work in this model. The United States does not contemplate separate religious and secular jurisdictions. The kinds of religious tribunals and dispute resolution processes used by religious Americans today are not employed to address ecclesiastical or sacerdotal matters of religious doctrine or church governance. Instead, religious parties seek to use faith-based arbitration to privately

Sharia Tribunals, Rabbinical Courts, and Christian Panels. Michael J. Broyde.

resolve very mundane disputes—conflicts over property, employment, and family; transactional and tort matters—using choice-of-law and choice-of-forum mechanisms to ensure that such cases will be resolved in accordance with their religious commitments. In this sense, then, modern American religious arbitration is fundamentally an expression of ordinary alternative dispute resolution, and works within the framework established by American arbitration law. Thus, the second root of contemporary faith-based arbitration is the development of private ADR in general and of private binding arbitration in particular.

This chapter focuses on the premodern use of religious courts to resolve ecclesiastical disputes within Western societies. Religious arbitration is by no means a new mechanism: it dates back hundreds of years. Societal acceptance of religious courts operating within the broader secular legal system is thus deeply ingrained in the Western tradition and in the common law tradition that forms the bedrock of American jurisprudence. The history of religious arbitration in Western societies is important because it helps contextualize and explain long-standing social, political, and legal comfort with religious groups engaging in various forms of alternative dispute resolution separate but not entirely outside societal laws. It is because of this historical familiarity that American law and policy has taken a permissive and even supportive attitude toward religious dispute resolution under the broad framework of the FAA. However, although its deep historical roots indicate that religious arbitration has stood the test of time, various practices and experiences associated with early forms of religious dispute resolution have led many people to be justifiably skeptical and wary of its place in modern secular societies.

A. HISTORICAL FOUNDATIONS OF RELIGIOUS ARBITRATION

In medieval Europe, the idea of church-state separation was far from reality. In fact, church and state were one and the same. Because church and state were one, "God and law were [also] intertwined."[1]

In England, there existed two branches of law: divine (religious) and secular.[2] In many cases, the line between them was blurred. For example, "[i]n 1489, the English Chancellor, ruling in a trust dispute, held that

1. Nicholas Walter, *Religious Arbitration in the United States and Canada*, 52 SANTA CLARA L. REV. 501, 505 (2012).
2. *Id.*

'each Law is, or ought to be, in accordance with the Law of God.'"[3] The infusion of religious principles into secular law is recurrent throughout much of English history.[4] France more explicitly placed religion under state control via "the *Déclaration du Clergé de France* (1682)," which "established Gallicanism in France."[5] Three years later, "the revocation of the Edict of Nantes . . . expel[led] Protestants."[6] As opposed to England's co-existing branches of law, with the secular branch oftentimes infused with the religious branch, in France, the king controlled religion, and "[t]hrough the king, religion and law were inextricably linked: *une foi, une loi, un roi*."[7]

The idea of religious arbitration is not that a country's body of law utilizes religious principles to settle disputes, but rather that religious arbitration serves as an alternative path to litigating disputes in the courts and under the laws of the state. Even with the blurring of the line between law and religion or even secular and religious law, premodern England and France served as the birthplaces of religious arbitration.[8] Although religious arbitration in premodern England and France was not identical to the religious arbitration we know today, it was similar in the sense that it was implemented by English and French religious authorities to "provide[] routes to justice that were an alternative to the state courts."[9] Like modern religious arbitration, following its implementation, religious arbitration and religious arbitral panels "competed directly with civil courts."[10] Unlike modern religious arbitration, the religious arbitral panels that existed in premodern England and France "exercised compulsory jurisdiction" over some issues.[11]

In England, the roots of religious arbitration were church courts. The blurred line between state and religion gave church courts more power and, in fact, "[b]y the fourteenth century, the church courts had adopted the practice of hearing appeals from the common law courts, and the monarch was obliged to enact a statute to prevent it."[12] Even with a statute to

3. *Id.* (quoting JOHN H. LANGBEIN ET AL., HISTORY OF THE COMMON LAW: THE DEVELOPMENT OF ANGLO-AMERICAN LEGAL INSTITUTIONS 313–14 (2009)).
4. *Id.*
5. *Id.* (quoting PHILIPPE SUEUR, 2 HISTOIRE DU DROIT PUBLIC FRANÇAIS 477–78 (1989)).
6. *Id.* (quoting SEUER, *supra* note 5, at 477–78).
7. *Id.* (quoting SEUER, *supra* note 5, at 476) ("One faith, one law, one king.").
8. *Id.*
9. *Id.*
10. *Id.* at 506.
11. *Id.* at 505.
12. *Id.* at 506 (citing First Statute of Praemunire, 27 Edw. 3, stat. 1, c. 1 (1353)).

protect against church-court overreach, however, "[u]p to the eve of the Reformation, the church still exercised jurisdiction over what we would today regard as quintessentially secular contract law."[13] Although this broad jurisdiction disappeared over time, the church courts continued to exist, with "the sixteenth and seventeenth century church courts hear[ing] matrimonial, probate, tithe, and defamation cases."[14] The church courts lost jurisdiction over most of these issues in the English Revolution, but "they survived with jurisdiction over matrimonial and probate disputes until 1857, when they finally surrendered control over all that is not considered 'secular.'"[15] Even so, church courts serve as a precursor to the rise of religious arbitration and, in particular, the way in which the practice can directly compete with state courts, especially under the guise of contract disputes, in which church courts proved competitive with royal ones.[16]

France shared much the same story as England—a "pattern by which church courts competed with royal courts, and gradually lost influence to them."[17] Where France differed, however, was in the number of courts fighting for their fair share of jurisdictional territory. Religious courts were known as ecclesiastical courts, one of four groups of courts in the thirteenth-century French judicial system.[18] The churches were in charge of organizing these. "*Officialités*, organized by the bishop of each diocese . . . heard cases where they could exercise either personal jurisdiction or subject matter jurisdiction."[19] Personal jurisdiction "could be established if a party was either a regular or secular clerk."[20] Even the subject matter jurisdiction of ecclesiastical courts was extremely broad, "extend[ing] to both civil and criminal cases: in the latter cases, the church could inflict any punishment known to the civil courts, with the exception of death."[21] In addition to these very inclusive categories, "[t]he church claimed subject matter jurisdiction over matters of faith, such as heresy and blasphemy; it also dealt with family law and marriage, and claimed a wide jurisdiction over disputes that had a mixed religious and secular character, such as contracts made under oath,"[22]

13. *Id.* (citing R.B. Outhwaite, The Rise and Fall of the English Ecclesiastical Courts 1500–1860, at 15 (2006)).
14. *Id.* (citing Outhwaite, *supra* note 13, at 20).
15. *Id.* at 507 (quoting Langbein, *supra* note 3, at 355).
16. *Id.* (quoting William Holdsworth, 12 A History of English Law 131 (1977)).
17. *Id.*
18. *Id.*
19. *Id.* (quoting Albert Rigaudiere, Histoire du Droid et Des Institutions Dans La France Medievale et Moderne 356–58 (4th ed. 2010)).
20. *Id.* (quoting Rigaudiere, *supra* note 19, at 357).
21. *Id.* at 507–08 (quoting Rigaudiere, *supra* note 19, at 358).
22. *Id.* at 508 (quoting Rigaudiere, *supra* note 19, at 359).

and even extended its jurisdiction to include "[a]ny 'grave transgression' against public morality."[23]

While ecclesiastical courts "reached the zenith of their power in the twelfth and thirteenth centuries," the massive amount of power they had grabbed drew the attention of the royal courts.[24] Starting in the fourteenth century, the royal courts slowly began to regain jurisdiction over cases that had been hijacked by the ecclesiastical courts, beginning with "cases involving church officials that involved serious crimes against the public order."[25] Shortly thereafter, the royal courts "established appellate jurisdiction over the church courts in cases where the church courts overstepped the bounds of their jurisdiction," and, "in the fifteenth century, this became a general appellate jurisdiction."[26]

The subject matter jurisdiction of the ecclesiastical courts continued to crumble in the sixteenth and seventeenth centuries. First, "[i]n 1539, ecclesiastical jurisdiction was dramatically curtailed by François I with the Ordonnance de Villers-Cotterêts, which provided that ecclesiastical judges could not hear 'actions pures personelles,' and left them with competence only over 'purely religious matters.' "[27] Louis XIV narrowed ecclesiastical court jurisdiction over even these in 1695, when he placed that jurisdiction under royal supervision.[28]

The power struggle between the ecclesiastical and secular courts in both England and France didn't just complicate the process of settling disputes through ecclesiastical courts; it actually pitted ecclesiastical and secular courts against one another. The secular courts, with strong government backing (based partially on the fear that ecclesiastical courts had gained too much power) consistently won these bouts. This led the governments of both England and France to slowly but surely chip away at the ability of individuals to choose to resolve their disputes in ecclesiastical courts. Although this certainly complicated the ecclesiastical-secular court dichotomy, many individuals remained loyal to the ecclesiastical courts and appreciated that they could settle their disputes in the way they wanted, through a lens tailored to religious values and in a tribunal

23. *Id.* (quoting RIGAUDIERE, *supra* note 19, at 359).

24. *Id.* (quoting BRIGITTE BASDEVANT-GAUDEMET & JEAN GAUDEMET, INTRODUCTION HISTORIQUE AU DROIT XIIIE–XXE SIECLES 175 (2000)).

25. *Id.* (quoting RIGAUDIERE, *supra* note 19, at 360).

26. *Id.* (quoting RIGAUDIERE, *supra* note 19, at 361).

27. *Id.* (citing *Ordonnance d'Août 1539 Prise par le Roi François I*, ASSEMBLEE NATIONALE, http://www.assemblee-nationale.fr/histoire/villers-cotterets.asp (last visited Oct. 26, 2011)).

28. *Id.* (quoting BASDEVANT-GAUDEMET & GAUDEMET, *supra* note 24, at 176).

utilizing the doctrines that shaped the way they lived. Therefore, when the first settlers arrived in the present day United States, they brought the idea of ecclesiastical courts with them.

B. RELIGIOUS ARBITRATION IN AMERICA

The importance of religious freedom to North American colonists cannot be overstated. Many fled their native countries in search of an opportunity to worship the god they wanted in the way they wanted. However, although the first colonists strongly considered the idea of freedom *of* religion, they failed to think about the freedom of individuals *from* religion. Most communities were structured around one religion or another. Some colonies actually went so far as to establish churches.[29] This, of course, was negated—at least by law—when, "[i]n 1789 the First Congress of the United States proposed to the states the First Amendment, which prevented an established church from reaching the same position in national American life as it had in Britain."[30] Even so, some states continued with established religions until 1833 when Massachusetts, the last, repealed the statute establishing its official religion.[31]

Although state-sponsored religions fell out of favor almost from the founding of the British colonies in North America, individuals took advantage of the free exercise clause of the First Amendment and quickly established religious arbitration as a means for settling disputes. Those in states with the deepest religious roots—many of which had, at one point or another, established a state-sponsored religion—were more likely to do so. Puritans in Massachusetts based their lives around their religion and established religious courts that "had powers that outstripped their English counterparts."[32] The secular and ecclesiastical court systems in Massachusetts quickly blurred together, with criminal cases often "end[ing] up in a church court,"[33] while secular courts maintained meaningful power even over church and religious disputes, "exercis[ing] jurisdiction over offenses that were purely religious, such as failure to attend church."[34] It is important to note, however, that church courts were not vehicles for arbitration, but

29. *Id.* at 509.
30. *Id.* (quoting 1 Stat. 97 (1789)).
31. *Id.* (quoting RELIGION AND THE NEW REPUBLIC: FAITH IN THE FOUNDING OF AMERICA 196 (James H. Hutson ed., 2000)).
32. *Id.* at 510.
33. *Id.* (quoting JEROLD S. AUERBACH, JUSTICE WITHOUT LAW? 22 (1983)).
34. *Id.* (quoting AUERBACH, *supra* note 33, at 22).

were instead driven by litigation, identical to their secular counterparts. This fostered an adversarial environment, which many Puritan colonists in Massachusetts found repugnant to their religious values. In fact, the colony as a whole "encouraged the settlement of disputes outside of the 'legal' framework."[35] This fostered the development of what would come to be known as arbitration, and religious arbitration in particular.

Although Massachusetts encouraged alternative methods of settling disputes, the colony did not construct any requirements for the practice. To the contrary, communities took it upon themselves to develop and utilize methods of arbitration. Communities began to do this as early as 1635, when a "Boston town . . . laid down an ordinance that no congregation members could litigate unless there had been a prior effort at arbitration."[36] One of the earliest cases involving religious arbitration came in 1640 and involved "a prominent lady and a carpenter."[37] In short, the prominent lady failed to abide by the church's arbitral decision—twice.[38] The dispute made its way into the ecclesiastical court, "which enforced it: not by seizing her property, which it could not do, but by excommunicating her."[39] This illustrates the power churches had—not granted to them by the state, but inherent in the faith of their members.

Ecclesiastical courts in Massachusetts always had a very clear set of parameters—including those outlining personal jurisdiction. For example, "Church courts in Massachusetts could only exercise jurisdiction in disputes where the parties were of the same congregation."[40] Especially as the colony moved away from an established religion, the decision to settle disputes in what had traditionally been known as church courts was left up to the parties. Aside from providing a venue in which disputes could be settled through the lens of an individual's religious beliefs, however, church courts—early examples of bodies utilizing religious arbitration—provided a number of benefits to the parties who chose to settle their disputes in them, as opposed to the secular civil courts. Church courts could settle disputes more quickly because they met year-round, as opposed to secular civil courts, which "sat only four times a year, and in the county seat."[41] Aside from being convenient, church courts were less formal, less expensive

35. *Id.*
36. *Id.* at 510–11 (quoting AUERBACH, *supra* note 33, at 23).
37. *Id.* at 511 (quoting AUERBACH, *supra* note 33, at 23–24).
38. *Id.* (quoting AUERBACH, *supra* note 33, at 23).
39. *Id.* (quoting AUERBACH, *supra* note 33, at 23–24).
40. *Id.* (quoting WILLIAM E. NELSON, DISPUTE AND CONFLICT RESOLUTION IN PLYMOUTH COUNTY, MASSACHUSETTS, 1725–1825, at 43 (1981)).
41. *Id.* (quoting NELSON, *supra* note 40, at 44).

(the parties needed not hire a lawyer), and, perhaps most important, the method of arbitration utilized by the church courts "was also divinely sanctioned: St. Paul exhorted the believers to settle disputes among themselves, urging them not to take cases to the courts of the 'unbelievers.'"[42]

The form of religious arbitration utilized in colonial America did not fare well following the American Revolution. So-called church courts lost nearly all of their power—except that of excommunication—to the secular courts, which "had effectively become 'the only institution that was available to adjudicate a dispute.'"[43] Although instances of disputes being settled by religious arbitration are documented, they are limited, and appear to be the exception, rather than the rule. For example, one finds records noting that "a church in Middleboro, Massachusetts in 1826 handled a dispute between two members concerning a dam."[44]

The likelihood of groups implementing religious arbitration, just like in colonial America, depended significantly on the uniformity of religious beliefs in their communities. As uniform communities began to take a back seat to those with a more diverse population, religious communities attempted to preserve the power of their members to avoid the secular courts and settle their disputes within the church by breaking off into their own subcommunities. Although examples of these groups abound, they were not limited to a particular geographical location. On the East Coast, one could find "the Oneida community in New York, a society of Christian Perfectionists, [which] was 'very averse to litigation and intended . . . to preclude the possibility of it.'"[45] Across the country in Aurora, Oregon, one could find "[a] Christian Utopian community made up of German immigrants."[46] Although this report is unconfirmed, this group "allegedly went nineteen years without recourse to the courts."[47] Although these communities were successful at settling their disputes within the church as opposed to doing so in the court system, there was no community in the nineteenth century as successful at placing a wedge between itself and the court system and, more generally, at being a stand-alone "Utopian" community, as were the Mormons in Utah Territory.[48]

The Mormons' affinity for, and trust in, the practice of arbitration can be gleaned from a quote from Brigham Young, who "summed up [the

42. *Id.* (quoting 1 *Corinthians* 6:6 (King James)).
43. *Id.* at 512 (quoting NELSON, *supra* note 40, at 76).
44. *Id.* (quoting NELSON, *supra* note 33, at 198 n.62).
45. *Id.* (quoting AUERBACH, *supra* note 33, at 51).
46. *Id.* (quoting AUERBACH, *supra* note 33, at 51).
47. *Id.* (quoting AUERBACH, *supra* note 33, at 51).
48. *Id.* (quoting AUERBACH, *supra* note 33, at 54).

Mormons'] views in 1857: 'There is not a righteous person, in this community, who will have difficulties that cannot be settled by arbitrators . . .'"[49] Young seriously disliked—one could even say he had disdain for—lawyers and the courts, "argu[ing] that civil courts wasted time and 'destroyed the best interests of the community,' . . . adding that courts were a 'kitchen of the devil, prepared for hell' and that lawyers were a 'stink in the nostrils' of every Latter-Day Saint."[50] Although the Mormons avoided the court system for a short time, migrating "to an area of the West that was largely unpopulated . . . they still had to compete with civil justice [after] . . . Utah was incorporated as a territory in 1850, [just] four years after the Latter-Day Saints traveled to the region."[51] With its new status came the creation of federal courts within the Utah Territory.[52]

After this, instead of seeking autonomy over the secular court system, the Mormons attempted to construct an environment where the ecclesiastical Mormon courts (arbitral bodies) could co exist. As one author notes, Joseph Smith, the founder of the Mormon religion, actually showed deference to the secular court system on at least on one occasion. "[F]ollowing a revelation . . . in 1831[,] [Smith established] that crimes such as murder and robbery were to be tried in civil courts by the 'law of the land.'"[53] Even with this showing of what could be called solidarity with the secular court system, however, Mormons, at least on a macro level, "generally preferred to deal with intra-community disputes themselves."[54] The weakening and eventual fall of the Mormon religious courts came not at the hands of the federal courts, but instead stemmed from growth in the Utah territory's population and the religious diversity that followed. Like the religious arbitral tribunals that preceded them, "the Mormon[] [religious courts] could only claim jurisdiction by consent of the parties, and as the territory (and later state) became more religiously diverse, the power of the religious courts weakened."[55] More than religious diversity, however, and identically to the fall of the many religious courts that preceded them, the fall of the Mormon religious courts was due to one glaring, persistent problem: "[R]eligious arbitration could not compete with the secular system without

49. *Id.* (quoting C. Paul Dredge, *Dispute Settlement in the Mormon Community: The Operation of Ecclesiastical Courts in Utah*, *in* 4 ACCESS TO JUSTICE: THE ANTHROPOLOGICAL PERSPECTIVE 191, 198 (Klaus-Friedrich Koch ed., 1979)).

50. *Id.* at 512–13 (quoting Dredge, *supra* note 49, at 199).

51. *Id.* at 513 (quoting Dredge, *supra* note 49, at 198).

52. *Id.*

53. *Id.* (quoting Dredge, *supra* note 49, at 194).

54. *Id.* (quoting Dredge, *supra* note 49, at 198).

55. *Id.* (quoting Dredge, *supra* note 49, at 214).

adopting a secular enforcement mechanism."[56] This lack would not be remedied by any Christian denomination, but by the Jewish community.

The Jewish community, historically speaking, like many of the aforementioned religious groups, "preferred to avoid the secular courts."[57] Jewish reliance on dispute resolution within their communities "dates to the second century, when the Roman administration in Palestine abolished official Jewish courts."[58] Jewish reliance on religious arbitration translated well from Palestine to Europe, where "Jewish communities . . . adopted *Batei Din* to avoid their disabilities in civic life, which sometimes prevented them even from testifying in court."[59] Generally speaking, at this point in time, "there was a general prohibition against settling disputes in gentile courts,"[60] a prohibition that "remains, according to some scholars."[61] The Jewish community continued to utilize religious arbitration, and eventually brought the practice to the United States.

In the early 1900s, "the New York Jewish community adopted a mode of arbitration under the auspices of the *Kehillah*, a newly-created community organization.[62] Reaching beyond ecclesiastical matters, "*Kehillah* tribunals settled both commercial and non-commercial disputes."[63] Like the many religious tribunal bodies that preceded them, the *Kehillah* tribunals eventually lost steam and "faded after World War I."[64] Unlike their predecessors, however, other religious tribunals quickly filled the void. The transition was made smoother—and arguably even driven—by a number of arbitral bodies created by proponents of Jewish religious arbitration, including the "Jewish Arbitration Court[,] [which] was created in 1929."[65] Its rival, the Jewish Conciliation Court of America, came within a year of the Jewish Arbitration Court's creation.[66] These organizations took advantage of the momentum gained by the Jewish religious arbitration movement, first in New York City, where "the passage of the Municipal Court Act of 1915 . . . made [the judgments of Jewish tribunals] legally binding."[67] Although the

56. *Id.* at 512.
57. *Id.* at 513.
58. *Id.* at 513–14 (quoting AUERBACH, *supra* note 33, at 77).
59. *Id.* at 514 (quoting AUERBACH, *supra* note 33, at 77).
60. *Id.*
61. *Id.* at 514 n.81 (quoting 1 EMANUEL QUINT, A RESTATEMENT OF RABBINIC CIVIL LAW 174 (1990).
62. *Id.* at 514 (quoting AUERBACH, *supra* note 33, at 79).
63. *Id.* (quoting AUERBACH, *supra* note 33, at 79).
64. *Id.*
65. *Id.* (quoting AUERBACH, *supra* note 33, at 83–84).
66. *Id.* (quoting AUERBACH, *supra* note 33, at 83–84).
67. *Id.* (quoting AUERBACH, *supra* note 33, at 160 n.20).

passage of the Municipal Court Act, in retrospect at least, may seem to be foundational to modern religious arbitration, the more pivotal historical landmark actually predated it by three years.

"Maryland courts enforced judgments from tribunals where both parties had agreed to be bound, which made it possible for a Jewish tribunal to begin operating there in 1912."[68] Although the Maryland decisions seem relatively menial—at least in the big picture of arbitration in the United States—they were actually quite pivotal to shaping the practice's future. They reiterated that parties had the freedom to contract amongst themselves, and that the terms of their agreement would hold sway should the parties' agreement—or its terms—later be challenged or disputed.

The distinction of being first to perfect religious arbitration in the United States thus belongs not to any Christian denomination, but rather to the Jewish community. It did this by finding the secular enforcement mechanism the practice so desperately needed within the well-established body of contract law. Although the Jewish community first found it, not just they, but other religious groups as well, have helped to perfect it both in the United States and abroad.

C. CONCLUSION

This chapter has briefly explored the history of religious dispute resolution in the Anglo-American tradition, focusing on the various forms that faith-based dispute resolution has taken in the United States from colonial times until the early twentieth century.

The early successes of various Jewish arbitration forums in the early 1900s set the stage for subsequent developments on faith-based arbitration in America. Local legislation and judicial willingness to uphold and enforce arbitral awards on the basis of parties' prior consent foreshadowed the 1924 Federal Arbitration Act (FAA), which embraced a contractual approach to alternative dispute resolution. Generally speaking, contract law in the United States gives contracting parties significant latitude in crafting their agreements. When faced with a challenge to a contract, courts will typically uphold an agreement so long as its purpose, terms, and imposed duties are not illegal, and so long as the terms of the agreement are actually agreed upon by both parties, as opposed to one party's

68. *Id.* (quoting B.H. Hartogensis, *A Successful Community Court*, 12 J. AM. JUD. SOC. 183, 183 (1929)).

consent being procured by fraud or duress. The argument goes that if any agreement—other than an illegal or fraudulent one—may stand, so too may an agreement to submit a contractual dispute to religious arbitration.

The contractual turn in American arbitration law is discussed more fully in Chapter Five. Before we do so, however, it is important to understand that the development of faith-based arbitration in America in the twentieth and twenty-first centuries under the contractual approach endorsed by the FAA represents a qualitatively different kind of religious dispute resolution than the earlier models. With the advent of the FAA, faith-based arbitration was transformed into just one more expression of the choice-of-law and choice-of-forum provisions typical in many kinds of contracts. In this sense, religious dispute resolution was no longer particular, unique, or especially different than other means of private dispute resolution. Indeed, it was no longer particularly religious in an ecclesiastical sense. Although many of the kinds of early American religious arbitration discussed in this chapter were parochially religious, contract-based religious arbitration that functions within American law's general arbitration framework is in many ways rather mundane, even secular. It essentially involves parties using contractual methods to agree to resolve a litigious conflict in a forum and in accordance with norms chosen by the parties. In the case of religious arbitration, such choices happen to embrace religious forums and religious laws, but are in essence no different than parties in the construction industry choosing to resolve a dispute before a board of construction industry experts in accordance with construction industry standards, or Olympic athletes or sponsors turning to the Court of Arbitration for Sport to adjudicate a disagreement about steroid testing standards in accordance with its own normative standards.

CHAPTER 5

Arbitration Law and Its Evolution

This chapter will focus on the evolution of arbitration law in the United States. The story begins in the early 1900s with Justice Benjamin Cardozo's endorsement of what was then the standard approach to ADR in the United States, which held parties could not arbitrate disputes or choose the law governing a dispute. This chapter will explain how American law has gradually moved away from that early view to the more modern approach, which favors arbitration as an ordinary expression of choice of law and choice of forum by contract. This chapter will also explain why the current approach is both economically and socially valuable to general society and is now a significant feature of every aspect of American commerce.

A. INTRODUCTION: WHY CARE ABOUT THE PARAMETERS OF ARBITRATION GENERALLY?

Church and state should be separate. This simple principle has been woven into the fabric of the United States since the first settlers landed on the country's shores to escape the religious persecutions of their native lands. Early Americans found the principle so important that they included it as part of the First Amendment of the United States Constitution: "Congress shall make no law respecting an establishment of religion, or prohibiting the free exercise thereof . . ."[1] The First Amendment's religion clauses have

1. U.S. CONST., amend. I.

Sharia Tribunals, Rabbinical Courts, and Christian Panels. Michael J. Broyde.

two thrusts: (1) the free exercise clause protects the right of individuals to practice the religion of their choice, free from government intervention; (2) the establishment clause prohibits the government from establishing a religion. The religion clauses can be summed up with the phrase "live and let live." They give individuals the choice of which—if any—religion to practice, and protect individuals from being coerced or forced into practicing a religion established by the government, giving individuals a guarantee of freedom of (freedom to practice) and freedom from (freedom to choose not to practice) religion.

How is this relevant to religious arbitration? Simply put, religious arbitration seems to commingle the law—which the state is charged with implementing and enforcing—and religion. This commingling, in turn, appears to run contrary to the principle that church and state should remain separate. However, when one takes a closer look at religious arbitration as it is used in contemporary society, it is readily apparent that the practice is not the product of a law enacted by the government, but instead finds its footing in the long-established and thoroughly developed area of contract law.

This chapter traces the story of how and why arbitration in general became acceptable in America, and why it is so common in many areas of law and life. This discussion about arbitration generally is important to understand the issues and parameters of religious arbitration in particular in light of the core holding of the U.S. Supreme Court in *Good News Club v. Milford Central School*,[2] as well as many other cases.[3] In *Good News*, the state rented out public school classrooms to any and all who wished, but not to religious institutions, and the Supreme Court ruled this to be unconstitutional discrimination against religion. Rights that are given generally to all—even when coming from a law and not the Constitution—must be given to religions and religious groups as well.

Based on this, there is good reason to suspect (and many courts hold and scholarly articles aver)[4] that a state cannot ban religious arbitration, either in the sense of ADR under a religious legal system or ADR by a religious tribunal, while simultaneously permitting secular arbitration. Given the federal government's mandate through the Federal Arbitration Act (FAA)

2. 533 U.S. 98 (2001).

3. *See* Awad v. Ziriax, 670 F.3d 1111 (10th Cir. 2012), as well as many others.

4. Mark C. Rahdert, *Exceptionalism Unbound: Appraising American Resistance to Foreign Law*, 65 CATH. UNIV. L. REV. 537 (2016); Note, *The Future of Sharia Law in American Arbitration*, 48 VAND. J. TRANSNATIONAL L. 891 (2015); James A. Sonne, *Domestic Applications of Sharia and the Exercise of Ordered Liberty*, 45 SETON HALL L. REV. 717 (2015); Eun-Jung Katherine Kim, *Islamic Law in American Courts: Good, Bad, and Unsustainable Uses*, 28 NOTRE DAME J.L. ETHICS & PUB. POL'Y 287 (2014).

to generally permit arbitration, arbitration by religious tribunals and under religious law must be permitted under the same rules, too.

B. A HISTORY OF ARBITRATION LAW IN AMERICA

The law, generally speaking and in any and every sense, seeks to provide parties with a framework and arena in which to settle their disputes. Traditionally and historically, disputes were almost unequivocally settled in courts through litigation, with the rare exception of the now arcane practice of dueling, and the even rarer trial by ordeal.[5] The combination of the official nature and binding finality of the judgment of courts made utilizing them favorable to disputing parties. As time passed, however, and America grew more diverse as a country in terms of both population and culture, so did the number and types of disputes. As they were settled by the court system and, sometimes, legislatures, the body of statutory and case law expanded exponentially. With this inflation, courts became less specialized and less effective at settling disputes in a manner satisfactory to parties. With more cases to hear, dockets also grew more crowded, rendering courts less efficient.

Moreover, as the nation grew and became more socially, culturally, and religiously varied, those areas of law (most important, family law) that depended on the many courts' having a crisp understanding of cultural norms found it impossible to fully reflect diversity. This was particularly the case in situations (such as marriage) where our legal and cultural norms permit the kind of cultural discrimination that is generally prohibited in most commercial settings.[6]

With courts' ineffectiveness and cultural inefficiency, individuals looked to established law to craft new methods of settling disputes. In particular, they looked to contract law. Through contract law, parties developed more innovative ways to settle disputes—alternative means by which they could have their disputes decided more effectively and efficiently than in the

5. *See generally* Harwell Wells, *The End of the Affair? Anti-deuling Laws and Social Norms in Antebellum America*, 54 VAND. L. REV. 1805 (2001); ROBERT BARTLETT, TRIAL BY FIRE AND WATER: THE MEDIEVAL JUDICIAL ORDEAL (1986).

6. For example, marriage selection remains one of the few areas of life where one can lawfully engage in what is otherwise illegal discrimination based on religious, ethnic, and other otherwise protected classes. *See* Elizabeth F. Emens, *Intimate Discrimination: The State's Role in the Accidents of Sex and Love*, 122 HARV. L. REV. 1307, 1310 (2009); Note, *Racial Steering in the Romantic Marketplace*, 107 HARV. L. REV. 877, 883–84, 889 (1994).

comparatively crowded and culturally deaf courts.[7] The idea was novel in the United States, but not entirely new from a historical perspective. These alternative methods came to be known, naturally, as ADR. Defined simply as "[a] procedure for settling a dispute by means other than litigation . . . "[8] ADR was embraced by many parties jaded by the courts.

Although contract law can generally be said to have served as the incubator for ADR, a foundational principal of contract law—*negotiation*—could rightfully be pointed to as the specific seed from which the practice of ADR sprouted. Negotiation, a method of dispute resolution in its own right, is "[a] consensual bargaining process in which the parties attempt to reach agreement on a disputed or potentially disputed matter" and "usually involves complete autonomy for the parties involved, without the intervention of third parties."[9] The purpose of negotiation is to bring parties to a mutually agreed-upon understanding.[10] The hope is that allowing disputing parties to negotiate will lead them to a mutually satisfactory resolution. Although negotiation plays a large role in ADR, from initially agreeing to settle disputes through ADR to—in some subsets of ADR—ultimately settling an arisen dispute, negotiation is neither the beginning nor the end of ADR. What truly makes ADR a viable alternative to litigation are not its foundations in the art of negotiation, but its subset practices.

C. THE DEVELOPMENT AND EVOLUTION OF ADR IN THE UNITED STATES

ADR is ably split into three subpractices: *conciliation*, *mediation*, and *arbitration*. Although strikingly similar, the subsets of ADR do differ in some respects. If taken at face value, these differences seem insignificant, but, in practice, they are actually quite important. The most notable are procedural—namely, how each subpractice resolves disputes and whether the decisions are final and binding. Examining each subpractice and laying out its definition is important to understanding what makes ADR a reasonable—and sometimes favorable—alternative to litigation.

7. Ori Aronson, *Out of Many: Military Commissions, Religious Tribunals, and the Democratic Virtues of Court Specialization*, 51 VA. J. INT'L L. 231 (2011).
8. BLACK'S LAW DICTIONARY 91 (9th ed. 2009).
9. *Id.* at 1136.
10. *Id.* at 1137.

Conciliation

Conciliation is the closest subpractice of ADR to negotiation. In particular, it is, first and foremost, "[a] process in which a neutral person meets with the parties to a dispute and explores how the dispute might be resolved."[11] On the spectrum of ADR, conciliation is "a relatively unstructured method of dispute resolution in which a third party facilitates communication between parties in an attempt to help them settle their differences."[12] Conciliation, with its lack of structure, does not lend itself to binding decisions and is not binding. Instead, the conciliator is charged with helping the disputing parties reach a mutually agreeable resolution. If such a resolution is not reached, the disputing parties may utilize other avenues to settle their disputes. Even if a resolution is reached, either party may choose to take the dispute to the traditional court system or, if agreed to by the parties, into a different ADR arena, such as mediation or arbitration.

Mediation

Almost identical in definition to conciliation, mediation is "[a] method of nonbinding dispute resolution involving a neutral third party who tries to help the disputing parties reach a mutually agreeable solution . . . ."[13] There is some disagreement among scholars as to the true difference between mediation and conciliation, but the easiest distinction to draw is that "conciliation involves a third party's trying to bring together disputing parties to help them reconcile their differences, whereas mediation goes further by allowing the third party to suggest terms on which the dispute might be resolved."[14] Regardless of the distinction, mediation has become more popular and, therefore, more visible than conciliation. The mediator's decision is non-binding and, as with conciliation, if a resolution is not reached, the disputing parties may utilize other avenues to settle their disputes. Also identically to conciliation, even if a resolution is reached in mediation, either party may choose to take the dispute into the traditional court system or, if agreed to, into the third arena of ADR: arbitration.

11. *Id.* at 329.
12. *Id.*
13. *Id.* at 1070–71.
14. *Id.* at 1071 (quoting BRYAN A. GARNER, A DICTIONARY OF MODERN LEGAL USAGE 554 (2d ed. 1995)).

Arbitration

Arbitration is "[a] method of dispute resolution involving one or more neutral third parties who are usually agreed to by the disputing parties and whose decision is binding."[15] In arbitration, parties submit their case to an impartial third party for a binding resolution, called an award.[16] Arbitration offers disputants a number of advantages over formal litigation, including informal procedures, privacy, economy, amicability, speed, and efficiency.[17] Arbitration also enables parties to come to authoritative resolutions of their disputes in accordance with standards they prefer to those offered by the law, which may fail to adequately reflect the parties' expectations or satisfactorily protect their interests.[18]

Although ADR is a relatively new phenomenon in the American legal system, the practice itself dates back centuries. ADR is not confined to a particular country or even continent, and has become widely acclaimed by legal systems across the globe as a reasonable alternative to litigation.

Leaders of the Mari Kingdom (a part of present-day Syria) were the first, at least in recorded history, to utilize it.[19] The Kingdom "used mediation and arbitration in [a] dispute with other kingdoms."[20] Although these subpractices of ADR would not take hold until much later in history, the Mari Kingdom's use of ADR set the foundation for the use of diplomacy and negotiation—as opposed to war—as tools for solving problems between parties.[21] The next iteration of ADR found life in India beginning in 500 B.C., as a system of arbitration known as *Panchayat*.[22] The Greeks followed suit in 400 B.C., using a "public arbitrator in city-states," whose decisions were "'published' on temple columns."[23] Aristotle would, one hundred years later, praise arbitration, and even argue that the practice was superior to that used by courts.[24]

15. BLACK'S LAW DICTIONARY, *supra* note 8, at 119.
16. *See, e.g.*, THOMAS E. CARBONNEAU, THE LAW AND PRACTICE OF ARBITRATION 1–2 (2d ed. 2007).
17. *See* PIETER SANDERS, QUO VADIS ARBITRATION?: SIXTY YEARS OF ARBITRATION PRACTICE 2–7 (1999).
18. *See* Richard Allan Horning, *Interim Measures of Protection; Security for Claims and Costs; and Commentary on the WIPO Emergency Relief Rules (in Toto): Article 46*, 9 AM. REV. INT'L ARB. 155, 156–57 (1998).
19. JEROME T. BARRETT & JOSEPH P. BARRETT, A HISTORY OF ALTERNATIVE DISPUTE RESOLUTION: THE STORY OF A POLITICAL, CULTURAL, AND SOCIAL MOVEMENT, at xxv (2004).
20. *Id.*
21. *Id.*
22. *Id.*
23. *Id.*
24. *Id.*

After its initial head of steam, the practice of ADR—with the exception of some mediation practices and basic negotiation—seemingly disappeared from the annals of recorded history until its re-emergence in Europe during the thirteenth century A.D., first in Spain at the direction of King Alfonso the Wise—who "direct[ed] the use of binding arbitration with the publication of *Siete Partides*"[25]—and then in Ireland, which, in 1632, became the first country to "provide [a] statutory basis for arbitration."[26] At around this time, ADR washed up on the shores of North America. One subset, arbitration, proved popular in the United States, but suffered significant opposition from the U.S. court system, which was skeptical of the practice.

Arbitration in the United States, as a practice and an alternative to litigation, dates back to a century before the American Revolution, and expanded during the colonial period. In particular, "'arbitration was in constant and widespread use in New York' between 1664 and 1783."[27] The reasons arbitration was initially implemented are similar to the reasons it is so widely used today. Colonial merchants utilized it to avoid the long and expensive process of litigation in the fledgling American court systems.[28] In addition to expedience, arbitration allowed parties to choose arbitrators "on the basis of their expertise in matters pertinent to specific disputes."[29] Arbitration was particularly helpful to merchant contract negotiations. Following merchant agreements, enforcement proved relatively simple, as "[p]ractices developed among merchants to enforce arbitration awards; the failure to comply with an arbitrator's decision resulted in threats to a merchant's reciprocal arrangements or to his reputation."[30] In turn, such decisions "were generally honored and the use of arbitration was effective."[31] Even some of the most notable leaders in early America utilized arbitration. In 1770, George Washington "place[d] [an] arbitration clause in his will."[32] Although many people embraced arbitration, U.S. courts, following

25. *Id.*

26. *Id.* at xxvi.

27. Roger S. Haydock & Jennifer D. Henderson, *Arbitration and Judicial Civil Justice: An American Historical Review and a Proposal for a Private/Arbitral and Public/Judicial Partnership*, 2 PEPP. DISP. RESOL. L.J. 141, 145 (2002) (quoting Bruce L. Benson, *An Exploration of the Impact of Modern Arbitration Statutes on the Development of Arbitration in the United States*, 11 J.L. ECON. & ORG. 479, 481 (1995)).

28. Bruce L. Benson, *An Exploration of the Impact of Modern Arbitration Statutes on the Development of Arbitration in the United States*, 11 J.L. ECON. & ORG. 479, 482 (1995).

29. *Id.*

30. *Id.* at 484.

31. See Haydock & Henderson, *supra* note 27, at 145.

32. *Id.*

the lead of English courts, initially harbored hostility toward it, and especially toward binding arbitration born out of contracts.

Court hostility toward arbitration "dates back to 1609 when an English court declared, in *Vynior's Case*,[33] that contracts to submit to arbitration were revocable."[34] Arbitration clauses continued to be treated as revocable by English courts, even as parties' intent began to be recognized as a significant factor in contract enforcement.[35] Early court decisions in the United States followed England's lead. For example, in an 1836 case before the U.S. Supreme Court in which the appellants argued the dispute was subject to arbitration, the Court "responded that arbitration, 'being to a mere amicable tribunal, . . . could not, in a case of this sort, be now insisted upon to bar the jurisdiction of the court. It is wholly unlike the case, where a positive law has fixed the mode of ascertaining the compensation.' "[36] Thus, the Court held, "[a] dispute settled by an arbitrator could be appealed to an American court and essentially be treated as though it had never been investigated before."[37]

Within a decade following *Hobart*, the U.S. Supreme Court "began to reconsider its position towards arbitration."[38] In an 1842 case, the Court concluded: "[I]n construing [an arbitration] agreement, we must look at what was the obvious intention of the parties."[39] Shortly thereafter, in 1854, the Court expanded its view, noting:

> Arbitrators are judges chosen by the parties to decide the matters submitted to them, finally and without appeal. As a mode of settling disputes, it should receive every encouragement from courts of equity. If the award is within the submission, and contains the honest decision of the arbitrators, after a full and fair hearing of the parties, a court of equity will not set it aside for error, either in law or fact. A contrary course would be a substitution of the judgment of the chancellor in place of the judges chosen by the parties, and would make an award the commencement, not the end, of litigation.[40]

33. 4 Eng. Rep. 302 (1609).
34. Haydock & Henderson, *supra* note 27, at 145.
35. *Id.* at 145–46 (citing Kill v. Hollister, 95 Eng. Rep. 532, 532 (K.B. 1746) (holding contract to arbitrate was attempt by the parties to "oust this court" of its jurisdiction and it was therefore unenforceable)).
36. *Id.* at 146 (quoting Hobart v. Drogan, 35 U.S. 108 (1836)).
37. Bruce L. Benson, *An Exploration of the Impact of Modern Arbitration Statutes on the Development of Arbitration in the United States*, 11 J.L. ECON. & ORG. 479, 484 (1995).
38. Haydock & Henderson, *supra* note 27, at 146.
39. Hobson v. McArthur, 41 U.S. 182 (1842).
40. Burchell v. Marsh, 58 U.S. 344 (1854).

The Supreme Court's favorable view of arbitration carried into the late nineteenth century, and arbitration was utilized to settle some of the most vexing conflicts faced by the United States, especially following the American Civil War. In particular, following the abolition of slavery in the southern states, General Oliver Howard "institute[d] arbitration in employment agreements between former slaves and former owners."[41] Although the effectiveness of such antebellum employment agreements is largely questionable due to enforcement issues, and Howard's motive for using such agreements is unrecorded, their use provided the foundation for laborers across the country, including labor unions, to use arbitration as an alternative to litigation. By the late 1800s, arbitration was becoming more credible. This credibility, in turn, led to a movement to implement statutes governing arbitration.

In 1888, the Arbitration Act was passed, which was likely "the first ADR statute in the United States providing voluntary arbitration."[42] Even with the passage of the Arbitration Act and early acceptance of the practice by the U.S. Supreme Court, United States judges remained skeptical of the wide latitude arbitration agreements gave to parties, fearing such latitude might be used by those with significant business savvy to take advantage of less knowledgeable parties. As a member of the New York Court of Appeals in 1914, Justice Benjamin Cardozo discussed his concerns about arbitration, noting:

> In each case . . . the fundamental purpose of the contract [of arbitration] is the same—to submit the rights and wrongs of litigants to the arbitrament of foreign judges to the exclusion of our own. Whether such a contract is always invalid where the tribunal is a foreign court we do not need to determine. There may conceivably be exceptional circumstances where resort to . . . courts of another state is so obviously convenient and reasonable as to justify our own courts in yielding to the agreement of the parties and declining jurisdiction . . . If jurisdiction is to be ousted by contract, we must submit to the failure of justice that may result from these and like causes. It is true that some judges have expressed the belief that parties ought to be free to contract about such matters as they please. In this state the law has long been settled to the contrary. The jurisdiction of our courts is established by law, and is not to be diminished, any more than it is to be increased, by the convention of the parties.[43]

41. Barrett & Barrett, *supra* note 19, at xxvi.
42. *Id.* at xxvii.
43. Meacham v. Jamestown, J. & C. R. Co., 105 N.E. 653, 655 (N.Y. 1914) (Cardozo, J., concurring) (internal citation omitted).

That case involved a contract with both a choice of law to an alternative legal system and a choice of forum to private arbitration.[44] In Cardozo's view, neither was permitted.

Cardozo was not alone. In fact, most Western legal systems were initially hostile to ADR forums operating apart from the state-sponsored justice system and resolving conflicts in accordance with substantive and procedural values different from those embraced by the law.[45] Giving parties the ability to govern their own agreements, including allowing them to agree to choice-of-law and choice-of-forum provisions therein, made opponents of ADR, including Cardozo, uneasy.

Notwithstanding Cardozo's venerable view, both choice of law and choice of forum (including private arbitration) would eventually be universally accepted by United States courts. One characteristic of the Uniform Commercial Code would prove central to the rise of arbitration law: almost any of an arbitration agreement's provisions may be modified by agreement of the parties.[46] Contract law—namely judges' familiarity with contract law as a doctrine—was the initial legal pivot point of arbitration. Judges, extremely familiar with the well-developed and constantly vetted body of American contract law, grew more comfortable with the practice of arbitration. Nonetheless, legislators—first at the state level and later at the federal level—saw the increased use of arbitration by their constituents, and felt it necessary to develop statutes custom-tailored to regulate the practice, as opposed to simply allowing it to rest on well-established contract law.

44. The contract stated:

> In order to prevent all disputes and misunderstandings between them in relation to any of the stipulations contained in this agreement, or their performance by either of said parties, it is mutually understood and agreed that the said chief engineer shall be and hereby is made arbitrator to decide all matters in dispute arising or growing out of this contract between them, and the decision of said chief engineer on any point or matter touching this contract shall be final and conclusive between the parties hereto, and each and every of said parties hereby waives all right of action, suit or suits or other remedy in law or otherwise under this contract or arising out of the same to enforce any claim except as the same shall have been determined by said arbitrator.

Id. at 347.

45. *See* Steven C. Bennett, Arbitration: Essential Concepts 12–13 (2002).

46. U.C.C. § 1-302 (1977) ("Variation By Agreement: Except as otherwise provided in subsection (b) or elsewhere in [the Uniform Commercial Code], the effect of provisions of [the Uniform Commercial Code] may be varied by agreement . . . . The presence in certain provisions of [the Uniform Commercial Code] of the phrase 'unless otherwise agreed', or words of similar import, does not imply that the effect of other provisions may not be varied by agreement under this section.")

Even with its detractors, arbitration practice continued to grow in the early quarter of the 1900s, driven initially by merchants, who had found it preferable to litigation, and eventually by attorneys who, as a class, found significant opportunity to expand their practice into an area that could ultimately take away some of their traditional clientele. As attorneys entered the fray, they realized that the implementation of arbitration statutes would "promote the use of attorneys in the process."[47] Although arbitration statutes had been adopted before—most notably the Arbitration Act of 1888—these would not be considered modern. The first modern arbitration law was adopted by the State of New York in 1920.[48] This statute is considered modern in the sense that it "provid[ed] for enforcement of agreements to arbitrate future disputes, as well as agreements to settle existing disputes."[49]

Even with statutes governing arbitration in some places, the public was still relatively wary of the practice. Business leaders established the Arbitration Society of America in 1922 "to educate the public about the benefits of arbitration and to lobby for more extensive arbitration legislation."[50] The lobbying efforts paid off in 1925 when Congress passed the FAA.[51] The Act was grounded in contract law, as evident in Section 2, which "provides that written agreements to arbitrate matters involving commerce or maritime transactions 'shall be valid, irrevocable, and enforceable, save upon such grounds as exist at law or in equity for the revocation of any contract.'"[52] Congress, in its enactment of the FAA, "specifically stated its intent to place arbitration agreements on par with other contracts and to help parties avoid the expense and delay of litigation."[53]

Interestingly, as one author points out, the FAA's provisions have remained "essentially unchanged since [its] enactment in 1925." However, its application "has dramatically expanded."[54] In particular, it has become "definitively established as a substantive federal law, preemptive and binding on the states, and articulating a federal policy extending to issues well beyond its literal terms."[55] However, it would take time for it to reach this

47. Haydock & Henderson, *supra* note 27, at 147.
48. *See id.* (citing N.Y.C.P.L.R. §§ 7501–14 (McKinney 2000) (originally enacted as Act of Apr. 19, 1920, ch. 275, 1920 N.Y. Laws 803)).
49. *Id.* (internal quotation omitted).
50. *Id.*
51. *Id.* at 148.
52. *Id.* at 149 (quoting 9 U.S.C. § 2).
53. *Id.* (quoting Ed Anderson & Roger Haydock, *History of Arbitration as an Alternative to U.S. Litigation*, Aug. 12, 1996 WEST'S LEGAL NEWS 8257, *available at* 1996 WL 449743).
54. *Id.*
55. *Id.*

status, and "[f]or years courts and commentators agreed that the statute applied only in the federal courts and so governed only the few contract suits that happened to involve diversity or admiralty jurisdiction."[56]

Shortly after the passage of the FAA, the Arbitration Society of America merged with the Arbitration Foundation to become the American Arbitration Association.[57] The Arbitration Foundation, which had been established in 1924, differed from the Arbitration Society of America in that it concentrated its efforts on research and "promoting the commercial interests of its constituents."[58] Although the approaches differed, the goals were the same. The groups believed the merger would allow them to pool their resources and "integrate their differing approaches."[59]

The passage of the FAA and the formation of the American Arbitration Association provided arbitration much-needed momentum. Arbitration proved particularly useful for settling disputes between laborers and employers during the 1920s, 1930s, and 1940s, and helped to solidify the position of labor unions in American society, which, in turn, led to an uptick in public employment.[60] Through the 1940s, arbitration continued to expand. However, "[b]eginning in the 1950s, a United States Supreme Court decision created an obstacle to the expansion of arbitration" that would not be fully dismantled until 1989.[61]

The 1953 case of *Wilko v. Swan*[62] involved "an agreement between a securities broker and a buyer whereby the parties had agreed to arbitrate controversies arising out of the transaction."[63] The buyer sued, alleging the seller made misrepresentations and omissions in the agreement. While the broker "moved to stay the trial of the action pursuant to § 3 of the United States Arbitration Act until an arbitration,"[64] the buyer "sought to continue with his suit in federal court arguing that the arbitration clause in the parties' agreement was an unenforceable waiver of his right to bring suit in court under section 14 of the Securities Act."[65] Section 14 stated that "[a]ny condition, stipulation or provision binding any person acquiring any security to waive compliance with any provision of this subchapter or of

56. *Id.* at 149–50.
57. *Id.* at 148.
58. *Id.* at 147–48.
59. *Id.* at 148.
60. Barrett & Barrett, *supra* note 19, at xxvii–xxviii.
61. Haydock & Henderson, *supra* note 27, at 150.
62. Wilko v. Swan, 346 U.S. 427 (1953).
63. Haydock & Henderson, *supra* note 27, at 150.
64. *Wilko*, 346 U.S. at 429.
65. Haydock & Henderson, *supra* note 27, at 150.

the rules and regulations of the Commission shall be void."[66] The Supreme Court held that this provided the purchaser of securities in the case with a right to "select the judicial forum"[67] that could not be waived, not even by contract.

The Court's reasoning and inferences, however, would do much more damage to arbitration than its holding. The Court reasoned that the effectiveness of the protections provided by the Securities Act would be diminished "in arbitration as compared to judicial proceedings."[68] It then pointed to the complicated nature of securities cases:

> Determination of the quality of a commodity or the amount of money due under a contract is not the type of issue here involved. This case requires subjective findings on the purpose and knowledge of an alleged violator of the Act. They must be not only determined but applied by the arbitrators without judicial instruction on the law. As their award may be made without explanation of their reasons and without a complete record of their proceedings, the arbitrators' conception of the legal meaning of such statutory requirements as "burden of proof," "reasonable care" or "material fact" cannot be examined. [Furthermore], [the] [p]ower to vacate an award is limited.[69]

This highlighted the Court's distrust of arbitrators' ability to handle complex issues and hinted at its skepticism of the arbitration process itself. In his dissent, Justice Felix Frankfurter pointed out that the Court had made certain leaps in logic to reach its ultimate decision, noting, "[t]here is nothing in the record before us, nor in the facts of which we can take judicial notice, to indicate that the arbitral system . . . would not afford the plaintiff the rights to which he is entitled."[70] He concluded that, absent a showing that arbitration would jeopardize the plaintiff's rights, the arbitration clause should be enforced.[71] The Court would eventually heavily favor enforcement of arbitration clauses, but would spend the next thirty years chipping away at the limitations *Wilko* placed on the flourishing practice of arbitration.

American arbitration is thus strongly grounded in contract theories. Parties' decisions to arbitrate private disputes should be upheld in order to promote and respect the contractual autonomy and freedom of private

66. *Wilko*, 346 U.S. at 430 n.6.
67. *Id.* at 435.
68. *Id.*
69. *Id.* at 435–36.
70. *Id.* at 439–40.
71. *Id.* at 440.

parties to order their private affairs in whatever way seems best to them. The contract law foundations of arbitration make the practice extremely customizable. Parties can essentially decide on all aspects of how their arbitration will be governed long before any dispute arises. Such customization can include framing rules of procedure, guidelines for the arbitrator—including whom it will be—and implementing substantive law outside the realm of traditional substantive law. The difficulty of parsing and understanding this customized substantive law gradually led parties to favor selecting arbitrators who were experts in the substantive law governing their dispute. This actually gives arbitration a leg-up over litigation, in which generalist judges decide disputes with which they are sometimes unfamiliar.

Some groups went a step further than specialized arbitrators and actually created their own arbitral bodies, comprised only of arbitrators who were experts in the types of disputes that would come before them. Today, countless such arbitral bodies exist. They have proved particularly useful to various industries such as real estate and construction, which have liberally utilized the practice.[72] Although the less visible and commercial nature of disputes handled by arbitral bodies developed by these industries has led to little or no critical reception, other groups have not managed to stay under the radar. As a result, arbitration is probably the best-developed of the three subsets of ADR, and certainly that which carries the most weight, despite also being the most controversial. Parties must agree to arbitrate a dispute, and may do so either before or after a dispute arises. It is typical, however, for parties to agree to arbitrate disputes prior to any dispute arising. It has become particularly common for parties to agree to arbitrate disputes through arbitration clauses in contracts, which mandate arbitration and allow the contracting parties to avoid litigation.[73] Of course, there is always a fear that a mandatory agreement to arbitration prior to a dispute arising is (as noted below) part of the problem: coercive arbitration is selected because the forum is naturally biased in favor of one of the parties.

Arbitration's most notable characteristic—and one that is not shared by other subsets of ADR—is its binding nature. Arbitration removes the ability of courts to review disputes that have validly been submitted to—and validly decided by—an arbitrator or arbitral body. This, in turn, allows arbitral bodies to serve in place of courts, which, for some time, made courts uneasy. Many in the judiciary remain uncomfortable with the binding

72. For more on this, see *Areas of Expertise*, Am. Arbitration Ass'n, https://www.adr.org/aaa/faces/aoe (last visited Jan. 20, 2017).
73. Black's Law Dictionary, *supra* note 8, at 120.

nature of the practice even today, as well as with the fact that arbitration, for all intents and purposes, supplants court jurisdiction over certain disputes.

Outside of the courts, arbitration has other critics who are concerned that arbitration negatively affects parties of limited means and favors sophisticated ones who learn to play the game by the rules very well, making it a game rigged to favor repeat players.[74] Even with its detractors, however, arbitration has been embraced by many and, one could say, perfected by the parties to arbitration themselves.

In the United States, the Federal Arbitration Act (FAA) and state-specific arbitration rules often based on the Uniform Arbitration Act create a legal framework in which private arbitration can operate with the support of the official court system.[75] The FAA protects the integrity of arbitration by ensuring that courts will enforce awards, which gives the arbitration process a derivative power of enforcement, transforming it from a form of dispute resolution, the efficacy of which is contingent on disputants' goodwill, into one that is ultimately backed by government enforcement powers.[76] This legal framework is premised on courts' power to enforce binding contracts.[77] If disputants agree to arbitrate rather than litigate a conflict, and commit themselves to abide by the decision reached by their designated arbitration forum, then a court can enforce that contract by requiring recalcitrant parties to arbitrate the case in accordance with the terms of the arbitration agreement and to abide by the arbitrator's ruling.[78]

74. *See* Jessica Silver-Greenberg & Michael Corkery, *In Arbitration, a "Privatization of the Justice System,"* N.Y. TIMES DEALBOOK (Nov. 1, 2015), http://www.nytimes.com/2015/11/02/business/dealbook/in-arbitration-a-privatization-of-the-justice-system.html (last visited Oct. 1, 2016).

75. *See* 9 U.S.C. §§ 1–16 (2012). Prior to Congress's enacting the Federal Arbitration Act, courts were often hostile to alternative dispute resolution, including arbitration. *See* Meacham v. Jamestown, F. & C.R. Co., 105 N.E. 653, 655 (N.Y. 1914) (Cardozo, J., concurring) (arguing that courts should not enforce contracts that grant jurisdiction to resolve disputes to private arbitrators rather than regular courts). Congress passed the Act to combat this hostility. *See* H.R. REP. NO. 68-96, at 1–2 (1924); Mitsubishi Motors Corp. v. Chrysler-Plymouth, Inc., 473 U.S. 614, 625 n.14 (1985); Southland Corp. v. Keating, 465 U.S. 1, 13 (1984) (citing H.R. REP. NO. 68-96, at 1–2 (1924)) ("The need for the [Federal Arbitration Act] arises from . . . the jealousy of the English courts for their own jurisdiction . . . This jealousy survived . . . and was adopted by the American courts.").

76. *See* IAN R. MACNEIL ET AL., FEDERAL ARBITRATION LAW: AGREEMENTS, AWARDS AND REMEDIES UNDER THE FEDERAL ARBITRATION ACT §§ 38.1.1, 38.2 (Supp. 1995).

77. *See* Cindy G. Buys, *The Arbitrators' Duty to Respect the Parties' Choice of Law in Commercial Arbitration*, 79 ST. JOHN'S L. REV. 59, 69–70 (2005).

78. *See* Volt Info. Scis. v. Leland Stanford Junior Univ., 489 U.S. 468, 476 (1989) ("[T]he federal policy [under the FAA] is simply to ensure the enforceability, according to their terms, of private agreements to arbitrate.").

Under the FAA, a court may vacate an arbitration award under a variety of circumstances. A court may refuse to enforce an award not issued pursuant to a valid agreement, as when no agreement to arbitrate exists or one was obtained through fraud or duress.[79] Similarly, a court may vacate an award if it is the product of fraud,[80] bias,[81] or corruption,[82] or was the result of misconduct by the arbitrators that violated the rights of any party.[83] A judge may also refuse to enforce an award if the arbitrators acted in excess of the powers granted to them under the agreement.[84] Finally, although courts are generally not permitted to question the substance of an arbitration award, the FAA does allow them to vacate arbitral rulings that are contrary to public policy, and some courts have held that an award may be vacated if its substance amounts to manifest disregard for the law.[85]

Arbitration in the Field of Labor Relations

The U.S. Supreme Court's first shots at *Wilko* came in the 1960 cases of *United Steelworkers of America v. American Manufacturing Co.*,[86] *United Steelworkers of America v. Warrior & Gulf Navigation Co.*,[87] and *United Steelworkers of America v. Enterprise Wheel & Car Corp.*[88] The facts of each case dealt with arbitration under the guise of a collective bargaining agreement, and each carved away at *Wilko*, but in markedly different ways.

American Manufacturing Co. dealt with collective bargaining and labor relations, and particularly questioned the role of the judiciary in collective bargaining under the Labor Management Relations Act of 1947 (LMRA). In its holding, the Supreme Court first warned that, under the auspices of a collective bargaining agreement, "[t]he function of the court is very limited when the parties have agreed to submit all questions of contract interpretation to the arbitrator. It is confined to ascertaining whether the

79. *See* 9 U.S.C. §10(a) (2002).
80. *Id.*
81. *Id.*
82. *Id.*
83. *Id.*
84. *Id.*
85. *See* Michael A. Helfand, *Religious Arbitration and the New Multiculturalism: Negotiating Conflicting Legal Orders*, 86 N.Y.U. L. Rev. 1231, 1254–58 (2011); Michael A. Helfand, *Litigating Religion*, 93 B.U. L. Rev. 493, 508 n.74 (2013); *see generally* Amanda M. Baker, *A Higher Authority: Judicial Review of Religious Arbitration*, 37 Vt. L. Rev. 157, 163–64 (2012).
86. United Steelworkers of Am. v. Am. Mfg. Co., 363 U.S. 564 (1960).
87. *Id.* at 574.
88. *Id.* at 593.

party seeking arbitration is making a claim which on its face is governed by the contract."[89] It then concluded:

> The courts ... have no business weighing the merits of the grievance, considering whether there is equity in a particular claim, or determining whether there is particular language in the written instrument which will support the claim. The agreement is to submit all grievances to arbitration, not merely those which the court will deem meritorious.[90]

Finally, in a nod to the expertise of arbitrators of labor disputes, the Court pointed out that "[t]he processing of even frivolous claims may have therapeutic values of which those who are not a part of the plant environment may be quite unaware."[91] *American Manufacturing Co.* not only indicated the Court's willingness to go along with agreements to arbitrate in collective bargaining agreements, but also highlighted a turning point in the Court's outlook on the practice of arbitration and the ability of arbitrators themselves. Contrary to its skeptical view in *Wilko*, the Court explicitly acknowledged that arbitrators were capable of understanding and settling disputes between parties and, with specialization, may even do a better job of settling complicated disputes than courts.

Instead of once again overlooking *Wilko* and using the LMRA as a shield, as it did in *American Manufacturing Co.*, the Court's holding in *Warrior & Gulf Navigation Co.*, faced the *Wilko* decision more directly. The Court noted the existence of a "federal policy ... to promote industrial stabilization through the collective bargaining agreement"[92] and its belief—derived from earlier case law—that "[a] major factor in achieving industrial peace is the inclusion of a provision for arbitration of grievances in the collective bargaining agreement."[93] This policy, and the importance of arbitration to the promotion of industrial stabilization, thus rendered "the run of arbitration cases, illustrated by *Wilko* ... irrelevant to our problem."[94] The Court acknowledged that parties have a "choice ... between the adjudication of cases or controversies in courts with established procedures or even special statutory safeguards on the one hand and the settlement of

89. *Id.* at 567–68.
90. *Id.* at 568.
91. *Id.*
92. United Steelworkers of America v. Warrior & Gulf Navigation Co., 363 U.S. 565 (1960) at 578.
93. *Id.*
94. *Id.*

them in the more informal arbitration tribunal on the other."[95] *Wilko*, the Court pointed out, was a commercial case, and in such cases, "arbitration is the substitute for litigation."[96] In cases such as the one at bar, however, the Court asserted "arbitration is the substitute for industrial strife."[97] Therefore, it continued:

> Since arbitration of labor disputes has quite different functions from arbitration under an ordinary commercial agreement, the hostility evinced by courts toward arbitration of commercial agreements has no place here. For arbitration of labor disputes under collective bargaining agreements is part and parcel of the collective bargaining process itself.[98]

Therefore, the Court drew a distinction between arbitration of labor disputes and arbitration of commercial disputes. Although this seems to be an instance where the Court was simply straining to distinguish the case at bar from *Wilko*, it made clear that arbitration, at least under the LMRA, was a favorable alternative to litigation. It went on to make this point, along with the role judges may play in construing arbitration clauses under the LMRA, abundantly clear:

> [T]he judicial inquiry under § 301 [of the LMRA] must be strictly confined to the question whether the reluctant party did agree to arbitrate the grievance or did agree to give the arbitrator power to make the award he made. An order to arbitrate the particular grievance should not be denied unless it may be said with positive assurance that the arbitration clause is not susceptible of an interpretation that covers the asserted dispute. Doubts should be resolved in favor of coverage.[99]

Although the Court's decision in *Warrior & Gulf Navigation Co.* was not revolutionary in its treatment of *Wilko*, essentially selecting to detour around it through a commercial dispute versus labor dispute distinction, it did provide clarity on broad powers arbitrators wielded under the LMRA, and confined the ability of courts to strip power from them. In a way, the Court was once again signaling its confidence in the arbitration process, along with those who arbitrate disputes under the LMRA, similar to what it did in *American Manufacturing Co.*

95. *Id.*
96. *Id.*
97. *Id.*
98. *Id.*
99. *Id.* at 582–83.

The third case in the United Steelworkers trilogy of cases was *United Steelworkers of America v. Enterprise Wheel & Car Corp.*[100] (hereinafter "*Steelworkers III*"). In *Steelworkers III*, the Court was faced with the issue of when, whether, and to what extent courts may review arbitration awards under labor agreements. The Court began by noting that "[t]he refusal of courts to review the merits of an arbitration award is the proper approach to arbitration under collective bargaining agreements. The federal policy of settling labor disputes by arbitration would be undermined if courts had the final say on the merits of the awards."[101] Following this limiting statement, the Court pointed out the limitations placed on arbitrators: "An arbitrator is confined to interpretation and application of the collective bargaining agreement; he does not sit to dispense his own brand of industrial justice," and "his award is legitimate only so long as it draws its essence from the collective bargaining agreement."[102] Taking a closer look at the facts of the case, the Court admitted that the arbitrator's opinion may have been ambiguous, but quickly diminished the importance of this concession by noting "[a] mere ambiguity in the opinion accompanying an award, which permits the inference that the arbitrator may have exceeded his authority, is not a reason for refusing to enforce the award. Arbitrators have no obligation to the court to give their reasons for an award."[103]

If nothing else, the Court's opinion in *Steelworkers III* reinforced its position that, at least in labor relations cases, arbitrators' awards and opinions should be given great deference, based both on the federal policy of settling labor disputes through arbitration and allowing parties to have their agreements to arbitrate enforced. In all, the Steelworkers Trilogy cleared the way for arbitration of labor disputes and arbitration clauses in collective bargaining agreements. However, it did nothing to open the doors for arbitration of commercial disputes—like the one in *Wilko*.

Arbitration of Commercial Disputes

It would be seven years before the Court would once again be asked to reexamine *Wilko*. In *Prima Paint Corp. v. Flood & Conklin Manufacturing Co.*,[104] the Court was faced with an agreement involving a commercial arbitration clause. The plaintiff argued fraud in the inducement of the contract.

100. 363 U.S. 593 (1960).
101. *Id.* at 596.
102. *Id.* at 597.
103. *Id.* at 598.
104. Prima Paint Corp. v. Flood & Conklin Mfg. Co., 388 U.S. 395 (1967).

After concluding that the contract fell "within the coverage of the [Federal] Arbitration Act,"[105] the Court moved on to the issue of "whether a claim of fraud in the inducement of the entire contract is to be resolved by the federal court, or whether the matter is to be referred to the arbitrators."[106] The Court quickly distinguished a claim for fraud in the inducement generally, and a claim for fraud in the inducement of an arbitration clause.

> [I]f the claim is fraud in the inducement of the arbitration clause itself—an issue which goes to the "making" of the agreement to arbitrate—the federal court may proceed to adjudicate it. But the statutory language [in the Federal Arbitration Act] does not permit the federal court to consider claims of fraud in the inducement of the contract generally.[107]

Therefore, the Court held, "in passing upon a § 3 application for a stay while the parties arbitrate, a federal court may consider only issues relating to the making and performance of the agreement to arbitrate."[108] Although this did little to undo the damage to commercial arbitration agreements by *Wilko*, it was at least a starting point.

Seven years after the Court's decision in *Prima Paint, Scherk v. Alberto Culver Co.*[109] reached the Court. The case seemed to be an opportunity for the Court to overrule *Wilko*. It involved an international contract and a plaintiff alleging the defendant violated the Securities Act. Given the argument's striking similarity to *Wilko*, the district court and court of appeals relied on the Supreme Court's reasoning in that case to hold the arbitration clause unenforceable.[110] The Court reversed, based on the fact that the "contract . . . was a truly international agreement."[111] The Court continued:

> Such a contract involves considerations and policies significantly different from those found controlling in *Wilko*. In *Wilko*, quite apart from the arbitration provision, there was no question but that the laws of the United States generally, and the federal securities laws in particular, would govern disputes arising out of the stock-purchase agreement. The parties, the negotiations, and the subject matter of the contract were all situated in this country, and no credible claim could have been entertained that any international conflict-of-laws problems would arise.

105. *Id.* at 402.
106. *Id.*
107. *Id.* at 403–04.
108. *Id.* at 404.
109. 417 U.S. 506 (1974).
110. Haydock & Henderson, *supra* note 27, at 154.
111. *Scherk*, 417 U.S. at 515.

> In this case, by contrast, in the absence of the arbitration provision considerable uncertainty existed at the time of the agreement, and still exists, concerning the law applicable to the resolution of disputes arising out of the contract.[112]

As Haydock and Henderson point out, the distinction drawn by the Court is interesting in a couple of ways. First, "[t]he Court distinguished *Wilko*, notwithstanding the fact that 'the laws of the state of Illinois were explicitly made applicable by the arbitration agreement.'"[113] Moreover, the Court's reasoning "seemed to indicate that in international commercial cases it is permissible to 'substitute' arbitration for litigation."[114] Although the Court's holding seemed like another stretch to avoid overruling *Wilko*, it did carve out a specific area in which commercial disputes could be arbitrated.

Arbitration of commercial disputes would continue to gain ground in the 1980s, even as the Court's *Wilko* decision stood. The Court also shed certain assumptions about the FAA and its reach. In *Moses H. Cone Memorial Hospital v. Mercury Construction Corp.*,[115] the Court held that no federal deference was due to parallel litigation brought in state court under the guise of the FAA,[116] as "Federal law in the terms of the Arbitration Act governs [arbitrability of a dispute] in either state or federal court."[117] The Court went on a year later in *Southland Corp. v. Keating*[118] to place further emphasis on the pre-emptive nature of the FAA. In Haydock and Henderson's article, they note, "[t]he significance of *Southland Corp.* is that it established the supremacy of federal law over arbitration contracts."[119] In its opinion, the Court noted:

> We discern only two limitations on the enforceability of arbitration provisions governed by the Federal Arbitration Act: they must be part of a written maritime contract or a contract "evidencing a transaction involving commerce" and such clauses may be revoked upon "grounds as exist at law or in equity for the revocation of any contract." We see nothing in the Act indicating that the broad principle of enforceability is subject to any additional limitations under state law.[120]

112. *Id.* at 515–16.
113. Haydock & Henderson, *supra* note 27, at 155.
114. *Id.*
115. 460 U.S. 1 (1983).
116. Haydock & Henderson, *supra* note 27, at 158 ("The state court suit involved the question of whether a stay should be issued under section 3 of the Federal Arbitration Act. The federal court suit, on the other hand, involved the question of whether an order to compel arbitration should be issued under section 4 of the Federal Arbitration Act.").
117. 460 U.S. at 24.
118. Southland Corp. v. Keating, 465 U.S. 1 (1984).
119. Haydock & Henderson, *supra* note 27, at 158.
120. 465 U.S. at 10–11.

This set of conclusions, when viewed together with the Court's holdings in *Moses H. Cone Memorial Hospital*, established the Court's strong stance that the FAA pre-empted conflicting state law. This stance, in turn, expanded the reach of the FAA beyond simply governing federal cases.

Like the *Moses H. Cone Memorial Hospital* and *Southland Corp.* cases, the 1985 case of *Dean Witter Reynolds Inc. v. Byrd*[121] involved pendant state issues and asked the Court to determine the validity of the "doctrine of intertwining." The Court explained this doctrine: "When arbitrable and nonarbitrable claims arise out of the same transaction, and are sufficiently intertwined factually and legally, the district court, under this view, may in its discretion deny arbitration as to the arbitrable claims and try all the claims together in federal court."[122] The Court agreed with the contrasting view that:

> the Arbitration Act divests the district courts of any discretion regarding arbitration in cases containing both arbitrable and nonarbitrable claims, and instead requires that the courts compel arbitration of arbitrable claims, when asked to do so. These courts conclude that the [Federal Arbitration] Act, both through its plain meaning and the strong federal policy it reflects, requires courts to enforce the bargain of the parties to arbitrate, and "not substitute [its] own views of economy and efficiency" for those of Congress.[123]

Although the Court's termination of the Intertwining Doctrine was notable, what made the *Dean Witter Reynolds Inc.* case particularly interesting were the factual commonalities it shared with *Wilko*. The plaintiff, "an investor, sued his broker in federal court, alleging violations of both *federal* securities laws and New York *state* securities laws."[124] Like the contract in *Wilko*, the agreement contained an arbitration clause "purporting to make arbitrable any dispute related to the contract."[125] Although the Court's decision to terminate the Intertwining Doctrine chipped away part of *Wilko*, it left part of the question unanswered. Following *Dean Witter Reynolds Inc.*, "securities claims arising under *state* law may not be sued out where they are arbitrable under an arbitration agreement."[126] The Court, in tailoring its decision to apply only to securities claims arising under state law, left *Wilko* to "govern[] the arbitrability of *federal* securities laws claims."[127]

121. Dean Witter Reynolds Inc. v. Byrd, 470 U.S. 213 (1985).
122. *Id.* at 216–17.
123. *Id.* at 217 (internal citations omitted).
124. Haydock & Henderson, *supra* note 27, at 159.
125. *Id.*
126. *Id.* at 160.
127. *Id.*

The true beginning of the fall of *Wilko* came in the 1985 case of *Mitsubishi Motors Corp. v. Soler Chrysler-Plymouth, Inc.*[128] The issue in *Mitsubishi* was "the arbitrability, pursuant to the Federal Arbitration Act, and the Convention on the Recognition and Enforcement of Foreign Arbitral Awards (Convention), of claims arising under the Sherman [Antitrust] Act, and encompassed within a valid arbitration clause in an agreement embodying an international commercial transaction."[129] Prior to *Mitsubishi*, "courts had followed the Second Circuit's opinion in *American Safety Equipment Corporation v. J.P. McGuire & Company*[130] that, in accordance with *Wilko*, claims under U.S. antitrust laws were 'of a character inappropriate for enforcement by arbitration.' "[131]

The Court held that all the claims involved in the case, including the antitrust claims, were arbitrable. The Court found "no warrant in the Arbitration Act for implying in every contract within its ken a presumption against arbitration of statutory claims."[132] To the contrary, "as with any other contract, the parties' intentions control, but those intentions are generously construed as to issues of arbitrability."[133] After courts establish the parties' intention to arbitrate a statutory claim, the Court directed that "a court should [then] examine the applicable statute to determine whether Congress intended to prohibit arbitration."[134] Continuing on, the Court noted:

> We must assume that if Congress intended the substantive protection afforded by a given statute to include protection against waiver of the right to a judicial forum, that intention will be deducible from text or legislative history. Having made the bargain to arbitrate, the party should be held to it unless Congress itself has evinced an intention to preclude a waiver of judicial remedies for the statutory rights at issue. Nothing, in the meantime, prevents a party from excluding statutory claims from the scope of an agreement to arbitrate.[135]

Because of this conclusion, "[t]he implication is that broad arbitration agreements will, after *Mitsubishi Motors*, be deemed to include statutory claims unless those agreements expressly exclude statutory claims from

128. Mitsubishi Motors Corp. v. Soler Chrysler-Plymouth, Inc., 473 U.S. 614 (1985).
129. *Id.* at 616.
130. Am. Safety Equip. Corp. v. J.P. McGuire & Co., 391 F.2d 821 (2d Cir. 1968).
131. Haydock & Henderson, *supra* note 27, at 161.
132. *Mitsubishi*, 473 U.S. at 625.
133. *Id.* at 626.
134. Haydock & Henderson, *supra* note 27, at 161.
135. *Mitsubishi*, 473 U.S. at 628.

their scope, or unless Congress has expressly prohibited arbitration of those claims in the relevant statute or legislative history."[136] The Court, however, narrowly avoided having to overrule *Wilko* by leaning on its decision in *Scherk* that "the international nature of the dispute compelled enforcement of the arbitration agreement as a forum selection clause."[137]

Two years after the Court's decision in *Mitsubishi Motors, Wilko* took another hit with the Court's holding in *Shearson/American Express, Inc. v. McMahon*.[138] In *McMahon*, the Court was faced with two issues:

> The first is whether a claim brought under § 10(b) of the Securities Exchange Act of 1934 [SEA] . . . must be sent to arbitration in accordance with the terms of an arbitration agreement. The second is whether a claim brought under the Racketeer Influenced and Corrupt Organizations Act (RICO), must be arbitrated in accordance with the terms of such an agreement.[139]

In holding both claims arbitrable, the Court utilized its two-step analysis to determine arbitrability of disputes.[140] First, it determined "whether the scope of the arbitration agreement was meant to include the statutory claims at issue."[141] Because the agreements "provided for the arbitration of 'any controversy arising out of or relating to' the accounts, transactions or the agreement itself, the claims fell within the scope of the agreement."[142] Second, the Court was faced with the issue of whether Congress intended to exempt claims under the SEA or RICO from the FAA. This issue, as Haydock and Henderson note, "was made more difficult by the Court's holding in Wilko that the Securities Act prohibited arbitration because it voided agreements waiving obligations under that statute."[143] Moreover, "[t]he SEA contained a similar prohibition on 'waiver.'"[144]

Even with its similarities to *Wilko*, "[t]he Court . . . held . . . that arbitration of claims under the SEA was permitted and not prohibited by Congress because the 'waiver' only applied to *obligations* arising under the SEA, and not the *jurisdiction* of the federal courts."[145] Therefore, "the parties were permitted to agree to adjudicate disputes over SEA obligations in

136. Haydock & Henderson, *supra* note 27, at 162.
137. *Id.*
138. Shearson/American Express, Inc. v. McMahon, 482 U.S. 220 (1987).
139. *Id.* at 222.
140. Haydock & Henderson, *supra* note 27, at 162.
141. *Id.*
142. *Id.*
143. *Id.*
144. *Id.* (quotations omitted).
145. *Id.*

an arbitration proceeding and were not required to use the federal courts to resolve those disputes."[146] The Court's holding noted a few reasons it was able to get around the *Wilko* holding "that the analogous waiver provision in the Securities Act did prohibit arbitration."[147] First, it noted that the *Wilko* holding:

> Can only be understood in the context of the Court's ensuing discussion explaining why arbitration was inadequate as a means of enforcing "the provisions of the Securities Act, advantageous to the buyer." The conclusion in *Wilko* was expressly based on the Court's belief that a judicial forum was needed to protect the substantive legal rights created by the Securities Act.[148]

At the time of the *Wilko* decision, "the plaintiff's waiver of the 'right to select the judicial forum' was unenforceable only because arbitration was judged inadequate to enforce the statutory' obligations created under the Securities Act."[149]

The Court's discussion then turned to the changing perception of arbitration since the *Wilko* decision in 1953. The Court acknowledged: "[I]t is difficult to reconcile *Wilko*'s mistrust of the arbitral process with the Court's subsequent decisions involving the Arbitration Act."[150] First, the Court noted, "courts generally recognized that arbitrators are competent to handle complex factual and legal issues without direction or instruction from the court."[151] Second, the Court pointed out, "arbitration procedures had been 'streamlined' to the extent that courts no longer fear that arbitration unfairly limits substantive rights of claimants."[152] Finally, "judicial review of arbitration awards, while limited, were still sufficient to ensure that arbitrators comply with the law."[153] Although *McMahon* did not overrule *Wilko*, the Court summarized its opinion by positing "even if *Wilko*'s assumptions regarding arbitration were valid at the time *Wilko* was decided, most certainly they do not hold true today for arbitration procedures subject to the SEC's oversight authority."[154] Even so, it would take one more decision for the Court to explicitly overrule *Wilko*.

146. *Id.*
147. *Id.*
148. Shearson/American Express, Inc. v. McMahon, 482 U.S. 220, 228 (1987).
149. Haydock & Henderson, *supra* note 27, at 163 (quoting *McMahon*, 482 U.S. at 228–29).
150. *McMahon*, 482 U.S. at 231–32.
151. Haydock & Henderson, *supra* note 27, at 164 (citing *McMahon*, 482 U.S. at 229).
152. *Id.*
153. *Id.*
154. *Id.*

Finally, in *Rodriguez de Quijas v. Shearson/American Express, Inc.*,[155] the Supreme Court overruled *Wilko*. The Court reasoned that although, at the time of the *Wilko* decision its reasoning may have been justified, "[t]o the extent that *Wilko* rested on suspicion of arbitration as a method of weakening the protections afforded in the substantive law to would-be complaints, it has fallen far out of step with our current strong endorsement of the federal statutes favoring this method of resolving disputes."[156] The Court also reasoned, "it . . . would be undesirable for the decisions in *Wilko* and *McMahon* to continue to exist side by side."[157] To do otherwise "would create confusion and inconsistency in precedent. After all, the 'waiver' provision construed in the SEA in *McMahon* is 'in every respect the same as that in' the Securities Act,"[158] and treating them differently would thus be "at odds with the principle that the 1933 and 1934 Acts should be construed harmoniously."[159]

The Court's decision to overrule *Wilko* in *Rodriguez de Quijas* "set the stage for the expanded use of arbitration."[160] Into the 1990s, cases continued to reach the Court, allowing it to clarify its previously confusing stances on arbitration. In the 1991 case of *Gilmer v. Interstate/Johnson Lane Corp.*,[161] the Court was faced with the issue of whether Age Discrimination in Employment Act (ADEA) claims were subject to arbitration.

After determining that "the scope of the arbitration clause was broad enough to encompass the ADEA claim, and [that] there was nothing in the text or legislative history to indicate Congress had intended to exempt ADEA claims from arbitration," the Court turned to the plaintiff's argument that "there was an inherent conflict between arbitration and the purpose of the ADEA which prohibited making those claims subject to compulsory arbitration."[162] The Court rejected this argument, citing two reasons in particular. First, EEOC administration of the ADEA "would not be hindered . . . by the enforcement of agreements to arbitrate ADEA claims."[163] The employee could still file a charge with the EEOC, and the EEOC could even investigate on its own in the absence of an employee's claim.[164] Second, the Court pointed to the fact that "the ADEA does not guarantee a judicial forum and the procedures available in an arbitration forum are sufficient to provide

155. Rodriguez de Quijas v. Shearson/American Express, Inc., 490 U.S. 477 (1989).
156. *Id.* at 481.
157. *Id.* at 484.
158. Haydock & Henderson, *supra* note 27, at 165 (quoting *Rodriguez de Quijas*, 490 U.S. at 482, 484).
159. *Rodriguez de Quijas*, 490 U.S. at 484.
160. Haydock & Henderson, *supra* note 27, at 164.
161. Gilmer v. Interstate/Johnson Lane Corp., 500 U.S. 20 (1991).
162. Haydock & Henderson, *supra* note 27, at 166.
163. *Id.*
164. *Id.*

relief."[165] Finally, the Court rejected the plaintiff's claim that an arbitrator might be biased in favor of the employer, noting that the rules governing his arbitration "provided protections in the unusual circumstance where a plaintiff believed bias to be an issue."[166]

Although the *Gilmer* decision was not as notable as *Rodriguez de Quijas*, it did give the Court an opportunity to "review[] the major complaints and concerns that had been voiced by those opposed to arbitration, and that had been raised in the lower courts."[167] As Haydock and Henderson note, "*Gilmer* closed almost all of the loopholes that had been used to avoid enforcement of arbitration agreements and made clear that arbitration agreements between businesses and individuals are readily enforceable."[168] Yet, questions regarding the Court's past decisions on arbitration still loomed.

Following the 1984 decision in *Southland Corp. v. Keating*, "state arbitration laws in conflict with the FAA were meant to be preempted by the federal law," yet "in the eleven years since that decision, several state courts navigated around *Southland Corporation* by construing the language of the FAA narrowly, avoiding conflict and thereby avoiding preemption of the state law."[169] This narrow reading of the FAA required that, for an agreement to be arbitrable under the FAA, the parties to a contract must have "contemplated a connection between their contract and interstate commerce."[170] For their agreement to be arbitrable, the alternative to this reading was a broad construction of the FAA holding arbitrable any agreement simply involving interstate commerce in fact.[171] In its 1995 decision in *Allied-Bruce Terminix Companies, Inc. v. Dobson*,[172] when presented with a choice between the two readings, the Court held the broader interpretation to be the correct one.

The Court, in construing the FAA to find congressional intent, "construed the words 'involving commerce' to mean 'affecting commerce,'" which, the Court concluded "was evidence . . . that Congress intended to exercise expansive powers over arbitration contracts."[173] Next, the Court construed "evidencing a transaction" to mean "that a contract involving interstate commerce in fact was sufficient to 'evidence a transaction' governed by the FAA."[174] After establishing congressional intent, the Court concluded that the FAA governed

165. *Id.*
166. *Id.* at 167.
167. *Id.*
168. *Id.*
169. *Id.*
170. *Id.*
171. *Id.*
172. Allied-Bruce Terminix Companies, Inc. v. Dobson, 513 U.S. 265 (1995).
173. Haydock & Henderson, *supra* note 27, at 168.
174. *Id.*

the contract at issue in the case. "Moreover, because the FAA conflicted with the Alabama statute that would have invalidated the arbitration clause, the Alabama law was preempted by the FAA."[175] The Court's decision in *Dobson* "resolved any further doubts about the ultimate reach of the FAA in governing arbitration agreements and signaled a further advancement in the use of arbitration agreements between businesses and consumers."[176]

Only one year after *Dobson*, the Court reinforced its support for *Southland Corp.* in *Doctor's Associates, Inc. v. Casarotto*.[177] *Casarotto* pivoted around a Montana statute "which required a specific type of notice on arbitration contracts."[178] The Montana Supreme Court held that the FAA did not preempt the statute.[179] The United States Supreme Court disagreed, pointing to the fact "that Montana's statute singled out arbitration contracts from other contracts."[180] This went directly against the FAA, under which "arbitration contracts must be placed on the same footing with all other contracts."[181] Therefore, the U.S. Supreme Court held, Montana's statute was in conflict with the FAA and was pre-empted thereby. The Court's decision in *Casarotto* not only reinforced its support for *Southland Corp.*, but also highlighted the difficulty states would have narrowing agreements to arbitrate by legislation without facing pre-emption by the FAA.

Turning the page to the new millennium, courts looked to combat another problem: arbitration clauses in consumer contracts of adhesion. The U.S. Supreme Court took its first swipe at such contracts in *Green Tree Financial Corp. v. Randolph*.[182] Randolph pivoted around consumer claims under the Truth in Lending Act and the Equal Credit Opportunity Act. The consumer in the case agreed to an adhesion contract drafted by a financial company. The contract contained an arbitration agreement. The consumer alleged that the "agreement was, in itself, a violation of her rights under the ECOA because she could not afford to pursue arbitration and therefore was prohibited from pursuing her statutory rights under the TILA."[183] The Court, therefore, was forced to face the issue of whether the lack of reference to arbitration costs in the arbitration agreement precluded enforcement of the agreement. Although Randolph "argued the 'risk' of prohibitive arbitration costs would force her to 'forgo' her claims against Green Tree and therefore

175. *Id.*
176. *Id.*
177. Doctor's Associates, Inc. v. Casarotto, 517 U.S. 681 (1996).
178. Haydock & Henderson, *supra* note 27, at 168.
179. *Casarotto*, 517 U.S. at 684.
180. *Id.*
181. *Id.*
182. Green Tree Fin. Corp. v. Randolph, 531 U.S. 79 (2000).
183. Haydock & Henderson, *supra* note 27, at 170.

preclude her from 'vindicating her federal statutory rights in the arbitral forum,'" she "failed to produce sufficient evidence of the costs she would actually incur in arbitrating her claims."[184] The Court therefore refused to invalidate the arbitration agreement. In sum, "[a]ll of the Justices in the *Green Tree* Court held that arbitration is a legitimate, acceptable method for businesses and consumers to resolve their differences."[185] More particularly, "arbitration is readily enforceable if it is fair, affordable, and accessible."[186]

The Court's consideration of arbitral practices quickly turned to arbitration in employment agreements. In *Circuit City Stores, Inc. v. Adams*,[187] the Court considered the scope of the FAA under the guise of employment contracts.[188] Section 1 of the FAA exempts "contracts of employment of seamen, railroad employees, or other class of workers engaged in foreign or interstate commerce."[189] In *Circuit City*, the Court narrowly construed this exemption such that only transportation workers' contracts are exempt. In narrowing the employment contract exemption, the Court stated:

> Unlike the "involving commerce" language in § 2, the words "any other class of workers engaged in . . . commerce" constitute a residual phrase, following, in the same sentence, explicit reference to "seamen" and "railroad employees." Construing the residual phrase to exclude all employment contracts fails to give independent effect to the statute's enumeration of the specific categories of workers which precedes it . . . .[190]

Therefore, the Court "once again construed the FAA such that more contracts, rather than fewer, fall within its scope. Instead of exempting all employment contracts from the reach of the FAA, the Court's construction of that Act exempts only the employment contracts of transportation workers."[191] This expanded the number—and kind—of contracts subject to arbitration beyond what was previously believed allowable.

Although the history of arbitration in the United States is a long and dynamic one, it appears the practice is here to stay, and will prove to be a useful tool for those who wish to avoid the expense—both in time and cost—of litigation in the future. Furthermore, as explained above, the

184. *Id.* at 171.
185. *Id.*
186. *Id.* at 172.
187. 532 U.S. 105 (2001).
188. *Id.*
189. Federal Arbitration Act, 9 U.S.C. § 1 (1947).
190. 532 U.S. at 115.
191. Haydock & Henderson, *supra* note 27, at 172.

structure of American First Amendment law will make it almost impossible to limit parties' ability to choose any legal system they wish in arbitration to non-religious ones. Practically, this means that the nationwide endorsement of arbitration as an alternative form of dispute resolution protects arbitration in all its forms, religious and secular.[192]

D. CONCLUSION

This chapter has laid out the development of American arbitration law from its early stance opposing private dispute resolution as an alternative to traditional adjudication, to its current approach, which endorses private dispute resolution and directs state and federal courts to enforce arbitral decisions issued in conformance with the requirements of the FAA. This neutral legal framework is critical to the current practice of faith-based arbitration in this country. Religiously observant individuals and communities in the United States have greatly expanded the opportunities for using faith-based arbitration to resolve all manner of co-religionist disputes. This expansion has relied on utilizing the general framework for legally recognized private dispute resolution gradually created under American law. It is the FAA's generally applicable arbitration framework that makes effective faith-based dispute resolution possible, and religious arbitration needs to be understood in that context.

As Chapter Six explains, however, the contractual bases for private arbitration under the FAA entail a number of requirements and restrictions on what courts and the law will recognize as legally legitimate and enforceable arbitration. In addition to ordinary contractual expectations that pertain to the viability of any private agreements to arbitrate, the FAA's arbitration framework also set basic procedural and some limited substantive requirements to ensure that, if courts are to enforce arbitration rulings, those private dispute resolution processes conform to basic due process and public policy norms. These requirements create special problems in the context of religious arbitration, where parties seek to resolve disputes in accordance with religious norms and principles and in religious communal contexts that may be inconsistent with these legal expectations. It is to this issue that the next Part of this book now turns.

192. *See, e.g.*, Asma T. Uddin & David Pantzer, *A First Amendment Analysis of Anti-Sharia Initiatives*, 10 First Amend. L. Rev. 363 (2012); Erin Sisson, *The Future of Sharia Law in American Arbitration*, 48 Vand. J. Transactional L. 891 (2015).

PART THREE

CHAPTER 6

Regulation of Arbitration Law in the United States

This chapter surveys the main limitations placed upon private arbitration processes by the FAA and the various state statutes at play in contemporary American arbitration law. These limits focus on three aspects of the arbitration process. First, arbitration law imposes various requirements on the formation of arbitration agreements. The chapter will then explain how a different set of limitations is needed to govern religious arbitration, including the remedies that a religious court can impose, proposing that with only a few exceptions in the area of child custody, religious arbitration should be limited to resolving matters through financial awards. Secular society must hold tightly onto the keys of coercive governmental authority and, even given contractual permission, religious arbitration should not be allowed any significant force. Second, great thought needs to be put into the question of what areas of law are outside the scope of arbitration, as we do not wish to have multiple standards. An example is racial discrimination, which should not be permitted even in religious communities, and cannot be arbitrated.

A. THE ARBITRATION AGREEMENT

The most important thing for religious groups looking to develop their own religious court system is to construct a tribunal whose decisions will be regularly upheld by secular courts. Fortunately, the law in the United States

Sharia Tribunals, Rabbinical Courts, and Christian Panels. Michael J. Broyde.

governing arbitration has become somewhat more objective as the practice has developed over the years. This objectivity leads to predictability for fledgling religious tribunals, and this predictability means more room for them to exercise their authority.

The FAA makes it clear that agreements to arbitrate are valid. In particular, it states:

> A written provision in any maritime transaction or a contract evidencing a transaction involving commerce to settle by arbitration a controversy thereafter arising out of such contract or transaction, or the refusal to perform the whole or any part thereof, or an agreement in writing to submit to arbitration an existing controversy arising out of such a contract, transaction, or refusal, shall be valid, irrevocable, and enforceable, save upon such grounds as exist at law or in equity for the revocation of any contract.[1]

The reach of this provision is more easily understood when one notes that the FAA defines "commerce" as

> commerce among the several States or with foreign nations, or in any Territory of the United States or in the District of Columbia, or between any such Territory and another, or between any such Territory and any State or foreign nation, or between the District of Columbia and any State or Territory or foreign nation, but nothing herein contained shall apply to contracts of employment of seamen, railroad employees, or any other class of workers engaged in foreign or interstate commerce.[2]

These provisions, taken collectively, reflect the law's long-held preference for courts honoring private agreements between parties.

Courts are required to honor agreements to arbitrate in most instances. If a court is presented with a suit or proceeding, "upon any issue referable to arbitration under an agreement in writing for such arbitration,"[3] it may review the agreement.[4] However, "upon being satisfied that the issue involved in such suit or proceeding is referable to arbitration under such an agreement," and so long as the applicant for the stay is not in default in proceeding with such arbitration, the court "shall on application of one of the parties stay the trial of the action until such arbitration has been had in

1. 9 U.S.C. § 2 (1990).
2. *Id.* § 1.
3. *Id.* § 3.
4. *Id.*

accordance with the terms of the agreement."[5] In all, this provision of the FAA expedites the arbitration process when a valid arbitration agreement exists.

Although the FAA provides certain parties—those with valid arbitration agreements—with a way out of unnecessary adjudication of their disputes within the court system, it also provides parties with a cause of action that allows them to petition the courts to compel arbitration arising from a valid arbitration agreement. If one party to an arbitration agreement allegedly "fail[s], neglect[s], or refuse[s] . . . to arbitrate under a written agreement for arbitration,"[6] the aggrieved party "may petition any United States district court which, save for such agreement, would have jurisdiction [over] . . . the subject matter of a suit arising out of the controversy between the parties, for an order directing that such arbitration proceed in the manner provided for"[7] in the parties' arbitration agreement.[8] Following proper service to the party in default—five days' notice in writing—the court may hear the parties' arguments in favor of (or against) compelling arbitration. Following a hearing, "upon being satisfied that the making of the agreement for arbitration or the failure to comply therewith is not in issue, the court shall make an order directing the parties to proceed to arbitration in accordance with the terms of the agreement."[9] If, however, "the making of the arbitration agreement or the failure, neglect, or refusal to perform the same be in issue, the court shall proceed summarily to the trial thereof."[10] This section, therefore, forces courts faced with a motion to compel arbitration to consider only one thing: whether the dispute at bar is over the making of an agreement for arbitration or the failure to comply therewith. If it is, the court may decide the dispute. If not, it must compel arbitration.

B. THE ARBITRATION PROCESS

Although the process of arbitration itself is left almost exclusively to the desires of the parties entering the agreement, the FAA does confront situations in which ambiguity is found in the arbitration agreement. For example, if an arbitration agreement does not appoint—or provide a method for

5. *Id.*
6. *Id.* § 4.
7. *Id.*
8. *Id.*
9. *Id.*
10. *Id.*

appointing—an arbitrator, or if one *is* provided but a party fails to appoint an arbitrator in a timely manner, then "upon the application of either party to the controversy the court shall designate and appoint an arbitrator . . . who shall act under the said agreement with the same force and effect as if he . . . had been specifically named therein."[11] Even in this instance, however, the court must consider only the conditions agreed to by the parties within the four corners of the arbitration agreement itself.[12]

Once arbitration begins, arbitrators, pursuant to the FAA, "may summon in writing any person to attend before them or any of them as a witness and in a proper case to bring with him or them any book, record, document, or paper which may be deemed material as evidence in the case."[13] These summons, as discussed in the FAA, are aligned with subpoenas to appear and testify before courts. In terms of procedure, they must "be served in the same manner as subpoenas."[14] If a person subject to a summons to testify "refuse[s] or neglect[s] to obey" it, the arbitrator may petition the federal courts to

> compel the attendance of such person or persons before said arbitrator or arbitrators, or punish said person or persons for contempt in the same manner provided by law for securing the attendance of witnesses or their punishment for neglect or refusal to attend in the courts of the United States.[15]

Although the power to subpoena witnesses is the furthest the FAA goes to align arbitrators with judges, it is a potent tool that arbitrators may use to more effectively and efficiently settle disputes between parties. In addition, the power to summon witnesses is necessary for the process of arbitration to maintain its place as a viable alternative to litigation. Taking this power away from arbitrators would render arbitration voluntary and give witnesses the power to affect the outcome by deciding on their own whether to show up.

Arbitration can serve as an alternative to the court system, but the two can sometimes become intertwined, either by consent of the parties or due to issues arising during arbitration. The FAA provides parties to an arbitration agreement an opportunity to have their arbitration award judicially reviewed.[16] Parties may, of course, agree in an arbitration agreement

11. *Id.* § 5.
12. For example, courts that designate an arbitrator must comply with the terms agreed to by the parties in the arbitration agreement.
13. 9 U.S.C. § 7 (1990).
14. *Id.*
15. *Id.*
16. *See id.* § 9.

to have a judgment entered by the courts upon an arbitrator's award.[17] However, the simple fact that parties do not do so does not mean that an arbitrator's award is immune from review and vacature.

Under the FAA, courts may vacate an arbitrator's award on four grounds.[18] First, a court may vacate an arbitrator's award "where the award was procured by corruption, fraud, or undue means."[19] This includes where an arbitrator's award was not pursuant to a valid arbitration agreement between the parties and, thus, no agreement exists. Second, an award may be vacated "where there was evident partiality or corruption in the arbitrators."[20] Third, a court may vacate an award stemming from arbitration "where the arbitrators were guilty of misconduct in refusing to postpone the hearing, upon sufficient cause shown, or in refusing to hear evidence pertinent and material to the controversy; or of any other misbehavior by which the rights of any party have been prejudiced."[21] Finally, courts may vacate an award stemming from instances "where the arbitrators exceeded their powers, or so imperfectly executed them that a mutual, final, and definite award upon the subject matter submitted was not made."[22] Many courts have taken an expansive view of this section of the FAA. For example, although the FAA does not generally permit courts to question the substance of an arbitration award, it has been interpreted to allow courts to vacate arbitral rulings that are contrary to public policy, and some courts have gone further to hold that an award may be vacated if its substance amounts to manifest disregard for the law, thus adding the objectivity of the law to an arbitrator's considerations.[23]

Aside from vacating an arbitrator's award, courts may modify or correct one on three grounds. The first is "[w]here there was an evident material miscalculation of figures or an evident material mistake in the description of any person, thing, or property referred to in the award."[24] Second, an arbitration award may be modified or corrected "[w]here the arbitrators have awarded upon a matter not submitted to them, unless it is a matter not affecting the merits of the decision upon the matter submitted."[25] The final, and probably broadest ground, is "[w]here the award is imperfect in

17. *Id.*
18. *See id.* § 10(a).
19. *Id.* § 10(a) (1).
20. *Id.* § 10(a) (2).
21. *Id.* § 10(a) (3).
22. *Id.* § 10(a) (4).
23. *See id.* § 10(a). *See also* Hall Street Assocs. LLC v. Mattel, Inc., 552 U.S. 576 (2008); Annie Chen, *The Doctrine of Manifest Disregard of the Law after* Hall Street: *Implications for Judicial Review of International Arbitrations in U.S. Courts*, 32 FORD. INT'L L.J. 1872 (2008).
24. 9 U.S.C. § 11(a) (1990).
25. *Id.* § 11(b).

matter of form not affecting the merits of the controversy. The order may modify and correct the award, so as to effect the intent thereof and promote justice between the parties."[26]

In addition to these general statutory grounds, courts consider the following in deciding whether to uphold a religious tribunal's decisions: "(1) the validity and scope of the arbitration agreement between the parties, (2) whether the arbitral proceedings observed proper procedures and due process, and (3) whether the resulting decision is irrational or void as against public policy." These criteria demonstrate the extent to which procedural guarantees of validity and fairness affect the viability of a religious tribunal in the eyes of its secular counterparts.[27]

C. UNCONSCIONABILITY AND DURESS

Courts considering arbitration cases engage in a three-question process. First, is the arbitration clause valid? Second, is the entire contract valid? Third, is the contract enforceable?[28] An arbitration clause may be valid even where some other aspect of the contract is invalid.[29] If a contract is valid on its face and contains an arbitration clause, courts will generally look no further into the circumstances of the contract and will send the parties to arbitration to further determine its validity.[30] The arbitrator then has jurisdiction to determine whether the arbitration clause is itself valid.[31] In other words, the arbitrator rules on whether he or she has the jurisdiction to rule over the contract in the first place. Although this may seem counterintuitive, it is a mirror of the power courts have to determine whether they have jurisdiction over a case.[32]

26. *Id.* § 11(c).

27. Lee Ann Bambach, *The Enforceability of Arbitration Decisions Made by Muslim Religious Tribunals: Examining the* Beth Din *Precedent*, 25 J.L. & RELIGION 379, 390 (2010).

28. Prima Paint Corp. v. Flood & Conklin Mfg. Co., 388 U.S. 395, 403–04 (1967).

29. *Id.*

30. *Id.*

31. *Id.*

32. There is some debate over the fairness of such a doctrine. If an invalid contract contains a mandatory arbitration clause and is thus sent to arbitration, and the arbitrator deems the contract itself invalid or unenforceable, the arbitration clause would also be invalidated. If the arbitration clause is invalidated, then the arbitrator never had any power to rule over the validity of the contract in the first place. Although we may feel comfortable when a judge, who was either voted in by election or appointed by an elected official and who has the required legal education and background, makes such a jurisdictional determination, some are less so where the arbitrator is not a part of the legal system.

Furthermore, as explained above, the FAA takes a strong pro-arbitration stance, limited only by a savings clause indicating that arbitration agreements are to be enforced "save upon such grounds as exist at law or in equity for the revocation of any contract."[33] This has widely been acknowledged to mean those grounds of contract law that would make a contract void, such as fraud, duress, or unconscionability.[34] Arbitration agreements, by virtue of their nature as contracts, are subject to these defenses.[35] These defenses apply to both the arbitration agreement itself and to the overlying contract, and each may be independently proven.[36] Mistake, incapacity, duress, undue influence, unconscionability, fraud, and frustration of purpose are all defenses to contract formation that may be used to void arbitration agreements.[37]

Contracts are governed by three main sources of law. As a matter of uniformity, the Uniform Commercial Code (UCC) governs business contracts over the sale of goods.[38] The common law governs contracts over other forms of business, including the sale of real estate, contracting for services, insurance, employment, and any intangible assets. The federal government and the states also legislate in areas of financial, employment, and civil rights issues.[39] State legislation and common law have almost exclusive jurisdiction over family law matters.[40]

Beyond the initial question of the validity of the arbitration agreement, it is necessary to split the discussion of arbitration contracts into the broader categories of commercial contracts and family law contracts. The defenses to contract formation as well as the defenses against enforcement of contracts differ between these two categories and are better addressed as separate issues.

This issue also brings up further concerns for agreements to arbitrate, which must be dealt with in the future. If there is a question that one of the parties did not agree to arbitrate or that the whole contract may be fraudulent, the party who is contesting the agreement did not agree to take the contest outside of the courtroom in the first place. To then demand they do so would be to allow fraudulent contractors to deny a contesting party their right to the courtroom and then bind them by an extra-legal authority they never agreed to be bound by in the first place.

33. 9 U.S.C. §§ 1–16 (1990).

34. Perry v. Thomas, 482 U.S. 483 (1987).

35. Doctor's Assocs., Inc. v. Casarotto, 517 U.S. 681, 686 (1996).

36. *Id.*

37. *Id.*

38. U.C.C. § 9-101 (1990).

39. 1-1 CORBIN ON CONTRACTS § 1.21 (2015).

40. Janet Halley, *What Is Family Law?: A Genealogy Part II*, 23 YALE J.L. & HUMAN. 189 (2011).

Unconscionability in Commercial Arbitration

Unconscionability is a contract defense that invalidates a contract that, by its terms, shocks the conscience.[41] Thus, a contract that is by all other definitions legal may be voided where the terms of the agreement are extremely unfair, such that no reasonable person would have agreed to them.[42] This determination is made by a judge in the courtroom or, where there is an agreement to arbitrate, by the arbitrator.[43]

The doctrine of unconscionability has historically been difficult to outline. Determining what constitutes an unconscionable contract is very much "knowing it when you see it." The decision is frequently based on local societal mores, which often vary greatly depending on the geography of the case.[44] As with any determination based on conscience and morality, what "shocks the conscience" in New York City will inevitably be different than what shocks the conscience in, for instance, rural Georgia. These differences thus make certain determinations of unconscionability difficult to comprehend on a national level. However, these difficulties are most likely to show up in the family law arena.

In order to understand how unconscionability relates to arbitration, it is necessary to understand how the analysis is broken down. Unconscionability can be brought as a defense to either the arbitration agreement alone or to the full contract.[45] The Supreme Court determined in *Prima Paint Corp. v. Flood and Conklin Manufacturing Corp.* that when dealing with a mandatory arbitration agreement purportedly induced by fraud, the court makes the determination as to unconscionability.[46] If the agreement is valid, the case should go to arbitration.[47] If not, the courts then have jurisdiction over the case. However, where the entire contract and not only the arbitration agreement is argued to be induced by fraud, the issue of unconscionability is left to the arbitrator.[48] In other words, where there is a claim that the agreement to arbitrate is itself unconscionable, the courts decide whether this is so. Where there is nothing wrong with the arbitration agreement

41. Eyre v. Potter, 56 U.S. (15 How.) 42, 60 (1853).
42. Restatement (Second) of Contracts § 208 (1981) (quoting Hume v. United States, 132 U.S. 406, 411 (1889) (quoting Earl of Chesterfield v. Janssen, 2 Ves. Sen. 125, 155, 28 Eng. Rep. 82, 100 (Ch. 1750)))).
43. *Id.*
44. *Id.*
45. Doctor's Assocs., Inc. v. Casarotto, 517 U.S. 681, 686 (1996).
46. 388 U.S. 395 (1967).
47. *Id.*
48. *Id.*

specifically, and it is some other aspect of the contract that is said to be unconscionable (for instance, an unfairly punitive liquidation penalty), the courts defer to the arbitrator as directed by the FAA.[49]

Prima Paint was the first in a series of cases that furthered support for arbitration. The second game-changer was *Southland Corp. v. Keating* in 1984.[50] Prior to *Southland*, there was a growing suspicion of arbitration among state courts as the use of arbitration clauses in contracts began to become popular, particularly as many judges read the FAA as being significantly less broad than it is now recognized to be.[51] As a result of their suspicion of arbitration, states began to pass laws banning arbitration over certain subject matter, or created their own boundaries and rules regarding when arbitration could be used.[52] The main concern was that arbitration might be used to deny parties their fundamental right to access the courtroom.[53] In *Southland*, in response to this growing trend, the Supreme Court definitively stated that Section 2 of the FAA, which dictates that arbitration clauses in commercial contracts are enforceable, is a substantive rule rather than a procedural one, and therefore preempts any state laws that attempt to make arbitration clauses illegal as a matter of course.[54]

Southland was followed some years later by *Circuit City Stores, Inc. v. Adams*, which closed off one of the last major defenses to arbitration.[55] *Circuit City* attempted to use the clause in Section 1 of the FAA that states that the FAA would not apply to "contracts of seamen, railroad employees, or any other class of workers engaged in foreign or interstate commerce."[56] This had previously been read broadly by many states to ban mandatory arbitration clauses in certain employment contracts, a reading that seemed reasonable given the Supreme Court's broad reading of Section 2 and, indeed, its more general expansion of the commerce clause.[57] However, *Circuit City* unequivocally upheld the Supreme Court's pro-arbitration stance.[58] Notably, the case was a racial discrimination case under Title VII of the Civil Rights Act, which clarified two separate points. The first

49. *Id.*
50. 465 U.S. 1 (1984).
51. Susan Landrum, *Much Ado about Nothing: What the Numbers Tell Us about How State Courts Apply the Unconscionability Doctrine to Arbitration Agreements*, 97 MARQ. L. REV. 751 (2014).
52. *Id.* at 757–58.
53. Armendariz v. Found. Health Psychcare Servs., Inc., 24 Cal. 4th 83 (2000).
54. 465 U.S. 1 (1984).
55. 532 U.S. 105 (2001).
56. *Id.* (quoting 9 U.S.C. § 1).
57. *Id.*
58. *Id.*

was that the FAA Section 1 exclusion for workers engaged in interstate commerce would be read extremely narrowly and would thus be virtually useless in challenging mandatory arbitration clauses in employment contracts.[59] The second was that, even for subject matter such as racial discrimination under Title VII, the Supreme Court was holding fast to its support for arbitration.[60]

This case crystallized one of the bigger criticisms of the Supreme Court's interpretation of Section 1 and Section 2 of the FAA—its use of the commerce clause. The initial criticism of the Court's reading of Section 2 of the FAA as supporting a broad reading of the commerce clause was that it problematically applied the modern, extremely broad view of the commerce clause to an act that clearly could not have taken into account this broad reading without assuming a level of legislative prescience that is unlikely at best.[61] *Circuit City* compounded this criticism when it chose a reading of the reference to the Commerce Power in Section 1 that was extremely narrow.[62] In other words, where the legislative intention of Congress in writing the FAA was logically to read both Section 1 and Section 2 as referencing the narrower understanding of the Commerce Power in 1925, the Supreme Court instead broadened the reading of Section 2 without also broadening the reading of Section 1, therefore expanding the reach of arbitration while ignoring the original legislative attempt to limit it.[63]

In a third case, *Doctor's Associates, Inc. v. Casarotto,* the Supreme Court confirmed that any state legislation that attempted to limit the reach of arbitration without also limiting other contractual agreements violated the FAA.[64] This meant that states could not legislate against what they saw as problems unique to arbitration clauses. These decisions confirmed that the Supreme Court was taking a hard pro-arbitration stance. They did not, however, mean that state courts were willing to give up their concerns. Although the Court's *Southland* decision closed off one avenue and *Circuit City* and *Doctor's Associates* another, there remained another option. This, then, is where unconscionability comes in.

Written into the FAA in Section 2, the same section in *Southland* that identified the enforcement of arbitration clauses as substantive law, is the qualifying phrase that requires arbitrations be enforced "save upon such

59. *Id.*
60. *Id.*
61. Aaron-Andrew P. Bruhl, *The Unconscionability Game: Strategic Judging and the Evolution of Federal Arbitration Law*, 83 N.Y.U. L. Rev. 1420, 1426–31 (2008).
62. *Id.*
63. *Id.*
64. Doctor's Assocs., Inc. v. Casarotto, 517 U.S. 681, 686 (1996).

grounds as exist at law or in equity for the revocation of any contract."[65] Left with few other options, the states turned to unconscionability to combat arbitration clauses. Although it was clear that the Supreme Court was taking a strong pro-arbitration stance, there was some wiggle room in contract law. As the Court noted in *Doctor's Associates*, "state law may be applied 'if that law arose to govern issues concerning the validity, revocability, and enforceability of contracts generally.' Thus, generally applicable contract defenses, such as fraud, duress, or unconscionability, may be applied to invalidate arbitration agreements without contravening § 2."[66]

States thus began to use the unconscionability doctrine, which falls under "grounds ... for the revocation of any contract,"[67] as a means of nullifying arbitration agreements where they triggered some broader potential unconscionability issue.[68] These included limitations on punitive damages, limitations on one-sided arbitration clauses that required only one party to go to arbitration while leaving the other free to litigate, clauses that allowed for a biased arbitrator, limitations on the extent of discovery, certain limitations on the potentially unfair allocations of arbitration costs, requirements for confidentiality, requirements that put a potentially unfair travel burden on a party, and provisions that allowed one party to unilaterally change the terms of the agreement.[69] Nearly all of these cases were based in the fundamental concern that a party with unequal bargaining power would force another party to agree to terms that were unfair and often against public policy.[70]

Although unconscionability is an accepted defense to contract enforcement, the nature of its use has always been difficult to define in concrete terms. There is, for instance, a difference in procedural unconscionability as opposed to substantive unconscionability.[71] This discussion is further complicated when referring to arbitration. Both procedural and substantive unconscionability issues have been argued in the use of unconscionability as a defense to arbitration.[72] Where it is argued, for instance, that an arbitration agreement was signed under unfair circumstances or compelled through the use of force, or where it was clearly impossible for the signor

65. 9 U.S.C. § 2 (1925).
66. *Doctor's Assocs.*, 517 U.S. at 686.
67. 9 U.S.C. § 2 (1925).
68. Landrum, *supra* note 51, at 772–73.
69. Bruhl, *supra* note 61, at 1438–39.
70. *Id.*
71. For a review of procedural and substantive unconscionability, see Arthur A. Leff, *Unconscionability and the Code*, 115 U. PA. L. REV. 485 (1967).
72. *See, e.g.*, Armendariz v. Found. Health Psychcare Servs., Inc., 6 P.3d 669 (2000).

to have read the arbitration agreement, there are issues of procedural unconscionability.[73] That is, the process of signing the contract was flawed. Alternatively, one of the main criticisms of arbitration is that the process is substantively unfair; that is, the very idea of signing away one's right to litigate certain contract disputes is in itself unbelievable to the point that the courts cannot, in good faith, enforce such an agreement.[74]

The most well-known of the unconscionability cases was the *Armendariz v. Foundation Health Psychare Services, Inc.* case of 2000.[75] *Armendariz* was a California case concerning an employment contract that contained an arbitration agreement requiring the employee to bring any claims for wrongful termination to arbitration.[76] In order to qualify as an unconscionable contract, the court required that the contract be both procedurally and substantively unfair, making it a useful case in parsing the difference between procedural and substantive fairness and a good example of the difficulty of qualifying what levels of unfairness might rise to the level of unconscionability.[77]

As unconscionability is generally defined by state law, the specific requirements for an unconscionability ruling are not uniform. Some states have more specific requirements, whereas others rely almost entirely on a fact-based analysis of each case. California requires that, in order to be considered unconscionable, the contract must first be a contract of adhesion—"a standardized contract, which, imposed and drafted by the party of superior bargaining strength, relegates to the subscribing party only the opportunity to adhere to the contract or reject it."[78] This, to some extent, is the procedural aspect of unconscionability.

If the court finds that the contract at issue is a contract of adhesion, then it may move on to consider whether the particular elements of the contract are "unduly oppressive or 'unconscionable.'"[79] Unconscionability may be determined based on a number of factors; California notes both the "reasonable expectations" standard and one of "oppressive" limitations.[80] The California court cites a "sliding scale" of unconscionability, wherein

73. Jeffrey W. Stempel, *Arbitration, Unconscionability, and Equilibrium: The Return of Unconscionability Analysis as a Counterweight to Arbitration Formalism*, 19 Ohio St. J. Disp. Resol. 757, 794–98 (2004).
74. *Id.*
75. *Armendariz*, 6 P.3d 669.
76. *Id.*
77. *Id.*
78. *Id.* (citing Neal v. State Farm Ins. Cos., 188 Cal. App. 2d 690, 694 (1961)).
79. *Id.* at 113.
80. *Id.*

both the procedural and substantive elements must exist; however, "they need not be present in the same degree."[81]

The court in *Armendariz* ultimately decided that the arbitration agreement was unconscionable.[82] It recognized that for most potential employees, an employment contract is one of adhesion wherein the employee needs the job and therefore cannot afford to argue over the inclusion of an arbitration clause.[83] It also recognized the inherent one-sidedness of an employer requiring arbitration from the employee without being mutually bound by the same restriction, as well as the limitations on damages to the employee that would normally be available by law for the same types of claims.[84]

Notably, the California court pointed out that, although some courts had refused to view contracts of adhesion with arbitration clauses as unconscionable due to the fear that such a move might be seen as targeting arbitration agreements specifically and therefore run afoul of the FAA, such an analysis in fact did not, because it applied equally to arbitration as well as non-arbitration contracts.[85] In other words, there are contracts of adhesion that do not contain arbitration clauses but may otherwise fall into unconscionability analysis. The court ultimately decided in favor of the employees and struck the arbitration agreement from the contract.

With California as the major exception, however, procedural unconscionability has proven to be largely ineffective as a defense to arbitration. *Prima Paint, Southland,* and *Circuit City* each supported the notion that, for better or worse, the Supreme Court considers arbitration to be an acceptable alternative to litigating in a courtroom, and the growing popularity of contracts of adhesion in all areas of contracting has made the procedural argument a much more difficult sell, despite popular criticisms regarding the feasibility of actually reading common but extremely long terms of use.[86] However, it was not until 2011 that the Supreme Court specifically addressed the use of unconscionability as a defense to arbitration.

AT&T Mobility LLC v. Concepcion, another California case, involved an arbitration contract that, in addition to the typical arbitration clause, disallowed class-action arbitration.[87] California courts have historically been consumer-protective and, as was the case in *Armendariz*, wary of contracts

81. *Id.* at 114.
82. *Id.* at 126.
83. *Id.* at 115.
84. *Id.* at 117–18.
85. *Id.* at 97–98.
86. AT&T Mobility LLC v. Concepcion, 563 U.S. 333 (2011).
87. *Id.*

that they perceive to be procedurally suspect.[88] *AT&T* fell squarely into this category. On the one hand were the Concepcions, a couple who argued that AT&T had cheated them when they were charged a $30.22 tax on what had been advertised as a free phone.[89] On the other hand was AT&T, a media conglomerate with comparatively endless funding and a contract of adhesion binding the Concepcions to individual arbitration. The California courts had held that a ban on class action arbitration was unconscionable, reasoning that California law considers contracts that do not allow class action lawsuits alleging fraud in consumer adhesion contracts where the individual damages are too small to feasibly litigate individually to be unconscionable contracts.[90] The Supreme Court disagreed.

In a 5-4 decision, the Supreme Court held that California's ban on arbitration clauses that denied class action arbitration was preempted by the FAA.[91] The opinion focused on the FAA's adamantly pro-arbitration stance, and went on to list a parade of horrors that might result if the Court were to allow states to apply their own public policy defenses to arbitration provisions, while reiterating the benefits of arbitration's expediency.[92] The decision effectively rendered the unconscionability defense unusable where there exists even the most remote possibility that the defense might be used more often against arbitration clauses. The Court cited its previous pro-arbitration stance as justification for this decision.[93]

AT&T would seem to have shut down the possibility of future use of the unconscionability defense in commercial arbitration. It is certainly true that, since the decision, the use of arbitration clauses mirroring the one in *AT&T* have promulgated fairly rapidly.[94] There is, however, another possibility at play. Federal courts have until now interpreted arbitration clauses solely under the banner of the FAA, as that was the only governing federal law supporting arbitration clauses. The vagueness of the wording combined with the Supreme Court's controversial interpretation of Sections 1 and 2 of the FAA has been the main governing law.[95] Consumers have thus had no option but to follow the Court's interpretation.

88. *Id.*
89. *Id.*
90. Laster v. AT&T Mobility LLC, 584 F.3d 849 (9th Cir. 2009).
91. *AT&T Mobility*, 563 U.S. 333.
92. *Id.* at 344.
93. *Id.*
94. Myriam Gilles, *Killing Them with Kindness: Examining "Consumer-Friendly" Arbitration Clauses after* AT&T Mobility v. Concepcion, 88 Notre Dame L. Rev. 825 (2012).
95. *AT&T Mobility*, 563 U.S. 333.

This may no longer be the case. The Consumer Financial Protection Bureau (CFPB), created by Congress under the Dodd-Frank Wall Street Reform and Consumer Protection Act, recently conducted the largest study yet on the use of arbitration agreements in business contracts, many of which are the kinds of contracts of adhesion that were implicated in the unconscionability cases.[96] The Act granted the CFPB the ability to issue regulations regarding arbitration clauses for the protection of consumers.[97] Likely as a direct result of the decision in *AT&T*, the CFPB paid particular attention to the relationship between consumer and business.[98] The results of that study were released in March 2015.[99]

Rather than supporting the Supreme Court's insistence that the benefits of arbitration outweighed its detriments, the study instead validated state courts' concerns that consumers were suffering from larger corporations wielding unequal bargaining power and forcing arbitration clauses in contracts of adhesion. The study cited the reality that very few consumers ever bring individual cases against corporations, either in litigation or in arbitration.[100] Rather, the most effective way to police corporations who are defrauding customers is by bringing a class action.[101] By requiring arbitration in contracts of adhesion, corporations were inoculating themselves against class action lawsuits and functionally taking themselves out of the legal system altogether. On May 5, 2016, the CFPB announced that it would be proposing rules to ban arbitration clauses that forbid class action lawsuits.[102]

The actions of the CFPB seem to show that the Supreme Court went too far in its support of arbitration in *AT&T*. This likely means that the future of unconscionability in arbitration is not as cut and dry as it seemed post-*AT&T*. Though it is too soon to say exactly how the CFPB rules will affect

96. Dodd-Frank Wall Street Reform and Consumer Protection Act (Dodd-Frank Act), Pub. L. No. 111-203, § 1011, 124 Stat. 1376 (2010) (codified at 12 U.S.C. § 5491 (2010)).

97. *Id.*

98. Arbitration Study: Report to Congress, pursuant to Dodd-Frank Wall Street Reform and Consumer Protection Act § 1028(a), at 4, *available at* http://files.consumerfinance.gov/f/201503_cfpb_arbitration-study-report-to-congress-2015.pdf.

99. *Id.*

100. *Id.* at 8.

101. Eric Goldberg, *CFPB Proposes Prohibiting Mandatory Arbitration Clauses That Deny Groups of Consumers Their Day in Court*, Consumer Financial Protection Bureau (May 5, 2016), http://www.consumerfinance.gov/about-us/blog/cfpb-proposes-prohibiting-mandatory-arbitration-clauses-deny-groups-consumers-their-day-court/.

102. *Id.* at 2.

arbitration, the fact that Congress has acted to limit arbitration clauses may resurrect the unconscionability argument once again.

However, the impact of these possible rules seems to be uniquely unsuited to regulating religious arbitration as they focus on the problems of contracts of adhesion and interactions between large commercial firms and small consumers—conditions that forestall class action lawsuits. None of these are concerns in the setting of religious arbitration.

The issues related to unconscionability in religious arbitration focus on a much more complex set of rules that are easy to outline but require a great deal more analysis: which procedural protections customarily granted to litigants really can be waived in the arbitration context, and which ones we as a society ought not permit parties to waive?

The more broadly the unconscionability doctrine or public policy is understood to apply, the less valuable it is. Helfand makes a strong case that the "no hearings on Sunday" rules that are present in many states ought to be waivable and that the court decisions focusing on Sunday hearings as unconscionable or violative of public policy are mistaken, a view that everyone involved in religious arbitration understands: Sunday is neither a Jewish nor a Muslim day of rest, and those religious tribunals should be open as a matter of policy.[103] But the case for unconscionability gets more complicated the deeper and more substantive the waiver. Consider the complexity of women's testimony in Islamic law as an example. I suspect that a court that frontally encounters an arbitral decision that discounts a women's testimony based on gender alone would rule that enforcing such a decision would be unconscionable: it is simply too deep an affront to the system of justice we hold dear in the United States, although this is really simply public policy masking itself as unconscionability.

Even in that situation, I am uncertain as to the proper approach to a contract that explicitly and directly contains an agreement to a biased tribunal or a biased law signed by the parties with no other evidence of duress. In the recent *NFL v. Brady*[104] case, the parties agreed that the final decision as to a dispute between the parties would be determined by the Commissioner of the National Football League—an employee of one of them. The Second Circuit noted that is not a problem, as both parties were well-represented and understood to what they had agreed. Saying "adjudicated according to

103. Michael A. Helfand, *Arbitration's Counter-Narrative: The Religious Arbitration Paradigm*, 124 Yale L.J. 2994, 3023 (2015) (discussing Justice Edgar Walker, *Decisions of Interest: Ruth Bauer, Petitioner v. Irving Bauer,* et al., *Respondents*, N.Y.L.J., June 26, 2014, *available at* http://prawfsblawg.blogs.com/files/bauer-nylj-decision.pdf.

104. NFL v. NFLPA & Brady, 820 F.3d 527 (2d Cir. 2016).

Islamic law" might be an underhanded way of saying "discounted women's testimony," and in that sense this can be unconscionable. But saying clearly and directly "WOMEN'S TESTIMONY IS DISCOUNTED" surely is not, and seems hardly less conscionable than saying, "IN CASES OF DISPUTE BETWEEN THE NFL AND A PLAYER, THE COMMISSIONER OF THE NFL, WHO IS AN EMPLOYEE OF THE NFL AND NOT NEUTRAL SHALL MAKE ALL FINAL DECISIONS"—which our legal system is completely comfortable with.

Unconscionability in Family Law and Policy

Although the Supreme Court's decision in *AT&T* appeared to halt the use of unconscionability in commercial contracts, the same cannot necessarily be said for family law. Unlike in commercial contract enforcement, it has traditionally been left up to the states to define family law relationships.[105] With certain rare exceptions, such as the recent decision in *Obergefell*,[106] states may determine the status of marriage, divorce, and child custody and support.[107] This is in large part because it is rare for multiple states to have a vested interest in the status of a family. Whereas modern commercial contracts frequently cross state borders and may affect many similar contracts, family law is more naturally limited to the size of a family, and tends to implicate religion and sociological mores to a more visceral and personal extent.[108]

It is also true that, although federal courts are more likely to address issues of commerce under Congress's commerce clause powers, issues of family law are more often dealt with in local courts and under local laws. The most common form of contract in family law is the prenuptial agreement.[109] A prenuptial agreement is a contract wherein two people create an enforceable agreement covering how they will deal with incidences in their marriage or divorce.[110] These may cover anything from property distribution in the case of divorce to the religion in which their children will be raised. Other common forms of family law contract involve those created

105. George K. Walker, *Arbitrating Family Law Cases by Agreement*, 18 J. AM. ACAD. MATRIMONIAL L. 429, 431 (2003).
106. Obergefell v. Hodges, 135 S. Ct. 2584 (2015).
107. United States v. Lopez, 115 S. Ct. 1624, 1630–31 (1995).
108. Anne C. Dailey, *Federalism and Families*, 143 U. PA. L. REV. 1787 (1995).
109. SAMUEL GREEN & JOHN V. LONG, MARRIAGE AND FAMILY LAW AGREEMENTS § 2.07 (1984 & Supp. 1997).
110. *Id.*

at the time of divorce, which may cover alimony and child support as well as custody agreements.

Although states are mostly willing to allow consenting adults to agree on the terms of their marriage and property distribution, there are certain areas of family law that the state retains control over, even where parties have agreed to arbitrate. These include child support, child custody, and, in certain cases, situations where one spouse would otherwise be left to the care of the state.[111]

When approaching an unconscionability analysis in family law, states look to the same signals of unfairness as in commercial law: unequal bargaining power, unfair surprise, and substantive unconscionability.[112] The major difference between commercial and family law arbitration, however, is the subject matter itself. Although, for instance, a court is likely to enforce financial contracts even where they may seem unfair, so long as the contracting process was procedurally fair, the same is not necessarily true for family law. Courts will not, for instance, enforce a contract that forbids divorce entirely, as that is considered a fundamental right of both parties.[113] Neither will courts enforce an agreement that forbids conversion to or from a religion, even where the rest of the contract is legitimate.[114] In these cases, courts are likely to strike the offending clause, but may choose to enforce the remainder of the contract if it can stand alone.

These issues are most likely to come up in the case of religious arbitration agreements in family law. As with commercial arbitration, courts will uphold arbitration agreements in family law contracts so long as the contract is superficially legitimate. The difference occurs not in the enforcement of the arbitration agreement itself but rather in the level of judicial review available to the parties. Courts in commercial agreements are largely unwilling to delve very far into the voluntariness of the contractors when an arbitration agreement has been signed.[115] Rather, they will allow the arbitrator to rule on this so long as the contract is superficially valid.[116] Unless the arbitrator comes to a decision that is grossly incorrect, the courts will generally enforce the decision.

111. AM. JUR. 2D DIVORCE & SEPARATION § 665 (2016).

112. *See* Parr v. Parr, 635 N.E.2d 1124 (Ind. Ct. App. 1994) (invalidating a prenuptial agreement due to the husband's severe non-disclosure, misrepresentation of his assets, and his attorney's failure to provide a copy of the agreement to the wife's counsel in advance).

113. Carey v. Population Servs. Int'l, 431 U.S. 678, 684–85 (1977).

114. U.S. CONST. amend. 1.

115. AT&T Mobility LLC v. Concepcion, 563 U.S. 333 (2011).

116. Doctor's Assocs., Inc. v. Casarotto, 517 U.S. 681, 686 (1996).

In family law, however, states have a vested interest in the status of children and marriages. For instance, in many states, a parent cannot waive his or her child's right to child support from the second parent, as it is the child's and not the parent's right to receive it.[117] States further have an interest in keeping children and their parents out of the welfare system. They will not generally allow the writing off of responsibilities for either a divorced spouse or a child where the end result will be the state taking over that burden.[118]

The other major difference between commercial and family law arbitration is the implication of fundamental rights. Although arbitration itself has been argued to implicate the right to access a courtroom, the federal courts have chosen not to interpret it in that way. However, fundamental rights to freedom of religion, marriage, and general autonomy are rights the courts do not allow a person to contract away. Therefore, even in cases where arbitration has been agreed upon, a court will not enforce an agreement that purports to destroy these rights.

In the field of religious arbitration, unconscionability as a claim for defeating arbitration is clearly a possibility, but the standard is high, and both substantive and procedural unconscionability must be shown as a general matter. As Helfand notes:

> [U]nconscionability is a doctrine well-suited to addressing this problem because it considers both whether parties are pressured into arbitration and whether the applied rules accord with general conceptions of arbitral justice. Although unconscionability is generally a losing argument, it has had a remarkable resurgence in the arbitration context. In fact, a number of recent statistical studies have demonstrated that courts employ the unconscionability doctrine in arbitration cases at a rate significantly higher than in other contract cases. Indeed, given recent developments in arbitration law, the unconscionability doctrine may serve as the preferred ground to vacate awards for judges looking to push back against the perceived inadequacies of arbitral justice.[119]

But, the standards for unconscionability would seem to be religiously neutral and focused on results that strike at the heart of that which a legal system can tolerate; certainly racial discrimination would be such an example.

117. *See, e.g.,* N.Y. C.L.S. Family Ct. Act § 413 (2016).
118. *Id.*
119. Michael A. Helfand, *Religious Arbitration and the New Multiculturalism: Negotiating Conflicting Legal Orders*, 86 N.Y.U. L. Rev. 1231, 1294 (2011).

Merely reaching a result that is different from what secular law would is certainly not unconscionable. Even more important, the religious nature of the arbitration would seem not to be the important datapoint—the nature of the award is mostly what determines unconscionability, and financial awards are almost never deemed unconscionable.

Related to unconscionability, but distinct, is the now widely discredited idea of arbitration awards not being enforced if they violate public policy. As explained in the next chapter in much greater detail, the United States is a system of many different laws, and in any situation in which a choice-of-law provision is permitted, one would be hard pressed to claim that choosing a different legal system—which certainly will generate different legal answers—violates public policy. The public policy application is best manifest in not allowing a choice of law or a choice of forum. Of course, selecting French or Islamic or Japanese or Jewish law will each generate different outcomes in certain cases—but public policy does not preclude doing so.

A classic example of this is the case of *Brisman v. Hebrew Academy of the Five Towns & Rockaway* [HAFTR],[120] where the Beth Din of America reinstated a Judaic Studies faculty member from his job in a Jewish school, returned him to his status as a tenured faculty member, and ordered that he be provided with back pay for the time he was not working. Justice Balter of the New York Supreme Court (the trial court) ordered the arbitration award to be vacated as it violated the public policy of the state of New York. The court observed that:

> [a]n arbitration award may not be vacated by a court .... unless: it clearly violates a strong public policy; is completely irrational; or if it manifestly exceeds a specifically enumerated limitation on the arbitrator's power, or unless the rights of a party were prejudiced by the partiality of the arbitrator.

The court then added simply:

> [T]he award is violative of public policy. The Beth Din's ruling sets a precedent that will impact and limit the ability of private schools to make and enforce routine employment decisions, as the award compels Respondent to reinstate an employee it does not wish to employ. It is noted by the Court, that a severance package, which amounted to *Chodesh L'Shanah* [severance of one month's salary for each year worked, which is customary under Jewish law] was offered

120. 25 Misc. 3d 913 (N.Y. Sup. Ct. Kings Cty. 2008). For the sake of full disclosure, I note that I was the appellate judge on this matter as a member of the Beth Din of America and wrote an opinion on this matter as a rabbinical court judge.

> by the Respondent upon termination of the Petitioner, which was rejected. Furthermore, the difficulty set forth by the determination of the salary at an amount exceedingly greater than Petitioner's co-workers is counterproductive to a harmonious and productive work environment.

The court in essence makes the following claim: the provision here—even though the parties could have agreed to it by contract—violated the court's understanding of what the rules ought to be, and as such violated public policy.

This case was appealed and was one of the well-litigated public policy cases of the last decade. The Appellate Division unanimously reversed the trial court judge and observed simply that HAFTR "failed to demonstrate the applicability of any of the statutorily enumerated grounds for vacatur of the award." In plain English, the appellate court held—quite correctly in this author's view—that "public policy" is not merely a showing that the court would have reached a different result. The exact reason the parties went to rabbinical court to be adjudicated based on Jewish law is that they wanted a different legal system. Rather, it has to be a much broader assertion of public policy.

Although unconscionability has never been the most popular of contract defenses, its place in the arbitration arena cannot be understated. *AT&T v. Concepcion* appeared to destroy this last defense against the expansive power of the FAA, but it appears that with the new rules awaiting passage by the CFPB in 2016 restricting arbitration clauses, protective restrictions on arbitration will likely see a resurgence. This is, however, of little importance to religious arbitration, where few if any of the concerns of the CFPB are actually present.

D. CONCLUSION

The legal arbitration framework provides an important means of empowering individuals and communities in the United States to conduct their internal affairs in accordance with their religious commitments.[121] Law-based faith traditions such as Islam and Judaism expect their adherents to order their lives and resolve their conflicts in accordance with their respective religious law norms, which necessitates turning to religious

121. *See generally* Nicholas Walter, *Religious Arbitration in the United States and Canada*, 52 SANTA CLARA L. REV. 501 (2012).

tribunals presided over by religious law scholars and jurists.[122] The secular legal framework for arbitration facilitates efficacious *religious* arbitration by ensuring that parties to such proceedings can employ coercive powers to enforce awards instead of their being forced to rely solely on the goodwill of the losing disputant. In order to enjoy the benefits of this secular legal framework for enforcing arbitration awards, religious arbitration tribunals must take steps to ensure that their decisions comply with the standards set by that framework and earn the respect of secular courts.

122. *See* Yaakov Feit, *The Prohibition against Going to Secular Courts*, 1 J. Beth Din Am. 30, 41 (2012) (discussing the Jewish law obligation for Jews to resolve disputes in rabbinic courts); Lee Ann Bambach, *The Enforceability of Arbitration Decisions Made by Muslim Religious Tribunals*, 25 J.L. & Religion 385 (2009–2010) (noting that the need for a religious forum for the resolution of disputes can be urgent for Muslims looking to closely observe *Shari'a*).

CHAPTER 7

Refining Religious Arbitration in the United States and Abroad

The Jewish Experience

The general framework established by American arbitration law creates various basic requirements for arbitration agreements to be recognized and arbitral awards to be enforced by courts. It is important to appreciate, however, that experience shows that there are really two elements at play in judicial enforcement of arbitration awards. On the one hand, there are the formal legal elements; courts will be legally incapable of enforcing the arbitral awards issued by religious tribunals if those tribunals fail to follow the basic legal demands imposed by the FAA and relevant state laws. Even if faith-based arbitrators have observed all the formal legal requirements, they must still convince state courts and judges that their religious dispute resolution processes are genuinely fair, effective, and worth upholding as an alternative form of just adjudication. In other words, courts must not only be legally able to enforce religious arbitration decisions, they must be willing to do so. In the context of religious arbitration, this latter concern poses special problems. Because faith-based dispute resolution involves essentially religious legal processes in which religious functionaries apply religious law and issue religious remedies, it can look very strange to traditional judges. In order to gain judges' confidence and convince American courts that religious dispute resolution process are just another form of legalistic adjudication, religious tribunals must undertake special measures to demonstrate

Sharia Tribunals, Rabbinical Courts, and Christian Panels. Michael J. Broyde.

their integrity, professionalism, and effectiveness. This chapter uses the Jewish-American arbitration experience to identify six measures that religious arbitration organizations can and should take in order to ensure an effective, legally viable, and judicially enforceable arbitration process.

A. JEWISH ARBITRATION TODAY

Judaism is a faith tradition grounded in the observance of legal norms based on God's revealed will. Like Muslims, Jews are obligated to resolve their disputes in religious courts,[1] called *batei din*,[2] which adjudicate commercial disputes, divorce and family matters, and other issues contemplated and regulated by *halakha*, or Jewish religious law.

For some time, rabbinical courts struggled to find their footing in the American legal system. Initially, secular courts were uncomfortable upholding and enforcing arbitral decisions issued in accordance with what they viewed as foreign, inaccessible substantive and procedural law.[3] One of the country's most prominent rabbinic courts, the Beth Din of America (BDA), was founded in 1960 to provide a more effective adjudicative forum for Jews committed to living in accordance with *halakha* in a secular American legal and social context. Today, the BDA provides a sprawling network of Jewish law courts that function as fully legal, *halakha*-compliant arbitration panels marked by expedience and affordability. Over time, by adopting a host of prudent measures designed to improve the transparency, consistency, equity, and professionalism of its arbitral process, the BDA has gained widespread acceptance among America's secular courts, which are comfortable enforcing its arbitral decisions, and which to date have never overturned a BDA-issued arbitration award.[4]

1. For a discussion of Jews' religious duty to resolve disputes in religious rather than secular courts, see Yaakov Feit, *The Prohibition against Going to Secular Courts*, 1 J. BETH DIN AM. 30 (2012).

2. *Beth din* or *bet din* (pl. *batei din*) translates literally to "house of judgment." For an overview of the *beit din* system, see MENACHEM ELON, THE PRINCIPLES OF JEWISH LAW 561–65 (2007). For a broader review of the evolution of Jewish law court, see Michael J. Broyde, *Jewish Law Courts in America: Lessons Offered to Sharia Courts by the Beth Din of America Precedent*, 57 N.Y.L. SCH. L. REV. 287 (2012–2013).

3. *See* Ginnie Fried, *The Collision of Church and State: A Primer to Beth Din Arbitration and the New York Secular Courts*, 31 FORDHAM URB. L.J. 633 (2004).

4. *See, e.g.*, Paul Berger, *In Victory for "Chained" Wives, Court Upholds Orthodox Prenuptial Agreement*, JEWISH DAILY FORWARD (Feb. 8, 2013), *available at* http://forward.com/articles/170721/in-victory-for-chained-wives-court-upholds-o/?p=all (noting that with respect to the religious prenuptial agreement developed by the BDA, the presiding judge "appeared to treat the Orthodox [BDA] prenup in the same routine way he would treat any other any [*sic*] secular prenuptial contract").

The BDA was originally founded in 1960 as part of the Rabbinical Council of America (RCA), one of the principal organizations of traditionally observant rabbis in the United States.[5] Although the BDA is now an over-fifty-year-old organization, its true metamorphosis into an effective arbitration venue respected by American courts began only in 1996, when it became autonomous from the RCA.[6] In the twenty years since, an independent board of directors has worked with the BDA's rabbinic leaders to craft an arbitration process that secular courts are comfortable upholding. This entailed creating an arbitral practice that operates within the legal framework established by American arbitration laws. The BDA directors also went beyond merely satisfying technical legal requirements and strove to earn secular court confidence in the legal character of their tribunals as well as in the professional competence of their rabbinic arbitrators.[7] Although the BDA's transformation into a respected arbitration organization required adaptations of the default *halakhic* procedures traditionally employed by *batei din*, these did not entail substantive alterations of Jewish law not permitted by the *halakhic* system itself.[8] The BDA gained judicial acceptance by presenting Jewish law and dispute resolution in a way that drew upon language, categories, and principles familiar to the secular legal establishment, allowing the latter to take confidence in the BDA process's transparency, legal sophistication, and fairness.[9]

These measures, discussed more fully below, illustrate the steps the BDA took in order to gain the respect of the broader legal community and ensure that its rulings would be enforced by secular courts. Although the sum total of these efforts has significantly altered the appearance of traditional *beit din* practice, each individual measure was undertaken with substantial support in earlier Jewish law precedents. By building on these permissible but innovative approaches, the BDA successfully navigates the complex relationship between secular and religious law in the United States, and is able to offer Jews an efficacious adjudicatory forum consonant with both Jewish and American law.

B. THE PILLARS OF SUCCESSFUL RELIGIOUS ARBITRATION IN AMERICA

The experiences of the BDA indicate that arbitration institutions that decide cases based on religious law can gain the respect of secular courts

5. *See Organization and Affiliations*, Beth Din of America, https://bethdin.org/about/ (last visited Nov 19, 2016).
6. *Id.*
7. *See* Broyde, *supra* note 2, at 288.
8. For an overview of traditional *beit din* processes, see Emanuel B. Quint, 1 A Restatement of Rabbinic Civil Law (1990).
9. *See* Broyde, *supra* note 2, at 288.

by structuring their arbitration processes around six principles. These "pillars" serve a dual purpose. First, they ensure that state judicial apparatuses will have the legal power to enforce awards by ensuring that the tribunals meet the formal requirements set by the secular arbitration law framework. Second, by engendering mutual respect between legal authorities in the religious and secular spheres and by promoting judicial familiarity with religion-based arbitral processes, these measures help ensure that awards *will actually* be enforced.

The legal viability of the BDA arbitration processes has come to rest on six main pillars common to reconstituted Jewish and Islamic arbitration processes. First, the BDA developed formal, sophisticated rules of procedure that protect parties' rights to due process. Second, both sets of religious arbitrators endorsed appellate processes that promote transparency and accountability. Third, the BDA exhibited respect for the secular legal systems in which it operates by respecting the ultimate legal authority of the state and concomitantly limiting the BDA's jurisdiction to certain kinds of cases, and by according primacy to parties' choice of law. Fourth, the tribunals embraced common commercial customs and principles of equity in order to give effect to the reasonable expectations of disputants and to craft remedies consonant with a broader, less parochial sense of fairness and justice. Fifth, the BDA demonstrated dual-system fluency by employing arbitrators familiar with both their respective religio-legal norms and those of state law, and by utilizing the expertise of religiously observant professionals familiar with factual issues raised by particular cases. Sixth, the BDA took an active role in governing and guiding their respective religious communities, and in representing the interests and concerns of their co-religionists to the broader society.

1. Publication of Formal, Sophisticated Rules of Procedure

By developing and publishing formal rules of procedure that constitute and govern its arbitration processes, the BDA gained the respect and acceptance of secular legal authorities. The American legal system places great importance on procedural fairness in both formal adjudicatory and ADR contexts. Indeed, although courts generally cannot refuse to enforce an arbitration award because a reviewing judge disagrees with the substance of the arbitral ruling, they can vacate arbitral awards for a variety of procedural irregularities and injustices in the arbitral process. Thus, when faced with motions to confirm arbitration awards and processes based on religio-legal norms, where the substantive fairness of the arbitral tribunal's application of its own religious norms may not be apparent to the court, a judge can nevertheless take confidence that the "procedural rules . . . protect vulnerable parties."[10]

Caryn Wolfe has identified several procedural protections that, if embraced by arbitration tribunals, result in American courts being willing to enforce their awards. They include the entitlement of parties to adequate notice that arbitration proceedings are underway, the right to representation by an attorney, the duty of arbitrators to disclose facts relating to their impartiality, and the inability of parties to agree to unreasonable restrictions on these basic protections.[11] If arbitration tribunals fail to formally provide for and protect these procedural safeguards, Wolfe argues, courts will regularly refuse to enforce their awards.[12]

Recognizing the basic truth of this concern for procedural fairness, the BDA adopted and published detailed procedural rules. Rather than attempting to justify the substance of each award by trying to explain to secular courts the religio-legal norms upon which the award is based, this institution has crafted rules and procedures that clearly explain what litigants can expect of the arbitration process: adequate notice, opportunities for discovery, standards for the admissibility of evidence, methods for challenging the impartiality of the arbitrators, and so on.

Therefore, when a court is asked to enforce a BDA award, it need not rely on the historical traditions and religio-legal corpuses of Judaism; instead, a secular judge can take confidence in the knowledge that these arbitral processes incorporate familiar important procedural guarantees.[13] In addition to these rules providing formal protections to parties, their structure and detailed nature comforts secular judges. Jewish and Islamic courts traditionally maintained fairly complex procedural standards. The BDA gained the confidence of secular courts by reformulating these using language and structure familiar to them.

Written in lawyers' English, and organized along lines similar to the procedural codes used by secular courts, the Rules and Procedures of the Beth Din of America outline an arbitration process that is largely recognizable to judges entrenched in American or British civil procedure. Additionally, the BDA has added new procedures that do not contradict Jewish law when

10. Caryn Litt Wolfe, *Faith Based Arbitration: Friend or Foe? An Evaluation of Religious Arbitration Systems and Their Interaction with Secular Courts*, 75 FORD. L. REV. 427, 458 (2006).

11. *Id.* at 458–59.

12. *Id.* at 459.

13. *See* Michael A. Helfand, *Religious Arbitration and the New Multiculturalism: Negotiating Conflicting Legal Orders*, 86 N.Y.U. L. REV. 1231, 1260–64 (2011).

such protections are considered absolutely necessary by prevailing state law. The development of formal rules of procedure by the BDA has thus been more a departure from traditional norms than an abrogation of the substance of religio-legal rules. The Beth Din of America has published these rules on its website, and they thus help a layperson understand what to expect procedurally during the process of religious arbitration.[14] To a lawyer or judge, these rules look much like the Federal Rules of Civil Procedure; they set out requirements such as the number of days between filing and response. They describe matters such as discovery, motion practice, transcription, and the appropriate place to file items. They also establish the proper language for hearings, the procedure for compiling a record, waiver doctrines, notice provisions, and other rules of procedure.[15]

Consistent with basic principles of fairness and due process in the arbitration context, as well as with traditional Jewish law, the BDA's rules provide that no party can be subject to arbitration in the BDA against his or her will. A dispute can come before the BDA in only one of two circumstances: either the case arises from a contract or other prior dealing subject to a valid arbitration clause in which the parties agreed to resolve their disagreement through the BDA arbitral process, or one party requests BDA arbitration after a dispute has arisen and obtains the opposing party's agreement through the execution of a legal arbitration agreement.[16] If a party declines to arbitrate before the BDA in violation of a previously executed arbitration agreement, the BDA will extend the permission required under Jewish law to the other party to proceed to a secular court for the enforcement of a default judgment.[17] Alternatively, the BDA might issue a *seruv*, which is a Jewish legal document publicizing the recalcitrant party's refusal to appear, as a means of bringing social pressure to bear with the

14. *The Rules and Procedures of the Beth Din of America*, BETH DIN OF AMERICA, *available at* https://bethdin.org/forms/ (last visited Nov. 19, 2016).

15. Perhaps the most startling thing one might encounter in a comparative study of the rules of the BDA, Christian ICC, and Islamic MAT is how similar they are. With but a few differences, they essentially address the same set of issues, namely the procedural rights of the parties in arbitration. Indeed, with but a few word changes, the rules of any one of them could serve as rules of each of them. Although this might incline one to think that they had a common author (which assuredly they did not, as I drafted the BDA rules myself many years ago, but did not write the ICC or MAT rules), the truth is that they are simply co-evolutionary identical responses to the pressures of the secular FAA (or perhaps the MAT and ICC used the BDA rules?)

16. *See The Rules and Procedures, supra* note 14, § 2. The BDA offers a standardized arbitration agreement that ensures compliance with both statutory requirements and Jewish law. *See Standard Binding Arbitration Agreement*, BETH DIN OF AMERICA, *available at* http://www.bethdin.org/forms-publications.asp (last visited Oct. 2, 2016).

17. *See The Rules and Procedures, supra* note 14, § 2(i).

hope of convincing the disputant to arbitrate.[18] If the parties did not previously sign a valid BDA arbitration agreement, a disputant has no obligation to appear, despite the other party's request that he do so, provided that the refusing party is willing to resolve the dispute through some other means sanctioned by Jewish law, such as in another *beit din*, or by using a third-party arbitrator.[19] Only if a Jewish disputant refuses to appear in any appropriate forum might the BDA issue a *seruv* against him in an effort to convince him to resolve the dispute through means sanctioned by Jewish law consistent with his religious obligations.[20] Consonantly with both American and Jewish law, however, under no circumstances will the BDA arbitrate a dispute unless both parties agree to do so.

Upon the commencement of arbitral proceedings, the BDA rules provide that the *Av Beth Din* (literally "The Head of the *Beth Din*"—the Chief Justice at the head of the BDA hierarchy) shall designate approved arbitrators from the BDA's list to hear the case.[21] Again, consistent with Jewish law and secular law due process requirements, the rules provide that the parties shall be given notice of the identities of the designated arbitrators, and that either party may seek to remove an arbitrator for bias or interest.[22] Additionally, the rules impose an obligation on each arbitrator to disclose any interest he may have in a case, irrespective of whether his impartiality is challenged by a party.[23]

Once the arbitrators have been chosen and the action commences, parties experience a process very similar to that of a secular court, but consistent with normative *halakha*. Parties may hold a preliminary conference during which they create a schedule for discovery, stipulate to undisputed facts, and identify documentary evidence to be produced and witnesses to be called.[24] The actual arbitration hearing consists of opening statements, followed by each party presenting its claims and evidence.[25] Before closing the hearing, the arbitrators must specifically inquire whether either party has anything to add, and the arbitrators may close the proceedings only upon negative responses by each party.[26] Under the rules, the BDA arbitration panel must issue a ruling within three months after closing the

18. *Id.*
19. *Id.* § 2(b)–(f).
20. *Id.* § 2(i).
21. *Id.* § 5.
22. *Id.* § 6(a).
23. *Id.* § 6(b).
24. *Id.* § 8.
25. *Id.* § 16(a).
26. *Id.* § 22(a).

hearings on a case; the award, which must be agreed upon by at least a majority, must be made in writing and in English, and must be personally served on the parties.[27]

The BDA rules also include clear procedures for taking evidence.[28] Parties may present any evidence they wish, including documents, witnesses, or affidavits, but the arbitrators retain the authority to determine the relevance and materiality.[29] Importantly, the rules state that evidence may only be taken in the presence of the entire arbitration panel and both parties, and that any ex parte communications between arbitrators and parties or arbitrators and witnesses is strictly prohibited.[30] In order to protect the integrity of the BDA arbitration process, any communications a party or witness wishes to convey to an arbitrator outside of a formal hearing must first be directed to the *Av Beth Din*, who determines whether to transfer the information to the arbitrator.[31]

BDA rules further require the *Av Beth Din* to arrange for the electronic recording of all arbitration proceedings unless both parties waive their right to such a record.[32] Additionally, at the request of any party, the *Av Beth Din* must arrange for the preparation of a written transcript from those electronic records.[33] Although normative Jewish law does not provide for the transcription of court proceedings, it does not prohibit it.[34] The BDA adopted this sensible practice in order to gain the respect of secular legal authorities, but also as a reasonable way of ensuring a more honest and transparent arbitration process. These English-language records serve as an inducement for BDA arbitrators to conduct proceedings with the utmost integrity, and also enable reviewing courts to assess whether BDA arbitrations do in fact comport with the procedural protections provided for in the BDA rules. The very existence and availability of such records help engender judicial confidence in the BDA.[35]

The BDA rules offer a number of other procedural protections that also ensure that the basic requirements of American due process are preserved, so that judges will have the legal authority and personal desire to enforce BDA awards. These include the right of each party to

27. *Id.* §§ 26–27.
28. *See generally id.* §§ 18–19.
29. *Id.* § 18(a).
30. *See id.* §§ 18(c), 25(a).
31. *Id.* § 25(a).
32. *Id.* § 10(a).
33. *Id.*
34. *See* Shulchan Aruch: Choshen Mishpat 13:2–3, 19:2.
35. *See* Broyde, *supra* note 2, at 291; *see also, e.g.*, Lang v. Levi, 16 A.3d 980 (Md. Ct. Spec. App. 2011) (citing and deferring heavily to the BDA's Rules and Procedures); Tal

be represented by counsel,[36] their right to an adversarial hearing before the tribunal before an award is rendered[37] and their right to adequate notice of the time and place of each significant stage in the proceedings.[38] Also, the BDA rules provide that all proceedings must be conducted in English, unless all the parties and arbitrators agree to use another language, and that each party has the right to use an interpreter or other aid to remedy a language barrier or other obstacle that may prevent that party from fully understanding the proceedings.[39]

Although the BDA rules place heavy emphasis on procedural due process, they are entirely opaque as to substantive law. Rule 3(c) states simply that "the Beth Din of America accepts that Jewish law as understood by the Beth Din will provide the rules of decision." There is no definition of the substance of Jewish law. By insisting that Jewish law as understood by the Beth Din is the law, substantive review becomes impossible, as whatever decision of Jewish law the BDA determines to be correct is by definition the Jewish law as understood by the Beth Din.

There are no clear rules of decision in the BDA that any court can review for consistency and proper application. Consider a simple hypothetical example concerning a commercial dispute between a kosher food provider and a customer about whether Jewish law considers pigs' feet to be kosher.[40] If the BDA were to determine that they were, a secular court could not review that determination to see if it was consistent with Jewish law, as it is "Jewish law *as understood by the Beth Din*" (emphasis added).[41] The decisions of arbitrators are not subject to review by secular courts for errors of law.

This fits well with our understanding of the role of secular courts in reviewing religious arbitration: they are limited to procedural review. American arbitration law pays little attention to notions of substantive due process. Neither the government nor the courts enforce a preconceived notion of the "right" substantive resolution of most any dispute if the parties contractually opt for a different resolution or a process that produces one.[42] Rather, the FAA and the myriad state laws that derive from it have a

Tours (1996) Inc. v. Goldstein, No. 5510-05, 2005 WL 2514967 (N.Y. Sup. Ct. Nassau Cty. Oct. 7, 2005) (same).

36. *See The Rules and Procedures, supra* note 14, § 12.

37. *Id.* §§ 16–17.

38. *Id.* § 9.

39. *Id.* § 11.

40. There is no view in Jewish law that considers them kosher, as the Bible explicitly states that pork is not kosher. *See Leviticus* 11:7 (King James).

41. *See* Rules and Procedures, *supra* note 14, § 3(c).

42. *See* Helfand, *supra* note 13, at 1256.

strong notion of procedural due process.[43] These statutes provide that there are certain things arbitration panels may and may not do in the course of decision-making: they may not call a hearing at 4:00 am on a federal holiday, they must provide litigants with a reasonable amount of notice,[44] they must conduct hearings in a language that the parties understand, arbitrators may not have a financial interest in the resolution of the case or financial involvement with the parties, and other basic dictates of procedural fair play.[45] Thus, secular courts can and do evaluate whether secular procedural due process was complied with, and whether general notions of fair play were observed, but they cannot decide the substantive rules of Jewish, Islamic, or Christian law.[46] Even if they could, religious arbitration organizations write their rules to prevent that review.[47] Arbitration law mandates that arbitration organizations have rules that protect basic procedural rights (not basic substantive rights), and they do: no other review is needed.

2. Development of an Internal Appellate Process

It is important that religious arbitration panels develop internal review processes. To err is human, and all arbitration panels sometimes err. Sometimes they err in judgment, sometimes in fact. Sometimes the errors are painfully obvious or even laughable, as even great people sometimes make simple mistakes. Sometimes there are errors in transcription. Many of these procedural errors can result in a court overturning an arbitration

43. *See* Michael A. Helfand & Barak Richman, *The Challenge of Co-religionist Commerce*, 64 Duke L. Rev. 769 (2014).

44. *See, e.g., JAMS Policy on Employment Arbitration: Minimum Standards of Procedural Fairness*, JAMS (July 15, 2009), *available at* http://www.jamsadr.com/files/Uploads/Documents/JAMSRules/JAMS_Employment_Min_Stds-2009.pdf. Of course, the JAMS policy is only binding when it is incorporated by contract, and the minimal obligations of the arbitrator under state law are considerably lower.

45. For a re-examination of the basic issues of due process and fairness in this context, see Bradley Dillon-Coffman, Comment, *Revising the Revision: Procedural Alternatives to the Arbitration Fairness Act*, 57 UCLA L. Rev. 1095 (2010).

46. Although in theory disputants could have a choice-of-forum provision that selects a state court and a choice-of-law provision that specifies Jewish law, in which case the state court might very well make a determination of what Jewish law is in the first instance, that is much different from a secular court being asked to review someone else's determination of Jewish law. For examples of this first phenomena, see Daniel Ashburn, *Appealing to a Higher Authority? Jewish Law in American Judicial Opinions*, 71 U. Det. Mercy L. Rev. 295 (1994).

47. By defining, for example, Jewish law not in reference to its historical meaning, but in reference to how this court understands it.

award. An appellate process is thus an important safeguard that allows an arbitral organization to correct its mistakes internally before they are brought to the attention of a reviewing court that may well vacate the tribunal's decision entirely.

Without an internal appellate process to correct one's own procedural mistakes, a court will step in and do it, pointing to the provisions of the FAA or state law.[48] An internal appellate procedure allows for a basic error correction process that produces regularly valid decisions. Good arbitration rules, then, spell out the grounds for error and procedures to initiate an appeal.

The BDA engendered greater judicial confidence in the fairness of its arbitration process by instituting a system of internal appellate review of awards. Over its long history, the BDA came to realize that, absent a form of internal review, courts asked to enforce BDA awards were much more likely to take an active role in reviewing the underlying arbitration for factual and procedural errors on the part of the arbitrators, as well as for the basic substantive fairness of the award. Because one of the chief goals of Jewish arbitration is for disputants to fully and finally resolve their conflict in accordance with Jewish law articulated by a *beit din* rather than secular law in a state court, the BDA included an appellate procedure in its arbitration process. This internal review thus provided a dual benefit: it helped keep the resolution of disputes within the *beit din* system by making it less likely that courts would overturn arbitral awards that had already been through one round of appellate review, and also helped promote judicial confidence in the BDA's competence by lending its arbitration process a more "legalistic" appearance.

The BDA's procedural rules permit any party to file a written petition for review and modification of an award within twenty days.[49] As with other filings, copies of the petition must be served on all other parties to the original arbitration, and those parties may file a written objection within ten days of being served.[50] The rules provide five grounds upon which the BDA may modify an award: (1) an error in the mathematical calculation of the award; (2) a mistaken description of a person, place, or thing in the award;

48. Consider the following example: The parties agree to a submission deadline of March 25. The arbitrator hearing the matter hastily jots down a squiggly five, which is later transcribed to the file as a three. The arbitrator then closes the matter on March 23, and, finding that one party failed to make a timely submission, issues an award on March 24, in favor of the other party. The arbitrator has committed a procedural error. A secular court judge presented with this case will find the award unenforceable, as the record should have remained open for another two days.

49. *See The Rules and Procedures, supra* note 14, § 31(a).

50. *Id.* § 31(b).

(3) the award's addressing an issue not submitted to the BDA for arbitration, provided such can be corrected without affecting the merits of the remainder of the award; (4) any other imperfection in the award that does not affect the merits of the decision; and (5) the *Av Beth Din*'s determination that the award is manifestly contrary to Jewish law.[51] These grounds, and the standard of review employed, are comparable to secular court appellate processes.[52] The BDA's internal appeals procedure thus gives secular courts confidence in the integrity and legality of BDA awards, even if the unfamiliarity and inaccessibility of the Jewish law rules upon which those awards are based might otherwise make judges wary of enforcing them.

Traditionally, Jewish law did not provide a formal right of appeal. The Talmud specifies that "one *beit din* cannot review the judgment of its fellow *beit din*."[53] Thus, the adjudication of a dispute was limited to the *beit din* of first instance, and parties were bound to abide by that tribunal's decision; no court was formally empowered to review, modify, or reverse the original ruling on a case.[54] Nevertheless, in practice, some organized *beit din* systems established a hierarchy of courts within their limited geographical jurisdiction, and provided for the possibility of appeals from local court rulings to more expert regional *batei din*.[55] In light of this historical Jewish law precedent and the pressing need to establish the credibility of Jewish religious arbitration tribunals in the United States, the BDA adopted internal appellate procedures, which contributed to courts' willingness to regularly uphold BDA awards.

Importantly, what we have under successful systems of arbitration is not only a process of appeal to a higher internal authority, but sometimes an elaborate procedure akin to a motion for reconsideration, in which a litigant who sees error in a decision can point out the error to the original panel, which may then correct itself.[56]

51. *Id.* § 31(a).

52. For a discussion of normative Jewish law standards of review for error by a *beit din*, see Shulchan Aruch: Choshen Mishpat 25; QUINT, *supra* note 8, at 169–72.

53. Babylonian Talmud, Bava Basra 138b.

54. *See, e.g.*, R. Moses Isserles, Darkei Moshe, Choshen Mishpat 25:1.

55. *See* J. DAVID BLEICH, CONTEMPORARY *HALAKHIC* PROBLEMS 17–45 (1995); J. David Bleich, *The Appeal Process in the Jewish Legal System*, 28 TRADITION 94 (1993).

56. The process of appeal is not unique to religious arbitration, of course. Part of a recent JAMS advertising campaign was aimed at dispelling "one of the biggest myths about arbitration," namely, "that there is no avenue to appeal." *See* JAMS, *Five Things You Didn't Know about Arbitration*, A.B.A. J. (Apr. 29, 2014, 5:04 PM), http://www.abajournal.com/advertising/article/five_things_you_didnt_know_about_arbitration/. The advertisement explains:

> Perhaps one of the biggest myths about arbitration is that there is no avenue to appeal. This is not the case, and hasn't been for many years. The International

Not surprisingly, the grounds used by successful religious arbitral bodies are essentially those that would cause a reversal under the secular law of the land, with the exception of particular provisions of the rules of the BDA,[57] which are modeled on the rules of the Rabbinical Courts of Israel, which also have this form of review, and which will be explained below.

One could easily advance a further point: a litigant who chooses not to use the error-correcting process provided by the arbitration panel and its rules could be said to have waived her right to allege that error in secular court under the well-known doctrine of exhaustion of administrative review. Although I am aware of no case law to make this point, it seems logical that, just as one cannot appeal the decision of an administrative agency to a court without first exhausting the review process internal to the agency, the same ought to be true of the appellate panel of an arbitration organization. As the classical law review article on this topic by Professor Raoul Berger noted in its opening sentences in 1939, "Administrative remedies must be exhausted before resort is had to the federal courts. The doctrine is as old as federal administrative law, and in the fifty years that have elapsed since the early decisions it has been expounded in a formidable mass of case law."[58]

It is reasonable to rule that an arbitration agreement (contract) that directs the parties to obey the process of arbitration should function like an administrative agency: before running to court, an unhappy disputant must exhaust the internal process. Indian tribes (whose resemblance to insular religious communities requires much further examination) already require this in their arbitration agreements.[59]

> Institute for Conflict Prevention and Resolution (CPR) and JAMS have, for many years, offered appellate procedures that provide a formal structure for appeal to either a single arbitrator or tripartite panel. The American Arbitration Association has recently issued its own Optional Appellate Arbitration Rules. Keep in mind that not every arbitration is well suited to an appeal, but incorporation of an appellate process can lessen the risks and provide some peace of mind.

Id.; see also Optional Appellate Arbitration Rules, AM. ARBITRATION ASS'N, *available at* http://images.go.adr.org/Web/AmericanArbitrationAssociation/%7B9e172798-c60f-4de0-9ebc-438e54e78af8%7D_AAA_ICDR_Optional_Appellate_Arbitration_Rules.pdf (last visited Oct. 2, 2016). In fact, CPR first published an arbitration appeals procedure in 1999. *See CPR Arbitration Appeal Procedure and Commentary 1*, INT'L INST. FOR CONFLICT PREVENTION, *available at* http://www.cpradr.org/Portals/0/Resources/ADR%20Tools/Clauses%20&%20Rules/CPR%20Arbitration%20Appeal%20Procedure.pdf (last visited Nov. 25, 2014).

57. Provision (e) of the rules of the BDA.

58. Raoul Berger, *Exhaustion of Administrative Remedies*, 48 YALE L.J. 981, 981 (1939).

59. *See, e.g.*, Tort Liability Ordinance, VIEJAS BAND OF KUMEYAAY INDIANS TRIB. CODE § 6.01 (Nov. 20, 2013), *available at* http://viejas.com/sites/default/files/Tort_

Indeed, it would be wise if religious arbitration panels were to make this clear by inserting the following additional sub-rule (as a new Section 31c of the BDA rules):

> Exhaustion of Modification of Award Process under this Rule: Litigants must first exhaust the Modification of Award process found in this rule before contesting the confirmation of any award issued by this tribunal in any other forum or court. Either party's failure to do so shall be deemed a waiver of the underlying claim that could have been the subject of a Modification of Award motion.

3. Respect for Both Religious and Secular Legal Norms

To convince secular courts to respect and enforce their awards, arbitration tribunals that base their awards on religio-legal norms need to demonstrate respect for the laws of the secular justice system in which they operate. This entails accepting and responding correctly to several realities attendant to arbitrating within a secular legal context. Arbitral tribunals must accept that secular courts will be powerless to enforce their awards unless they satisfy the minimal technical requirements set by the secular law arbitration framework. This framework establishes that the jurisdiction of an arbitration tribunal is premised on the voluntary agreement between disputants to submit their case to it and to abide by its decision. Thus, arbitral courts applying religio-legal norms should only act pursuant to a valid arbitration agreement. Also, because jurisdiction is premised on the voluntary agreement of the parties, arbitral tribunals must accept the contractual choice of the parties as to the substantive and procedural rules that will govern. If arbitration tribunals fail to follow these requirements, secular courts will lack the jurisdiction to enforce their awards, no matter how much judges may want to do so.

Moreover, arbitration tribunals must accept that the secular laws under which they operate impose jurisdictional limits on their ability to handle certain kinds of cases. Typically, in Western countries, only state courts can grant civil divorces,[60] and thus arbitral tribunals need to appreciate that

Liability.pdf ("Exhaustion of Tribal Dispute Process. Claimant must first exhaust the Viejas Band's Tribal Dispute Process for resolving a Claim as provided in Sections 6 and 7. Claimant's failure to do so or to strictly comply with any aspect of the Tribal Dispute Process shall result in Claimant's loss of any right to pursue a Claim against the Viejas Band by arbitration or any other legal action.").

60. *See* Ann Laquer Estin, *Unofficial Family Law*, 94 Iowa L. Rev. 449, 463 (2009) ("[C]ivil divorce belongs to the state . . . .").

their granting or arranging a religious divorce between disputing spouses does not suffice to dissolve the parties' civil marriage in the eyes of the state.[61] Similarly, secular law usually claims exclusive jurisdiction over criminal matters and monopolizes the use of force, prohibiting private law institutions from imposing corporal sanctions upon even those subjects willing to suffer them.[62] Arbitral tribunals that apply religio-legal norms, therefore, must neither attempt to adjudicate claims of criminal conduct covered by secular criminal law nor impose corporal sanctions even when their own religio-legal commitments instruct that they do so.

The BDA has accepted these realities. In order to ensure that secular courts will have the legal authority to enforce its awards, the BDA scrupulously abides by the legal arbitration framework established by the FAA and state rules. The BDA thus only arbitrates disputes pursuant to valid arbitration agreements, and utilizes an arbitration process that protects the basic due process rights of disputants, such as equal treatment, counsel, notice, and an opportunity to present evidence and be heard by unbiased arbitrators. Importantly, the BDA remained and remains fully committed to Jewish law, and is not willing to abrogate Jewish law by respecting secular law standards in order to gain legitimacy in the eyes of state court judges. Instead, the BDA embraced due process requirements largely by implementing what are in any case basic requirements for valid adjudication under Jewish law, albeit using forms and language that make it apparent to secular judges that secular arbitration law is being respected.[63]

A practical recognition of the secular legal context in which it operates required the BDA to admit certain jurisdictional barriers not contemplated by Jewish law itself. Because the state claims exclusive authority over at least some spheres, arbitration—whether based on religio-legal or other norms—will come up lacking with respect to some kinds of disputes. Arbitral tribunals therefore cannot provide an effective substitute for secular court action. In some cases, religious litigants will be forced to resolve their disputes in secular courts because they are the only forums capable of addressing the issues presented or providing the relief sought.[64] Such jurisdictional limits are perhaps most pronounced in the realm of family

61. *Id.* at 463–65.

62. *See* David Wolitz, *Criminal Jurisdiction and the Nation-State: Toward a Bounded Pluralism*, 91 Or. L. Rev. 725, 730–31 (2013); John Witte, Jr., *The Future of Muslim Family Law in Western Democracies*, *in* Sharia in the West? 287 (Rex Ahdar & Nicholas Aroney eds., 2010) (noting "only the state and no other social or private unit can hold the coercive power of the sword").

63. *Id.*

64. *See* Broyde, *supra* note 2, at 296.

law where, for example, no amount of arbitration will permit a religious divorce to serve in lieu of a civil one.[65] The BDA accepts this proposition as an unavoidable necessity, and therefore requires couples seeking a Jewish divorce from the *beit din* to also obtain a civil divorce from a secular court.[66] Indeed, at the conclusion of a Jewish divorce proceeding, the BDA issues each former spouse a document stating that the couple has received a Jewish divorce, and that each is "free to marry provided that s/he is also civilly divorced."[67]

Arbitral tribunals that operate in accordance with religio-legal norms in a Western legal context must also respect secular law jurisdictional bars on the resolution of criminal matters and the meting out of corporal punishment, even when such measures are warranted or required by religious laws.[68] In the United States, as well as other Western countries, the state has exclusive jurisdiction to adjudicate alleged criminal offenses, and enjoys a complete monopoly on the use of violence.[69] Thus, the BDA admits no arbitral power to resolve claims covered by secular criminal codes, even though such claims and remedies may be contemplated by *halakha*. Importantly, in respecting secular legal requirements by refusing to resolve criminal cases or impose corporal sanctions for violations of Jewish or Islamic law, the BDA is not acting contrarily to its own religio-legal norms. *Halakha* obligates Jews to respect the laws of their host countries provided such laws do not mandate clear and active violations of Jewish law. Thus, respect for the secular legal system need not require religious courts to compromise their ecclesiastical legal obligations, at least if they wish to be part of a Western legal society.

Additionally, operating within the context of a secular legal system means that arbitration panels that enforce religio-legal norms must accept that religious principles will not excuse religious parties from criminal and other forms of liability under the relevant secular legal system.[70] As Professor John Witte, Director of the Center for the Study of Law and

65. *See* Michael J. Broyde, Marriage, Divorce, and the Abandoned Wife in Jewish law 32 (2001).

66. *See* Broyde, *supra* note 2, at 296.

67. Louis Jacobs, The Jewish Religion: A Companion 132–33, 188 (1995).

68. *See* Fried, *supra* note 3, at 649 (quoting Rakoszynski v. Rakoszynski, 663 N.Y.S. 2d 957, 961 (Sup. Ct. 1997) ("While the parties may elect to arbitrate their differences in a religious tribunal, the tribunal cannot abrogate to itself exclusive jurisdiction over all civil and criminal matters involving the parties.").

69. See Witte, *supra* note 62, at 9 (noting that "only the state and no other social or private unit can hold the coercive power of the sword").

70. S.D. v. M.J.R., 2 A.3d 412 (N.J. Super. Ct. App. Div. 2010), a recent New Jersey case that evoked nationwide criticism of Islamic law and the relationship between

Religion at Emory University, observes, "even the most devout religious believer has no claim to exemptions from criminal laws against actions like polygamy, child marriage, female genital mutilation, or corporal discipline of wives, even if their . . . particular religious community commands it."[71] In order to garner the respect of the secular justice system by genuinely respecting secular law, arbitration institutions must educate their communities on the necessity of adhering to general legal norms.

The BDA procedural rules also accommodate choice-of-law provisions in arbitration agreements in accordance with the demands of the secular law arbitration framework. Under secular arbitration law, the power and jurisdiction of an arbitration tribunal is created and defined by the arbitration agreement entered into by the parties. Thus, if an arbitration agreement selects a particular tribunal, and also chooses a particular body of substantive law as the set of norms that will regulate that tribunal's decision, the arbitral panel's authority is limited to issuing an award based on

Muslim religious norms and the American justice system, illustrates this reality, and the importance of Islamic arbitral courts' teaching their communities about the importance of following American law, even when it prohibits acts that may be permitted under religious law. The case involved domestic violence charges against a Muslim husband for allegedly beating his nineteen-year-old wife. At trial, the judge heard testimony from the couples' imam, who explained that under Islamic religious law a wife has a duty to accede to her husband's sexual demands. In light of this evidence, the court acquitted the husband of the charges. *Id.* at 417–18. The trial judge reasoned that although the husband had engaged in multiple instances of nonconsensual sexual intercourse with his wife, his personal religious commitment to Islam and his consequent honest belief that he had a legal right to sex with his wife precluded him from having the requisite intent to be culpable for the charged offense. *Id.* at 427–28. Although the trial judge's decision was ultimately overturned by a New Jersey appellate court, which held that the husband's religious beliefs could not excuse him from state criminal laws, *id.* at 442, the case sparked a deluge of critical commentary regarding the incompatibility of Islamic law with American law, *see, e.g.*, Donna Leinwand, *More States Enter Debate on Sharia Law*, USA Today (Dec. 9, 2010, 10:29 AM), http://www.loonwatch.com/2010/12/more-states-enter-debate-on-sharia-law/; Maxim Lott, *Advocates of Anti-Shariah Measures Alarmed by Judge's Ruling*, Fox News (Aug. 5, 2010), http://www.foxnews.com/us/2010/08/05/advocates-anti-shariah-measures-alarmed-judges-ruling/, and has since served as a banner for opponents of Islamic religious arbitration and of Islamic religious practice, *see, e.g.*, Robert Spencer, *Sharia in New Jersey: Muslim Husband Rapes Wife, Judge Sees No Sexual Assault because Islam Forbids Wives to Refuse Sex*, Jihad Watch (July 24, 2010, 6:20 AM), http://www.jihadwatch.org/2010/07/sharia-in-new-jersey-muslim-husband-rapes-wife-judge-sees-no-sexual-assault-because-husbands-religio.html; *see also* Jeffrey Breinholt, *Courtroom Jihad and the Defense "I Am a Muslim"*, Int'l Assessment & Strategy Ctr. (Oct. 29 2007), http://www.strategycenter.net/research/pubID.172/pubdetail.asp. This case and the popular responses to it highlight the importance of religious arbitration institutions taking an active role in educating their communities on the need to respect and adhere to American law as a means of garnering the respect and understanding of the American public generally, and of the American legal-political community in particular.

71. *See* Witte, *supra* note 62.

the selected body of substantive norms.[72] Early on, the BDA recognized that there would be cases in which parties selected the BDA to resolve their dispute but also agreed that the case should be resolved in accordance with substantive norms other than those provided by Jewish law.[73] In such instances, the BDA would not issue an award based on Jewish law, as doing so would overstep the limited jurisdiction granted to it by the parties' arbitration agreement, and preventing secular courts from enforcing the award. The BDA rules thus include a provision that honors choice-of-law provisions to the greatest extent permitted by Jewish law.[74] Because Jewish law permits general freedom of contract, and maintains that the financial (non-ritual) relationships of parties are governed by their voluntary contractual agreements, substantive Jewish law norms notwithstanding,[75] in practice, this means that the BDA will virtually always abide by litigants' choice-of-law provisions, at least with respect to commercial matters.

4. Acknowledgment of Commercial Customs and General Equity

Religious courts (of any flavor) functioning as arbitration panels that wish to take advantage of secular law's endorsement and enforcement have to be sensitive to both religious and secular norms in order to get cases right. More particularly, religious arbitration panels have to be right in three senses: religiously, legally, and culturally.[76] Being right religiously means that the panel

72. See Cindy G. Buys, *The Arbitrators' Duty to Respect the Parties' Choice of Law in Commercial Arbitration*, 79 St. John's L. Rev. 59, 67–69 (2005).

73. Indeed, such cases have been contemplated by Jewish legal scholars throughout history, who often dealt with actual cases presenting such issues by ordering a *beit din* to resolve disputes in accordance with substantive rules other than those provided by *halakha. See, e.g.*, Babylonian Talmud, Bava Metzia 83a ("What is the rule concerning one who hires workers and orders them to arrive at work early or to stay late? In a location where the custom is to not come early or stay late, the employer is not allowed to compel them [to do so] . . . All such terms are governed by local custom."); R. Joseph Kolon, Responsa Maharik, no. 102; R. Samuel di Medina, Responsa Maharashdam, no. 108.

74. *See The Rules and Procedures, supra* note 14, § 3(d):

> In situations where the parties to a dispute explicitly adopt a "choice of law" clause, either in the initial contract or in the arbitration agreement, the Beth Din will accept such a choice of law clause as providing the rules of decision governing the decision of the panel to the fullest extent permitted by Jewish law.

75. On the *halakhic* permissibility of Jewish parties choosing to resolve a dispute in a *beit din* in accordance with secular substantive law rather than *halakha*, see Feit, *supra* note 1, and especially sources cited at n.34.

76. The virtues of dual-system fluency are not merely in adjudication, of course. In my conversation with Justice Menachem Elon of the Israeli Supreme Court, he

is correctly applying the technical rules of the faith to the problem at hand. Being right legally means producing a decision that the secular legal system will enforce.

Being right culturally is the hardest to understand, but just as important. When an arbitration panel loses—within its own religious community—the appearance of religious legitimacy (that deep sense of the community of the faithful that this religious court is part of that community), community members will refuse to participate in its workings. On the other hand, and equally so, if the secular legal community (which is ultimately the source of the religious panel's coercive authority, through contract enforcement) senses that the religious tribunal cannot be trusted to genuinely adhere to the procedural norms needed to guarantee enforcement,[77] then it will remove this arbitration panel from access to the commonwealth of justice, either on a case-by-case or wholesale basis.

But, in truth, there is a deeper problem in the dual-system issue: it is quite possible that religious tribunals lose track of what is actually occurring on a commercial level. Sometimes in the Jewish law world, rabbinical courts are applying Jewish law faithfully but the community is not: it has already adopted the commercial law norms of the general society in which it lives and works and has fully integrated secular law norms with the Jewish law. Thus, the religious arbitrators ought to be people who are comfortably

observed many times that when he would lecture on Jewish law in medieval Europe he would explain that, centuries ago, Jews could engage in international commerce when no one else could, as they were dual-system fluent. He would observe that a Polish Catholic who wanted to sell a product in Protestant Germany was not able to, because the seller and the buyer could not agree on a law, a language, or a court to resolve disputes should they arise. But the Jews, with their cross-border commonalities of a language (Yiddish), a law (Jewish law), and a legal system (the rabbinical courts), could serve as middle men. Thus, a Polish Catholic could sell merchandise to a Polish Jew in accordance with Polish law, and the Jew could take the product to Germany and sell it to a German Jew in their shared language of Yiddish, in accordance with Jewish law and subject to adjudication in the shared legal system they both honored. The German Jew would then sell it to a Protestant German merchant in accordance with German law. Having a common language, legal system, and religious tribunals allows for the resolution of common disputes and builds community. Of course, the existence of a formal transnational mercantile law in premodern times is a subject of great historical dispute, but Justice Elon's point reflects at least one of the perceived strengths of Jewish law in premodern times.

77. Because they do not know how to conform to basic secular standards, or because they choose not to for either religious reasons or, most commonly, because they have no one who can explain to them how to conform to secular norms, as they do not think those norms are valuable religiously.

enmeshed in the community and also follow the details of what is actually occurring commercially.[78]

The Jewish law story is probably typical of many faiths. In Jewish law, (1) any condition that is agreed upon with respect to monetary matters is valid,[79] and (2) customs established among merchants acquire Jewish law validity,[80] provided that the practices stipulated or commonly undertaken are not otherwise ritually prohibited.[81] These two principles are arguably interrelated; commercial customs are sometimes said to be binding because business people implicitly agree to abide by them.[82] The Code of Jewish Law (*Shulchan Aruch*) makes it clear that common commercial practices override many default Jewish law rules that would otherwise govern a transaction.[83] Moreover, these customs are valid even if the majority of the businesspeople establishing them are not Jewish, simply because they are the norm. As Rabbi Moses Feinstein explains:

> It is clear that these rules which depend on custom . . . need not be customs . . . established by Torah scholars or even by Jews. Even if these customs were established by non-Jews, if the non-Jews are a majority of the inhabitants of the

78. The Jewish tradition has a long and storied interaction with secular law and elaborate doctrines of incorporation, as this chapter notes. Islamic law is beginning that process, as its history is not as a diaspora religion residing in a secular environment. For more on this, see KATHLEEN M. MOORE, THE UNFAMILIAR ABODE: ISLAMIC LAW IN THE UNITED STATES AND BRITAIN (2010).

79. *See generally* ENCYCLOPEDIA JUDAICA, THE PRINCIPLES OF JEWISH LAW 880–87 (Menachem Elon ed., 1975).

80. *Id.*

81. For example, Jewish law prohibits a debtor from offering a "pound of flesh" as collateral for a loan, and even if the borrower, the lender, and the general community of merchants accept such a practice, Jewish law would nonetheless prohibit it. *See* Rabbi Shiloh Yosef Zemin, *Mishpat Shylock Lefi Ha-Halakhah [Shylock in Jewish law]*, *in* LE-OR HA-*HALAKHAH*: BE'AYOT U-VERURIM 310 (2d ed. 1957) (Isr.).

82. As explained in note 73, this is the classical Jewish law. Indeed, doctrinally, this is not a modern addition to Jewish law, and dates to the establishment of recorded Jewish law itself. The Mishnah (200 C. E.) pronounces the validity of commercial customs. It states:

> What is the rule concerning one who hires workers and orders them to arrive at work early or to stay late? In a location where the custom is to not come early or stay late, the employer is not allowed to compel them [to do so] . . . . All such terms are governed by local custom.

THE OXFORD HANDBOOK OF JUDAISM AND ECONOMICS 373 (Aaron Levine ed., 2010) (quoting Babylonian Talmud, Bava Metzia 83a). This ancient doctrine is central to how Jewish law works.

83. Rabbi Yosef Karo, Choshen Mishpat 331:1, in Shulchan Aruch (Ketuvim ed. 1992) (Isr.). *See also* Talmud Yerushalmi: Bava Metzia 7:1(11b) (statement of Rav

> city, Jewish law incorporates the custom. It is as if the parties conditioned their agreement in accordance with the custom of the city.[84]

Most authorities rule that such customs are legally valid according to Jewish law even if they were established because secular law required the particular conduct.[85]

A religious tribunal not only has to know the religious law and secular law; it has to be familiar with the street law, so as to know which legal code—or hybrid—is actually being followed. Sometimes, truth be told, no legal code is being followed at all, just a commercial custom.

Allow two illustrative examples: Jewish law rules that when one steps into a supermarket and picks up a jar of spaghetti sauce to put it in one's cart and the jar slips and breaks, the one who broke it purchased it and has to pay for it.[86] On the other hand, the accepted practice in American law is clear that such is not the case and the customer has not yet purchased the item.[87] In theory, were one to run a supermarket according to Jewish law, one could hang a sign that said, "If you're Jewish and you break an item, you bought it as per Jewish law; if you're a Gentile, the U.C.C. governs and it's on the house." But Jewish tradition recognized centuries ago that shopkeepers were not in fact acting this way: the common commercial practice

Hoshaya, ha-minhag mevatel et ha-*halakhah* [Custom supersedes *halakhah*]); Rabbi Joseph Colon, Responsa of Maharik no. 102; Rabbi Samuel di Medina, Responsa of Maharashdam no. 108.

84. Rabbi Moses Feinstein, Hoshen Mishpat 1:72, in Iggerot Moshe; see also Rabbi Yehiel Michel Epstein, Hoshen Mishpat 73:20, in Arukh ha-Shulhan; *see generally* Rabbi Steven H. Resnicoff, *Bankruptcy: A Viable* Halachic *Option?*, 24 J. HALACHA & CONTEMP. SOC'Y 5, 10–14 (1992) (discussing this issue at great length).

85. *See, e.g.*, Feinstein, *supra* note 84; Rabbi Isaac Blau, Pithei Hoshen, *Din*ei Halva'ah, ch. 2, P 29 n.82; Rabbi Isaac Aaron Ettinger, Maharyah ha-Levi 2:111; Rabbi David Hazzan, Nediv Lev no. 12; Rabbi Eliyahu Hazzan, Nediv Lev no. 13; Rabbi Abraham Kahana-Shapiro, Dvar Avraham 1:1; Rabbi Israel Landau, *Beit* Yisrael no. 172. For example, Rabbi Joseph Iggeret, Divrei Yosef no. 21, states:

> One cannot cast doubt upon the validity of this custom on the basis that it became established through a decree of the King that required people to so act. Since people always act this way, even though they do so only because of the King's decree, we still properly say that everyone who does business without specifying otherwise does business according to the custom.

There is no reason to assume that these customs would not be valid if international law gave rise to such practices. *See* Michael J. Broyde, *Public and Private International Law from the Perspective of Jewish Law, in* THE OXFORD HANDBOOK OF JUDAISM AND ECONOMICS 373 (Aaron Levine ed., 2010).

86. This is called *kinyan mishicha*. *See* Karo, *supra* note 83, at 198:1. It is possible that there is also an action here in tort for damages, but more importantly, a sale has occurred.

87. *See* U.C.C. § 2-204 (1977), for an indication as to why this might be the case.

was to defer to secular law norms on many matters of sale law, because Jews participated in an integrated economy and it was easier to adopt those secular norms. Though there are occasional exceptions,[88] the Jewish tradition generally is to buy, sell, and otherwise conduct business according to the norms and practices of the secular marketplace.[89] If rabbinical courts of arbitration do not understand this, decisions are not resolved "correctly."

The real world contains far more complex cases, where determining what really is the law and the custom is far from clear. Consider, for example, the sale of marijuana in the United States. It is a federal crime to sell marijuana, medical or otherwise.[90] Per the supremacy clause of the U.S. Constitution, federal law supersedes state statutes, and states cannot abrogate federal law.[91] Yet, in several states, there are in fact medical marijuana dispensaries in which bona fide commercial transactions take place; in some states, such sales are "legal" even outside a pharmacy.[92] Are these sales legal or illegal as a matter of Jewish law? How should a rabbinic court consider a debt collection action for merchant credit extended to purchase marijuana? Is it a valid debt because Jewish law does enforce a contract of payment for an illegal action?[93] Is it invalid because secular law prohibits, through the clean hands doctrine, lawsuits for relief in illegal transactions?[94] Is it valid because state law validates the sale,[95] or valid because people on the street are actually doing this?[96] Or is it an illegal transaction, as it violates federal law, and the Jewish tradition validates such illegality through the "law of

88. For example, a rabbi's contract of employment might be adjudicated purely in accordance with Jewish law.

89. This tradition is very old, and traces itself back to the Talmudic attempt to harmonize itself with Roman law on the issue of market overt. *See* Babylonian Talmud, Bava Kama 115a (E.W. Kirzner trans.), *available at* http://halakhah.com/pdf/nezikin/Baba_Kama.pdf (last visited Nov. 25, 2014); Michael Broyde & Stephen Resnicoff, *Jewish Law and Modern Business Structures: The Corporate Paradigm*, 43 WAYNE L. REV. 1685 (1997).

90. *See* Controlled Substances Act, 21 U.S.C. §§ 801–904 (1970).

91. U.S. CONST. art. VI, § 2 ("The Laws of the United States . . . shall be the supreme Law of the Land . . . .").

92. *See Medical Cannabis in the United States*, WIKIPEDIA, http://en.wikipedia.org/wiki/Medical_cannabis_in_the_United_States (last modified Sept. 25, 2014, 7:57 PM) (particularly the entry under Colorado, which notes that all recreational sales are legal in that state).

93. *See* Karo, *supra* note 83, at 225:5.

94. *See* Gonzales v. Raich, 545 U.S. 1, 29–33 (2005), which notes that such laws are void under the supremacy clause.

95. *See, e.g.*, Vivian Cheng, Comment, *Medical Marijuana Dispensaries in Chapter 11 Bankruptcy*, 30 EMORY BANKR. DEV. J. 105 (2013) (arguing that state law legality is enough).

96. *Id.* at 128 (noting that Colorado "has more medical marijuana dispensaries than McDonalds [*sic*] and Starbucks combined" (footnote omitted)).

the land" doctrines that would point to federal law?[97] Is the Jewish law in Georgia, then, different from that in Colorado? One cannot answer these questions in the abstract.[98] The point of this example is not to discuss marijuana sales and Jewish law but to emphasize that to successfully arbitrate, one needs to know not only one's own religious tradition and law, and secular law, but also the facts on the ground that craft the commercial question that people are actually confronting.

But, one might ask—and reasonably so—what is so bad about wrong decisions? They are nonetheless legally binding through secular arbitration law, so how do "wrong" decisions detract from the legitimacy of religious arbitration? The answer is clear: a pattern of "wrong" outcomes undermines legitimacy because litigants simply will not repeatedly use any process that produces binding but wrong results, even if they sometimes win unjustly. When a businesswoman wins a case that she knows she should have lost, she says to herself, "Wow, thank goodness I won this time. But, I'm never going back to this panel, because in the next case that I should win, I very well might lose." Arbitral decisions that are enforced, but thought of as wrong by the community, undermine the community's sense that its judicial process is fair, reasonable, and useful—whether or not it is binding. Community members simply will not consistently use a process that is binding but irrational.

BDA experience points to the importance of crafting arbitral awards that are consistent with the common commercial practices and standards that reflect the reasonable expectations of disputants and incorporate commonly accepted notions of equity. Over time, the BDA found that many Jews do not conduct their business dealings in accordance with *halachic* default rules; common commercial customs often play an important role in business relationships. Because litigants often construct business relationships on the basis of expectations created by customary industry practices, the BDA decided to acknowledge and, wherever possible, uphold common

97. As the Jewish law doctrine of "the law of the land" might mandate that federal law be followed per the supremacy clause. Or maybe not, and the law of the land doctrine mandates that one follow the law of one's home state only.

98. I, for example, think that Jewish law would enforce a merchant debt entered for the purchase of marijuana in a state where such a sale is legal, even as it violates federal law, and hope to write a future article explaining the issues in such a case. This is grounded in the two-sided idea that Jewish law expects people to obey the law of the land as enforced and that the common commercial custom is to consider such transactions as valid in those states that permit it, notwithstanding the Supreme Court's clear rule to the contrary in *Gonzales*, 545 U.S. at 29–33. Obviously, the religious obligation to obey the law of the land is made much more complex when various portions of the law are intentionally left unenforced by secular authorities.

commercial practices in its arbitral awards.[99] Accordingly, the BDA added the following language to its Rules and Procedures:

> The Beth Din of America provides a forum where adherents of Jewish law can seek to have their disputes resolved in a manner consistent with the rules of Jewish law (halacha) and with the recognition that many individuals conduct commercial transactions in accordance with the commercial standards of the secular society. These Rules and Procedures are designed to provide for a process of dispute resolution in a Beth Din which is in consonance with the demands of Jewish law that one diligently pursue justice, while also recognizing the values of peace and compromise. The Beth Din of America adjudicates disputes in a manner consistent with secular law requirements for binding arbitration so that the resolution will be enforceable in the civil courts of the United States of America, and the various states therein.[100]

Upholding commercial customs is not required by the American arbitration framework, and failure to do so would not affect the technical enforceability of BDA decisions. Yet, commercial standards often govern litigants' commercial dealings and their expected resolution of commercial disputes. Failing to resolve commercial disputes in accordance with the relevant commercial customs might therefore result in a legally sound award, but nevertheless leave the parties dissatisfied. In all likelihood, the losing party in such a case would walk away displeased, believing that he or she should have won, and the winning party would rejoice in its immediate success, but know better than to bring further disputes before the BDA for fear of not having such good fortune in the future. In a short time, word of mouth would result in people avoiding the BDA arbitration process, undermining the ability of the BDA to be an effective and trustworthy forum for Jewish disputants to resolve conflicts in accordance with their religious obligations.[101]

Notably, recourse to commercial standards as a basis for arbitral rulings by the BDA does not entail any departure from *halakha*; indeed, Jewish law often incorporates common business customs into its rules of decision in commercial cases.[102] This legal principle of common commercial custom (called in rabbinic terminology, *minhag ha-sochrim*, literally "the custom of merchants"),

99. American law, too, places significant stock in upholding commercial customs that presumably form the basis of parties' agreements. *See, e.g.*, U.C.C. § 1-205(5) ("An applicable usage of trade in the place where any part of performance is to occur shall be used in interpreting the agreement as to that part of the performance.").

100. *See The Rules and Procedures*, *supra* note 14, Preamble.

101. *See* Broyde, *supra* note 2, at 297–99.

102. ELON, *supra* note 2, at 561–65.

creates the presumption that businessmen informally and implicitly rely on established commercial practices in negotiating their agreements, and that such terms are legally binding under the principle that Jewish law upholds private contracts in monetary matters that do not undermine any ritual law.[103] Commercial customs are held to be a fortiori binding on parties when contracts and other business documents are written in compliance with the regulations that determine common practice.[104]

The BDA has also learned from experience that when it resolves cases in accordance with Jewish law, it is best to inject principles of general equity and fairness into the decision-making process as a means of developing solutions that, at least nominally, satisfy all parties. Traditionally, *batei din* decided cases in strict accordance with Jewish law, assuming that by submitting their dispute to a *beit din* the parties were signaling their preference for a ruling based purely on Jewish law (*din*), rather than for a compromise-based solution formulated with regard for the applicable Jewish law principles (*p'shara krova l'din*).[105] When a case is decided according to *din*, the party that proves his or her case by a preponderance of the evidence will recover 100 percent of the amount in dispute. A case decided according to *p'shara krova l'din*, by contrast, may result in recovery of a lesser amount, depending on the relative equities of the parties' claims.[106]

The opportunity to creatively craft equitable solutions to disputes is often considered one of the prime reasons for pursuing arbitration instead of adjudication.[107] By resolving disputes with an eye toward equity, then, arbitration tribunals help ensure that all parties to a dispute, and not just the "winner," walk away from the arbitration experience nominally satisfied with the results and willing to return if they find themselves embroiled

103. *See* Babylonian Talmud, Kiddushin 19b (ruling that "one who makes a stipulation contrary to the law of the Torah, his stipulation is void," and that "every stipulation one makes with respect to money stands."); ELON, *supra* note **2**, at 880–87.

104. For an in-depth analysis of this concept, see Resnicoff, *supra* note 84.

105. Traditionally, Jewish arbitration was conducted in accordance with *din*, Jewish law. Today, the Rules and Procedures of the Beth Din specify that cases will be decided in accordance either with *p'shara* (a compromise in which *dayanim* consider the issue in *according* with Jewish law principles) or *p'shara krova l'din* (compromise or settlement related to Jewish law). Beth Din of Am., *supra* note 14, § 3. Under the latter framework, *dayanim* are more flexible to consider the parties' relative equities and to craft an appropriate remedy, whereas awards decided in strict accordance with *din* are necessarily a zero-sum game.

106. *See generally* R. JACOB BACK REISCHER, 2 RESPONSA SHEVUS YAAKOV § 144 (quoted in R. Avraham Zvi Eisenstadt, Pischei Teshuva, Choshen Mishpat 12:2).

107. *See* Mona Rafeeq, Comment, *Rethinking Islamic Law Arbitration Tribunals: Are They Compatible with Traditional American Notions of Justice*, 28 WISC. INT'L L.J. 108, 115 (2010). Amy J. Schmitz, *Ending a Mud Bowl: Defining Arbitration's Finality through Functional Analysis*, 37 GA. L. REV. 123, 160–65 (2002).

in a litigious conflict. For these reasons, as well because of technical Jewish law considerations,[108] the BDA decided that it would commit itself only to resolving disputes in a manner "consistent" with the rules of Jewish law, rather than in accordance with Jewish law.[109] The BDA thus decides cases under the rubric of *p'shara krova l'din* (Jewish law filtered through common commercial practice, customs, and equity).[110]

As in the case of the BDA's reliance on common commercial customs, its decision to rule based on *p'shara krova l'din* is not intended merely as a means to further some practical purpose or curry favor with litigants or American judges. *P'shara krova l'din* is a well-established principle of Jewish law adjudication whose foundation may be traced back to legal codes written in the Middle Ages.[111] In fact, some *halakhic* scholars consider this

108. *See generally* Shulchan Aruch: Choshen Mishpat § 12 (discussing the benefits of judges resolving cases based on compromise and equity rather than in accordance with the strict letter of the law).

109. *See The Rules and Procedures, supra* note 14, Preamble.

110. Footnote to § 3(b) of Rules and Procedures of the Beth Din of America helps define this term as:

> Compromise or settlement related to Jewish law principles (*p'shara krova l'din*), is a process in which the relative equities of the party's claims are considered in determining the award. For example, in Jewish law (*din*), the party that proves the "truthfulness" of its case "more likely than not," as well as proving the Jewish law basis for its entitlement, is qualified to recover 100% of the amount sought, whereas in compromise or settlement related to Jewish law principles (*p'shara krova l'din*) such a party would not necessarily recover 100% of the amount sought, depending on that party's conduct throughout the matter under dispute. So too, in a case where neither party proves the "truthfulness" of its case "more likely than not," or does not prove the Jewish law basis for its entitlement, Jewish law (*din*) would not provide for an award, whereas compromise or settlement related to Jewish law principles (*p'shara krova l'din*) could provide for an award in that case.
>
> Remedies also might be different. In a case governed by the principles of compromise or settlement related to Jewish law principles (*p'shara krova l'din*) an award could require a public apology, or other remedies not required in Jewish law (*din*). Even in a case decided under the compromise or settlement related to Jewish law principles (*p'shara krova l'din*) it is quite possible that one litigant will triumph completely and be fully vindicated.
>
> Among the factors not considered in compromise or settlement related to Jewish law principles (*p'shara krova l'din*) in a financial dispute are: levels of religiosity, relative wealth of the parties, or gender.
>
> Compromise (*p'shara*) alone shall not be subject to these restrictions.
>
> It is the policy of the Beth Din of America to encourage the parties to adjudicate matters in accordance with compromise or settlement related to Jewish law principles (*p'shara krova l'din*).
>
> In those cases in which Jewish law mandates that compromise (*p'shara*) alone provide the basis for the resolution of the dispute, no explicit acceptance of such shall be required.

111. *See* R. Avraham Zvi Eisenstadt, Pitchei Teshuva, Choshen Mishpat § 12:3–4.

approach preferable in some respects to a procedural posture grounded in *din*, because they deem it presumptuous for Jewish judges to purport to reach certain decisions that correctly track God's law.[112] Thus, by deciding to rely on *p'shara krova l'din* in an effort to reach equitable decisions based on Jewish law principles, the BDA decided to prefer one permitted mode of Jewish law dispute resolution to another because it would be more effective at securing the BDA's goals under the conditions in which it operates.

5. Reliance on Arbitrators with Broad Dual-System Expertise

Partially to address these complexities, successful religious arbitration panels pick arbitrators who are experts not only in their own religious law and secular law, but also in the particular matter at hand. Thus, when dealing with building construction matters, they employ an expert in building construction matters. And for dental malpractice, an expert in dentistry. Similarly, if a religious tribunal expects to hear matters of child custody, having a child psychologist present (either with the panel or on the panel) would seem helpful and increases the likelihood of secular affirmance.[113]

In recognition of this, Jewish law does not strictly require that arbitrators be rabbis, but allows the parties to accept panel members who are qualified in other ways.[114] Because of this, and given that the Jewish tradition allows panels of three, one does not have to find a single individual who is a Jewish law scholar, an American law scholar, and a skilled dentist (though such experts undoubtedly exist); rather, the arbitration panel can be composed of various subject matter experts, who together reach a resolution.

This complexity is part and parcel of the problem of religious arbitration of both commercial and family law matters: by default, the arbitration panel must include people who are fluent in more than one legal system and more than one cultural reality. American law does not require this level of expertise and does not have to. Because the dominant legal culture

112. *See, e.g.*, SEFER MITZVOS HAGADOL, POSITIVE COMMANDMENT 177 (quoted in R. YOEL SIRKES, BAYIS CHADASH, CHOSHEN MISHPAT 12:6) ("Thank God, that our biblical jurisdiction to rule in matters of monetary law has been abolished, for since we are have neither the depth or breadth of knowledge, we should not accept upon ourselves to rule in accordance with the law of the Torah, and thereby save ourselves from punishment were we to err.").

113. *See, e.g.*, Michael J. Broyde, *What's Love Got to Do with It? (Part I): Loving Children in Cases of Divorce or Death in the Jewish Tradition, in* THE BEST LOVE OF THE CHILD: BEING LOVED AND BEING TAUGHT TO LOVE AS THE FIRST HUMAN RIGHT 253, 261 (Timothy P. Jackson ed., 2011).

114. *See* Karo, *supra* note 83, at 7:1–2.

reasonably assumes that all adhere to its social, cultural, and legal norms, judges need not wonder if the parties actually intend to follow the common law of the land. Furthermore, consistently with its contractarian model, the FAA does not restrict arbitrators to experts—it even allows parties to pick three blind mice, more or less.[115]

But litigants who live in more than one cultural norm will not use a service that selects single-system experts; only multi-system experts will succeed, and only those able to determine which system provides the proper rules for the case at hand will actually be successful. So this is a balance not just of what arbitration law allows, but the reality of what sophisticated consumers in a narrow religious community will insist upon, which is arbitrators who understand the very complex legal, social, and cultural mores of religious communities in America. Although some religious communities are totally separatist and look to secular law and culture for virtually nothing, most religious communities are not. These communities are in a perpetual dynamic relationship with secular law and secular society, incorporating secular legal rules and ideas into their commercial and family law—and to do justice, the arbitrators chosen by these communities ought to be engaged with that dynamic interaction.[116]

The BDA's twenty years of experience with arbitration in the American legal context has shown that, in the United States, an arbitration tribunal's success rests in large part on its ability to navigate not only its own substantive and procedural norms, but also those of the secular legal systems in which it operates. Secular judges are more receptive to enforcing arbitral decisions that rely exclusively on religio-legal norms if the awards are couched in American legal terminology and reference familiar legal categories and doctrines that parallel religious norms. Also, the BDA has discovered that arbitration opinions that evidence arbitrators, understanding of secular law are afforded greater deference by secular court judges, and

115. Of course, neither the American nor the Jewish tradition actually allows mice to serve as arbitrators. *See* Karo, *supra* note 83, at 7, for a list of the minimal qualifications to be arbitrators.

116. Let me add that within the traditional Jewish community that I am part of, secular law norms have made greater inroads in the area of commercial law than in the area of family law. This is, I suspect, typically true of conservative religious faiths, but is not axiomatically correct. One could construct a sexually progressive but economically conservative religion as well. *See, e.g.*, Heresy and Authority in Medieval Europe (Edward Peters ed., 1980) (arguing that Catharism was such a faith). This point is worthy of emphasis: The ideas presented in this section are useful not only for conservative religions but liberal ones. The question of how to structure one's community when secular law is not to the liking of one's faith is universal. *See, e.g.*, Posik v. Layton, 695 So. 2d 759 (Fla. Dist. Ct. App. 1997), *reh'g den'd*, 699 So. 2d 1374 (Fla. 1997).

that arbitrators with formal education in secular law are considered more credible by judges. Additionally, the BDA's experience has shown that, in order to correctly resolve cases in accordance with commercial customs or choices of law made by the parties, arbitral panels must often include professionals familiar with both Jewish law and the practices and standards of the parties' respective lines of work. Religious arbitration institutions, therefore, must not only talk the talk by couching decisions based on religious law in American "legalese," but also walk the walk by actually issuing awards that preserve parties' contractual agreements and reasonable commercial expectations. To gain the confidence and respect of secular courts, arbitration tribunals that apply religio-legal norms must therefore produce and utilize trilingual arbitrators fluent in American law, professional practices, and the laws of their respective religions.

Providing litigants with access to such a fluid framework requires more than a willingness to acknowledge outside legal systems. Traversing the gap between Jewish law and secular law demands the cultivation and participation of arbitrators who are American lawyers, and skilled ones at that. Today, the BDA almost never presides over a case without the arbitral panel having at least one well-trained lawyer who is comfortable with both American and Jewish law.[117]

Legal training, however, is only one of many professional backgrounds necessary to cultivate a pool of skilled arbitrators. As noted in the previous section, the success of the BDA's commercial arbitration practice relies in large part on its willingness to honor common commercial customs when doing so does not conflict with *halakha* or secular law. Unlike secular laws, trade customs are rarely memorialized in writing and are, therefore, not readily discernible to outside observers. Accordingly, in addition to religious and legal scholars, the BDA often employs *dayanim*, or judges, who in addition to their rabbinic work are also engaged in various trades and are familiar with the commercial practices of those fields.[118] As *beit din* arbitrators, these rabbi-professionals provide other arbitrators on the same panel with a proper grasp of the factual issues raised by different cases. Thus, a BDA's panel for a construction dispute might include a Jewish contractor,

117. The most recently published partial list of Beth Din arbitrators names twenty-six *dayanim*. Of those individuals, twenty-one are rabbis and nine are lawyers. However, seven of the lawyer-*dayanim* are also ordained rabbis. This list used to be posted on the Beth Din of America website and is cited to that effect at Broyde, *supra* note 2, at n. 71, and can now can now be found at http://ip-50-63-248-10.ip.secureserver.net/Dayanim.asp (last visited Nov. 19, 2016).

118. *See Staff Biographies*, Beth Din of America, http://www.bethdin.org/staff-bio.asp (last visited Oct. 1, 2016).

the panel for a dental malpractice case will include a Jewish dentist or doctor, and so on, and the panel for a child custody case may consist of two rabbi-lawyers and one Jewish child psychologist. Beyond providing a level of institutional expertise that contributes to substantively sound arbitration awards, this dual-system fluency contributes to the perceived legitimacy of those decisions. As a result of this approach, no BDA award has ever been overturned by a secular court;[119] this is true even with respect to family law arbitration awards, which secular courts typically review with particular vigor.[120]

6. Assumption of an Active Role in Internal Communal Governance and External Communal Representation

Although this phenomenon is worthy of a paper of its own, religious leadership that resolves disputes between parties ultimately serves a role in shaping the community, no differently than judges in any society. What flows from this observation is less of a requirement than a consequence, but any discussion of what happens when judicial structure is introduced into a religious community would be incomplete without it. Religious tribunals, once up and running, begin to assume roles in communal governance; this should seem clear to any who look at a history of Catholic religious tribunals in the United States, which never resolved disputes between Catholic individuals over commercial matters, but focused on church governance matters and ecclesiastical disputes.[121] It is not enough for a faith—or even a legal system—to have rules; it has to have a judicial process (that is, arbitration panels) that applies those rules to the reality it confronts.

When this system is respected by peer religious organizations within the same faith as producing religiously reliable and functionally realistic answers to pressing questions, this adjudicative body becomes the location

119. This proposition acknowledges that one BDA-issued award has been overturned by a trial court, but was restored on appeal. *See, e.g., In re* Brisman v. Hebrew Acad. of Five Towns & Rockaway, 887 N.Y.S.2d 414 (N.Y. App. Div. 2008) (vacating an award of the Beth Din of America), *rev'd*, 895 N.Y.S.2d 482 (2010) (restoring it).

120. *See, e.g.*, Glauber v. Glauber, 192 A.D.2d. 94, 97 (N.Y. App. Div. 1993) (finding that "the court must always make its own independent review and findings" in child custody cases, despite an arbitration award addressing the issue); *see also* Fawzy v. Fawzy, 199 N.J. 456 (2009) (finding a N.J. constitutional right to child custody arbitration).

121. Indeed, this is much more part of the mission of the canon law courts than any other. *See, e.g., Code of Canon Law*, VATICAN, http://www.vatican.va/archive/ENG1104/_INDEX.HTM (last visited Nov. 25, 2014).

members of the religious community go to when they have disputes, not just about buying and selling houses or marriage and divorce, but about territorial, jurisprudential, and even theological matters that co-religionists sometimes disagree about. Without this, even members of the same faith, who share an identical vision of the grander questions of community, life, and God, will sometimes fight about the mundanely parochial, and even about the more important issues that can generate institutional conflict.

Dispute resolution for the faithful will resolve not only mundane disputes but also communal disputes. Within the Jewish tradition, this has clearly happened, and it is a consequence of building structure: many religious institutions prefer law to politics as a method of dispute resolution, and if there is a court that shares their religious values, they will use it. This will build a tighter cooperation among the community of the faithful, as the organs of justice will share their religious values. Over time, this gives the community increased structure, stability, and cohesiveness. I expect this to be true not only of particular Jewish law courts, but of a wide variety of religious and values-oriented forums for dispute resolution. The Catholic model in America—which is uniquely hierarchical and thus does not serve as a general precedent for most American faiths—can be built into other faiths as well by this process, but most likely will not.[122]

An increased role within a religious community also entails increased responsibility within the broader society. Secular court recognition of the legitimacy of religious arbitral tribunals presupposes a broad tolerance of legal pluralism, albeit one that accepts the ultimate functional supremacy of one system over all others. Thus, although the American legal system, and American society more generally, is usually accepting of a plurality of private law systems, arbitral awards will be accepted by state judges only when, to use a *halakhic* aphorism, they stand within the "four cubits of the (secular) law."[123] Moreover, in working to gain the respect of a secular legal system, it is important for litigants who use faith-based arbitration to be seen as integrated, participating members of the broader secular society so that courts do not view such arbitral tribunals as promoting isolation and factionalism.[124] Arbitration organizations that enforce religio-legal norms

122. Because the Catholic model has but one mother church and expects full obedience to it by all of its subsidiaries. This model does not fit the religious ideology of most American faiths, in that the Catholic Church is so broadly interconnected as a single whole church, whereas almost all other American faith groups expect and grant their local communities much more religious, legal, and ideological autonomy.

123. Babylonian Talmud, Berachos 8a.

124. *Cf.* Helfand, *supra* note 13, at 1237.

must therefore create a system of joint governance in conjunction with secular legal authorities, demonstrating that those who use such tribunals, as well as the tribunals themselves, "jointly belong to more than one community, and will accordingly bear rights and obligations that derive from more than one source of legal authority."[125]

Membership in more than one community, however, entails more than merely formally recognizing the authority of multiple legal systems; it also entails becoming a genuine participant in multiple social communities.[126] Since 9/11, many attempts have been made to prevent arbitration in accordance with Islamic law due to a pervasive fear of Muslim religious fundamentalism.[127] These measures demonstrate that the level of legal and social legitimacy possessed by faith-based arbitral tribunals is often commensurate with how effective they are at internally governing their respective constituent communities, and with their ability to successfully represent their communities to the broader society.

For this reason, the BDA transformed itself from being just one forum for Jewish law arbitration among a relatively disjointed network of independent *batei din* operating in America into one of America's pre-eminent rabbinic authorities. By taking an active role as a source of *halakhic* rulings and adjudications, the BDA became an important building block in the creation of an internally cohesive and coherent *halakhic* community in America. The BDA is now viewed by many *halakha*-observant Jews, as well as by external—including governmental—organizations, as a dependable and just arbitrator whose opinions are regularly upheld by secular courts. As a result of its reputation for resolving disputes in a manner that is predictable, professional, and uncompromisingly adherent to *halakha*, the BDA is frequently called upon to play a larger role than the sum of its individual arbitrations. Today, the organization performs an important stabilizing function within the Jewish community, and also represents and advocates for that community within the larger society.[128]

The Jewish community as a whole periodically calls upon the BDA to perform such functions. In 2007, for example, the BDA played a prominent role in a nationwide revision and regulation of the process for conversion

125. Ayelet Shachar, Multicultural Jurisdictions: Cultural Differences and Women's Rights 13 &, n.12 (2001).

126. Joel A. Nichols, *Religion, Marriage, and Pluralism*, 25 Emory Int'l L. Rev. 967, 970–71 (2011).

127. *See* Awad v. Ziriax, 670 F.3d 1111 (10th Cir. 2012) (holding that a proposed amendment to the Oklahoma Constitution forbidding courts from considering Sharia violates the First Amendment).

128. *See* Broyde, *supra* note 2, at 301.

to Judaism.[129] Previously, conversions to Judaism were conducted by individual rabbis on a case-by-case basis, often based on varying *halakhic* standards.[130] The disorganization of that ad hoc conversion process rendered the system susceptible to inconsistency and fraud.[131] As a result, the Jewish community turned to the BDA and the Rabbinical Council of America to address this issue. Together, these two organizations developed uniform *halakhic* standards to govern the conversion process in the United States,[132] and created a network of authorized *batei din* that agreed to follow these procedures and continue to work closely with the BDA to ensure compliance.[133] *Batei din* outside this network continue to follow their own conversion practices,[134] and are certainly free to do so within the *halakhic* system, but for many Jews, the BDA's work has lent a degree of predictability and consistency to this important process, and allows them to rely on the BDA's expertise and professionalism in determining which conversions to accept as legally effective.[135]

129. *See RCA and Israeli Chief Rabbinate Announce Historic Conversion Agreement*, RA BBINICAL COUNCIL OF AMERICA, http://www.rabbis.org/news/article.cfm?id=100905 (last visited Nov. 23, 2011).

130. See Michael J. Broyde, "On Conversion, the True Issue Is Standards," The Jewish Week, August 2, 2016. http://www.thejewishweek.com/editorial-opinion/opinion/conversion-true-issue-standards (last visited Jan. 24, 2017).

131. *Id.* ("Of course, the centralization controversy and the standards controversy are somewhat inter-related. A fully centralized system must have a uniform standard for acceptance and allows much less individualization both by the local rabbi and the local rabbinical court. On the other hand, a decentralized system tends to have more flexible standards with a rabbinical court made up of local communal rabbis who self-validate and who find a level of observance for the convert that reflects the needs of the local community. This approach is more ad hoc and less consistent from case to case.")

132. *See Geirus Policies and Standards Governing the Network of Regional Batei Din for Conversion* (Apr. 20, 2007), http://www.judaismconversion.org/geirus-policies-and-standards/.

133. *See* http://www.judaismconversion.org/ under "About GPS" and http://www.judaismconversion.org/RCA_Conversion_Network_Recognized.html, which states: "The network accomplishes multiple goals. First and foremost it ensures that its converts will be assured that their status as Jews will not be questioned in the future, whether in Israel or in other major mainstream Orthodox communities. In addition it introduces long overdue standardization and comprehensive record-keeping into the conversion process. The courts follow clearly understood policies and practices. Candidates for conversion will know what to expect and what will be expected of them."

134. *Id.* ("In any case an individual rabbi can still elect to do conversions outside of the national network. Such conversions will not automatically come with the endorsement of the RCA. But that is nothing new. The RCA has not previously given blanket endorsements to the conversions of its members.").

135. *See* Broyde, *supra* note 2, at 301 ("Rabbis around the globe would be assured that conversions done through these centrally organized rabbinical courts would not adopting [*sic*] understandings of Jewish law that fall outside the range of normative accepted halacha. Finally, converts could be confident that their conversions would be

Many organizations outside the Jewish community have also come to recognize the BDA's prominence as a leading rabbinic authority and representative of the observant Jewish community in America. Following the September 11 attacks on the World Trade Center towers, the City of New York found itself in a quandary with respect to its Jewish community. Among the suspected victims of the attacks were several observant Jews whose deaths could not be confirmed with the certainty required by Jewish law. Without incontrovertible evidentiary support to confirm these individuals' whereabouts at the time of the attacks, the victims' wives faced a fate known as *iggun*:[136] they would be unable to remarry.[137] In the months following the tragedy, the BDA worked closely with the New York Medical Examiner's Office to locate and identify fingerprints, dental records, and DNA from the wreckage, in the hopes of compiling sufficient evidence to make a definitive Jewish law ruling regarding the missing. Not only did the medical examiner's office supply the BDA with daily updates by fax, but members of the BDA were also granted personal access to the office's files.[138] Even representatives of *USA Today* met with members of the BDA to compare notes on the attacks.[139] In the end, the cooperation between the BDA and these other organizations enabled the resolution of each case.

C. CONCLUSION

Over time, Jewish religious arbitration, represented by the practices and processes of the Beth Din of America, has become a form of faith-based alternative dispute resolution that is both effective and authoritative for its constituents, as well as legally credible in the eyes of American courts. In a purely formal sense, it is critical that all religious arbitration tribunals follow the basic legal requirements set forth by the FAA and other applicable laws discussed in Chapter Six. However, abiding by the technical requirements for valid arbitration agreements and fair process may not be enough to ensure that judges will routinely enforce faith-based arbitration awards. The FAA provides a floor, not a ceiling, on judicial expectations for private

universally accepted precisely because they could be certain that the halachic standards used were normative.").

136. Literally, "chained."

137. *See* Yona Reiss, *The Resolution of the World Trade Center* Agunot Cases *by the Beth Din of America: A Personal Retrospective*, *in* CONTENDING WITH CATASTROPHE: JEWISH PERSPECTIVES ON SEPTEMBER 11TH 14–15 (Michael Broyde ed., 2011).

138. *Id.* at 22.

139. *Id.* at 21.

dispute resolution. The experience of the Beth Din of America shows that it has gained the respect and confidence of American courts by adopting six measures that go beyond the minimum requirements prescribed by the FAA. These measures include the adoption and publication of formal, law-like rules of procedure; the development of a system of internal review and appeal; demonstrated respect for secular law and policy in addition to religious norms and values; the use of common commercial custom and equitable principles in its decision-making process; the employment of arbitrators who have expertise in both religious law and relevant secular fields such as law, psychology, finance, and business; and the assumption of an active leadership role within the religious communities that it serves. These measures have helped show American courts and judges that BDA arbitration is professional, law-like, fair, effective, consistent, transparent, and reliable. This gives courts confidence in the Jewish arbitration process, and increases judges' willingness to routinely uphold BDA awards.

CHAPTER 8

Refining Religious Arbitration in the United States and Abroad

The Muslim and Christian Experience

Religious arbitration in the United States has come a long way from its early ecclesiastical forms. Under the FAA, faith-based arbitration was transformed from something particularly sacerdotal and religious into what is in essence just another form of general arbitration that just happens to utilize religious courts and religious norms as its relevant choice of law and forum. Through the Beth Din of America experience described in the previous chapter, moreover, religious arbitration has evolved in creative ways that help ensure that faith-based dispute resolution processes will be viewed favorably and respectfully by American courts and judges.

Although basic frameworks for successful religious arbitration thus exist, religious communities—and the growing American Muslim community in particular—still face challenges in implementing their own ADR systems effectively. This chapter describes some of these challenges, as well as the ways in which they may be effectively addressed. It looks to the example set by the Muslim Arbitration Tribunal, a U.K.-based Islamic arbitration organization that has successfully adopted and adapted the Beth Din of America approach to religious arbitration, as a likely model for American Muslims to build on in constructing their own ADR processes. In addition, this chapter notes that Christian communities in the United States also face challenges in their attempts to implement effective faith-based arbitration, though these challenges are somewhat different than those dealt with by the more law-centered Jewish and Muslim traditions. In any case, Christian communities have responded to these challenges by creating their own religious arbitration models that, like the BDA framework, conform to the technical legal requirements of the FAA while also portraying a professional dispute resolution process that secular judges and courts can be thoroughly comfortable with and confident in enforcing.

A. THE CHALLENGE OF ISLAMIC ARBITRATION IN AMERICA

Private dispute resolution has long been an accepted legitimate alternative to formal adjudication in Islamic religio-legal practice.[1] The history of Islamic law[2] includes a rich tradition of formal and informal methods for resolving litigious conflicts.[3] The *Qur'an* and *Hadith* include numerous references to the importance of using human judgment regulated by Islamic religio-legal norms to resolve disputes,[4] and *fiqh* books of practical religio-legal rules include extensive discussions of adjudicatory procedures and judicial methodology.[5] For Muslims, traditional, religiously-sanctioned methods of dispute resolution include *sulh*, negotiated settlement;[6] *tahkim*,

1. For one example, see G.R. Hawting, THE FIRST DYNASTY OF ISLAM: THE UMAYYAD CALIPHATE A.D. 661–750, at 24–33 (2d ed. 2000).

2. As used here, the term "Islamic law" refers to *fiqh*, the sacred religious law of Islam as developed by the main schools of Islamic religio-legal jurisprudence, and not to the state law of Muslim-majority countries, which although often informed in some respects by religious law principles and concepts, more closely tracks the substance and organization of various European legal codes imposed on Muslim populations during the colonial era.

3. *See, e.g.*, KNUT S. VIKOR, BETWEEN GOD AND THE SULTAN: A HISTORY OF ISLAMIC LAW 168–221 (2005).

4. *See, e.g.*, QUR'AN 4:35 (Abdel Haleem trans., 2010) ("If you [believers] fear that a couple may break up, appoint one arbitrator from his family and one from hers."); *id.* at 4:105 ("We have sent down the Scripture to you [Prophet] with the truth so that you can judge between people in accordance with what God has shown you."); *id.* at 38:26 ("David, We have given you mastery over the land. Judge fairly between people."); *id.* at 49:9–10 ("If two groups of the believers fight, you [believers] should try to reconcile them . . . make a just and even-handed reconciliation between the two of them: God loves those who are even-handed. The believers are brothers, so make peace between your two brothers and be mindful of God, so that you may be given mercy.").

5. *See, e.g.*, AHMAD IBN NAQIB AL-MISRI, RELIANCE OF THE TRAVELER: A CLASSIC MANUAL OF ISLAMIC SACRED LAW 624–38 (Nuh Ha Mim Keller trans., rev. ed. 1997).

6. MARC GOPIN, HOLY WAR, HOLY PEACE: HOW RELIGION CAN BRING PEACE TO THE MIDDLE EAST 135–43 (2002).

binding arbitration;[7] *qada*, formal adjudication in which a judge, or *qadi*, decides cases by determining the relevant facts and applying Islamic legal norms articulated by *muftis*, or scholar-jurists, who clarify points in response to questions posed by litigants or judges, and adjudication in state-run *mazalim* and *shurta* courts that apply public-policy-based rules under the jurisprudential rubric of *siyasa-shariya*, or Islam-inspired societal constitution and regulation.[8]

Today, observant Muslims living in the United States face the challenge of developing effective and respectable religious courts as a means of fulfilling their obligation to abide by Islamic law while living in a secular Western political, social, and legal context. On the one hand, Muslims have a religious duty to live in accordance with Islamic legal norms, which in turn necessitate the ability to order relationships and resolve disputes through religiously acceptable dispute resolution procedures rather than the secular judicial system.[9] On the other hand, the American Muslim community's ability to fulfill this religious imperative faces some significant obstacles. First, although historically, and in some places even today, Islamic law tribunals could enforce their own decisions, Islamic courts in the United States must rely on the goodwill of disputing parties. Second, whereas American law maintains a legal framework that provides a means of making private arbitration rulings enforceable by the state, at present, Islamic law arbitral tribunals often fail to operate within it. Also, to the extent that Islamic tribunals do operate within American law's formal arbitration guidelines, secular judges often remain wary of enforcing their decisions because they perceive Islamic arbitration as foreign, discriminatory, arbitrary, "informal, closed, and secret."[10] Finally, significant segments of American society maintain general distrust of Islamic law and courts, as evidenced by

7. Ahmed S. Moussalli, *An Islamic Model for Political Conflict Resolution: Takhim (Arbitration)*, in PEACE AND CONFLICT RESOLUTION IN ISLAM: PRECEPT AND PRACTICE (Abdul A. Said ed., 2001).

8. *See* 8 FRANK E. VOGEL, ISLAMIC LAW AND LEGAL SYSTEM: STUDIES OF SAUDI ARABIA 173 (2000).

9. *See* IMAM KHASSAF, ADAB AL-QADI: ISLAMIC LEGAL AND JUDICIAL SYSTEM 1–2 (Munir Ahamad Mughal, trans., 2004); MARION BOYD, DISPUTE RESOLUTION IN FAMILY LAW: PROTECTING CHOICE, PROMOTING INCLUSION 57 (2004), *available at* http://www.attorneygeneral.jus.gov.on.ca/english/about/pubs/boyd/fullreport.pdf (quoting Sept. 10, 2004 submission of His Highness Prince Aga Khan Shia Imami Ismaili National Conciliation and Arbitration Board of Canada: "[W]hen differences of opinion or disputes arise between them, these should be resolved by a process of mediation, conciliation and arbitration within themselves in conformity with the Islamic concepts of unity, brotherhood, justice, tolerance and goodwill").

10. Michael C. Grossman, *Is This Arbitration?: Religious Tribunals, Judicial Review, and Due Process*, 107 COLUM. L. REV. 169, 179 (2007).

periodic popular outcries when American courts uphold Islamic arbitral awards and by recent attempts in some states to prohibit courts from applying or enforcing *Shari'a*.[11] Apprehensions about "creeping Sharia"[12] and the impending "Islamization of America"[13] make it politically difficult for Islamic arbitration to gain the respect it needs for its arbitral awards to be regularly and routinely upheld and enforced by American courts.[14] If American Muslims decide to cultivate more respectable and efficacious religious-law arbitration processes in the United States, they will have to look toward developing institutions that both conform to the formal legal requirements of the American arbitration framework and engender understanding of and respect for Islamic law in the American legal-political community and American society more generally.

There have been some efforts by American Muslims to accomplish these ends,[15] but much remains to be done. In particular, a more systematic consideration of the factors that contribute to religious arbitration tribunals' gaining the acceptance of secular courts may be warranted. In this respect, American Muslims seeking to develop Islamic dispute resolution processes that will be respected by American courts might benefit by learning from the experience of the religiously observant American Jewish community, which has successfully built its own arbitration institutions based on Jewish law.

A similar phenomenon has occurred in the United Kingdom with respect to Islamic law arbitration. Muslim religious courts have functioned there for decades, resolving matters under Islamic family and personal law, as well as some commercial disputes, but these informal "Shari'a Councils" did not follow any set procedural rules or operate within any secular legal

11. Abed Awad, *The True Story of Sharia in American Courts*, THE NATION, June 13, 2012, *available at* http://www.thenation.com/article/168378/true-story-sharia-american-courts#.

12. Matthew Schmitz, *Fears of "Creeping Sharia"*, NAT'L REVIEW REV. (June 13, 2012), *available at* http://www.nationalreviwe.com/article/302280.

13. PAMELA GELLER, STOP THE ISLAMIZATION OF AMERICA: A PRACTICAL GUIDE TO THE RESISTANCE (2011).

14. Although American courts do regularly enforce the provisions of Islamic marriage agreements as valid, legally binding contracts in civil divorce proceedings, judges are far more apprehensive about respecting and enforcing the outcomes of Islamic religious arbitrations, which the law provides may be voided for a variety of reasons linked to the propriety of the arbitral process and the consistency of the award with public policy.

15. *See, e.g.*, *Islamic Arbitration: Guidelines and Procedures*, ASSEMBLY OF MUSLIM JURISTS OF AMERICA, http://www.amjaonline.org/en/our-services/international-convention/19-imams-conference/47-islamic-arbitration-guidelines-and-procedures (collection of papers delivered at the 2010 Imams' Conference of the American Muslim Jurists Association, entitled "Islamic Arbitration: Guidelines and Procedures").

framework.[16] Consequently, the decisions of these early Islamic tribunals were not legally enforceable, and litigants had to rely solely on the goodwill of the parties to adhere to the religious court's decisions. The Muslim Arbitration Tribunal (MAT) was established in 2007 to provide British Muslims with a more effective alternative for resolving disputes in accordance with Islamic law, drawing on, among other things, the BDA's experiences.[17] In 2008, the British government formally recognized the MAT's network of *Shari'a* courts, ensuring that its decisions would be enforced by the secular courts.[18]

As the American Muslim community continues to develop and refine its own religious courts as effective forums for resolving disputes in accordance with Islamic law, it may wish to consider the BDA experience as a useful navigation tool for how to establish a system of respectable religious courts in the United States. Likewise, American Muslims might look to the MAT's experience in the United Kingdom for precedent. Specifically, American Muslims may note six pillars on which the BDA and MAT have constructed their religious arbitration processes, which have allowed them to garner respect and endorsement from the secular courts: (1) publishing legally sophisticated rules of procedure, (2) developing an internal appellate process; (3) exhibiting respect for both religious and secular legal norms, (4) acknowledging common commercial customs and equitable standards, (5) utilizing arbitrators with broad professional expertise in both religious and secular disciplines, and (6) taking an active role in governing and representing their constituent religious communities.

B. ISLAMIC ARBITRATION IN THE UNITED KINGDOM: THE MUSLIM ARBITRATION TRIBUNAL MODEL

In the United Kingdom, binding arbitration takes place under the aegis of the Arbitration Act of 1996.[19] Like its American counterpart, the Act

16. For a discussion of the structure and procedures of these *Shari'a* Councils, see John R. Bowen, *How Could English Courts Recognize Shariah?*, 7 U. St. Thomas L.J. 411, 418–21 (2010).

17. *See* Bilal M. Choksi, Comment, *Religious Arbitration in Ontario—Making the Case Based on the British Example of the Muslim Arbitration Tribunal*, 33 U. Pa. J. Int'l L. 791, 812 (2012) (arguing, "[In establishing the MAT], Shaykh Siddiqi followed the Jewish example of the *Beit Din* rabbinical court.").

18. *Id.* at 812–13.

19. The Arbitration Act of 1996, available at http://www.legislation.gov.uk/ukpga/1996/23/contents.

is premised on the notion that "parties should be free to agree how their disputes are resolved, subject only to such safeguards as are necessary in the public interest."[20] Under the Act, courts must respect parties' contracts and enforce awards issued by an arbitral tribunal pursuant to a valid arbitration agreement.[21] The Act allows courts to refuse to enforce arbitration awards under circumstances constituting "serious irregularity."[22] These include a tribunal's failure to conduct the arbitration pursuant to a valid agreement and arbitrators' failure to ensure the procedural protections relating to impartiality and fairness required under the Act.[23] When a reviewing court finds such irregularities, the Act permits it to remit the award to the arbitral tribunal for reconsideration, set aside the award, or decline to enforce the arbitral decision.[24] This legal arbitration framework provides one important means of empowering individuals and communities to conduct their internal affairs in accordance with their religious commitments.[25] In order to enjoy its benefits, arbitration tribunals applying religious legal norms must take steps to ensure that their decisions comply with the standards set by that framework and earn the respect of secular courts.

The MAT was established in 2007 to provide British Muslims with the opportunity to effectively resolve disputes in accordance with Islamic legal norms.[26] Although Islamic courts have existed in the United Kingdom for many decades, both under the institutional umbrella of the Islamic *Shari'a* Council and as privately sponsored tribunals presided over by local religious scholars, these forums did not follow formal, transparent procedures or operate within any secular legal framework. As a result, their decisions were not legally enforceable, and litigants had to rely on the willingness of the disputants to adhere to tribunals' decisions.[27] To remedy this, Sheikh Faiz Siddiqi, a barrister and the founding principle of Hijaz College, and Shamim Qureshi, a practicing Muslim and English District Judge, founded the MAT to provide British Muslims with a more effective means of dispute resolution in accordance with Islamic law.[28]

20. *Id.* § 6 (b).
21. *Id.* § 30(1).
22. *Id.* § 68(1)–(2).
23. *Id.* § 33.
24. *Id.* § 68(3).
25. *See generally* Nicholas Walter, *Religious Arbitration in the United States and Canada*, 52 Santa Clara L. Rev. 501 (2012).
26. *See* Maria Reiss, Note, *The Materialization of Legal Pluralism in Britain: Why Shari'a Council Decisions Should Be Non-binding*, 26 Ariz. J. Int'l & Comp. L. 739, 768 (2009).
27. *See* Choksi, *supra* note 17, at 811.
28. *Id.* at 812–13.

The MAT operates pursuant to Section 1 of the Arbitration Act of 1996, which provides that "parties should be free to agree how their disputes are resolved, subject only to such safeguards as are necessary in the public interest."[29] Like the BDA, the MAT developed innovative processes in order to ensure that its arbitrations would conform to the formal requirements of the Arbitration Act, garner the respect of British courts, and make judges more comfortable enforcing its rulings. Some of these measures represented significant departures from the *fiqh*-based procedural rules of traditional Islamic adjudication,[30] as well as from traditional *tahkim* processes, which are far less formal than MAT proceedings.[31] Muslim scholars have observed, however, that Islamic law can be understood to provide ample room for such procedural innovations as a means of enabling Islamic tribunals to operate effectively in a non-Muslim political and legal context.[32] By building on viable avenues for innovation in Islamic law, the MAT, like the BDA, has crafted an arbitration process that gives British Muslims the opportunity for effective dispute resolution services consistent with both British and Islamic law.

The MAT, like the BDA, has adopted a variety of legally sophisticated procedural protections designed to ensure fairness in a way that puts secular court judges at ease, yet that also remain within the bounds of Islamic law. Consistent with traditional Islamic adjudicatory practices,[33] and in accordance with secular arbitration laws, the MAT will not proceed on a matter until both parties have signed a legally valid arbitration agreement, which

29. *See* Arbitration Act of 1996 § 1(1).

30. For a discussion on traditional procedures in Islamic adjudication, see WAEL B. HALLAQ, *SHARI'A*: THEORY, PRACTICE, TRANSFORMATIONS 342–54 (2009); VIKOR, *supra* note 3, at 168–221; ABDUR RAHIM, THE PRINCIPLES OF MUHAMMADAN JURISPRUDENCE ACCORDING TO THE HANAFI, MALIKI, SHAFII AND HANBALI SCHOOLS 364–82 (1911).

31. For a review of the traditional *tahkim* process, see MOHAMED M. KESHAVJEE, ISLAM, SHARIA AND ALTERNATIVE DISPUTE RESOLUTION: MECHANISMS FOR LEGAL REDRESS IN THE MUSLIM COMMUNITY 67–69 (2013).

32. *See, e.g.*, TABA JABIR AL-ALWANI, ISSUES IN CONTEMPORARY ISLAMIC THOUGHT 202 (2005) ("*Shari'a* does not provide for a specific procedural system, but leaves such details to the ijtihad and understanding of those responsible for ensuring that justice is done."); *see generally id.* at 196–225; TAHA JABIR AL-ALWANI, TOWARDS A *FIQH* FOR MINORITIES: SOME BASIC REFLECTIONS (Anas S. Shaikh-Ali & Shiraz Khan eds., 2003) (developing a framework for a renewal of *ijtihad*, or direct engagement and interpretation of the primary sources of Islamic law, in order to develop religious law doctrines that take into account the conditions and realities of life for Muslims living in non-Muslim political and legal contexts).

33. *See* MOHAMMAD KESHAVJEE, ISLAM, SHARIA, AND ALTERNATIVE DISPUTE RESOLUTION: MECHANISMS FOR LEGAL REDRESS IN THE MUSLIM COMMUNITY 67–68 (2013).

commits them to abiding by the MAT's ultimate decision and provides an adequate basis for enforcement of any award issued by the MAT in a British court.[34] Once an arbitration agreement is in place, a plaintiff can commence MAT proceedings by submitting a formal request asking the MAT to hear the case.[35] This written filing must state the plaintiff's claims and arguments in support thereof, contain the names of opposing parties and contact information for all the parties, and, if possible, list the documents and witnesses the plaintiff anticipates using as evidence in any arbitration hearing.[36] The rules provide that the MAT then serves notice on the defendant on behalf of the plaintiff, providing the defendant with information about the plaintiff's claims and evidence, thereby permitting the defendant an opportunity to prepare an adequate response.[37]

The MAT rules expressly provide for several key procedural protections considered indispensable to a fair adjudication by English law. Thus, the tribunal must give all parties adequate notice of all hearings,[38] permit litigants to be represented by attorneys,[39] and provide each party with an adequate opportunity to be heard by presenting claims and evidence and by rebutting the arguments and proofs offered by their opponents.[40] The MAT rules further provide standards for taking evidence; although parties may present oral or documentary evidence in support of their cases, the tribunal is prohibited from considering any evidence that is not made available to all parties.[41] The MAT rules also work to gain respect from the secular courts by providing that every arbitration tribunal must consist of at least one Islamic law scholar and one barrister or solicitor of England or Wales, thus ensuring that the arbitration process is conducted in accordance with both British ADR law and Islamic *fiqh*.[42]

Of course, the content of substantive law remains unclear—just like in the BDA. The MAT steadfastly refused (as did the BDA and the Institute for

34. *See* Mona Rafeeq, Comment, *Rethinking Islamic law Arbitration Tribunals: Are They Compatible with Traditional American Notions of Justice*, 28 Wisc. Int'l L.J. 108, 125 (2010).
35. *See Procedure Rules of the Muslim Arbitration Tribunal* § 2(1) (2010), Muslim Arbitration Tribunal, *available at* http://www.matribunal.com/rules.php (last visited Oct. 3, 2016).
36. *Id.* § 2(1)–(4).
37. *Id.* § 3(1).
38. *Id.* § 12.
39. *Id.* § 13(1)–(2).
40. *Id.* § 17.
41. *Id.* § 14(1)–(6).
42. *Id.* § 10(1).

Christian Conciliation (ICC)) to allow the reviewing secular court to consider what substantive Islamic law it applies. A MAT rule states that

(1) In arriving at its decision, the Tribunal may consider but not be bound by any previous decision of the Tribunal.
(2) In arriving at its decision, the Tribunal shall take into account the Laws of England and Wales and the recognized Schools of Islamic Sacred Law.[43]

Because decentralization is an internally important feature of Islamic law,[44] the traditional Islamic adjudication process also did not include a formal right of appeal. Traditionally, the Islamic judicial system was not formally hierarchical,[45] and the decision of any *qadi* was considered final and binding. The MAT, unlike the BDA, has chosen not to break with this traditional practice, and does not include an internal appellate procedure. Nevertheless, acknowledging that its arbitration process operates within the legal framework created by British law, MAT rules expressly acknowledge that a party may apply for judicial review of its arbitral awards.[46] In this respect, the MAT follows in the footsteps of some Islamic arbitration panels in Ontario, which, before being banned under a 2006 law, did not provide for internal appellate processes, but expressly permitted parties to appeal awards to a Canadian court.[47] Although an internal appellate procedure might give courts greater confidence in the procedural fairness of the MAT arbitration process, the lack of internal review has apparently not negated the MAT's legal credibility in the eyes of English judges, nor has it led to British courts refusing to enforce MAT awards.

Similarly, the MAT conducts its own arbitration processes in accordance with the legal requirements of British arbitration law to ensure that secular courts will have the legal authority to enforce its awards. In respecting these secular law standards, the MAT does not see itself as disregarding traditional *fiqh* procedures, but as building on Islamic law's normative adjudicatory framework in light of contemporary views about what procedures best protect litigants and ensure just outcomes.

43. *Id.* § 8.
44. *Cf.* MOHAMMAD HASHIM KAMALI, PRINCIPLES OF ISLAMIC JURISPRUDENCE 257 (3d ed. 2003).
45. *Cf.* AL-ALWANI, *supra* note 32, at xiii–xiv (2003).
46. *See Procedure Rules of the Muslim Arbitration Tribunal, supra* note 35, § 23.
47. *See* Donald Brown, Comment, *A Destruction of Muslim Identity: Ontario's Decision to Stop Shari'a-Based Arbitration*, 32 N.C.J. INT'L L. & COM. REG. 495, 522 (2007).

Like the BDA, the MAT has evidenced its respect for the secular legal environment in which it functions by admitting certain limitations on its own ability to act, based on the requirements of British law. Thus, the MAT affirms that "we believe in the co-existence of both English law and personal religious laws. We believe that the law of the land in which we live is binding upon each citizen . . . *Shari'a* does however have its place in this society where it is our personal and religious law."[48] Similarly, the Islamic *Shari'a* Council (ISC), a pre-eminent source of Islamic legal authority for British Muslims and an institution heavily involved in the facilitation of Islamic divorces, maintains that a couple must first document its receipt of a civil divorce from English judicial authorities before it will begin religious divorce proceedings.[49]

Similarly, although the MAT will exercise arbitral jurisdiction over civil and personal matters and resolve such cases in accordance with Islamic law, it will not adjudicate claims of criminal misconduct or apply corporal punishments prescribed by Islamic law for certain offenses.[50] Indeed, Islamic law precludes Muslim jurists from judging criminal matters or imposing corporal punishments for religious offenses in the absence of their being appointed to do so by the prevailing political authorities.[51]

The MAT, too, has embraced common commercial customs and equitable principles in its arbitration process, both to satisfy litigants and to gain the respect of British courts. Thus, MAT rules of procedure provide that "in arriving at its decision, the Tribunal shall take into account the Laws of England and Wales and the recognized Schools of Islamic Sacred Law."[52] The MAT's rules of decision include both Islamic and British standards, and it applies both, where appropriate, in order to arrive at effective legal solutions. The MAT's approach follows in the footsteps of the ISC, which holds itself not bound to apply the established rules of any particular school

48. *Values and Equalities of MAT*, Muslim Arbitration Tribunal (2010), http://www.matribunal.com/values.html. This exact sentence is no longer on the website. For a similar set of sentiments, see http://www.matribunal.com/values-and-principles.php (last visited Jan. 23, 2017).

49. *See* Application to File an Islamic Divorce (Dissolution/Khula/Talaq), *available at* http://www.islamic-sharia.org/wp-content/uploads/2014/05/Khula_Application0216.pdf (last visited Mar. 3, 2017).

50. *Compare generally* Leo Landman, Jewish Law in the Diaspora; Confrontation and Accommodation: A Study of the Development, Composition and Function of the Concept of Dina D'Malkhuta Dina—the Law of the Kingdom (The State) Is the Law (1968); *see also* R. Avraham Dov Kahane Shapiro, Teshuvot D'var Avrohom, no. 1:1 (3) (ruling that criminal matters are within the province of governmental authority and beyond legitimate *beit din* jurisdiction).

51. *See, e.g.*, ibn Naqib al-Misri, *supra* note 5, at 638.

52. *Procedure Rules of the Muslim Arbitration Tribunal, supra* note 35, § 8(2).

(*madhhab*) through *taqlid*,[53] but instead decides cases using *takhayyur*, an Islamic jurisprudential doctrine that urges jurists to rely on any of the traditional schools of Islamic law, or on marginal minority opinions about the law, in order to achieve compelling solutions in particular cases.[54] Additionally, the MAT and other Islamic arbitral tribunals have, according to Ihsan Yilmaz, been employing a sort of "neo-*ijtihad*," which enables Muslim jurists to issue rulings based on direct engagement with the primary sources of *fiqh*—the *Qur'an* and *Hadith*—in light of contemporary conditions in the United Kingdom, instead of relying on the rules already established by the various schools of Islamic law.[55] This approach enables the MAT to incorporate accepted standards of equity and commercial customs into its decisions in a way that is consistent with both the substance and the broader methodological concerns of Islamic jurisprudence.[56]

As in the case of the BDA, the MAT's success has been due in part to its ability to procure dual-trained individuals to head its tribunals. The MAT's founder, Hazrat Allama Pir Faiz-ul-Aqtab Siddiqi, is a British Muslim scholar and a barrister; he is also the principal of Hijaz College, a British Muslim school that combines traditional Islamic education with the British National Curriculum. The school also offers students the opportunity to receive an LLB degree, which qualifies graduates for the Bar-at-Law Finals and the Solicitors Law Society Legal Practitioners Course, which allows one to practice law in England.[57] Another MAT presiding judge, Shamim Qureshi, is also a judge in the Wolverhampton Magistrates' Court.[58]

53. *Taqlid* (literally, "imitation") refers to a method of Islamic legal decision-making in which the jurist relies on the rules of law contained in the principal codified works of his respective *madhhab*, rather than by directly engaging and interpreting the *Qur'an* and *Hadith*, the principle primary sources of Islamic law norms. *See* Kamali, *supra* note 44, at 493–94, 501–03.

54. *See* Ihsan Yilmaz, *Law as Chameleon: The Question of Incorporation of Muslim Personal Law into the English Law*, 21 J. MUSLIM MINORITY AFFAIRS 304 (2001).

55. *See* Ihsan Yilmaz, *Muslim Alternative Dispute Resolution and Neo-ijtihad in England, 2 Alternatives*, TURKISH J. INT'L REL. 117, 119–20 (2003). For more extensive discussions on neo-*ijtihad*, and the possibility of deriving Islamic religious law rulings directly from primary source interpretation in light of contemporary conditions for Muslim communities in the West, see generally JABIR AL-ALWANI, *supra* note 32; SHAMMAI FISHMAN, *FIQH AL-AQALIYYAT*: A LEGAL THEORY FOR MUSLIM MINORITIES IN RESEARCH MONOGRAPHS ON THE MUSLIM WORLD (Hudson Inst., Ser. No. 1, Paper No. 2, 2006), *available at* http://www.futureofmuslimworld.com/docLib/20061018 MonographFishman2.pdf.

56. *See* Rafeeq, *supra* note 34, at 124–25.

57. *See About Us*, HIJAZ COLL., http://www.hijazcollege.com/about.php; *LLB Law and BA Islamic law*, HIJAZ COLL., http://www.hijazcollege.com/llb-law.php (last visited Jan. 23, 2017).

58. *See* Robert Barr, Press Release, The Lord Chief Justice, Muslim Arbitration Tribunal, http://www.dailymail.co.uk/news/article-3391501/Crown-judge-

Although some MAT arbitrators are dual-system-fluent themselves, MAT rules further ensure that every MAT arbitration panel is competent in both British and Islamic law by providing that each shall consist of a minimum of one scholar of Islamic law and one solicitor or barrister of England and Wales.[59] The MAT also requires all of its arbitrators to be trained in a number of subjects related to dispute resolution, such as how to deal with adversarial parties, proper court behavior, and effective writing.[60] This training is meant to parallel the expertise that secular legal education provides British judges.[61] Although Islamic courts traditionally consisted of only a single judge, the MAT's reliance on multiple judges with complementary fields of expertise is not entirely unprecedented. Muslim judges, or *qadis*, have always been expected to be fully competent in a wide range of judicial skills, and have been directed to be aware of their own limitations and to consult experts whenever necessary.[62] In the early twentieth century, Bediuzzaman Said Nursi argued that individual judges were no longer effective due to the complexities of the modern era, and that committees of jurists would be better.[63] More recently, Fethullah Gülen, a Turkish scholar whose work focuses on Islam and Islamic law in the modern era, argued strongly for the use of *ijtihad* committees consisting of scholars from different disciplines and with different areas of expertise, reasoning that it is no longer possible for individuals to master all subjects.[64]

The MAT has taken an active role in the internal governance and external representation of the British Muslim community.[65] In addition to serving as a dispute resolution forum, the MAT has taken an active role in developing religio-legal standards for British Muslims by instructing them about what *Shari'a* might require in an Anglo context. For example, the MAT has become a leader in the field of dealing with forced arranged

rule-sharia-cases-court-set-hardline-cleric-led-demonstration-against-Charlie-Hebdo.html (last visited Jan. 23, 2017).

59. *See Procedure Rules of the Muslim Arbitration Tribunal, supra* note 35, § 10(1).

60. *See* Rafeeq, *supra* note 34, at 124–25.

61. *Id.*

62. *See generally* Ghulam Murtaza Azad, *Qualifications of a* Qadi, 23 Islamic Stud. 249 (1984).

63. *See* Ihsan Yilmaz, Muslim Laws, Politics, and Society in Modern Nation States: Dynamic Legal Pluralisms in England, Turkey, and Pakistan 135 n.3 (2005).

64. *See id.* at 176.

65. *See* Choksi, *supra* note 17, at 828 ("The MAT plays an active role in educating the Muslim and broader British community about the true nature of *Shari'a* law by dispelling myths that evolve through the conflation of religious law with cultural customs.").

marriages between British Muslim citizens and spouses in Muslim-majority countries such as Pakistan.[66] To alleviate this problem, the MAT suggested that British Muslims who want to bring a foreign spouse into the country first provide testimony before a panel of Muslim judges to establish that the arrangement is truly consensual.[67] The MAT also continues to work to educate the Muslim community that forced marriages are a cultural rather than religious phenomenon, and that they violate Islamic law.[68]

Additionally, in July 2013, the MAT assumed another internal religious and communal leadership role by undertaking an investigation in response to reports of the contamination of some meat certified as halal with pork. The MAT published its findings so as to offer British Muslims guidance and ideas for future improvements to halal certification.[69]

Beyond leading within the Muslim community, the MAT also serves as an effective representative for it to the British government and public by portraying Islamic law as sophisticated, nuanced, effective, and contemporarily relevant. Sadakat Kadri, a well-known barrister and author of the book *Heaven on Earth: A Journey through* Shari'a *Law from the Deserts of Ancient Arabia to the Streets of the Modern Muslim World*,[70] has argued that Islamic courts such as the MAT are good for the British Muslim community, because they put *Shari'a* on a transparent, public footing and make it more widely accessible to those who want it.[71] As a result of the MAT's efforts, British society has begun to accept Islamic arbitration, despite initial Islamophobia. In 2010, the MAT reported a 15 percent rise in the number of non-Muslims using *Shari'a* arbitration courts in commercial cases.[72]

66. *Id.* at 819–23.

67. *See Procedure Rules of the Muslim Arbitration Tribunal*, *supra* note 35, at 13.

68. *Id.* at 26; *id.* at 44 ("Arranged marriages have some grounding in Islamic law, but forced or coerced marriages have no foundations in Islamic law and shall be nullified under the edicts of Islamic tenets.").

69. *See Findings of a Public Community Inquiry*, MUSLIM ARBI. TRIB. (July 8, 2013), *available at* http://www.matribunal.com/downloads/MAT%20Public%20Declaration.pdf.

70. SADAKAT KADRI, HEAVEN ON EARTH: A JOURNEY THROUGH *SHARI'A* LAW FROM THE DESERTS OF ANCIENT ARABIA TO THE STREETS OF THE MODERN MUSLIM WORLD (2013).

71. David Shariatmadari, *Sharia Law Compatible with Human Rights, Argues Leading Barrister*, GUARDIAN (Jan. 15, 2012), http://www.guardian.co.uk/world/2012/jan/16/sharia-law-compatible-human-rights.

72. Afua Hirsch, *Fears over Non-Muslim's Use of Islamic Law to Resolve Disputes*, GUARDIAN (Mar. 14, 2010), http://www.guardian.co.uk/uk/2010/mar/14/non-muslims- sharia-law-uk.

C. ISLAMIC ARBITRATION IN THE UNITED STATES

There are approximately 2.6 million religiously observant Muslims in the United States today, up from about 1 million in the year 2000.[73] The number of mosques and other Islamic institutions in the United States has also grown, with over 2,100 congregations reported.[74] At present, Muslims who regularly attend mosque services are found in nearly 600 counties throughout the United States.[75]

The recent dramatic growth of the Muslim population in America has been accompanied by an increase in the need for Islamic arbitration to resolve Muslims' financial disputes, family conflicts, and marriage and divorce issues, all of which are governed by traditional *fiqh*. Islam has no official church and no institutional or organizational religious hierarchy that ties together the diverse Muslim communities throughout the United States. Instead, each congregation and each individual practices Islam in accordance with the religious and legal teachings of his or her chosen leaders.[76] Consequently, Islamic dispute resolution practices differ widely between communities and individual adjudicators, and there is little systematic understanding of the precise state of Islamic arbitration in the United States today on the macro or micro level.[77]

The few studies examining Islamic court practices in Canada and England may be taken as a general indication of the diversity among tribunals in the United States.[78] One 2004 study, sponsored by the Canadian Attorney General's office, solicited information about internal dispute resolution procedures from a variety of faith groups, and sheds light on the arbitral

73. *See* Meghan Neal, *Number of Muslims in the U.S. Doubles since 9/11*, N.Y. Daily News (May 3, 2012), http://www.nydailynews.com/news/national/number-muslims-u-s-doubles-9-11-article-1.1071895. These figures are based on numbers of people who self-identify as Muslim, and who regularly attend religious worship services. *Id.*

74. *Id.*

75. *See* U.S. Membership Report: Religious Traditions (2010), http://www.thearda.com/rcms2010/r/u/rcms201099USname2010.asp.

76. *See generally* Frank E. Vogel, Islamic Law and Legal System: Studies of Saudi Arabia 1–25 (Ruud Peters & Bernard Weiss eds., 2000).

77. For some indication of the diversity of Islamic religious court practices in connection with family law matters, see Asifa Quraishi & Najeeba Syeed-Miller, *No Altars: A Survey of Islamic Family Law in the United States*, *in* Women's Rights and Islamic Family Law: Perspectives on Reform 181–83 (Lynn Welchman ed., 2004).

78. Of course, the MAT, with its centralized organizational authority and its willingness to conduct religious arbitration proceedings in a variety of cities throughout England, has lent some measure of macro-level systemization to the Islamic dispute resolution scene in the United Kingdom.

procedures of one Sunni Muslim congregation, the Masjid El-Noor in Toronto.[79] A typical arbitration tribunal at the Masjid El-Noor consists of three members—the *imam*, one man, and one woman—selected from the mosque's mediation board, which includes the *imam* and six other members equally divided between men and women. Most board members are professionals who use their expertise to help resolve cases between members of their religious community.[80] The Masjid El-Noor arbitral board deals primarily with family matters, though it occasionally resolves commercial conflicts as well, employing a continuum of negotiation, mediation, and arbitration.[81] The study notes, however, that Canadian Muslims report that Islamic arbitration practices differ widely from tribunal to tribunal, and are often not as transparent, consent-based, or well-structured as those of the Masjid El-Noor, and that some Islamic courts in Canada flout state civil and criminal law with impunity.[82]

The state of Islamic courts in the United Kingdom further illustrates the diversity—and sometimes heavily veiled practices—of Islamic dispute resolution processes. Although today the MAT provides a network of relatively formal and transparent arbitral tribunals for British Muslims, it is not the only available forum. The Islamic *Shari'a* Council (ISC)[83] is a network of Islamic law decision-makers who operate outside the British arbitration framework and resolve family and civil disputes in accordance with Islamic law. The ISC follows more traditional *fiqh* procedures than the MAT, with fewer accommodations for English substantive and procedural laws.[84] Similar services are offered by other Islamic tribunals in England, including the Muslim Law Shariah Council,[85] as well as an extensive number of unconnected private Islamic law decisors who issue rulings to their followers using the procedural and substantive standards of their own respective

79. *See* Marion Boyd, Dispute Resolution in Family Law: Protecting Choice, Promoting Inclusion 59–68 (2004), *available at* http://www.attorneygeneral.jus.gov.on.ca/english/about/pubs/boyd/fullreport.pdf.

80. *Id.* at 60.

81. *Id.* at 61.

82. *See id.*; *see also* Brown, *supra* note 47, at 519–23.

83. *See* The Islamic Shari'a Council, http://www.islamic-sharia.org/ (last visited Jan. 23, 2017).

84. *See* Christopher R. Lepore, *Asserting State Sovereignty over National Communities of Islam in the United States and Britain: Sharia Courts as a Tool of Muslim Accommodation and Integration*, 11 Wash. U. Global Stud. L. Rev. 669, 682–85 (2012); *see also* Edna Fernandes, *Sharia Law UK: Mail on Sunday Gets Exclusive Access to a British Muslim Court*, Mail Online (July 4, 2009), http://www.dailymail.co.uk/news/article-1197478/Sharia-law-UK-How-Islam-dispensing-justice-side-British-courts.html.

85. *See* The Islamic Shari'a Council, http://www.islamic-sharia.org/ (last visited Jan. 23, 2017).

schools of Islamic law.[86] Islamic dispute resolution processes are likely even more diverse and hidden from the public eye in the United States than they are in England or Canada.[87]

Islamic arbitration is regarded with some suspicion by many Americans, as well as by segments of the United States' political and legal communities. These feelings of distrust result from uncertainty about much of what actually takes place in Islamic arbitrations in the United States, coupled with popular misunderstandings about the nature of Islamic law, and from Islamophobia fueled by a number of very vocal groups.[88] In 2010, Oklahoma passed a state constitutional amendment prohibiting state courts from recognizing or applying "*Shari'a* law."[89] Although this amendment was quickly enjoined and ultimately struck down by a federal court on First Amendment grounds,[90] more than a dozen other states are working to pass similar legislation with the hope that more careful drafting may enable it to pass constitutional muster.[91] A number of advocacy groups, through print, Internet, and advertising media, are attempting to discredit Islamic law and dispute resolution in America.[92] Canada has taken similar steps. The province of Ontario amended its arbitration laws in 2006 so as to effectively ban Islamic and other forms of religious arbitration.[93] England has been one of the Western countries most accommodating to Islamic religious dispute resolution, having incorporated MAT arbitral processes within the ambit of its own arbitration laws.[94] Nevertheless, some British lawmakers and public commentators have urged that limits be placed on

86. *See* Jonathan Wynne-Jones, *Sharia: A Law unto Itself?*, THE TELEGRAPH (Aug. 7, 2011), http://www.telegraph.co.uk/news/uknews/law-and-order/8686504/Sharia-a-law-unto-itself.html.

87. *See* QAMAR-UL HUDA, THE DIVERSITY OF MUSLIMS IN THE UNITED STATES: VIEWS AS AMERICANS (U.S. Inst. of Peace, Special Report 159, Feb. 2006), *available at* http://www.usip.org/sites/default/files/sr159.pdf (last visited Dec. 2, 2013); Christopher R. Lepore, *Asserting State Sovereignty over National Communities of Islam in the United States and Britain: Sharia Courts as a Tool of Muslim Accommodation and Integration*, 11 WASH. U. GLOBAL STUD. L. REV. 669, 685–86 (2012).

88. *See generally* WAJAHAT ALI ET AL., FEAR, INC.: THE ROOTS OF THE ISLAMOPHOBIA NETWORK IN AMERICA (2011), *available at* http://www.americanprogress.org/wp-content/uploads/issues/2011/08/pdf/islamophobia.pdf.

89. *See* Awad v. Ziriax, 670 F.3d 111 (10th Cir. 2012).

90. *Id.* at 119.

91. *See* John Witte, Jr. & Joel A. Nichols, *Who Governs the Family?: Marriage as a New Test Case of Overlapping Jurisdictions*, 4 FAULKNER L. REV. 321, 331–32 (2013).

92. *See, e.g.*, PAMELA GELLER, STOP THE ISLAMIZATION OF AMERICA: A PRACTICAL GUIDE TO THE RESISTANCE (2011) (warning of the creeping encroachment toward introducing Islamic law into the United States); ATLAS SHRUGS, http://atlasshrugs2000.typepad.com; JIHAD WATCH, http://www.jihadwatch.org (last visited Jan. 23, 2017).

93. *See* Choksi, *supra* note 17, at 791.

94. *Id.* at 810–18.

Islamic arbitration and that such processes be more rigorously scrutinized by secular authorities, and have proposed legislation to that effect.[95]

In recent years, some Muslim organizations have taken steps to better systematize and regulate Islamic dispute resolution processes in the United States. In 2010, the Assembly of Muslim Jurists of America (AMJA) at its annual Imams Conference considered the state of Islamic arbitration in the United States.[96] There, Islamic law scholars, as well as a Muslim attorney, presented papers on the theory and practice of Islamic dispute resolution, and on proposed improvements to Islamic arbitration practices in the American legal and social context. The Tabah Foundation, an Islamic law think tank based in Abu Dhabi, has also published a working paper that outlines a general framework for how Muslims living in Western countries might develop more effective and consistent dispute resolution processes consistent with Islamic law.[97]

The six pillars of effective religious arbitration in a secular legal context that have been used by the BDA, and adapted to Muslim needs by the MAT, offer observant Muslims living in the United States a roadmap for how they might construct their own arbitration institutions in a manner that will both satisfy the formal requirements of American arbitration law and promote understanding of and respect for Islamic dispute resolution processes. By developing procedural models that enable established Islamic arbitration organizations to function in accordance with the legal requirements of the American arbitration framework, American Muslims will make it legally possible for secular courts to enforce awards issued by Islamic arbitral tribunals.

However, the satisfaction of legal formalities, although necessary, is not sufficient to insure viable and efficacious Islamic arbitration for American Muslims. Muslims—like any community that seeks to develop effective internal ADR—must ensure that American courts are not only legally capable of, but also willing to, enforce Islamic arbitral awards.[98] In order to

95. *See* Amy S. Fancher, Note and Comment, *Policies, Frameworks, and Concerns Regarding* Shari'a *Tribunals in the United States—Are They Kosher?*, 24 REGENT U.L. REV. 459, 483–85 (2011).

96. TMO Stringer, *Imams' Conference Held in Houston*, MUSLIM OBSERVER (Oct. 21, 2010), http://muslimmedianetwork.com/mmn/?p=7103.

97. MUSA FURBER, ALTERNATIVE DISPUTE RESOLUTION: ARBITRATION & MEDIATIONS IN NON-MUSLIM REGIONS (Tabah Foundation, Tabah Analytic Brief No. 11, 2011), *available at* http://www.tabahfoundation.org/research/pdfs/Tabah_Research_ab_en_011.pdf.

98. The fact that a court has the formal power to enforce an arbitral award under the relevant state laws does not mean it will be willing to do so absent an understanding of and a respect for the arbitral process at issue. If this is true for ordinary ADR

develop arbitral institutions on par with the BDA and MAT, Muslims in the United States might therefore pursue a broader program for demonstrating that Islamic dispute resolution is not only technically legal, but also fair, professional, judicious, and respectful—in a word, respectable. The BDA and MAT experience shows that this goal may be achieved by following the six-pillar model outlined above (see pages 139–170). American Muslim religious arbitrators can help ensure the legal viability and effectiveness of their dispute resolution processes by (1) publishing legally sophisticated rules of procedure, (2) developing an internal appellate process, (3) exhibiting respect for both religious and secular legal norms, (4) acknowledging common commercial customs and equitable standards, (5) utilizing arbitrators with broad professional expertise in both religious and secular disciplines, and (6) taking an active role in governing and representing their constituent religious communities.

Importantly, the development of these kinds of arbitration processes need not require Muslims to reject their deep commitment to Islamic law. With expertise, creativity, and ingenuity, Islamic jurists interested in using the six-pillar model will be able to develop arbitral systems that conform

processes, it is doubly so with respect to arbitrations based on religio-legal norms. This is illustrated by the contrast between two recent cases in which American courts considered the enforceability of Jewish and Islamic religious marriage contracts. In one case, *Soleimani v. Soleimani* (Kan. Dist. Ct., Johnson Cty., No. 11CV4668, Aug. 28, 2012), *available at* http://www.volokh.com/wp-content/uploads/2012/09/soleimani.pdf, a Kansas court refused to uphold a *mahr* agreement when issuing a divorce decree to a Muslim couple. Although the court was empowered to enforce the couple's Islamic religious marriage contract—even under the state's now-infamous prohibition on its courts applying religious law, *see* Kan. Sess. Laws, Chap. 136, p. 1089–90 (2012)—the trial judge declined to do so for a variety of reasons related to public policy. *See generally* Eugene Volokh, *Court Refuses to Enforce Islamic Premarital Agreement That Promised Wife $677,000 in the Event of Divorce*, VOLOKH CONSPIRACY (Sept. 10, 2012, 8:19 AM), http://www.volokh.com/2012/09/10/court-refuses-to-enforce-islamic-premarital-agreement-that-promised-wife-677000-in-the-event-of-divorce/. In *Light v. Light*, 2012 Conn Super. LEXIS 2967 (Dec. 6, 2012), a Connecticut judge chose to enforce a religious prenuptial agreement developed for Jewish couples by the BDA. Notably, despite First Amendment arguments put forward by the husband, the judge in *Light* deigned to treat the religious document just like any other legally binding contract. *See* Paul Berger, *In Victory for "Chained" Wives, Court Upholds Orthodox Prenuptial Agreement*, JEWISH DAILY FORWARD (Feb. 8, 2013), http://forward.com/articles/170721/in-victory-for-chained-wives-court-upholds-o/?p=all. These cases illustrate—if only anecdotally—the importance of not only making sure that religious acts, whether contractual agreements or arbitral awards, are technically enforceable, but also of creating an environment in which the presiding judge feels comfortable enforcing that religious act. Absent such comfort, judges are likely to find some technical deficiency or broad "public policy" incompatibility that provides them with a way to avoid enforcement. *Cf.* Michael A. Helfand, *Religion's Wise Embrace of Commerce*, FIRST THINGS (Feb. 7, 2012), http://www.firstthings.com/onthesquare/2013/02/religionrsquos-wise-embrace-of-commerce.

to the requirements of American law while remaining firmly committed to Islamic religio-legal ideals. Thus, with respect to the practical implementation of the suggestions offered here, this author respectfully defers to the judgment of qualified Islamic law decisors, and merely recommends those measures which, based on the BDA's experience, would facilitate the full acceptance of Islamic arbitration by American courts.

In a 2011 brief that addresses the issue of Islamic dispute resolution in non-Muslim countries, Sheikh Musa Furber suggested that it might proceed along either of two legal approaches.[99] One would be for American Muslims to resolve conflicts through *qada*, a litigious adjudicatory process in which disputants offer claims and evidence before a *qadi* (official, communally appointed judge) who issues a final, binding verdict based on his or her own assessment of the facts and evidence and the applicable rules of Islamic law. Alternatively, it might proceed through *tahkim*, a less formalistic arbitral process in which disputants select third-party decision-makers and commit themselves to adhere to the arbitrators' *hukm*, or ruling issued in accordance with Islamic legal norms.[100] Both *qada* and *tahkim* largely rely on the same default rules of procedure and evidence.[101]

The chief distinction between *qada* and *tahkim* relates to the source of authority in the respective decision-making processes. *Qada* is grounded in public authority, and the power of the *qadi* to resolve a case derives from his appointment by the *imam* or *caliph*, or by the community over which he has jurisdiction. *Tahkim*, however, is based on private authority; the power of a *hakam*, or arbitrator, to issue binding decisions derives from the consent of the disputants who voluntarily appoint him or her to resolve a specific conflict.[102]

These different sources of adjudicatory authority suggest that *tahkim* rather than *qada* may be a more appropriate approach for American Islamic dispute resolution processes. *Qada* would entail the appointment of Muslim judges by discrete Muslim communities, and the case-by-case agreement by

99. *See* FURBER, *supra* note 97.

100. *See* NAQIB AL-MISRI, *supra* note 5, at 624 ("It is permissible for two parties to select a third party to judge between them if he is competent for judgeship . . . It is obligatory for them to accept his decision on their case."); SHEIKH BURHANUDDIN ABI AL HASAN ALI MARGHINANI, THE *HIDAYA*: COMMENTARY ON THE ISLAMIC LAWS 752 (Charles Hamilton, trans., Zahra Baintner, ed., 2005) ("If two persons appoint an arbitrator, and express their satisfaction with the award pronounced by him, such award is valid; because as these two person [*sic*] have a power with respect to themselves, they consequently possess a right to appoint an arbitrator between them, and his award is therefore binding upon them.").

101. *See* Mahdi Zahraa & Nora A. Hak, Tahkim *(Arbitration) in Islamic law within the Context of Family Disputes*, 20 ISLAMIC L.Q. 2, 3 (2006).

102. *Id.*

disputants to allow such communal authorities to resolve their conflicts. However, appointing communal judges and ensuring their continued support by the community would require a degree of communal organization and consensus that would be difficult to obtain and even harder to sustain, particularly in light of the internal diversity of American Muslim communities.[103] Also, the development of established, formal communal courts within the Muslim community might only appear to confirm popular suspicions that Muslims in America seek to set up a parallel society in which Islamic courts will impose *Shari'a* on unwilling subjects.[104] This would likely undermine attempts to promote understanding and respect for Islamic law in American courts, and would leave Muslims in the United States in no better a position than before. It may even result in Muslims losing ground in the battle for social acceptance in the American public sphere.[105]

Islamic dispute resolution institutions modeled on the *tahkim* framework would largely avoid these difficulties. Disputants could choose to rely on the services of any arbitration tribunal that met their needs in terms of location, nature of the dispute, character and expertise of the arbitrators, and *madhhab*. Organizations offering *tahkim* would not need to wait for elusive communal endorsement, or be concerned about maintaining communal support beyond properly resolving individual cases. Also, a system of independent arbitration organizations offering dispute resolution services to American Muslims on a voluntary basis would be unlikely to create the impression of a parallel justice system.[106]

Islamic arbitration organizations can satisfy American arbitration law requirements and earn the respect of American judges by developing and publishing sophisticated rules of procedure to regulate their dispute resolution processes, and to provide litigants with a clear indication of what to expect. American law rests heavily on guarantees of procedural due

103. *See* Fancher, *supra* note 95, at 479–80 (observing that the diversity within Islam due to the several different schools of law has resulted in some British Muslims opposing established religious courts out of concern that they will impose the *fiqh* of one *madhhab* on Muslims who adhere to another).

104. *Id.* at 459, 483 (noting that Islamic religious tribunals' styling themselves as courts with inherent authority has resulted in criticism, suspicion, and backlash in Britain).

105. *Id.* at 481–83.

106. *Tahkim* may also be a useful avenue for pursuing effective Islamic arbitration in the United States because the framework for *tahkim* in traditional *fiqh* is, like arbitration in American law, based largely on disputants' agreement to submit their case to a third-party arbitrator, and is also heartily endorsed by all schools of Islamic jurisprudence, albeit with some minor disagreements as to some related issues. *See* Rafeeq, *supra* note 34, at 121–22.

process, and courts will likely not feel comfortable upholding the decisions of Islamic arbitrators unless their tribunals adopt and implement certain procedural safeguards. To develop formal, legalistic rules of procedure, Islamic arbitral tribunals might restate traditional Islamic procedural rules in legalistic English familiar to American judges, and publish codes of Islamic procedural law that mimic the structure and format, if not the content, of American ones. This could help the American legal community better understand the legal nature of Islamic arbitration, and help American judges feel more comfortable enforcing the results of that process.

However, simply translating traditional Islamic procedural law into terms and formats familiar to American lawyers will not be sufficient. To empower courts to enforce their awards, Islamic arbitration tribunals will have to respect the procedural requirements imposed by the FAA, which include basic due process rights to notice, representation by counsel, and the right to a fair and impartial hearing. Although arbitrators possessing adequate dual-system fluency may find that traditional *tahkim* practices will satisfy some of these requirements, they may not fulfill them all.[107] If so, Islamic jurists in the United States might consider whether various devices of Islamic jurisprudence (*usul-ul-fiqh*) might justify procedural changes to traditional *tahkim*. For example, Muslim jurists might consider the possibility that *darurah* (need and the prevention of harm) or *maslahah* (the functional ends served by Islamic legal rules) might justify the use of alternative procedural rules consonant with American legal requirements under the principle of *istisan* (the articulation of exceptions from existing legal norms). Alternatively, jurists might consider whether the jurisprudential principle that *urf* (generally accepted customary practice) can be a source of law that might permit the adoption of procedural rules considered normative in the West, as well in many Muslim-majority countries, but not included as part of traditional procedural *fiqh*.[108] Here, American Muslims might choose to follow the example of the MAT.

107. One commonly raised concern about the incompatibility of Islamic law norms with legal requirements of the American arbitration framework includes gender inequalities related to the disparate weight given to the testimony of male and female witnesses, and their respective rights to appear before an Islamic tribunal.

108. For a brief but poignant treatment of the possibility of using *istisan* premised on *darurah, maslahah,* or custom to override normative *fiqh* even absent textual support in the *Qur'an* or *Hadith* for such alternative rulings, see generally MOHAMMAD HASHIM KAMALI, EQUITY AND FAIRNESS IN ISLAM 36–44 (2005). *See also id.* at 7 (discussing the possibility of *istisan* serving as a basis for permitting changes to traditional Islamic rules of evidence recognizing only oral testimony in light of the modern evidentiary possibilities created by film, and sound recording, and DNA, fingerprint, and other laboratory testing for physical evidence).

Islamic dispute resolution tribunals in the United States should also accept that if they want their rulings upheld by American courts, they cannot operate in a vacuum. If American Muslims want judges to respect their Islamic arbitration processes, those processes must in turn demonstrate respect for American law and the American legal system. Islamic arbitration processes must also offer due consideration for prevailing commercial customs and principles of equity and fairness, which may be used to temper the strict requirements of normative *fiqh*.

In the eyes of American courts, Muslim litigants that come before Islamic arbitral tribunals, as well as the Muslim arbitrators themselves, are subject to American law. Thus, if Islamic arbitral tribunals want their awards upheld by American courts, they will have to accept jurisdictional limitations imposed by American law, which may preclude them from resolving some kinds of cases or offering certain kinds of remedies, even if such matters are within the jurisdictional competence of traditional Islamic courts. Use of the *tahkim* model as the paradigm for Islamic dispute resolution in the United States may help alleviate some of these tensions. Although Islamic law generally authorizes disputants to select third-party arbitrators to resolve disputes, it also prohibits arbitrators from deciding cases involving offenses against God—the so-called *hudud* crimes that necessitate corporal punishment. Muslim arbitrators in the United States might thus avoid incurring a religious obligation to perform judicial functions prohibited by American law by constituting arbitral tribunals as a form of *tahkim* rather than *qada*.

Respect for the exclusive jurisdiction of the secular justice system to address criminal offenses and impose criminal penalties is also likely unproblematic from the perspective of traditional *fiqh*. In American law, criminal proceedings and punishments are premised on the prosecution by the public itself of offenses against society. Islamic law, by contrast, does not contemplate the notion of offenses against the public, or the prosecution of a claim by any collective body. Instead, traditionally, Islamic courts only resolved private actions between individuals, and left public-law matters such as the prosecution of criminal offenses against society to the *siyasa-Shari'a* courts and laws of Muslim rulers. Thus, American Muslim jurists can likely find ways to constitute formal, institutionalized arbitration tribunals to enforce most aspects of Islamic law between Muslims while also respecting the exclusive jurisdiction of state authorities over criminal matters.

Furthermore, as some prominent organizations that issue fatwas for Muslims living in America have noted, Muslims have a religious duty to abide by the laws of the country they live in, especially when those laws do not directly contradict their religious duties.[109] Consequently, Muslim arbitrators may avoid resolving criminal matters by respecting their religious duty to abide by American law, which prohibits nonstate actors from exercising criminal jurisdiction. This is particularly so in light of the fact that many jurists maintain that Islamic courts constituted in Western countries do not have an absolute religious duty under Islamic law to exercise jurisdiction, even over *hudud* offenses.[110]

Unlike *halakha*, Islamic law does not embrace custom (*urf*) as a formal source of law.[111] American Muslims would thus not likely be able to follow the path taken by the BDA of incorporating prevailing commercial practices into their arbitral rulings on the grounds that such customs themselves constitute the substance of religio-legal norms. However, Islamic law *does* recognize that commercial customs may establish the implicit terms under which parties engage in a wide range of commercial relationships: "What is known among merchants is as if stipulated among them."[112] Islamic law thus incorporates the common expectations and practices prevalent in a particular place at a particular time into all matters of interpersonal relationships, especially with respect to commerce.[113] Islamic arbitral tribunals might thus use the concept of *urf* in order to respect common commercial customs, which often form the foundation of disputants' relationships and condition their expectations. Incorporating prevailing commercial customs into their decisions will also help Islamic arbitral tribunals earn the respect of the secular courts as the latter will come to recognize Islamic ADR as a familiarly legalistic dispute resolution process.

Islamic legal history further suggests that Muslim arbitrators in the United States could decide to employ equitable solutions in cases where rulings in strict compliance with normative *fiqh* would be viewed as unfair by American courts. One example may be taken from Islamic inheritance law, an area of *Shari'a* that has faced considerable public criticism in the

109. *See, e.g., Plural Marriage in the U.S.*, ASSEMBLY OF MUSLIMS JURISTS OF AMERICA (Sept. 6, 2010), *available at* http://www.amjaonline.org/fatwa-82452/info.

110. Shaykh Abdullah bin Bayyah, *Muslims Living in Non-Muslim Lands* (speech delivered Santa Clara, CA, July 31, 1999), *transcript available at* http://www.sunnah.org/articles/muslims_in_nonmuslim_lands.htm ("rules . . . such as the penal code of the Muslims . . . are not the concern of those people who are living in a land in which there is not a legitimate state authority of Muslims.").

111. *See generally* GIDEON LIBSON, JEWISH AND ISLAMIC LAW: A COMPARATIVE STUDY OF CUSTOM DURING THE GEONIC PERIOD (2003).

112. The Medjelle of Ottoman Civil Law, art. 44 (W.E. Gringby trans., London, Stevens and Sons 1895); *see also id.* at art. 33 ("What is accepted custom is like a stipulated condition."); *see generally* KAMALI, *supra* note 44, at 369–83 (2003).

113. *See* Gideon Libson, *On the Development of Custom as a Source of Law in Islamic Law*, 4 ISLAMIC L. & SOC'Y 131, 152–54 (1997).

West.[114] Normative rules dictate that the uterine brothers of a deceased female take one-third of her estate, whereas germane brothers have only a residuary interest in whatever remains of the estate after all other heirs receive their respective portions. In one case, however, the Caliph Umar al-Khattab ruled that both a half brother from a common mother, as well as a full brother, should take a collective third of the estate as an equitable measure.[115] Although this rule was adopted by some Islamic *madhhabs* and rejected by others, it, along with other examples,[116] suggests that Islamic jurists in the United States might find ways to temper the strict application of normative rules in order to achieve results that are more equitable to the parties, and that seem more just to American judges.

American Muslims seeking to create Islamic arbitration panels whose awards will be upheld by American courts may want to cultivate a group of arbitrators trained in both traditional *fiqh* and American law. The BDA found that arbitration awards based on religio-legal norms invoke more cursory review by American judges when they are arrived at and written by arbitrators with secular legal training. Judges tend to assume that arbitral awards written using familiar legal terminology and reasoning are reasonable and legally sound, even when such forms are mere window dressing for rulings grounded in unfamiliar religio-legal rules. Accordingly, Islamic arbitration tribunals would benefit from the professional expertise of Muslim lawyers trained at recognized American law schools. Not only will American judges come to trust the arbitral decisions issued by fellow members of the bar, but the presence of Muslim lawyers on Islamic arbitration panels will assist Islamic tribunals in navigating the American legal field. American Muslims might also find it useful to follow the BDA and MAT by employing arbitrators who are both Islamic jurists and trained lawyers. The Muslim community in the United States might take a special interest in sending students of traditional *fiqh* who want to work as Islamic arbitrators to study in American law schools, or in helping Muslim attorneys pursue rigorous *fiqh* training.

Additionally, like the BDA and the MAT, Islamic arbitral organizations may want to cultivate a cadre of observant Muslims trained in various

114. *See, e.g.*, Maria Reiss, Note, *The Materialization of Legal Pluralism in Britain: Why Shari'a Council Decisions Should Be Non-binding*, 26 Ariz. J. Int'l & Comp. L. 739, 756–58 (2009).

115. *See* Kamali, *supra* note 108, at 44.

116. *See, e.g.*, *id.* at 61 (relating that the Caliph Uthman equitably permitted a divorced woman to inherit from her deceased husband's estate despite the normal rule that a divorce cuts off a wife's right to inherit because, in that case, the husband divorced his wife while on his deathbed as a means of preventing her from taking a share in his estate after his death).

professions and trades, and encourage such individuals to take an active role in the Islamic arbitration process. Muslim doctors, accountants, finance experts, psychologists, construction workers, merchants, and laborers might function as arbitrators alongside Islamic jurists and trained lawyers, serve as "court witnesses" for established tribunals, and provide reliable, non-adversarial expert testimony to ensure that Muslim arbitrators make decisions with a complete picture of all the relevant facts and after having addressed all the issues raised by particular cases. Reliance on such experts has ample precedent in traditional Islamic dispute resolution, and Sheikh Taha Jabir al-Alwani has argued that reliance on experts is essential if Muslim jurists are to reach correct decisions when applying normative *fiqh* in American contexts.[117]

The BDA's experience shows that there must be more than just formal juridical rapprochement between *Shari'a* and American law if the Muslim-American community is to establish arbitration tribunals that can work in harmony with the American legal system. Muslim-Americans will also have to show that their hyphenated identity is not a contradiction. Muslims must ensure that Americans do not view Islam as a threat to their culture, but rather as a religion that should be protected under the First Amendment. The need for Muslim-Americans to "prove" themselves to be non-threatening, contributing members of American society is not unique to the Muslim experience. Many religious communities, including Jews, were seen as a threat when they first tried to establish themselves on American soil, and Muslim-Americans can learn from their religious compatriots' experiences in this area. For example, Catholic-Americans were for a long time forced to bear the anti-Catholic biases of many Protestant Americans,[118] and Mormons, though part of American society, are still subject to significant prejudice and, in some cases, mockery.[119]

The *Fiqh* Council of North America, an important organization of American Islamic law scholars that issues *fatwas* on many matters of concern to Muslims living in the United States, has taken measures to legitimate Muslims and Islam in American society by demonstrating that Muslims are religiously obligated to be good citizens. For example, the Council has confirmed for the American Muslim community that "Islamic

117. *See generally* JABIR AL-ALWANI, *supra* note 32.

118. PHILIP JENKINS, THE NEW ANTI-CATHOLICISM: THE LAST ACCEPTABLE PREJUDICE 23 (2003).

119. J. Spencer Fluhman, *Why We Fear Mormons*, N.Y. TIMES, June 3, 2012, at A25, *available at* http://www.nytimes.com/2012/06/04/opinion/anti-mormonism-past-and-present.html.

teachings require respect of the laws of the land where Muslims live as a minority groups, including the Constitution and the Bill of Rights, so long as there is no conflict with Muslims' obligation for obedience to God. We do not see any such conflict with the U.S. Constitution and Bill of Rights."[120]

D. CHRISTIAN DISPUTE RESOLUTION IN AMERICA

There is an important difference between Christian arbitration in the United States and the faith-based dispute resolution processes of Islam and Judaism. Both Judaism and Islam are nomos-centric religion traditions. This means that in each of these faiths, religious virtue is most typically understood to be a function of adherents' observance of a range of behavioral norms, and that these norms are determined using jurisprudential systems of sources and methods that in numerous respects mimic secular law. This is important because it means that the religious arbitration processes of nomos-centric faith traditions are basically legalistic, and embrace many of the procedural protections and substantive forms of ordinary adjudication. Even when religious norms and procedures depart from secular standards—as they inevitably do—the basic contours of Jewish and Islamic dispute resolution are easily recognizable for what they are: a kind of rule of law system in which litigants' conflicts are resolved by third-party decision-makers applying relatively stable and known rules in predictable and methodologically consistent ways.

Christian arbitration in the United States has a somewhat different character. Most forms of Christianity are not law-based in the same way as are Judaism and Islam. Although Judaism and Islam are concerned with rules and principles, decision-making procedures, judicial institutions, and normative religio-legal authority, law is not the central feature of Christian—and certainly not Protestant Christian—religious life. As we have observed elsewhere:

> The Christian (and particularly Protestant) mindset simply does not view "laws," "rules," or "obligations," as the central framework upon which to consider complex issues of [religious] society. Many other virtues, including "love" and

120. Muzammil Siddiqi, *Being Faithful Muslims and Loyal Americans*, Fiqh Council of North America, http://fiqhcouncil.org/node/10 (last visited Jan. 23, 2017).; *see also* Marshall Breger, *Why Jews Can't Criticize Sharia Law*, Moment Mag., 1 Jan./Feb. 2012, at 18 ("Muslim jurists have always drawn on sharia to mandate that fellow Muslims obey the laws of the land in matters that sharia does not prohibit.").

"piety" successfully compete with "rules" or "precedent" for the heart and soul of society in a Christian community, and serve as central features of Christian jurisprudence."[121]

Certainly, there is nothing wrong with a jurisprudence of love. It may be an appropriately lofty religious ideal. However, when such a broad and vague principle is used as a basis for normative judgments and dispute resolution, almost any disposition can be reasonably justified. Arguably, then, Christian faith-based dispute resolution can be less rigorous and less legalistic—though certainly just as religiously important to Christians—than the kinds of Jewish or Islamic arbitration described above.

Despite this lack of formal legal materials and methods upon which to base their processes and decisions, some Christian arbitration organizations have affirmatively adopted measures like the BDA and MAT's rules in order to create a more regulated, transparent, and predictable process that will respect secular law arbitration requirements. The Institute for Christian Conciliation (ICC), for instance, has developed the kind of rules-governed arbitration process that gives secular court judges confidence in the professionalism, objectivity, and reasonableness of this religious dispute resolution method. The Rules of the Institute for Christian Conciliation provide for the selection of arbitrators, discovery procedures, adequate notice for parties regarding upcoming arbitration meetings, limits on communication between parties and arbitrators to preserve impartiality, the transcription of proceedings to better ensure transparency and fairness, opportunities to present and rebut evidence and arguments, and opportunities for appeal and reconsideration.[122]

Perhaps most important, the ICC's rules expressly consider the potential for conflicts between the rules and secular state or federal law, as well as tensions between the substantive norms and values the Christian arbitrations seek to uphold and standards set forth in secular law. In both cases, the ICC's rules affirm the essentially religious nature of its faith-based dispute resolution process, while also conceding ultimate legal authority to the laws of the state. Rule 42, for instance, provides that if "these Rules vary from state or federal arbitration statutes, these Rules shall control except where the state or federal rules specifically indicate that they may not be superseded." Rule 4 likewise seeks to strike a delicate integrative

121. *See* Michael J. Broyde, *Faith-Based Private Arbitration as a Model for Preserving Rights and Values in a Pluralistic Society*, 90 Chi.-Kent L. Rev. 111 (2015).
122. *See* http://peacemaker.net/wp-content/uploads/2015/02/F-GUIDELINES-PART-IV-RULES-OF-PROCEDURE-FOR-CC-V-4.6.pdf.

balance between religious commitments and secular norms. It states that "Conciliators shall take into consideration any state, federal, or local laws that the parties bring to their attention, but the Holy Scriptures (the Bible) shall be the supreme authority governing every aspect of the conciliation process."

E. CONCLUSION

In terms of gaining acceptance in the eyes of the American legal and social community, there is a difference between the path taken by the Jewish community and the ones that the Muslim community might pursue. This difference is due to the disparate historical backgrounds of the two minority groups. The Jewish community transitioned from being a minority in one country (or countries) to being a minority in another. Therefore, it was able to utilize the tools it had already developed to acclimate to its new surroundings. Culturally and juridically, Jews had already accepted the position of being a diaspora population even before they landed on American soil. Muslim-Americans, on the other hand, like the Catholic and Mormon communities, have had to adjust to being a minority in American society after spending centuries (in the case of the Mormons, a century) as the controlling, majority population in the areas they inhabited. This difference is not only one of degree, in the sense that due to their diasporic experience, Jews were able to more quickly integrate themselves into American society. Rather, the manner in which Jewish and Muslim inclusion into the American mainstream becomes possible is different given their different social and cultural backgrounds.

The Muslim-American community may wish to acknowledge that, though it is similar to the Jewish community in terms of sharing a religio-legal foundation, the Jewish-American community may not be a good model for the purpose of social integration. A better model may be found in the Muslim-British community, which has had to deal with the specific issue of how to transition from being a part of a majority or controlling population to being a minority one.

Religious liberty is ingrained into the American legal and cultural psyche by the First Amendment, which prohibits both the proscription of religion (i.e., any action that unduly burdens a person's conscience, restricts his or her religious expression and activity, discriminates against religion, or undermines the autonomy of religious bodies), as well as prescriptions of religion (i.e., any action that coerces a person's conscience, mandates religious expression and activity, discriminates in favor of a religion or improperly allies government with a religious body).[123] The ideals of the First Amendment, however, cannot fully protect in fact religions that are seen to threaten American society.[124] Particularly in this day and age, Islam has a long list of detractors. If the Muslim-American community wishes to effectively establish Islamic arbitration courts in America, it might first and foremost address its social and cultural notoriety before it considers the juridical sacrifices it must make. This does not mean that Muslim-Americans must totally assimilate or abandon their identities; rather, it means demonstrating that there is no inconsistency between loyalty to America and loyalty to Islam. The Muslim spirit, the product of the Islamic religion and Muslims' experiences, must be seen as essentially modern and essentially American.

It is very important to appreciate the unique boons conferred on religious freedoms through the FAA, which protects private dispute resolution though arbitration by religious communities. This protection provides a viable option for maintaining religious communities that wish to organize themselves around values they no longer share with an increasingly tolerant and neutral secular law.

Traditional communities ought to recognize that, in matters regarding which they hold cultural values that are different from the majority of the polity, they can—and, if they are to stay viable, sometimes must—opt out of society's legal structure to avoid being suffocated. Private arrangement of family matters can be a viable option for those who, for example, do not believe in unilateral no-fault divorce, do not believe in divorce, or do not believe in marriage. This is true whether one is speaking about Jewish courts, *Shari'a* courts, Evangelical Christian courts, Catholic canon law courts, or Hindu tribunals. Whatever the differences, if religious communities avoid suffocating in this secular atmosphere, it will be because the secular society recognizes the right of parties to contract out of the general law. Those communities wise enough to take advantage of the six principles necessary to successfully opt out and build religious arbitration tribunals will flourish. These communities will be gloriously different, each in its own way, each sharing its religious values in a grand whole, and each exercising the freedom to maintain its own set of beliefs and practices within the majestic mosaic of diverse communities that make up our United States.

123. John Witte, Jr., *The Future of Muslim Family Law in Western Democracies*, *in* Sharia in the West? 289 (Rex Ahdar & Nicholas Aroney eds., 2010).

124. There is a long history of the tension between protecting religious liberty and protecting the American ethos. For a colonial example where the religion that threatened America was Catholicism, see *id.* at 74.

PART FOUR

CHAPTER 9

The Case against Religious Arbitration

A. INTRODUCTION

For nearly twenty years, I served as an arbitrator in the Beth Din of America, first as the consultant hired to write the rules that are still used by the BDA, then as the director, and then as one of the four standing members of the rabbinical court. During that time, I grew to appreciate what a successful religious court did, and how it helped shape a religious community. As in all communities, "justice" and "law obedience" are very important values within the Jewish tradition, and as in many communities, crafting a process for enforcing religious norms that are successful is not a simple task. Communities that fail to provide justice to their members consistently and regularly, one suspects, fail as thicker communities. Religious communities also fail when they are not sources of justice, both on a theoretical level and a practical one. So the virtues of having a functioning religious legal system, including a court system, that can "compel" (at least after the litigants agree to be "compelled") plays a very important role in community formation and development—and even more so to those religious communities that are law based.

The first few chapters of this work go far to demonstrate that the formation of religious communities in America is dramatically assisted by the modern rise of contract law as the central touchstone of dispute resolution: arbitration law works to provide religious legal systems with a model of secular law with which it can successfully interact.

This is in contrast to a secular legal system that functions based on its sacrament—not only marriage sacrament, but sacrament in all areas of the

Sharia Tribunals, Rabbinical Courts, and Christian Panels. Michael J. Broyde.

law—which looks at people and communities with alternative legal rules and denies them the right to be adjudicated by any legal rules other than the law of the state, because the state's legal rules are sacred, so that even if the parties wish to apply them, the legal system refuses to do so.[1]

If Justice Benjamin Cardozo (in his classic work *The Paradoxes of Legal Science*) is correct that law is a search for truth in the same manner that science is a search for truth, then he is also correct when he tells us that "If jurisdiction is to be ousted by contract, we must submit to the failure of justice that may result from these and like causes." And he is also correct then when he disallows all arbitration.[2] But, as we have explained in various prior chapters, this is not the pathway our American legal system has taken. Rather, both choice of law and choice of forum (including private arbitration) are considered proper. For example, if there is one characteristic of the Uniform Commercial Code that is central, it is that almost any of its provisions may be modified by agreement of the parties.[3] Our American legal system is moving faster and faster into contract as the foundational doctrine.

Under a system that takes contract as a foundational doctrine, religious communities with well-written religious arbitration contracts will grow, thrive, and prosper.

1. For an example of this, see Shelley v. Kraemer, 334 U.S. 1 (1948), which applies to racial matters. Although this requires more analysis, *Shelley* is undoubtedly correct in its analysis of racial matters exactly because the choice to discriminate based on race is constitutionally suspect. The single greatest challenge politically to religious arbitration agreements remains, I suspect, the sense (perhaps even true in certain settings) that religious arbitration discriminates based on values that secular society views as not proper to discriminate. I would suggest however, that *Shelley* is unusual in that the contract in *Shelley* was designed to impact those who had not signed it (by creating covenants that ran with the land). Parties ought to have the right to construct their more private matters with values that otherwise discriminate. For example, most states have doctrines of sexual freedom that protect the right to commit adultery (see, for example, People v. Onofre, 415 N.E.2d 936, 943 (N.Y. 1980)), but that does not mean that parties cannot agree in a prenuptial agreement that such conduct is to be financially penalized by contract. *See also* Note, *Racial Steering in the Romantic Marketplace*, 107 HARV. L. REV. 877 (1994) (discussing societal tolerance for racial steering in personal ads).

2. Meacham v. Jamestown, J. & C. R. Co, 105 N.E. 653, 655 (N.Y. 1914) (Cardozo, J., concurring) (emphasis added) (internal citation omitted).

3. Variation By Agreement:

> Except as otherwise provided in subsection (b) or elsewhere in [the Uniform Commercial Code], the effect of provisions of [the Uniform Commercial Code] may be varied by agreement.
>
> . . .
>
> The presence in certain provisions of [the Uniform Commercial Code] of the phrase "unless otherwise agreed", or words of similar import, does not imply that the effect of other provisions may not be varied by agreement under this section.

U.C.C. § 1-302 (1977).

But, what has yet to be addressed is whether this is really a good idea from the perspective of a Western liberal society. Is the rise of religious arbitration a good idea for the general liberal community? This chapter and the next are an attempt to answer that question in the affirmative and explain why a secular society ought to encourage—actually promote the growth of—religious arbitration (albeit within contractual limits). We begin in this chapter by outlining the case against religious arbitration.

B. ONE LAW FOR ONE PEOPLE

Contemporary Western societies are diverse places. Individuals are often bound up in a complex array of cross-cutting authorities and normative allegiances owing to concurrent national, cultural, ethnic, racial, class, gender, and religious identities. According to many commentators, although it is important for the liberal state to be respectful of this de facto normative pluralism, the state should not afford such multiple, conflicting normative systems the status of law. In this regard, there is a valuable distinction to be made between "normative pluralism" on the one hand, and "legal pluralism" on the other. Legal pluralism connotes the idea that "multiple legal systems exist alongside state law on equal footing, and that citizens of the state have a wide amount of discretion to choose which legal system should apply to their lives."[4] Normative pluralism, by contrast, refers to the idea that although it may be important for the state to be respectful of the various nonstate norms and value systems to which individuals feel bound, the state ought not to grant those systems the force of state law.[5] Proponents of religious arbitration typically advocate for a legally pluralistic relationship between the state and other normative systems observed by its citizens, but opponents of secular enforcement of religious arbitration push for a more limited, normative pluralism model.

Normative pluralism opponents of secular recognition of religious arbitration have offered a number of arguments supporting this position. First, some contend, quite sensibly, that it is necessary for any society to have only a single legal order in which all citizens are bound by, and for all societal relationships to be governed by the same set of norms.[6] Law is a reflection of and a means of actualizing policy, and policy, in turn, represents society's

4. Amanda M. Baker, *A Higher Authority: Judicial Review of Religious Arbitration*, 37 Vt. L. Rev. 157, 190 (2012).

5. *See* William Twinning, *Normative and Legal Pluralism: A Global Perspective*, 20 Duke J. Comp. & Int'l L. 473, 475–85 (2010).

6. *See* Charles Taylor, *The Politics of Recognition*, *in* Multiculturalism: Examining the Politics of Recognition 25, 43–44 (Amy Gutmann, ed., 1994).

collective vision of the substantive, procedural, and constitutional terms on which public-sphere—and even many private-sphere—relationships should be ordered. Permitting the simultaneous existence of multiple conflicting legal orders, many of which may be reflective of deeply differing values, undermines society's ability to structure itself in accordance with majoritarian preferences.[7] Moreover, such legal factionalism undercuts one of the more important bonds that helps hold liberal societies together: a common commitment to core norms and values.[8] Liberal societies value individual autonomy, disagreement, debate, and conflicting visions of the good all vying for public recognition. Despite such dissonance, liberal democracies largely manage to hold together very diverse populations made up of numerous interest groups precisely because all are committed to contingently abide by the legal and political results of democratic processes. You may win today's election or today's legislative vote, but I will have the opportunity to effect change more in line with my own preferences next time around, and I can expect that you will abide by the results of my political successes precisely because I agree to abide by the results of your own. Permitting discrete groups to opt out of societal laws and policies through religious arbitration undermines this sense of collective commitment to make society work. Rather than playing by the rules and respecting the results, religious groups are allowed to simply withdraw from the game and play by themselves whenever they happen to not like the outcome.

Additionally, opponents of religious arbitration contend that legal pluralism rests on a very thin theory of justice, one that is inadequate to meet the standards of contemporary liberal commitments. At its root, the kind of legal pluralism that would support secular recognition and enforcement of alternative legal systems through religious arbitration views numerous normative systems as equally valid. Not only should individuals and communities be able to abide by such systems on a purely voluntary basis, but the state should even hold people to the commitments they make to such systems. Such a theory of justice is basically a procedural one. It maintains that society ought not to make substantive value judgments about the content of the norms and values that citizens wish to live by.[9] Instead, as long as individuals have made free-willed choices to order their lives and affairs in accordance with certain rules, the state ought to respect those

7. *Cf.* BRIAN BARRY, CULTURE AND EQUALITY (2001) (arguing that the multicultural agenda undermines liberalism's core commitment to equality).

8. *See generally* Michael A. Helfand, *Religious Arbitration and the New Multiculturalism: Negotiating Conflicting Legal Orders*, 86 N.Y.U. L. REV. 1231, 1272–76 (2011).

9. As explained in Chapters Five and Six of this book.

decisions, and even enforce such commitments in order to protect the interests of those for whose benefit they were made. This thin theory of justice is incompatible with many contemporary theories of liberal justice, which hold that the rule of law is not merely procedural, and that societal norms cannot be grounded in consent alone. Instead, these theories hold that societal commitments are, at least in important part, about maintaining a commitment to certain fundamental rights that cannot and should not be alienated.[10]

In truth, the "one people one law" argument presented above is likely the weakest challenge to secular enforcement of religious arbitration. In the United States in particular, the claim rings hollow. Like it or not, there is not now, nor has there ever really been only one law of the land in the United States. This country's basic federalist framework is built on the idea that there is no single "correct" law that should apply to all Americans all the time. Unlike many other nations that have uniform national laws, the United States maintains a much deeper commitment to substantive federalism in which there are fifty states, each with its own laws, an overlay of federal law, Indian tribal law, and a maddening patchwork of overlapping local codes and regulations at the county, city, and town levels. This diversity provides Americans with myriad opportunities to choose which kinds of legal regimes they will use to order their lives. Americans make such choices of law by deciding what states, cities, or counties to live in; where to organize and register their business entities; where to practice their professions; and where to marry, divorce, and raise their children. U.S. Supreme Court Justice Louis Brandeis noted that, although messy and perhaps inefficient, this legally pluralistic approach serves an important purpose. It permits various semi-autonomous legal systems to act as "laboratories of democracy" wherein citizens can experiment with law and policy solutions at a local level.[11] Good, workable laws might be adapted and adopted in other jurisdictions, whereas poor, unworkable laws can be replaced without broader adverse consequences to the whole nation.

In some states, there are even different official legal regimes that provide citizens with the opportunity to choose which of several state law frameworks they wish to use to organize their affairs. In some states, for instance, there is a two-tiered system of marriage and divorce law. When obtaining a marriage license, couples may choose to structure their union as a "covenant marriage," which is governed by more traditional and stringent

10. See Chapter Four.
11. *See* New State Ice Co. v. Liebmann, 285 U.S. 262 (1932) (Brandeis, J., dissenting).

rules relating to the formation and dissolution of the marital relationship. Alternatively, Louisiana couples may choose to enter into a more modern "contractual marriage," in which the formation and dissolution of the relationship resembles the making and breaking of a private contractual relationship. Both marriage frameworks are encoded into Louisiana state law, and the state will enforce the terms of whichever of the two unions marrying parties choose to create.[12]

Similar opportunities to choose the legal system by which one will be bound are afforded by American contract law, which provides contracting parties the benefit of choosing the laws that will govern their contractual relationship. Parties can agree to structure their relationship not only under New York or California law, but under Canadian, French, or Chinese law as well. This strong trend favoring freedom of contract and contractual autonomy suggests that the United States is very much a choice-of-law country. People and organizations regularly choose the state's laws under which they wish to order their affairs on given matters. The availability of legal choices of this kind is so ingrained in American civic, commercial, and family life that the forces of law strongly favor the idea that people can and should be able to use contractual mechanisms to select the normative systems that will govern their affairs, regardless of whether the choice is between New York, Delaware, or California law, or if it is between the laws of the state of New York and the norms and values of Judaism, Islam, or Christianity.[13] Importantly, the ability to contractually choose the laws under which contractual relationships shall be governed is not unique to the United States. It is embraced to a greater or lesser extent by many other common law and civil law jurisdictions as well.[14]

Of course, even in the United States, such choice of law is not absolute. No state system could function under conditions of perfect legal pluralism. Instead, the United States' constitutional system reflects the idea that choices about which legal regime one should order one's affairs under should be permitted except in those relatively rare situations in which the kind of very broad national consensus ultimately reflected in overarching constitutional norms pre-empts and precludes the

12. Katherine S. Spaht, *Louisiana's Covenant Marriage: Social Commentary and Legal Implications*, 59 La. L. Rev. 63 (1998), *available at* http://faculty.law.lsu.edu/katherine-spaht/covenantmarriage.htm.

13. *See* Ed Anderson & Roger Haydock, *History of Arbitration as an Alternative to U.S. Litigation*, Aug. 12, 1996 West's Legal News 8257, *available at* 1996 WL 449743.

14. *See* Friedrich K. Juenger, *Contract Choice of Law in the Americas*, 45 Am. J. Com. L. 195 (1997).

simultaneous existence of alternative legal regimes.[15] Likewise, in the context of arguments over secular recognition of religious arbitration, the notion that the adoption of a legally pluralistic stance entails complete normative anarchy is a bit of a straw man. No serious argument in favor of religious arbitration actually maintains that states ought to enforce all the results of all religious proceedings all the time. Actual claims in support of religious arbitration are far more modest. Much as there are substantial limits placed on choice of law in the secular realm, based in part on constitutional requirements grounded in broad and strong national consensus, reasonable limits on what a religious arbitral tribunal can do to resolve disputes and how they can do so may be perfectly compatible with an overall commitment to legal pluralism.

Not all countries maintain the kind of federated choice-of-law system embraced for largely historical reasons by the United States. Nevertheless, the largely well-functioning existence of such a regime in the United States undercuts some of the more salient concerns posed by critics of legal pluralism in general, and of secular recognition of religious arbitration more specifically. First, the American experience suggests that legal pluralism, or the ability to choose which state-enforced legal system one will use to order one's affairs, does not undermine societal order and predictability. On the contrary, it tends to enhance these values, as well as broader liberty interests. Enabling individuals to be bound by legal systems they directly choose to adopt allows them to predictably order their affairs and constitute legal relationships based on the norms that they regard as conducive to their own interests and needs, the future applications and consequences of which they feel better equipped to plan for and anticipate.

Additionally, the American approach to legal pluralism does not merely reflect a thin, consent-based theory of legal justice, but remains consistent with thicker liberal conceptions of substantive justice. As discussed above, American legal pluralism is not absolute; the United States' constitutional system places significant substantive limits on what alternative legal regimes and choices can be made available through diverse state and local laws. No laws can contradict the positive requirements and negative limits created by constitutional rights and governmental frameworks. To the extent that they apply, federal laws pre-empt and are superior to state and local laws. The substantive terms of these superseding federal

15. *See* Helfand, *supra* note 8, at 1254–58; Michael A. Helfand, *Litigating Religion*, 93 B.U. L. Rev. 493, 508 n.74 (2013); *see generally* Baker, *supra* note 4, at 163–64.

and constitutional norms represent precisely the kind of thicker theory of justice that some supporters of normative pluralism argue is lacking in a legally pluralistic regime. Despite its wide purview for choice of law, justice in the United States is not merely a function of individual contractual agreements. Choices of law cannot contravene basic substantive commitments to human rights and societal order. For example, a party cannot contractually absolve another of criminal liability by agreeing to be murdered, and parties could not effectively structure a real estate conveyance with a racially-based restrictive covenant merely because local ordinances permit the same in violation of the U.S. Constitution and federal law. Put differently, the state can recognize and uphold citizens' choices to structure their lives using various alternative legal systems without completely abrogating substantive limits on what kinds of alternative norms society will be willing to permit people to adopt. Secular legal systems can and in practice do uphold thick, substantive conceptions of justice and the rule of law consistent with liberal principles while also respecting and upholding a plurality of different legal regimes that citizens can turn to in structuring their affairs.

C. RELIGIOUS ARBITRATION PRODUCES SUBSTANTIVE INJUSTICE

Many of the most substantiated and well-placed concerns about religious arbitration relate to alleged injustices perpetuated through the religious arbitration process. These claims are considered in this and the following two sections. This section reviews some of the main arguments that religious arbitration works substantive injustices by applying and enforcing norms and values that are often substantially at odds with contemporary liberal rights commitments maintained by secular laws and societies. The next section turns to the issue of procedural justice, and explores concerns that religious arbitration proceedings lack the requisite procedural protections necessary to ensure fair and impartial dispute resolution. The last section discusses the concern that, although it is supposed to be voluntary, at least some parties to religious arbitration are often forced to participate in these proceedings under significant communal pressure that approximates genuine duress.

One of the most common arguments offered in opposition to secular enforcement of religious arbitration awards is the claim that religious norms and values very often include commitments that clash severely with contemporary liberal notions of gender equality, religious liberty, freedom of choice, personal privacy, and distributive justice.[16] The much-publicized 2005 ban on religious arbitration enacted in Ontario, for instance, was pushed by a broad coalition of different interest groups arguing that the practice and implementation of religious norms through religious arbitration produces substantive injustices to women and other traditionally disadvantaged parties.[17] Such concerns are particularly acute in the context of religious family law arbitration. In both the Jewish and Islamic legal systems, for example, divorces can generally only be granted by a husband to a wife. Traditional Jewish law maintains that to be considered divorced, a woman must have received a ritual bill of marital separation, called a *get*, which must be given to the wife by the husband of his own volition. The giving of a *get* cannot be directly coerced by rabbinic arbitrators, and in virtually all circumstances there is no recourse in Jewish law for judicial divorce or annulment. Moreover, Jewish law discriminates between the statuses and consequences of extramarital relationships by still-married Jewish men and women. It is possible—if difficult—for a Jewish man that has not divorced his wife with a *get* to obtain religious permission to marry again, and that marriage will be regarded as technically valid.[18]

A woman that has not received a *get*, by contrast, cannot marry another under Jewish law; any relationships she may engage in will be considered adulterous, and any children produced from such relationships will be considered illegitimate and unable to marry under Jewish law. In practice, this religious legal framework affords husbands substantial leverage in divorce settlement negotiations. Jewish wives are often compelled to accede to their husbands' demands for inequitable property divisions and child custody arrangements in order to secure the willing giving of a *get*.[19] According to some opponents of religious arbitration, such inequities resulting from religious legal frameworks should not be recognized or enforced by secular courts.[20]

Islamic law, too, contains family law norms that are viewed by opponents of religious arbitration as prejudicing the legitimate interests of women and children. Like in Jewish law, divorce in Islamic law is largely

16. As discussed above in Chapter Eight.

17. As discussed above in *id.*

18. *See generally* MICHAEL J. BROYDE, MARRIAGE, DIVORCE, AND THE ABANDONED WIFE IN JEWISH LAW (2001).

19. *See* AVIAD HACOHEN & BLU GREENBERG, THE TEARS OF THE OPPRESSED: AN EXAMINATION OF THE *AGUNAH* PROBLEM: BACKGROUND AND *HALAKHIC* SOURCES 20–23 (2004).

20. *See* Caryn Litt Wolfe, *Faith-Based Arbitration: Friend or Foe? An Evaluation of Religious Arbitration Systems and Their Interaction with Secular Courts*, 75 FORD. L. REV. 427, 460–61 (2006).

dependent on the husband. Typically, a divorce is affected through *talaq*, a voluntary thrice-repeated statement by the husband declaring his intent to divorce his wife. Although it is possible for a wife to request that an Islamic religious court broker a judicial divorce, absent a failure of the husband to uphold his marital duties, such a divorce—called a *khul*—typically necessitates the wife's giving the husband some form of material consideration. Thus, unlike the Muslim husband, who can unilaterally effect a *talaq* divorce whether or not his wife is at fault for the breakdown of the marriage, a wife will usually have to pay her unwilling husband to grant a divorce, likely in the form of an inequitable property settlement, and may only be able to do so for cause.[21] Gender inequalities are present in other aspects of Islamic family law as well. Many conservative Muslim scholars may permit some forms of physical coercion by a husband against a wife.[22] In the event of a divorce, there is also a strong presumption favoring paternal rather than maternal custody of children after they reach the age of seven or eight years old.[23]

Substantive incongruities between the religious norms likely to be applied by religious arbitration tribunals and those of secular law go beyond the realm of family law. Many Christian arbitration organizations explicitly commit themselves to resolving disputes brought before them in accordance with biblical principles. It is not too difficult to imagine, however, how in some Christian arbitrations such principles might clash sharply with contemporary liberal legal commitments in commercial and other contexts. Consider, for example, the case of a Christian-owned bakery, which as part of its standard custom baking contract includes an arbitration clause. After entering such a contract with a customer to bake a cake for a wedding, and just shortly before the cake is scheduled to be delivered, the baker discovers that the wedding will be that of a same-sex couple, and refuses to perform under the contract. The customer might seek legal redress for this breach of contract, but find him- or herself bound to resolve the dispute through Christian Conciliation or some similar religious dispute resolution forum that applies what it regards as biblical norms and values. Religious arbitrators might find squarely in favor of the baker, holding that no valid

21. *See* Sebastian Poulter, *The Claim to a Separate Islamic System of Personal Law for British Muslims*, *in* ISLAMIC FAMILY LAW 147, 161 (Chibli Mallat & Jane Connors eds., 1990).

22. *See generally* Azizah Y. al-Hibri, *An Islamic Perspective on Domestic Violence*, 27 FORD. INT'L L.J. 195 (2003).

23. *See* Aayeesha Rafiq, *Child Custody in Classical Islamic Law and Laws of Contemporary Muslim World*, 4 INT'L J. HUM. & SOC. SCI. 267 (2014).

agreement could be made to provide support services for a union that contravenes what they view as biblical principles and values.

Although the above scenario is, to the best of my knowledge, only a hypothetical, there are actual examples of religious arbitrations reaching results that depart substantially from what might be considered contemporary liberal substantive justice. In one case, an arbitration award issued by the Institute for Christian Conciliation applied what it regarded as biblical values in holding that a Christian religious school wrongfully fired its principal without first notifying her of her impending dismissal, or attempting to resolve the matter through direct negotiations or by resorting to third-party dispute resolution.[24] As a result, the arbitrator awarded the principal nearly $150,000 in damages for wrongful termination, harm to her reputation, and lost future earnings. In challenging the award, the school argued that the award was substantially inconsistent with the normative standards governing employer-employee relationships under applicable state law, which would have permitted the school to fire its principal, an at-will employee, without cause and without first seeking reconciliation as required by the biblical standards applied by the arbitrator. The reviewing court rejected this argument, affirming the general American law rule that "the fact that the remedy ordered by an arbitrator is inconsistent with state law is not grounds for vacating an award."[25] The court's decision, however, merely begs the question: Why should secular courts enforce arbitral awards that apply norms and values that are substantially inconsistent with those embraced as sound policy by state law? Opponents of religious arbitration could argue that, from the perspective of society's laws, the arbitrator in this case worked a significant distributive injustice by ordering the school to pay the fired principal money that, under the legally-enshrined public policy of the state, it should not have had to pay. Religious arbitration in that case resulted in a structuring of the employee-employer relationship along very different lines from the ones envisioned by secular society.

Similar inconsistencies between religious and secular substantive law can be found in other ecumenical systems as well. As Michael Helfand has noted, for example, traditional Jewish law rules restricting certain kinds of competitive business practices can be viewed as conflicting with U.S. antitrust laws and policies designed to promote competition and any particular business concern from gaining monopolistic control over particular

24. *See* Prescott v. Northlake Christian Sch., 141 Fed. Appx. 263 (2005).
25. *Id.* at 272.

markets.[26] Both Jewish and Islamic law, moreover, contain substantial restrictions on contractual autonomy. Islamic law, for instance, does not recognize contracts based on speculation, such as agreements for the future sale of goods or most kinds of insurance arrangements, as well as loans and other transactions that include interest payments. Traditional Jewish law includes price controls and restrictions on interest- based lending, and departs from common law doctrines in matters of land use and nuisance, torts, and other areas. In these and other matters, the results of religious arbitration proceedings may well differ significantly from the results parties might expect to receive in secular courts. More important, however, the societal enforcement of such arbitral awards would undermine the degree to which secular notions of substantive justice actually order commercial relationships in society.

It is worth noting that the thrust of substantive justice arguments against religious arbitration is blunted somewhat by the fact that this problem is not limited to the religious arbitration context. Many commentators have observed that traditionally vulnerable parties are often placed at substantial disadvantages by non-religious arbitration as well. Especially with respect to arbitration in consumer and employment matters, consumers and employees often find themselves bound by decisions that strongly favor retailers, wholesalers, manufacturers, and employers in ways that cut against contemporary progressive notions of distributive justice and fair dealing.[27] One notable example of this phenomenon is the use of arbitration agreements in service contracts for credit cards, cable and Internet services, and online retail commerce to preclude class action suits. Research has shown that as a result of this move by banks, credit card companies, and retailers to prevent consumer class actions, most people with claims against these companies did not pursue them. Typically, class action suits are the only pragmatically cost-effective way of pursuing most claims for predatory lending, wrongful billing, wage theft, and discrimination. Oftentimes these claims are each too small to make litigation practical; the only practical way of pursuing them is through class actions. Such lawsuits are a critical means of holding corporations to account for misbehavior, and the public status of such court actions are a valuable source of data that helps government regulators better uncover patterns of corporate

26. *See* Helfand, *supra* note 8, at 1258–60.

27. *See, e.g.*, Elizabeth J. Jensen, *Using Arbitration to Eliminate Consumer Class Actions: Efficient Business Practice or Unconscionable Abuse?*, 67 L. & CONT. PROB. 75 (2004); Herman Schwartz, *How Consumers Are Getting Screwed by Court-Enforced Arbitration*, THE NATION (July 18, 2014), https://www.thenation.com/article/how-consumers-are-getting-screwed-court-enforced-arbitration/.

abuse and misconduct.[28] The legal enforcement of these kinds of arbitration agreements and the results of such arbitral proceedings undermine an important aspect of American law and public policy—the reliance on class action lawsuits to help ensure good corporate conduct. Of course, these commercial arbitrations are not religious at all; they are decidedly secular. Nevertheless, they too produce results that reflect deep incompatibilities with contemporary notions of substantive justice.

The danger of religious norms and values displacing secular standards of justice is further reduced by existing arbitration law frameworks. In the United States, arbitration awards that seriously conflict with the law can be vacated by a reviewing court. As the United States Supreme Court has held, "a substantive waiver of federal civil rights" in an arbitration agreement "will not be upheld."[29] Additionally, American courts have long held that arbitration awards—whether secular or religious—can and should be vacated by courts when the substance of such awards are contrary to "public policy." This practice helps protect important public interests in cases where a disputant participating in an arbitration proceeding has privately agreed to alienate certain legal rights that are intended to protect the public generally.[30] In such cases, courts often refuse to enforce the arbitration award, reasoning that the waiver of substantive rights is not merely a matter of private contract, but implicates broader societal interests that ought not be permitted to be abrogated through private agreements. Importantly, the Supreme Court has held that public policy vacatur may be implicated not only when an arbitration award contradicts important policies enshrined in positive legislation or constitutional norms. Even arbitration decisions that conflict with broader, but not strictly *legal* policy concerns, may be vacated on these grounds.[31] Thus, some courts have refused to enforce arbitration decisions regarding child custody matters, holding that such issues must be dealt with by state courts for public policy reasons.[32] In Canada too, arbitration awards may be vacated if they are found to violate substantive provisions of the Canadian Charter of Rights and Freedoms.

28. *See* Jessica Silver-Greenberg & Robert Gebeloff, *Arbitration Everywhere: Stacking the Deck of Justice*, N.Y, Times, http://nyti.ms/1KMvBJg (October 31, 2015).

29. 14 Penn Plaza, LLC v. Pyett, 129 U.S. 1456, 1474 (2009).

30. *See* Helfand, *supra* note 8, at 1254.

31. *See* E. Assoc. Coal Corp. v. United Mine Workers of Am., 531 U.S. 57, 63 (2000).

32. *See, e.g.*, Berg v. Berg, No. 25099/05, 2008 WL 4155652, at *11 (N.Y. Sup. Ct., Sept. 8, 2008); Rakoszynski v. Rakoszynski, 663 N.Y.S.2d 957 (Sup. Ct. 1997). *See also, In re* Marriage of Dajani, 251 Cal. Rptr. 871 (Cal. Ct. App. 1988) (refusing to enforce a prenuptial contract because the contract's provision of a dowry only in the event of divorce encourages divorce, and is therefore void for public policy).

D. RELIGIOUS ARBITRATION PRODUCES PROCEDURAL INJUSTICE

Opponents of religious arbitration further argue that religious dispute resolution often lacks the kinds of procedural protections necessary to ensure a fair and unbiased arbitration process.[33] Existing arbitration law frameworks provide that parties to arbitration proceedings are entitled to certain basic procedural protections that help ensure the fairness of the proceedings and protect vulnerable parties. These protections include the right to have notice of when and where a hearing will take place, the right to have an attorney present for the proceedings, the right to be heard and present and impeach evidence, the right to a fair and impartial tribunal, and the right to have the tribunal consider relevant evidence.[34] More generally, standard liberal conceptions of the rule of law assume that legitimate adjudicatory processes entail limited judicial discretion in applying the law to resolve specific disputes.

In many cases, the selection of religious arbitration also entails selection of the procedural rules posited by that particular religious tradition. Unlike in ordinary commercial arbitration, where parties are largely free to contractually choose the procedural rules that will be applied in the proceedings, in a religious arbitration setting, procedures derived from religious norms and values are typically part of the whole package. Opponents of secular recognition of religious arbitration argue that religious arbitration processes are often unfair because religious procedural rules fail to provide the kinds of protections for vulnerable parties and even playing fields that we have come to expect from contemporary due process standards. Both traditional Jewish and Islamic law, for instance, maintain formal procedural distinctions between men and women in a number of respects. Under traditional Jewish law, women cannot serve as rabbinic court judges, which means that Jewish religious arbitration panels are typically all-male. Women are also formally ineligible from offering witness testimony in rabbinic courts, along with unrepentant sinners, relatives of litigants, and others with financial interests in the outcome of a case.[35] Traditional Islamic law accords different weight to the verbal testimony of men and women, and religiously inspired conceptions of female modesty lead some Islamic

33. *See* Wolfe, *supra* note 20, at 463–65.
34. *See, e.g.*, Revised Uniform Arbitration Act § 16.
35. *See* 1 Emanuel Quint, A Restatement of Rabbinic Civil Law 52, 275–300 (1990).

courts and tribunals to compel female litigants, advocates, and lawyers to take a less public and obtrusive role in religious proceedings.[36]

Religious law rules of evidence and burdens of proof may also be taken as being inconsistent with secular notions of how to protect disadvantaged parties, ensure fair dealing, and produce truthful results in dispute resolution settings. In Islamic jurisprudence, for instance, burdens of proof typically depend on which of the litigants in a given case ends up being procedurally classified as the plaintiff, and which as the defendant.[37] In contrast to most every other legal system, however, these designations may not correlate to which party brought the action or is seeking a change to his or her current circumstances. Instead, the plaintiff, who is the party that typically bears the higher burden of proof, is usually the party who in the arbitrator's assessment is advocating a legally weaker claim, and who must therefore bear the burden of demonstrating by an additional showing of fact and law that his or her claims should prevail.[38] From a policy perspective, it can be argued that this kind of procedural posturing runs counter to standard notions of due process. It can encourage frivolous or dishonest litigation on the part of claimants who expect to successfully shift the burden of proof to defendants who may be unable to reach it.

Moreover, in both Jewish and Islamic law, burdens of proof can be shifted, and in some cases entire claims can be sustained or refuted as a matter of law by various parties taking ritual oaths as to the truth of their own factual assertions.[39] This method of "fact finding" is at odds with secular notions of due process and good judicial procedure under which objective considerations of the weight of evidentiary proofs are the principal determinants of facts to which the law will be applied.

Some religious traditions also oppose the inclusion of counsel or attorneys in dispute resolution proceedings.[40] Unlike common law systems premised on the discovery of truth through attorney-driven adversarial processes, many modes of traditional religious adjudication are more inquisitorial and judge-driven. In this model, which is embraced by Jewish and Islamic law, as well as modern Christian Conciliation organizations,

36. *See* HAUWA IBRAHIM, PRACTICING SHARIAH LAW: SEVEN STRATEGIES FOR ACHIEVING JUSTICE IN SHARIAH COURTS 140–41 (2012).

37. *See* THE ASHGATE RESEARCH COMPANION TO ISLAMIC LAW 83–84 (Rudolph Peters & Peri Bearman eds., 2016).

38. *See id.*

39. *See id.* at 84; THE PRINCIPLES OF JEWISH LAW 615–19 (Menachem Elon ed., 2007).

40. *See* C. Paul Dredge, *Dispute Resolution in the Mormon Community: The Operation of Ecclesiastical Courts in Utah*, *in* 4 ACCESS TO JUSTICE: THE ANTHROPOLOGICAL PERSPECTIVE 191, 198 (Klaus-Freidrich Koch ed., 1979); MICHAEL J. BROYDE, THE PURSUIT OF JUSTICE AND JEWISH LAW 14–20 (1996).

the goal of the dispute resolution process is not merely—or perhaps even primarily—to reach the most accurate, formally legalistic resolution of a dispute. Instead, religious arbitration processes seek to promote fairness, reconciliation, acknowledgment of wrongdoing, and the establishment of equitable and peaceful relations between disputants. Within this framework, the inclusion of lawyers and other kinds of counsel is often seen as counterproductive, as the goal of the dispute resolution process is not to enable each party to press its right to the furthest extent of the law, but to help each litigant fulfill his or her religio-legal and moral obligations to others.[41] Some religious arbitration tribunals proscribe the involvement of lawyers, in direct contradiction to the legal framework for arbitration established by many secular law regimes. Among those tribunals that do permit attorney involvement in the proceedings, many do not make this fact clear to litigants upfront.

This general religious preference for equitable, conciliatory dispute resolution results in religious dispute resolution processes taking on highly flexible postures in which results are often not determined by the religious norms parties may have bargained for. Jewish law, for example, encourages rabbinic arbitrators to resolve disputes with an eye toward equity and amicable settlement, a procedural posture called *peshara*, or "compromise," which stands in contrast to *din*, or dispute resolution strictly in accordance with the law.[42] This authorization for flexible decision-making gives rabbinic arbitrators wide discretion in crafting decisions based largely on their own senses of fairness, and also creates opportunities for judicial abuse. This potential is enhanced by the fact that Jewish law also empowers rabbinic courts to do away with its own default rules of evidence and procedure in order to flexibly achieve pragmatic and just results in specific cases, repeatedly authorizing arbitrators to act "in accordance with what appears in the eyes of the judge."[43] Likewise, many Islamic arbitration tribunals operate using a procedural posture called *tahkim*, which typically involves a flexible, less law-based arbitral process in which decisions are grounded in *maslahah*, or equitable, pragmatic policy. Although this sort of flexible, result-oriented dispute resolution helps achieve the kinds of conciliatory results preferred by many religious systems, it also leaves disputants subject to the vagaries of arbitrators' personal subjectivities in ways that secular standards of due process are intended to prevent.[44]

41. *See* BROYDE, *supra* note 40, at 11–14.
42. *See supra* Chapter Four at 27-33.
43. *See* Shulchan Aruch § 2.
44. *See supra* Chapter Eight (B–C).

It should be pointed out, however, that the very existence of religious procedural laws that govern religious arbitration proceedings does offer litigants procedural protections not always afforded to parties in commercial arbitrations, regardless of the degree to which these rules comport with standard societal conceptions of due process. One of the more salient critiques of arbitration in general has been that many commercial arbitral proceedings are plagued by unfairness, informal preferences favoring corporate parties, and uncertainty about applicable rules of procedure and evidence.[45] Research has shown that because corporate parties often arbitrate regularly in the same forums, their attorneys are often on friendly terms with arbitrators. Arbitrators, in turn, often owe their own jobs to the willingness of corporate clients to continue to appear in front of them time after time. The employees and consumers who are typically forced to bring their claims against corporations to arbitration, by contrast, are single-use players in these forums. Arbitrators have much to gain and little to lose by producing favorable outcomes for their corporate clients.[46] This potential for unfairness and bias is exacerbated by the fact that, unlike religious tribunals, commercial arbitration organizations do not typically consider themselves bound to any particular procedures. Although parties can in theory prescribe the use of certain procedural rules in their arbitration agreements, oftentimes arbitrators get to make it up as they go along. The admission and consideration of evidence, selection of arbitrators, procedures for making arguments and countering opponents' claims, discovery, and other procedural matters can be—and at times are—thus crafted in ways that favor corporate parties. Rather than protect vulnerable disputants, the procedures (or lack thereof) employed in many secular arbitration contexts often disadvantage consumers and employees in ways that can be appalling to standard notions of adjudicatory due process.[47]

Although the existence of religiously prescribed procedural rules can help alleviate some of the concerns that exist in the procedural vacuum of commercial arbitration, religious dispute resolution does suffer an important disadvantage that undermines the likelihood of fair dealings. Specifically, religious arbitration is often far less professional than its secular counterpart. Pastors, ministers, rabbis, and imams are spiritual teachers and leaders, not legal practitioners. Although some notable religious arbitration organizations make sure that their arbitrators are trained in

45. *See* Jessica Silver-Greenberg & Michael Corkery, *In Arbitration, a "Privatization of the Justice System,"* N.Y. TIMES (November 1, 2015).
46. *See id.*
47. *See id.*

dispute resolution, law, and other related disciplines, and may also include experts in specific fields on arbitral panels hearing matters that fall within those subject areas, many others offer no such professionalism or expertise. In such forums, decision-making can be highly informal, haphazard, and without sufficient attention to the kinds of procedural subtleties that professional legal experience has shown to be important to ensuring fair proceedings and just results.

E. RELIGIOUS ARBITRATION IS OFTEN COERCIVE AND IS USED TO ENTRENCH UNJUST POWER RELATIONS IN RELIGIOUS COMMUNITIES

Another concern raised by opponents of secular enforcement of religious arbitration is the problem of coercion. The legitimacy of all arbitration is premised on the parties' voluntarily agreeing to submit their dispute to a nonjudicial forum. Although all citizens have the right to have cases resolved by state courts in accordance with state laws, contemporary commitments to freedom of contract permit individuals to waive this right, and to instead choose to have their conflicts adjudicated in the forum and according to the law of their own choosing. Based on these theoretical underpinnings, standard arbitration laws provide that arbitration agreements, like all contracts, are void if secured through coercion or duress.[48] At least in the United States, the standard for voiding a contract procured through duress is that courts will invalidate agreements produced by means of "improper threats by the other party that leaves the victim no reasonable alternative" but to enter into the coerced contract.[49]

Problematically, however, courts have a poor track record of recognizing various forms of pressure exerted by religious communities to get individuals to agree to arbitrate disputes before religious tribunals as legal duress. Traditional Jewish law, for instance, maintains that Jews are obligated to resolve their disputes with co-religionists in rabbinic courts in accordance with Jewish law. Jewish litigants who refuse to appear before a rabbinic tribunal when summoned in response to a complaint being filed may be subject to a *seruv*, a public declaration that such parties are in contempt of court. The practical ramifications of a *seruv* vary widely from community to community, but can include exclusion from participation in religious

48. *See, e.g.*, 9 U.S.C. § 10(a)(1).
49. Restatement (Second) of Contracts § 175(1) (1981).

services, denial of the rights and privileges of membership in the Jewish community, and expulsion of one's children from private religious schools. Additionally, an individual's being subject to a *seruv* may result in other members of the Jewish community refusing to do business with him or her, and thus have real economic consequences.

In some communities, refusal to consent to resolve disputes in rabbinic courts, and resorting to secular adjudication, can result in a party being ostracized by friends and family. In numerous instances, parents who seek to leave the observant Jewish community and refuse to adjudicate divorce, property division, and child custody matters in a religious forum have had the full financial and political resources of some Jewish communities brought to bear against them in secular court proceedings, sometimes resulting in their loss of custody or visitation rights. Despite the very real consequences of refusing to arbitrate a dispute in a rabbinic court, American courts have regularly held that a *seruv* does not constitute legal coercion, and that arbitration agreements signed under threat or actual issuance of a *seruv* are not void for duress.[50]

Jewish law and some Jewish communities use the *seruv* as a formal procedural means of pressuring members of the community to appear before a religious arbitration tribunal. Although similar mechanisms may not necessarily exist in other religious systems, many other religious communities exert all kinds of informal communal pressure to compel members of the faith—as well as those who no longer wish to remain members—to resolve litigious matters internally. Cases have been reported in which members of tight-knit Christian communities who refuse to arbitrate disputes in a religious forum have lost jobs in churches and religious schools, been made unwelcome in their places of worship, and been socially ostracized by friends and neighbors.[51] The more highly organized and isolationist a religious community is, the more harmful such pressure can be, and the more effectively it can be brought to bear in order to compel a recalcitrant member of the community to resolve a dispute internally.

The ways in which some well-organized religious groups have dealt with allegations of sexual abuse committed by religious leaders is illustrative, although not strictly an instance of religious arbitration. Such allegations have been rippling through Catholic, Jewish, and more recently Muslim communities for some time. In many cases, the religious establishments in these communities seek to resolve such matters internally, without

50. *See* Ginnie Fried, Comment, *The Collision of Church and State: A Primer on Beth Din Arbitration and the New York Secular Courts*, 31 FORD. URB. L.J. 633, 652–53 (2004).
51. *See* Wolfe, *supra* note 20, at 460–65.

involving secular law enforcement authorities. The Catholic Church has used a variety of different means to convince alleged victims and whistleblowers to keep such matters within Church disciplinary channels.[52] In one headline-making case of alleged sex abuse of a minor girl by an unlicensed community therapist and rabbi, communal leaders enacted numerous measures to punish the victim and her family for handling the matter through the secular criminal justice system. The victim and her family received threatening calls and were ostracized by neighbors, and the victim's husband had his local business boycotted and was forced to close.[53]

Despite the prevalence of such tactics to compel members of religious communities to agree to participate in religious arbitration proceedings, courts rarely recognize such pressures as constituting duress. One commentator has summarized the view of American courts on the matter: "if a religious body applies religious pressure on an individual to do something, it is not duress because that individual can reasonably refuse and abstain from religious pressure to do an act."[54] Opponents of religious arbitration can argue, however, that this approach badly misunderstands the nature of individuals' religious commitments, and their social, familial, and economic ties to their religious communities. Many religious traditions maintain that adherents are bound to resolve their disputes in religious courts and in accordance with religious norms and values.[55] Such duties exert genuine pressure upon faithful members of the community to accede to even unfair, unprofessional, and biased religious arbitration proceedings.

Rejecting this religious duty can often entail serious consequences to one's standing in the community, and in the mind of the individual adherent, to his or her standing in the eyes of God as well. Although this sense of obligation to abide by religious arbitration proceedings may not be the result of duress in the external sense typically contemplated by the law, for the religious individual there is often no reasonable alternative but to conform to the norms and values of his or her faith community. Leaving the faith, moreover, is often less of a choice than courts may be willing to

52. *See* Anna Stolley Persky, *Prosecutors Battle the Wall of Silence around Sex Assault in Religious Communities*, ABA J. (Dec. 1, 2013), http://www.abajournal.com/magazine/article/the_religious_wall_of_silence.

53. *See* Josh Saul, *Sex Abuse Victim Shamed during Synagogue Prayers*, N.Y. Post (Sept. 9, 2013), http://nypost.com/2013/09/09/sex-abuse-victim-shamed-during-synagogue-prayers/; Hella Winston, *Weberman Abuse Case Exposes Role of Shadowy "Modesty Committees,"* Jewish Week (Dec. 10, 2012), http://www.thejewishweek.com/news/new-york-news/weberman-abuse-case-exposes-role-shadowy-modesty-committees.

54. Fried, *supra* note 50, at 652. *See also*, Greenberg v. Greenberg, 656 N.Y.S.2d 369 (App. Div. 1997); Golding v. Golding, 581 N.Y.S.2d 4 (App. Div. 1992).

55. *See* Wolfe, *supra* note 20, at 440–41.

acknowledge. It is rare for religious communities to physically prevent an individual from leaving the fold, but abandoning one's religion and religious community nevertheless can lead to one's being ostracized by friends and family, loss of access to one's children, and severe financial hardship, especially for those seeking to leave isolationist communities where the teaching of secular education and skills for functioning in secular society are kept to a minimum.

F. RELIGIOUS ARBITRATION CANNOT BE ADEQUATELY POLICED OR REGULATED IN LIBERAL SOCIETIES COMMITTED TO RELIGIOUS FREEDOM

The challenges to religious arbitration discussed in the previous three sections are limited in a very important sense. Although concerns for substantive injustice, procedural unfairness, and coercive pressure to appear before religious tribunals are indeed quite real, they can—at least in theory—be addressed through secular judicial oversight over the religious arbitration process. Secular law arbitration regimes such as the Federal Arbitration Act provide for judicial review of arbitration agreements, procedures, and awards. Such review might also be—and in practice often is—applied by state courts to evaluate the validity and enforceability of religious arbitration proceedings as well.[56]

Arbitration agreements are subject to the ordinary rules of contract law, and can therefore be voided if procured through coercion or duress. Arbitration law also requires arbitration proceedings to respect basic norms of procedural due process. Arbitrators cannot be biased or have interests in the cases they decide; they are required to hear and take cognizance of relevant evidence, give all parties adequate notice of proceedings and an opportunity to be heard, and respect other basic notions of procedural fairness. Additionally, courts will not typically uphold arbitration agreements in which parties agree to alienate basic procedural due process rights protected by the Constitution. Moreover, secular law arbitration frameworks often include provisions empowering courts to review the substance of arbitration awards, and to vacate those awards if they are contrary to public policy. In theory, these legal limits on the judicial recognition and enforcement of all arbitration decisions can greatly limit the occurrence of coercive, unfair, and substantively unjust, but still legally binding religious

56. *See supra* Chapter Six (A).

arbitration proceedings. Moreover, to the extent that current legislative limits prove inadequate to address special concerns arising in the religious arbitration context, lawmakers can modify existing frameworks for judicial review of arbitral proceedings to better resolve such problems.[57]

Although existing legal frameworks from judicial review of arbitration may help prevent substantive and procedural unfairness and duress in theory, in practice, courts are highly deferential to religious arbitrators.[58] Such deference significantly heightens the concern that individuals may be pressured to participate in religious proceedings that are unfair, lack important procedural protections, and produce results that are at odds with standard notions of substantive justice. Judicial deference to arbitral proceedings is not only a concern in religious dispute resolution. Courts regularly uphold commercial and other non-religious arbitration agreements and awards, often with only cursory review. The United States and many other arbitration-friendly jurisdictions have clear policies favoring the use of private arbitration to resolve litigious conflicts outside state courts. These policies are grounded in several different concerns, including personal autonomy and freedom of contract; a desire to keep cases out of overworked and clogged court systems; the belief that private arbitration can often be used to craft better results more consonant with parties' expectations and interests; and a belief that arbitration is often cheaper, faster, and more efficient than formal adjudication. As a result of this broad, overarching public policy favoring arbitration, courts are often hesitant to void arbitration agreements or vacate arbitral awards.

When it comes to judicial review of religious arbitration, however, courts appear to be even more hesitant. This is largely a result of free exercise and religious establishment concerns, which give courts significant pause at the prospect of telling parties to religious arbitration proceedings what the norms and values of particular faith traditions are, and whether or not they may contract with each other to resolve private disputes accordingly.

In the United States, these concerns take the form of the "religious question doctrine." The origins of the religious question doctrine date back to the late nineteenth century, when the Supreme Court considered an appeal from a lower federal court ruling enjoining the enforcement of a state court decision that resolved a property dispute between two church factions. In upholding the lower court's refusal to permit a judicial disposition of the dispute, the Court held that, because the case turned on an interpretation

57. For examples of such proposals, see Baker, *supra* note 4, at 197–201.
58. *See* Baker, *supra* note 4.

of church doctrine, a state authority could not resolve the issue without infringing on important First Amendment principles. Instead, the Court ruled, such matters must be resolved by relevant ecclesiastical authorities, to which state courts must then defer.[59] Almost a century later, in *Presbyterian Church v. Mary Elizabeth Blue Hull Memorial Church*, the Supreme Court affirmed this doctrine. In that case, the Court reversed a ruling by the Georgia Supreme Court that awarded church property to two local congregations because it found that the broader institutional church organization failed to uphold its own tenets of faith and practice. In reversing the Georgia court's decision, the Supreme Court held that state authorities cannot determine the truth or falsity of religious doctrine.[60]

The religious question doctrine places major limitations on courts' abilities to review religious arbitrations for duress or procedural or substantive injustice. The Federal Arbitration Act, for instance, provides that courts may vacate an arbitration award issued as the result of arbitrators exceeding their authority as provided by the litigants' arbitration agreement.[61] In the secular context, this might mean that if parties to an arbitration agreement had provided that their dispute should be resolved according to French law, and instead, the arbitrators flipped a coin, it would be appropriate for a court to vacate the award because the arbitrators overstepped their grant of authority. Pursuant to the arbitration agreement, the arbitrators' authority was limited to resolving the parties' dispute in accordance with their understanding of French law. Although a court would likely not expect the arbitrators to resolve the case exactly as a French judge might, a coin-flip would clearly be a means of dispute resolution that the arbitrators were not contractually authorized to utilize.

Strangely, however, the religious question doctrine may prevent courts from making similar kinds of judgments with respect to religious arbitration proceedings. Courts have explicitly held that where arbitrators purport to have based their decisions on religious norms and values, courts cannot decide whether those religious standards actually support the award.[62] Under current applications of the religious question doctrine, courts may not make judgements about what religious laws and values *really* are or require; they cannot second-guess the purported religious determinations of ecumenical officials. Doing otherwise would amount to

59. *See* Watson v. Jones, 80 U.S. 679 (1872).

60. *See* Presbyterian Church v. Mary Elizabeth Blue Hull Memorial Church, 393 U.S. 440 (1969).

61. *See* 9 U.S.C. §10(a)(4) (1925).

62. *See, e.g.*, Lang v. Levi, 16 A.3d 980 (2011).

the government's making determinations about what are and are not correct statements of the teachings and commitments of particular faith traditions, essentially establishing some interpretations of those traditions and not others as normative. To avoid such governmental encroachments on the integrity and independence of religions, courts typically avoid any review of religious arbitral proceedings that would involve making substantive judgments about the underlying religious issues or laws.

Similar judicial review problems exist with respect to questions of duress and procedural fairness in religious arbitration proceedings. Evaluating the degree to which communal pressure and formal religious doctrines such as the rabbinic *seruv* unduly coerce parties to agree to arbitrate disputes in religious forums would require courts to examine and make judgments about religious values. Not only is there good reason to think that courts are simply bad at such determinations, but they may be barred from doing so under religious freedom doctrines. By default, such restrictions leave vulnerable parties unable to seek redress through the courts in the ways that existing legal frameworks for arbitration anticipate.

For the same reasons, there is good reason to think that legal standards for judicial review of arbitration are largely ineffective at protecting vulnerable parties from procedural unfairness in religious proceedings. Arbitration laws often provide for vacating arbitration awards if arbitrators refused to hear and consider relevant material evidence with respect to the dispute they are resolving.[63] In religious contexts, questions such as evidence, pleading procedures, and the way arbitrators ought to go about resolving cases are often determined by religious law. If a court is asked to vacate a religious arbitration award because the arbitrators failed to properly evaluate material evidence, or otherwise prejudiced the rights of the litigants, it would have to interpret and make determinations about relevant religious norms. The judge would have to decide what the relevant religious system says about what kinds of evidence are or are not material in order to determine whether the arbitrator—who by the terms of the arbitration agreement is supposed to apply religious law—failed to consider evidence that the religious laws he or she is supposed to apply consider to be material. Likewise, reviewing courts would have to consider what procedural rights the relevant religious laws and values afford to each litigant in order to determine whether the arbitrators acted in a manner that prejudiced such rights. Under many standard contemporary approaches to the religious question doctrine in particular, and government determinations of

63. *See* 9 U.S.C. §10 (a) (1925).

religious norms and standards in general, however, judges could not make such determinations. Rather than reviewing such claims of procedural unfairness and duress, state judges would have to defer to the religious arbitrators' decisions, leaving vulnerable litigants without meaningful recourse to ensure the truly volitional nature, and procedural and substantive justice of religious arbitration proceedings.

G. SECULAR ENFORCEMENT OF RELIGIOUS ARBITRATION VIOLATES DISPUTANTS' RIGHTS TO FREEDOM OF RELIGION

Opponents of secular enforcement of religious arbitration proceedings further argue that the use of state resources—and ultimately state coercion—to give force to religious arbitration represents a serious violation of individuals' right to the free exercise of religion. By recognizing and enforcing religious arbitration agreements and the decisions of religious arbitration tribunals, secular courts compel recalcitrant parties to participate in what are essentially religious practices, or abide by religious norms and values that they may not hold.[64]

For example, the 1999 case of *Encore Productions, Inc. v. Promise Keepers*.[65] In that case, Promise Keepers, a Christian organization that conducts meetings and conferences for men in large venues across the United States, entered into a contract with Encore Productions under which Encore would provide production and consulting services for Promise Keepers' events. The agreement included an arbitration clause in which the parties agreed that disputes between them would be resolved through binding arbitration in accordance with Christian Conciliation procedures.

When the relationship between Encore and Promise Keepers broke down, Encore sued Promise Keepers, and the defendants moved to have the action dismissed and sent to Christian arbitration pursuant to the parties' original service contract. In ruling to dismiss the claim, the court rejected an argument made by Encore that compelling it to engage in and abide by the decision of a Christian Conciliation proceeding would violate its rights to the free exercise of religion. Encore argued that its agents and employees could not be compelled to participate in a religious proceeding conducted in accordance with the tenets and values of a faith to which they did

64. *See* Jean R. Sternlight, *Creeping Mandatory Arbitration: Is it Just?*, 57 STAN. L. REV. 1631, 1635 (2005).

65. Encore Productions v. Promise Keepers, 53 Fed. Supp. 2d 1101, (D. Colo. 1999).

not subscribe. The court rejected Encore's argument. The presiding judge found that enforcing the results of the Christian Conciliation proceedings would not violate the freedom of religion rights of Encore or its employees because they had already "voluntarily signed a contract containing a written arbitration agreement that clearly and expressly disclosed that arbitration would be submitted to Christian Conciliation."[66] This, the court found, manifested Encore's decision to waive any rights it may have had to refuse to participate in a religious proceeding or abide by the religious norms and values that would form the basis of any arbitral award.

Encore illustrates what many have noted is a serious challenge to religious freedom posed by secular court enforcement of religious arbitration agreements and awards. From one perspective, religious arbitration helps enhance religious freedom. It gives members of particular faith traditions the opportunity to order their lives and affairs in accordance with the norms and values of their own ecumenical convictions. Secular recognition of religious arbitral decisions, moreover, helps concertize such religious commitments by providing a sometimes necessary enforcement mechanism. But religious freedom is a two-way street. The right to believe in a faith tradition and observe its practices also entails the right to choose to not believe or practice any specific faith against the dictates of one's own conscience. As James Madison put it, and as American courts have confirmed time and again, "The Religion . . . of every man must be left to the conviction and conscience of every man; and it is the right of every man to exercise it as these may dictate."[67] The right to believe or not believe in a religion, moreover, assumes the right to change one's beliefs. Opponents of secular enforcement of religious arbitration argue that courts' compelling individuals to participate in and abide by the decisions of religious arbitration proceedings abridges this right.

The problem raised by *Encore* can be highlighted by the following hypothetical. Consider the case of an individual who has decided to become a member of a particular religious faith. Imagine that, as part of its ritual for admitting new members, this faith requires that members make firm commitments to remain faithful adherents of this religion for life. This commitment is memorialized in a legally binding contract that provides for financial and social consequences in the event that the new convert

66. *Id.* at 1113.

67. James Madison, *Memorial and Remonstrance against Religious Assessments, in* Constitutional Debates on Freedom of Religion: A Documentary History 48, 50 (John J. Patrick & Gerald P. Long eds., 1999). *See also* Wallace v. Jaffree, 472 U.S. 38, 53 n.38 (1985).

decides to leave the faith or stop practicing the religion. Imagine, moreover, that this tradition requires those who are already members of the faith to periodically renew this commitment by signing such contracts as part of important life-cycle events and other religious ceremonies. Under the court's reasoning in *Encore*, it is not unreasonable to suppose that the state might be put in the position of having to enforce such contracts and apply such penalties, which most certainly abridge and restrict individuals' ability and freedom to choose their own religious practices and beliefs.

Indeed, it is unnecessary perhaps to resort to such hypotheticals in order to illustrate the problem. Religious groups often place various hurdles before those who wish to leave the faith, and impose consequences on community members who are less than scrupulous in their religious observances and beliefs.[68] Although in modern liberal societies such religious communities do not have any direct enforcement powers, they often eventually make use of secular court enforcement of religious arbitration agreements, arbitral proceedings, and other contracts, to help bind individuals to the religious community. As mentioned earlier, some isolationist Jewish communities use various forms of communal pressure, consequences, and informal religious supervision councils to keep adherents on the correct religious path. Ultimately, members of such communities are strongly discouraged from leaving by the likelihood of their facing serious economic and familial consequences at the hands of communal religious authorities acting as arbitration panels to resolve divorce, child support, custody, and property division matters. Communal pressure is used to get community members who have decided to leave the faith or become less strict in their religious observances to appear before religious arbitrators whose determinations will be enforced by secular courts. The likelihood of such eventualities places a serious bar on individuals' freedom to change their religious beliefs and practices or convert out of their religious community.

Similar problems have been recorded in connection to the Church of Scientology. In some reported instances, the Church has obligated its members to sign dozens of legally binding arbitration agreements that provide that any disputes between members and the Church will be resolved through binding arbitration conducted by arbiters who are church members in good standing, and in accordance with rules and procedures established by the Church itself. Church members who question or rebel against Church teachings or who seek to leave the Church of Scientology

68. *See* Ann Laquer Estin, *Embracing Tradition: Pluralism in American Family Law*, 63 Md. L. Rev. 540, 600 (2004).

are labeled "Subversive Persons." According to Church doctrine, members of the Church in good standing, including friends, family, and business associates, are prohibited from dealing, speaking, or otherwise interacting with such Subversive Persons, and they too can face sanctions for doing so. The arbitration agreements signed by Church members, and the significant membership dues, donations, and tuition for Church courses and lectures that members are expected to pay, place significant, legally enforceable burdens on church members' freedom to practice or change their religious affiliations and practices.[69]

Secular enforcement of parties' commitments to participate in and abide by the decisions of religious arbitration proceedings can limit the right to freedom of religion in more direct ways too. In particular, it can be used to actually compel individuals to perform religious rituals or engage in religious practices that they may be unwilling, as a matter of conscience, to participate in. A recent Canadian case is illustrative. *Marcovitz v. Bruker* involved a civil divorce settlement agreement between two spouses in which both agreed to appear before a rabbinical arbitration court in order to secure and arrange for the giving of a *get*, or Jewish bill of divorce.[70] At the time they entered the agreement, both parties were traditionally observant Jews and ostensibly committed to abiding by Jewish law, which prescribes that in the event of a divorce, a Jewish wife may only remarry after having received a *get* that is voluntarily given by her husband. Following their civil divorce in Canadian court, the defendant waited for over nine years to receive her *get*, which the plaintiff, her ex-husband, refused to provide, and she finally began legal proceedings for breach of the original divorce settlement.

Several years later—fifteen years after the couple's civil divorce—Marcovitz gave the *get*, finally permitting Bruker to remarry under religious law. Bruker, however, sued for damages for breach of the original divorce agreement. The matter wound its way through the courts, and ultimately the Canadian Supreme Court ruled that the promise to give the *get* was a justiciable matter. The Court reasoned that the divorce settlement was an ordinary secular contract within the purview of the courts, and the fact that the agreement included a promise to perform a religious rite did not prevent the court from hearing an action for damages for breach of

69. *See* Michael Corkery & Jessica Silver-Greenberg, *In Religious Arbitration, Scripture is the Rule of Law*, N.Y. Times (Nov. 2, 2015), http://www.nytimes.com/2015/11/03/business/dealbook/in-religious-arbitration-scripture-is-the-rule-of-law.html.

70. Marcovitz v. Bruker, 3 S.C.R. 607 (Can.) (2007).

that contract, claims of religious freedom to not perform a religious ritual such as the giving of a get notwithstanding.[71]

The action in *Marcovitz* was for damages rather than for specific performance of the promise to give a *get*. Nevertheless, it is worth considering what may have happened had Bruker asked the court to compel her ex-husband to give the *get* itself, arguing perhaps that no amount of financial compensation would qualitatively compensate her for her inability to remarry under Jewish law. Some commentators have argued that it is unlikely Bruker could have prevailed in a legal action to compel Marcovitz to appear before a rabbinical court or to give the *get*, as this would have been "an impermissible breach of the husband's constitutionally protected freedom of religion."[72] The fact remains, however, that courts do in fact routinely compel recalcitrant parties to uphold their obligations under arbitration agreements. They can be compelled, under threat of being in contempt of court, to appear before religious arbitration tribunals, and can be forced to obey the decisions of religious arbitration tribunals that have been converted into judicial orders enforceable by court marshals and the state. This raises serious questions about whether and to what extent secular enforcement of religious arbitration can be achieved without seriously abridging individuals' rights to freely choose, change, and practice religion as their own consciences dictate.

H. SECULAR RECOGNITION OF RELIGIOUS ARBITRATION PROMOTES ISOLATION AND NON-INTEGRATION AMONG RELIGIOUS COMMUNITIES

Some commentators have argued that societal recognition and enforcement of religious arbitration is a problematic social ill that undermines important interests in the assimilation of religious communities into secular society. Some others have argued that the recognition of religious arbitration helps promote a multicultural society in which numerous religious groups can better maintain their own identities, cultures, and practices. However, opponents of religious arbitration—including members of some religious communities—have countered that such multiculturalism is to be avoided rather than encouraged.[73] Even from a standard liberal perspective,

71. *Id.*
72. Ayelet Shachar, *Privatizing Diversity: A Cautionary Tale from Religious Arbitration in Family Law*, 9 Theoretical Inq. L. 573, 595 n.52 (2008).
73. *See* Wolfe, *supra* note 20, at 461–63.

these commenters argue that by permitting religious groups to remain insular and unintegrated into mainstream societal norms, secular enforcement of religious arbitration actually highlights and widens gaps between ordinary members of society and religiously observant "others."[74] Rather than encourage isolation and factionalism, society ought to encourage minority groups and cultures to more fully integrate into a broader societal ethos. At least in part, this means that all members of society ought to order their lives and affairs under the same sets of norms and values; or, at the very least, they should not be given encouragement and government support for avoiding doing so.

Religious isolationism within secular societies, moreover, correlates to a number of serious communal ills within religious communities that ought to be discouraged and if possible avoided. Some of the most often-referenced concerns relate to the subjugation and oppression of traditionally disempowered members of religious communities, especially women and children. Feminist criticisms of religious group autonomy within secular societies maintain that, by giving faith communities limited powers of self-government through the legal enforcement of religious arbitration, the state entrenches traditional power structures and puts vulnerable parties at greater disadvantages within their communities.[75] This is especially true in connection with secular recognition of religious dispute resolution. By legally enabling internal problem-solving through communal channels, many abuses and problems within religious groups are kept in-house. Victims of domestic violence, sexual abuse, predatory lending, unfair business and real estate practices, poor education, and religious coercion to conform to communal norms can be effectively pressured to keep their complaints within the community, where oftentimes they will not be effectively addressed. Indeed, in some isolationist communities, members may not even understand or be aware of alternative options.[76] Although there are numerous factors that contribute to such internal communal dynamics, secular recognition and enforcement of religious arbitration helps enable and give force to some of the kinds of communal institutions and authority structures that make them possible.

Another, possibly counterintuitive, argument against secular enforcement of religious arbitration, suggests that enabling religious communities

74. *See* Shahnaz Khan, *Canadian Muslim Women and* Shari'a *Law: A Feminist Response to "Oh! Canada,"* 6 CAN. J. WOMEN & L. 52, 62–63 (1993).

75. *See* Ayelet Shachar, *Religion, State, and the Problem of Gender: New Modes of Citizenship and Governance in Diverse Societies*, 50 MCGILL L.J. 49, 58 (2005).

76. *See* Fried, *supra* note 50, at 646–47; Nicholas Pengelley, *Faith Based Arbitration in Ontario*, 9 VINDOBONA J. INT'L COM. L. & ARB. 111, 122 (2005).

to be more autonomous and separate from the broader society actually hampers such groups from preserving and transmitting their religious practices and cultures. In order for religious traditions to remain relevant sources of norms and values, those traditions must offer compelling accounts of the world in which their adherents live and which they experience. Doing so, however, requires religions to take cognizance of, and perhaps interact with the real-world contexts in which they are situated. Such interaction produces subtle but unmistakable interpretive evolutions in religious thinking and practice. Dogmas and rituals deeply irreconcilable with societal norms and values are negotiated, cabined, and sometimes marginalized.

At the same time, religious values enter into public discourses, and societal sensibilities and cultures take on traditional elements. In short, by being forced to interact and contend with societal realities, religions organically adapt to their environments in a way that keeps them relevant and vibrant, but also integrous and true to their roots and traditions. Opponents of religious arbitration argue, however, that to the extent that secular institutions permit religious communal autonomy, they also enable religious groups to avoid such dialectical interactions with the wider contexts in which they exist. The result can often be the development of static and archaic religious traditions and practices that have no resonance for many of their adherents and the real world. Such faiths become dead letters rather than meaningful mediums for communicating values and structuring human relationships with each other and with the divine.[77] Put differently, the kind of religious autonomy facilitated through secular recognition of religious arbitration fosters an ossification of faith. Rather than bend and adapt, minority religions and cultures are more apt to break. By denying religious communities dispute resolution autonomy based on ecumenical norms and values, society can actually help religious traditions remain relevant.[78]

77. *See* Suzanne Last Stone, *The Intervention of American Law in Jewish Divorce: A Pluralist Approach*, 34 Isr. L. Rev. 170, 202–05 (2000).

78. *See* Wolfe, *supra* note 20, at 462–63.

CHAPTER 10

Religious Arbitration as a Secular Value

The Case for Religious Arbitration

In the previous chapter, the arguments against religious arbitration were laid out, examined, and parsed for their strengths and weaknesses. This chapter does the same for the case in favor of religious arbitration.

A. RECOGNIZING RELIGIOUS ARBITRATION IS A RELIGIOUS FREEDOM IMPERATIVE

The foregoing discussion offers a powerful case against secular law recognition and judicial enforcement of religious arbitration agreements and awards. Commitments to religious liberty and religious non-establishment may require liberal states to give religious arbitration the benefit of the same legal protections offered to commercial and other non-religious dispute resolution. If society wishes to enable and encourage citizens to utilize private dispute resolution forums rather than state courts to resolve litigious conflicts, then it must do so by putting both religious and non-religious arbitration mechanisms on equal footing. Any other result would amount to a government attempt to disestablish religion in favor of irreligion, a serious constitutional problem, at least in the United States. From this perspective, secular societies ought to create frameworks for legally enforceable religious arbitration, not because they want to, but because they have to. Either all forms of arbitration must be permitted, or else none may be.[1]

The doctrine of government neutrality between religion and irreligion is firmly established in American law and policy. In several important cases, the Supreme Court has held that this kind of neutrality is an important aspect of First Amendment limits of government involvement with religion. The establishment clause of the United States Constitution provides that "Congress shall make no law respecting an establishment of religion."[2] In addition to its prohibiting the government from creating an official state church, lending aid to particular religious faiths, or incorporating particular religious doctrines, practices, or teachings into law, this provision has also been understood as precluding attempts by government to establish or privilege secularism or irreligion over religion. In short, it requires the state to take a neutral stance toward religion, neither supporting it nor hamstringing it. As Justice Hugo Black wrote in *Everson v. Board of Education of the Township of Ewing*: "'The Establishment Clause' requires the state to be a neutral in its relations with groups of religious believers and nonbelievers; it does not require the state to be their adversary. State power is no more to be used so as to handicap religions than it is to favor them."[3]

This sentiment has been confirmed numerous times by American courts. In *Lemon v. Kurtzman*, in which the Supreme Court established an important test for determining whether government actions violate the establishment clause, the Court held that the state cannot enact laws whose principal or primary effect either advances or inhibits religion.[4] Likewise, in one concurring opinion, Justice Sandra Day O'Connor urged that "[e]very government practice must be judged . . . to determine whether it constitutes an endorsement or disapproval of religion."[5] In *Grand Rapids School District v. Ball*, the Supreme Court invalidated two state educational programs that provided classes to religious private school students on religious school premises and using public school teachers. The Court found that these programs principally advanced religion by relieving private religious schools of the burden of paying for such instruction themselves, making

1. *See* Nicholas Walter, *Religious Arbitration in the United States and Canada*, 52 Santa Clara L. Rev. 501, 563–67 (2012).

2. U.S. Const., amen. I.

3. Everson v. Bd. of Educ. of the Township of Ewing, 330 U.S. 1, 18 (1947). *See also* Committee for Public Ed. & Religious Liberty v. Nyquist, 413 U.S. 756, 792–93 (1973) ("A proper respect for both the Free Exercise and the Establishment Clauses compels the State to pursue a course of 'neutrality' toward religion.").

4. *See* Lemon v. Kurtzman, 403 U.S. 602, 613 (1971).

5. Capitol Square Rev. & Advisory Bd. v. Pinette, 515 U.S. 753, 778 (1995) (O'Connor, J., concurring).

the religious school more educationally compelling, and freeing up private school funds to be used for additional religious purposes. In making its ruling, however, the Court reasserted the importance of a neutral approach to religious establishments in general, ruling that "[if] . . . identification [of the government with religion] conveys a message of government endorsement or disapproval of religion, a core purpose of the Establishment Clause is violated."[6]

To date, there have not been any cases that have explicitly raised the issue of government favoring irreligion over religion that have been decided on establishment clause grounds. More typically, such cases involve government actors, such as public schools and universities, discriminating between religious and non-religious groups or interests in providing public funding or public space. In *Rosenberger v. Rector and Visitors of the University of Virginia*, for example, the Court reviewed the policy of a public university that provided funds to student organizations that met certain criteria, but that denied such funding to a group that met those qualifications because the group planned to use the funds to publish a Christian magazine.[7] Another case concerned a policy by some New York public schools to permit residents of the school district to use school facilities for after-school educational or artistic programming, but that denied an application to use school facilities for meetings of a religious group.[8]

In both cases, the schools argued that their discrimination against religious groups was grounded in their desire to avoid infringing on the establishment clause; they believed that they could not provide public money or facilities to religious groups to further religious purposes without violating the First Amendment. In both cases, the Supreme Court ruled the schools' actions unconstitutional, not because the schools had impermissibly favored irreligion over religion, but because both had engaged in illegal restrictions on free speech based on the viewpoints that the religious groups sought to express. Underlying the Court's rulings in such cases is a concern that discrimination against religious speakers or viewpoints risks "fostering a pervasive bias or hostility to religion, which could undermine the very neutrality that Establishment Clause requires."[9]

A legal framework that permitted and enforced non-religious arbitration while not giving the same benefit to religious dispute resolution would likely not implicate free expression concerns. Nevertheless, based

6. Grand Rapids School Dist. v. Ball, 473 U.S. 373, 472 (1985).
7. Rosenberger v. Rector and Visitors of the Univ. of Virginia, 515 U.S. 819 (1995).
8. Good News Club v. Milford Central Sch., 533 U.S. 98 (2001).
9. *Rosenberger*, 15 U.S. at 845–46.

on the United States Supreme Court's establishment clause jurisprudence, it seems reasonable to say that such a discriminatory arbitration regime could not pass constitutional muster. It is almost beyond doubt that a scheme in which courts were instructed to enforce religious arbitration agreements and awards, but not irreligious ones, would constitute an unlawful establishment of religion because it would endorse and advance religion. But "if giving special benefits to religion is favoritism, advancement, and endorsement, then discriminating against religion is hostility, inhibition, and disapproval."[10] Therefore, if American law is to permit private arbitration that meets certain qualifications, it cannot categorically refuse to recognize and enforce religious dispute resolution processes that satisfy the same requirements.

There are, however, important limits on governments' constitutional obligations to respect religious practices and commitments. These qualifications permit the state to burden religious practices, provided that is does so in a neutral, generally applicable way. This doctrine enables the state to address many of the salient concerns for the procedural and substantive justice of religious arbitration processes without impermissibly treading upon constitutional guarantees of free exercise or prohibitions on religious establishments. This doctrine was first articulated by the United States Supreme Court in *Employment Division v. Smith.*[11] The case concerned two individuals who had used the drug peyote as part of a Native American religious ritual. The individuals were fired for using the peyote, which was a crime under state law. The Court ruled that it was not unconstitutional to criminalize peyote use or to apply the criminal statute to the Native American religious users in that case.[12] This decision was based on the understanding that the free exercise clause does not "relieve an individual of the obligation to comply with a 'valid and neutral law of general applicability on the ground that the law proscribes (or prescribes) conduct that his religion prescribes (or proscribes).'"[13] *Smith* thus stands for the important idea that facially neutral, generally applicable and otherwise valid laws not designed to either advance or inhibit religion or religious practice, but that nevertheless burden the ability of religious individuals or communities to fully observe their faiths, do not violate the First Amendment.

10. Eugene Volokh, *Equal Treatment Is Not Establishment*, 13 NOTRE DAME J. L., ETHICS & PUB. POL'Y 341 (1999).
11. Employment Division v. Smith, 494 U.S. 872 (1990).
12. *See id.*
13. *Smith*, 494 U.S. at 879 (quoting United States v. Lee, 455 U.S. 252, 263 n.2 (1982) (Stevens, J. concurring).

Following *Smith*, then, it would be perfectly valid for the state to refuse to respect or enforce all private arbitration awards, both religious and non-religious, as that would be a neutral and generally applicable law that only happens to burden religious practice.[14] Likewise, laws designed to ensure the fairness and justice of all arbitration proceedings—such as many of the existing provisions of federal and state arbitration frameworks—would likely pass constitutional muster even if they did restrict the ability of some religious groups to fully observe and implement the totality of their respective traditional judicial and dispute resolution processes and remedies.[15] Indeed, it is not hard to imagine a secular law arbitration framework that imposed such onerous requirements on all arbitration proceedings so as to make religious arbitration—at least arbitration that would comply with traditional religious norms and values—practically impossible. Such laws could require arbitration panels to follow state rules of evidence or pleadings, regardless of religious laws to the contrary. They might also provide that religious tribunals must respect the same kinds of equality rules respected in secular adjudication, such as the inclusion of women as arbitrators or not drawing gender, age, or faith distinctions between the statuses of the testimony of different witnesses. State laws could also prohibit arbitration panels from enforcing norms or ordering remedies that are substantially at odds with secular notions of substantive and distributive justice embraced by societal law and policy. Such rules would substantially restrict the actual practice of many forms of traditional religious dispute resolution without actually violating either free exercise or establishment concerns.

Of course, not all jurisdictions maintain the kinds of strict establishment limits that exist in the United States; nor are such restrictions on states' privileging religion over non-religion or irreligion over religion strictly necessary from a standard liberal perspective. Modern Western nation-states have adopted a range of different approaches to this issue, ranging from American-style neutrality; to freedom or religion alongside an official state church, as in the United Kingdom; to the affirmative secularism and public hostility toward religious practice seen in countries such as France. In many cases, the United States included, these commitments are products of unique historical experiences.[16]

14. *See* Walter, *supra* note 1, at 563–54.
15. *See* Amanda M. Baker, *A Higher Authority: Judicial Review of Religious Arbitration*, 37 Vt. L. Rev. 157, 197–98 (2012).
16. *See generally* Stephen V. Monsma & J. Christopher Soper, The Challenge of Pluralism: Church and State in Five Democracies (2009).

Canadian restrictions specifically on religious dispute resolution are illustrative. In 2006, Ontario moved to place a total ban on faith-based arbitration in family law matters. This move, grounded in a variety of different concerns about Islamic arbitration, was reinforced by a more general policy in Canada that permits public restrictions on religious practices or religious access to public institutions, provided that such restrictions are applied in an even-handed way, and do not privilege or burden any particular faith more than any others.[17]

In any case, it seems reasonable to say that not all societies should be expected to enforce religious dispute resolution as a non-establishment necessity. Even in the United States, the First Amendment likely does not absolutely require societal enforcement of religious arbitration agreements and awards. Establishment concerns provide some basis for arguing that religious arbitration must be permitted and judicially enforced, even as there are good reasons to be wary of it. However, free exercise doctrine under *Smith* suggests that states can severely restrict the practice of traditional religious arbitration, provided they do so in a religiously neutral manner.

B. RELIGIOUS ARBITRATION OFTEN RESOLVES DISPUTES BETTER THAN SECULAR ADJUDICATION

Even if affording wide latitude and strong legal backing to religious dispute resolution processes may not be legally required—and certainly not in all jurisdictions—there are a number of strong policy reasons for why secular societies *should* judicially enforce religious arbitration. One such claim is highly pragmatic, and speaks to an important personal liberty interest that undergirds much of liberal law and policy. Put briefly, by allowing religious arbitrators rather than state courts to resolve disputes between parties who choose to appear and litigate is such forums, society can better ensure that conflicts are resolved judiciously, and that those resolutions reflect as much as possible the understandings and expectations of the parties involved.

As discussed above, the religious question doctrine often prevents courts from addressing and deciding questions that touch on religious issues. Despite the fact that disputes that arise between religiously observant individuals or within religious institutional or organizational contexts often raise such religious questions, and despite the fact that such

17. *See* Walter, *supra* note 1, at 506.

questions must be answered in order to resolve such matters, courts in the United States are often hesitant to address them lest they become entangled in making normative judgments about correct religious dogma or practice.[18] Whether courts are willing to address them or not, however, such matters represent genuine disputes between individuals and organizations that must be resolved if people are to exist and function together in society. It is important to realize that these kinds of conflicts *will* get resolved. The critical question is whether society wants such matters dealt with internally by religious authorities without any legal oversight.

If there are legitimate concerns about unfairness, injustice, duress, and discrimination against disadvantaged parties in even legally-recognized and nominally legally-compliant religious arbitration proceedings, such concerns are only exacerbated by forcing religious dispute resolution underground. It is important, therefore, for society to provide ways in which such conflicts can be addressed. If they cannot be dealt with by the courts because doing so would infringe on important interests in maintaining strict separations between religion and state, then the law ought to provide for other avenues of dispute resolution. Legally recognizing and judicially enforcing religious arbitration agreements and awards provides such an outlet. Indeed, American courts have noted repeatedly when invoking the religious question doctrine that religious disputes should properly be resolved by religious authorities.[19]

Of course, the religious question doctrine does not bar courts from addressing all disputes that touch on ecumenical concerns. American courts have held that they may adjudicate religious issues if they can do so using "neutral principles of law." This doctrine was announced in *Jones v. Wolf*, a case involving a property dispute between a local church and its broader umbrella organization.[20] The Court did not refuse to resolve the case on account of its being an essentially religious dispute between two ecumenical institutions and implicating religious documents, such as the general church's bylaws. Instead, the Court held that judges can resolve religious conflicts if they can do so using neutral principles of law. The property dispute in *Jones* could have been disposed of by applying ordinary

18. *See, e.g.*, Presbyterian Church v. Mary Elizabeth Blue Hull Mem'l Presbyterian Church, 393 U.S. 440 (1969). *See also* Jared A. Goldstein, *Is There a "Religious Question" Doctrine? Judicial Authority to Examine Religious Practices and Beliefs*, 54 CATH. U. L. REV. 497 (2005).

19. *See Serbian Orthodox Diocese v. Milivojevich,*426 U. S. 696, 426 U. S. 710 (1976); *Maryland & Va. Churches v. Sharpsburg Church,* 396 U. S. 367, 396 U. S. 368 (1970).

20. *See* Jones v. Wolf, 443 U.S. 595 (1979).

contract and statutory interpretation doctrines to the bylaws and agreements that existed between the church and its parent body. As no doctrinal or theological questions had to be considered in order to resolve the matter, the Court found that it could be adjudicated, even if the basic dispute was a religious issue.[21]

The neutral principles of law doctrine has been applied numerous times to permit state courts to address questions that touch on religious concerns without running afoul of constitutional limits. Indeed, in one case, a court went so far as to hold that an agreement to arbitrate a dispute before a "beth din"—without specifying which particular rabbinical court was intended—could be enforced under the neutral principles of law doctrine. This was despite the fact that enforcing the contract would require a court to make decisions about whether a particular dispute resolution tribunal qualified as a *beth din* and did or did not satisfy the terms of the agreement.[22]

Even as courts can and do address religious issues, there is good reason to think that perhaps they should not do so: that such matters may be better resolved through religious arbitration processes.[23] One of the main objectives of secular arbitration frameworks is to provide dispute resolution forums that will be able to approach specific kinds of cases with more focused expertise in the relevant facts and concerns than can state courts. There are arbitration panels with special expertise in construction, international trade, consumer credit, various professional and vocational trades, education and school administration, and numerous other fields. This helps ensure that disputes arising in these fields get resolved as efficiently and effectively as possible, and with a close correlation between adjudicatory results, parties' understandings and expectations, and the actual realities of the fields in which conflicts arise.

Religious disputes are no different. Many of the conflicts that arise between religiously observant parties are situated in particular religious and communal contexts that are best—and perhaps really only—understood by those who are themselves situated within those same contexts. As Caryn Litt Wolfe has observed, many people turn to faith-based arbitration precisely because they feel that religious arbitrators will understand their problems and the nature of their dispute better than secular judges. Likewise, disputants often view religious arbitrators as being better positioned to reach effective solutions to litigious matters because arbitrators

21. *See id.*
22. *See* Meshel v. Ohev Shalom Talmud Torah, 869 A.2d 343 (2005).
23. *See supra* Chapter Three.

will be situated within the same communal contexts, ecumenical worldviews, and intuitive understandings of the workings of the religious community as the litigants.[24] "[J]ust as people prefer bringing commercial disputes to arbitration because the arbitrator will have specific knowledge of the area, parties utilize religious arbitration because the arbitrator is better equipped to deal with religious issues."[25]

The notion that religious arbitration ought to be legally recognized because it helps secure dispute resolution more in line with the understandings and expectations of religious litigants is reinforced by general legal preferences for freedom of contract and respect for parties' contractual autonomy. Many contemporary legal systems are premised on the idea that individuals should as a matter of principle be able to enter into whatever contracts they like, and be able to rely on those agreements to be binding on other contracting parties as well as themselves. There are limits to this, of course. Contractual autonomy cannot be used to consent to be the victim of violence in order to absolve the perpetrator of criminal liability, and courts will refuse to enforce contracts made freely but under circumstances in which there were large differences between the relative bargaining powers of contracting parties, or where parties contract extremely unfair terms. However, in general, the law presumes that people are the best judges of their own interests, and respects their contractual choices and preferences.[26]

One of the chief reasons for this respect for contractual freedom is a policy stance that views contracting parties as being the ones best positioned to really understand their own needs and preferences, and to form agreements that meet those interests and expectations. This policy of regard for individuals' own assessments of their interests and understandings of their circumstances suggests that judicial enforcement of religious arbitration may be appropriate. When parties have chosen to have a dispute resolved by a religious tribunal, there is good reason to assume that they did so precisely because religious arbitrators are more likely to understand the critical subject-matter subtext of the underlying facts, conflict, and sought-after remedies, and will therefore craft better decisions.

As discussed extensively in Chapter Three, there is good reason to think that religious arbitrators can better address cases arising in religious

24. *See* Caryn Litt Wolfe, *Faith-Based Arbitration: Friend or Foe? An Evaluation of Religious Arbitration Systems and Their Interaction with Secular Courts*, 75 FORD. L. REV. 427, 441 (2006).
25. *Id.*
26. *See* Walter, *supra* note 1, at 559–61.

contexts even when the religious question doctrine would not preclude secular courts from adjudicating such matters. Indeed, there are numerous examples of judges reaching the wrong decisions in these kinds of matters precisely because they are not well-situated to understand the religious issues at hand—and cannot become fully conversant without treading upon religious freedom concerns. Judicial treatment of Islamic *mahr* agreements, and Jewish *ketubah* contracts in the family law context, as well as the *heter iska* in commercial settings, are but a few examples of this concern. Courts dealing with such matters often reach inconsistent results, and also issue rulings that respond poorly to litigants' actual needs and interests.

In a recent and particularly glaring example, federal courts considered an appeal by a Jewish prison inmate who was denied a request to engage in group Torah study with two other Jewish prisoners.[27] Although the prison regulations at issue permit such study in order to allow prisoners to observe their faiths, the prison warden reached the conclusion that Judaism only permits Torah study to take place with a rabbi, or else in the presence of a *minyan*, a quorum of ten adult Jewish men. In upholding the prison warden's policy, a trial court found that the policy did not substantially burden the inmate's religion because he could still engage in private worship.[28] The court reasoned that as the inmate's own religion dictated certain conditions for group study, it could not be burdensome to his religion to require those conditions be met before such study would be permitted in the prison.[29] This case highlights how badly courts or other government officials can misunderstand religion. Simply put, the prison warden's understanding of Jewish law is astoundingly incorrect. Torah study, whether individually or in groups, does not require either the presence of a rabbi or of a *minyan* quorum. Jews everywhere can and do study alone, with partners, in small groups, with and without rabbis, for millennia. Moreover, it is also incorrect to suppose that significant restrictions on a Jewish prisoner's ability to engage in Torah study do not substantially burden his or her religious practice. Torah study is a basic feature of Jewish life and practice for clergy and laity alike. Jewish law prescribes that Jews must maintain set times to study Torah each and every day, and the culture of Torah learning is one of the most prominent features of traditionally-observant Jewish life. Although it is certainly possible that a Jewish prisoner's interest in studying Torah could be outweighed by concerns for prison safety and order,

27. *See* Ben-Levi v. Brown, 60 Fed. Appx. 899 (4th Cir. 2015) (*cert. denied*, Ben-Levi v. Brown, 577 U.S. _ (2016)).

28. *See* Ben-Levi v. Brown, 577 U.S. _ (2016) (Alito, J. dissenting at *6–7).

29. *See id.* (Alito, J. dissenting at *8–9).

it is plainly incorrect to think that not being able to study does not place substantial burdens on Jewish religious practice.

Some have suggested that the law might draw a distinction between religious and secular disputes. These commentators argue that, although religious disputes should be resolved through religious arbitration for many of the reasons discussed above, secular conflicts ought not to be submitted to faith-based dispute resolution processes. This scheme would accommodate the need to have religious matters dealt with by those most familiar and best situated to address them fully and properly, while also limiting the potentials for injustice and abuse in religious dispute resolution processes.[30] This approach misses the fact that, for many religious individuals and communities, there is no such thing as a purely secular dispute. Although some religious traditions, such as Catholicism, distinguish between ecumenical concerns governed by religious law and secular matters governed by societal norms, other faiths, including Judaism, Islam, and others make no such distinction. This does not mean, of course, that Judaism and Islam posit that secular law is never binding; it merely suggests that for many observant Jews and Muslims, religion means resolving all private disputes in accordance with religious rules in religious courts. In these traditions, religious norms and values govern virtually all aspects of life, and impact the ways in which many religious people think about how they ought to order their affairs in both the conventionally "ecclesiastical" and the secular realms. Drawing what is from religious perspective an artificial distinction between purely secular and purely religious disputes denies the very real normativity of religious systems for their adherents who often feel genuinely bound to such rules in all aspects of their private affairs and relationships. It does little to help religious people and communities resolve what they regard as important religious issues through religious channels, and also signals to them that the state and society do not respect, understand, or accommodate their genuine religious commitments.

C. RELIGIOUS ARBITRATION IS NECESSARY FOR RESOLVING RELIGIOUS PROBLEMS

The foregoing section considered the value of religious arbitration for cases that courts either cannot address due to religious question doctrine,

30. *See, e.g.*, Walter, *supra* note 1, at 552–54.

or should not resolve due to their lack of expertise and immersion in the religious contexts from which such disputes arise. In some of these cases, secular societies should provide for legally enforceable religious arbitration because courts will be constitutionally incapable of addressing religious issues, and societal order demands that there be some normative means of binding third-party dispute resolution. In other cases, although courts adjudicate them in theory, religious arbitration offers a model of dispute resolution that will resolve such conflicts in ways that best reflect the understandings, intentions, and needs of religious parties. Religious dispute resolution is important in a third category of cases as well. There is a class of cases that state courts *could* decide based on neutral principles of law without violating the religious question doctrine, but the nature of these questions is such that secular judicial rulings would have no religious effect in the eyes of religiously observant disputants. These matters typically involve the fulfillment of ritual obligations that can only be ordered by religious authorities. Even if and when courts dispose of such cases, from the perspective of religious individuals and communities, such judicial resolutions would not solve the basic religious problem. Court rulings in such cases would leave parties no better off—and indeed sometimes even worse off—than before.

Perhaps the most famous example of this phenomenon is the "*agunah* problem" in Jewish law.[31] As discussed earlier, traditional Jewish law prescribes that a divorce can only be effected by the willing giving of a *get*, or bill of divorce written in a prescribed ritual manner, by the husband to the wife. Because the *get* must be given willingly, and because except in the rarest and most exceptional circumstances Jewish law does not provide for the judicial dissolution of marriage, husbands can and sometimes do use their refusal to grant a *get* as leverage in divorce proceedings. Without the *get*, the wife will continue to be considered religiously married, and will not be able to marry anyone else under rabbinic law, and any romantic relationships she subsequently has with other men will be considered adulterous, with serious religio-legal and communal implications for both herself and any future children she may have. A woman whose husband refuses to grant her a *get* after the practical dissolution of the marital relationship is called an *agunah*, a "chained woman." She remains metaphorically chained

31. *See* Rabbi Irving Breitowitz, Between Civil and Religious Law: The Plight of the *Agunah* in American Society (1993); Michael J. Broyde, Marriage, Divorce, and the Abandoned Wife in Jewish law: A Conceptual Understanding of the *Agunah* Problems in America (2001).

to her husband and a dead marriage, unable to move on with her life within the framework of Jewish religious observance.[32]

Because the *get* must be given willingly, a rabbinic court cannot directly compel a husband to give the *get*, nor can it unilaterally dissolve the marriage. Moreover, because Jewish law places fewer bars and consequences on a man marrying or having a sexual relationship with more than one woman than on a woman marrying or having a sexual relationship with more than one man, husbands have an upper hand in religious divorce proceedings. A husband can withhold a *get* from his religiously observant wife and thereby impose very substantial handicaps on her life without suffering reciprocal harms to himself.[33] Traditionally, rabbinic courts operating in Jewish communities that enjoyed some measure of legal autonomy within their host societies could apply certain kinds of pressure permitted by Jewish law in order to convince the husband to agree to give the *get*. In modern times, however, rabbinic courts in most jurisdictions have no such authority. Indeed, exerting such pressure would violate secular criminal laws, as one recent case in the United States illustrates.[34] This situation has resulted in what is called the "*agunah* problem," the phenomenon of husbands refusing to give their wives *gets*, even after the effective dissolution of their marriages and the completion of civil divorce proceedings, in order to compel their wives to agree to more favorable property division, custody, and child support settlements.

Jewish communities have attempted to address the *agunah* problem in a variety of different ways. Some have advocated changes to the contemporary practice of Jewish law. According to this approach, the *agunah* problem could be solved by adopting some non-normative legal opinions that permit rabbinic courts to unilaterally annul marriages in certain cases.[35] Others have proposed doing away with formal marriage entirely, and structuring relationships under Jewish laws of contract rather than the more ritualistic framework of marriage. This would enable contractual "marital" relationships to be dissolved without the need for a *get*, thereby removing husbands' leverage over their wives.[36] Both of these proposals

32. *See supra* Chapter Three (D).
33. *See* BROYDE, *supra* note 31, at 17–27.
34. *See* https://www.fbi.gov/contact-us/field-offices/newark/news/press-releases/orthodox-jewish-rabbi-sentenced-to-more-than-three-years-in-prison-for-role-in-conspiracy-to-violently-extort-divorce-consent-from-reluctant-husband (December 14, 2015) (last visited Jan. 23, 2017). *See generally* AVIAD HACOHEN & BLU GREENBERG, THE TEARS OF THE OPPRESSED: AN EXAMINATION OF THE *AGUNAH* PROBLEM: BACKGROUND AND *HALAKHIC* SOURCES 20–22 (2004).
35. *See* BROYDE, *supra* note 31, at 11–12.
36. *See id.* at 12–13.

have been widely rejected within observant Jewish communities, in large part because their adoption would threaten to undermine the sanctity and significance of Jewish marriage and committed Jewish family life as an important religious good.[37]

A third approach has been to get states to pass secular legislation that either bars individuals who are preventing their spouses from obtaining a religious divorce to obtain a civil divorce, or penalizes spouses who prevent the giving of a *get* as part of civil divorce decrees.[38] The first of these solutions is New York State's 1984 Get Law. This law provided that a plaintiff will not be granted a civil divorce until he or she has removed all barriers to the other spouse's ability to remarry. Although the law was facially neutral, it was designed to put pressure on Jewish husbands who refused to give their wives *gets* by preventing them from obtaining a civil divorce settlement.[39] In 1992, New York passed another Get Law, which directed courts to consider "the effect of a barrier to marriage" as one of the thirteen factors that must be considered when adjudicating a division of marital assets. In effect, the law permitted courts to award a wife a larger portion of the marital assets than she would otherwise be entitled to if her husband had not withheld her *get*.[40]

The New York *get* laws attempted to do through legislation what courts had been doing for decades through a variety of other legal theories. In some cases, courts have found legally enforceable agreements between husbands and wives that obligate the giving of a *get*. In most of these cases, the courts have declined to order the specific performance of such promises due to constitutional concerns for religious freedom, but have upheld the imposition of fines and other penalties upon recalcitrant husbands.[41] In one case, a court refused to grant any affirmative legal requests by the recalcitrant spouse—in that instance, the wife—until she fulfilled her contractual obligations to accept the *get*.[42] In *Waxstein v. Waxstein*, a New York court went so far as to directly order specific performance of an agreement in which the husband had promised to give the wife a *get*.[43] Other courts have held that husbands are legally obligated to give their wives *gets* based

37. *See* HACOHEN & GREENBERG, *supra* note 34, at 21.
38. *See* BROYDE, *supra* note 31, at 12–13, 35.
39. *See generally* Zornberg, *supra* note 39, at *Beyond the Constitution: Is the New York* Get *Legislation Good Law*, 15 PACE L. REV. 703, 728–33 (1995).
40. *See* BROYDE, *supra* note 31, at 35.
41. *See, e.g.*, Marguiles v. Marguiles, 344 N.Y.S.2d 482 (1973).
42. *See* Rubin v. Rubin, 348 N.Y.S.2d 61 (1973). *See also* Pal v. Pal, N.Y. L.J., July, 1973 at 13.
43. *See* Waxstein v. Waxstein, 395 N.Y.S. 2d 877 (1976) (*aff'd* 394 N.Y.S.2d 253 (1977).

on an implied contractual promise in the *ketubah*, or Jewish religious marriage contract. The *ketubah* includes language in which the husband promises to take his spouse as a wife "in accordance with the laws and Moses and Israel." At least one court has held that this language implies a contractual promise to grant a *get* in those cases in which Jewish law—the Law of Moses and Israel—requires it.[44] Finally, some courts have attempted to compel recalcitrant Jewish husbands to give their wives *gets* by treating the refusal to give a *get* as a tort, such as fraud or the intentional infliction of emotional distress.[45] Those courts have not directly ordered the giving of a *get*, of course, but they have sustained causes of action by wives seeking financial compensation from their husbands who refuse to give them *gets*. Both legislation and judicial actions on *get* cases evince a societal interest in remedying a serious religious problem through secular legal mechanisms.[46]

These efforts by secular law to remedy the *agunah* problem highlight one of the chief deficiencies inherent in dealing with some kinds of religious problems in secular courts, and with not affirmatively empowering religious arbitrators to address them effectively and decisively. In short, when American courts attempt to administer the *get* giving process or interfere with this tightly regulated religious sacrament, their efforts at helping may actually do more harm than good. The specific problem is that, according to traditional Jewish law, a *get* is only valid if given willingly by the husband. The use of coercive measures against a recalcitrant husband, especially by a secular court or legal authority, will typically result in the *get*'s being considered null and void under traditional rabbinic law. Although Jewish law does permit rabbinic courts with the authority to use certain coercive measures against recalcitrant husbands, such measures must be applied only by rabbinic authorities pursuant to a rabbinic court's ruling that the giving of a *get* is legally required in that specific case. According to many contemporary Jewish law authorities, *gets* issued as a result of penalties imposed through secular legislation or by the order of state courts are thus invalid; they do not result in a religiously recognized divorce.[47] Even more bizarrely, a husband's giving such a court-ordered *get* would likely help him avoid further legal penalties or liabilities—this despite the fact that, from a religious law perspective, his invalidly given *get* has accomplished nothing for his observant and religiously still-married wife.

44. *See* Stern v. Stern, 5 Fam. L. Rep. (BNA) 2810 (1979).
45. *See, e.g.*, Weiss v. Goldfeder, N.Y.L.J., Oct. 26, 1990 at 21 (1990).
46. *See generally* Zornberg, *supra* note 39, at 721–27.
47. *See* Broyde, *supra* note 31, at 103–16.

An alternative approach to dealing with the *agunah* problem focuses on utilizing existing secular law arbitration frameworks to put religiously permitted pressure on husbands to give *gets* to their wives. Generally speaking, this approach involves using legally compliant arbitration agreements in which both spouses agree to adjudicate their religious divorce in a *beit din*, a rabbinic court. One early example of this model is the 1954 case of *Koeppel v. Koeppel*, where the parties had signed a prenuptial agreement that required both spouses to appear before a rabbinic court in the event of a dissolution of their marriage.[48] Although the court in that case found the agreement enforceable, it also concluded that the *beit din* provision was too vague to warrant a ruling for specific performance of the promise. Several decades later, however, a court upheld the enforceability of an innovative clause inserted into the *ketubah* contracts of some Jewish couples that required both spouses to appear before a *beit din* and abide by its decision, subject to financial penalties.[49]

Another arbitration-based solution was developed by the Rabbinical Council of America, a major Orthodox rabbinic association in the United States. This approach (the "RCA Prenup") utilizes a prenuptial agreement in which the husband makes a legally binding promise to fulfill the spousal marital support obligations incumbent upon him under traditional Jewish law from such time as the marital relationship effectively ends until the giving of a *get*.[50] Combined with an arbitration agreement that commits both parties to appear before a specific *beit din* to arbitrate their divorce settlement in accordance with Jewish law, this contractual approach to mitigating the *agunah* problem uses religious arbitration to establish a husband's religious duty to give a *get*, which in turn causes the clock to begin running on a daily spousal support obligation that can be enforced in court.[51] Critically, because this prenuptial agreement only imposes spousal support payments that the husband would otherwise be religiously obligated to provide for the duration of the couple's marriage, these payments do not amount to the kind of coercion that would invalidate the *get*, even when such support duties are enforced by a secular court. In effect, this arbitration-based response to the *agunah* problem—unlike solutions grounded in state legislation or judicial action—checks most of the necessary boxes. It ensures that the giving of a *get* will only be done pursuant to the finding of a competent religious tribunal rather than a secular court. It

48. *See* Koeppel v. Koeppel, 138 N.Y.S.2d 366 (1954).
49. *See* Avitzur v. Avitzur, 58 N.Y.2d 108 (1983).
50. *See* http://theprenup.org/prenupforms.html.
51. *See* BROYDE, *supra* note 31, at 66–70.

utilizes secular contract and arbitration law to impose religiously acceptable penalties upon a recalcitrant husband.[52] Most important, this solution seems to work. To date, there do not seem to be any cases of long-term *get* refusal by husbands who have previously signed this prenuptial arbitration agreement. Indeed, the spousal support provision of the RCA Prenup was recently upheld and enforced by a Connecticut state court in *Light v. Light*, leading to the husband giving the wife a *get*.[53]

The religious ineffectiveness of secular court adjudication in Jewish law is indeed far broader than just semi-sacral matters of marriage and divorce. Traditional rabbinic jurisprudence maintains a fairly strict bar on Jewish individuals and institutions litigating disputes with fellow Jews in secular courts. This religious restriction applies even if non-Jewish courts were to resolve such cases in accordance with substantive Jewish law norms and principles. Some Jewish legal sources go so far as to characterize the collection of secular court judgments against fellow Jews as theft.[54] In this view, state court judgements are fundamentally ineffective from a religious perspective; even in "secular" matters, religiously observant Jews can fulfill their religious responsibilities only by abiding by the rulings of rabbinic adjudicators. A system of secular law that does not provide for the effective faith-based resolution of disputes between Jewish individuals through arbitration is thus insufficient from a religious perspective.

This idea is not limited to Jewish law. Similar commitments exist in other religious systems as well. Muslim jurists have long held that Islam strongly encourages, if not requires, that disputes between Muslims that come within the ambit of Islamic religious law be resolved by Muslim judges or arbitrators in accordance with Islamic norms and values.[55] Some scholars have indeed held that Muslims may utilize secular courts under the religiously non-ideal conditions of Muslims living in non-Muslim societies without access to Islamic judges and courts. However, this is recognized merely as a stop-gap measure to facilitate the normal functioning of Muslim communities in secular contexts.[56] In principle, the religious

52. *See* Rahel Levmore, *Rabbinic Responses in Favor of Prenuptial Agreements*, 42 TRADITION 29 (2009).

53. *See* Light v. Light, 2012 WL 6743605 (Sup. Ct. Conn., 2012).

54. *See* Yaacov Feit, *The Prohibition against Going to Secular Courts*, 1 J. BETH DIN AM. 30 (2012).

55. *See, e.g.*, Qur'an 5:44 ("And whosoever does not judge by what God has revealed [and instead judges by other laws], such [people] are unbelievers . . ."), *id.* At 5:49–50.

56. *See, e.g.*, Shaykh Sa'd al-Humayd, Fatwa no. 11592, https://islamqa.info/en/11592 (last visited Jan. 23, 2017). (permitting a Muslim plaintiff to litigate a claim against a Muslim defendant in state court after exhausting alternatives and where no *Shari'a* court was available).

duties of observant Muslims toward each other and to God can only be fulfilled through the adjudication of those obligations through religious processes. Likewise, for many Christians, there is a strong belief that even basically secular disputes ought to be resolved by religious authorities and in accordance with biblical norms and values. Here too, dispute resolution in secular courts is religiously deficient.[57]

Thus, although it is often possible for state courts to resolve many of the conflicts between religious individuals consistent with constitutional norms and religious establishment concerns, the fact that such rulings may be legally valid from the perspective of society does not mean that they will also be regarded as religiously valid for observant litigants. For members of many faith traditions, the only way to effectively resolve disputes consistent with their religious duties is through faith-based arbitration. To the extent that secular society recognizes the value of ensuring that conflicts are resolved in a manner that provides closure and effective, non-violent social ordering for disputants, it also has an interest in facilitating effective and enforceable religious alternatives to state adjudicatory processes.

D. SECULAR RECOGNITION OF RELIGIOUS ARBITRATION HELPS MODERATE AND INTEGRATE RELIGION

The foregoing two sections have argued that secular recognition and enforcement of religious arbitration is important to the well-being of religion and religious individuals living in societies in which the general courts do not understand, embrace, or enforce their faith commitments. This section continues that line of argument by suggesting that religious interactions and negotiations with secular norms and values through their participation in alternative dispute resolution frameworks regulated by secular law can help faith traditions evolve and grow in ways that keep them meaningful and relevant in contemporary, non-religious contexts. But, this section also takes the claim one step further. Religious arbitration is not only good for religion, and it is not only a necessary consequence of secular commitments to religious freedom: religious arbitration is also good for secular societies. This section will contend that secular arbitration frameworks can help promote more complex and moderate modes of religious thought

57. *See* Judith M. Keegan, *The Peacemakers: Biblical Conflict Resolution and Reconciliation as a Model Alternative to Litigation,* 1987 J. Disp. Res. 11, 16–19 (1987).

and practice among religious minority groups in secular societies. This, in turn, helps ensure that religious individuals and communities view themselves as partners in a broader societal project that transcends parochial identities, and do not come to view their relationships with general society in oppositional terms. Secular societies ought to facilitate effective faith-based arbitration because by doing so they will encourage their constituent religious communities to become more integrated into society, and more moderate in their ecumenical convictions and practices.

One of the main concerns of liberal, multicultural polities is that various interest and identity groups within those societies will isolate themselves from general society. In doing so, such minority communities may reject the norms and values of the general society, and order their internal affairs in accordance with their own parochial preferences—often in ways that are deeply antithetical to the behavioral standards and mores that society seeks to uphold.[58] Oftentimes, these groups will be puritanically loyal to extreme understandings of their own practices and traditions. Fault lines may develop between isolationist communities and the general society, especially in the realm of individual rights, where the practices of insular groups tend to diverge from societal norms in ways that violate what society has determined to be fundamental individual rights and interests that government is obligated to protect. Minority communities following their own norms and values may treat people—even if just their own members—in ways that society feels it should not and cannot tolerate, especially in areas such as education, religious freedom, treatment of women and children, bodily integrity, and family matters. When this happens, government must step in to correct what it views as severe injustices perpetrated by such groups against their members or others. Entire internally-cohesive communities thus become resentful of what they view as societal oppression and overreaching, and develop antagonistic relations with other citizens, societal institutions, behavioral norms, and values. This, in turn, creates unhealthy, systematic tensions and discord that can undermine the foundations of civil societies from within.

Many scholars have noted that the incidence of religious isolationism and extremism is often related to the quality and quantity of religious freedom and autonomy that societies afford to their various constituent faith communities. There are, in truth, two schools of thought on this issue.

58. *See* Richard W. Garnett, *Do Churches Matter?: Towards an Institutional Understanding of the Religion Clauses*, 53 VILL. L. REV. 273, 292–93 (2008) (describing the importance that religious communities place on opportunities for self-governance).

According to some, dangerous, non-integrative expressions of religious thought and practice tend to flourish in the absence of religious freedom.[59] In this view, restrictions on the freedom to observe faith traditions within a given society tend to encourage religious individuals and communities to reject prevailing social norms and values, and to isolate themselves from societal participation. In such contexts, religious practitioners see little value in integrating into a society and culture that views their own deeply cherished commitments with suspicion or derision. This outlook then tends to produce an oppositional attitude toward the broader society, and isolationist religious tendencies. Restrictions on religious freedom signal societal opposition and disregard for religion. This often leads religious groups and individuals to reject prevailing societal norms and values, and to turn inward, isolating themselves from external influences.[60]

Restrictions on religious freedom and the resulting tendency of religious communities to isolate themselves from their host societies can also contribute to the development and adoption of more puritan and extremist approaches to religious thought and practice. In part, this is because when religious communities reject and isolate themselves from society, they avoid engaging with society's mores, values, and behavioral standards as genuine religious concerns. By not engaging with the broader societies in which they are situated—indeed by regarding those societies as irrelevant, or even dangerous—such isolationist religious cultures tend to cultivate more extreme modes of understanding and practicing of their faith, contributing to a cycle of increasing tension between religious communities and individuals and their societies.

Some other scholars maintain that there is an inverse relationship between religious freedom on the one hand, and religious isolationism and extremism on the other. On this view, unrestricted freedom of religion actually encourages religious communities to become more isolated from general society, and ultimately to become more puritanical and extreme in their religious commitments.[61] Freedom to practice and believe in one's

59. *See* Jean Bethke Elshtain, *On Religious Freedom and Religious Extremism* (Sept. 9, 2011), The Religious Freedom Project, The Berkley Center for Religion, Peace, and World Affairs, https://berkleycenter.georgetown.edu/essays/jean-bethke-elshtain-on-religious-freedom-and-religious-extremism.

60. This was the thrust of much of The Fundamentalism Project of the University of Chicago in the late 1990s and early 2000s, and the subject of an excellent edited work by the director of that project entitled "Fundamentalism Comprehended" edited by Martin E. Marty & R. Scott Appleby (1995, University of Chicago Press).

61. *See, e.g.*, Frederick Mark Gedicks, *The Recurring Paradox of Groups in the Liberal State*, 2010 UTAH L. REV. 47, 51–55 (2010); Henry J. Steiner, *Ideals and Counter-Ideals in the Struggle over Autonomy Regimes for Minorities*, 66 NOTRE DAME L. REV. 1539, 1551–55 (1991).

faith as one sees fit without any societal limits or oversight can be, and sometimes is, interpreted as an endorsement of total normative relativism, of "freedom for belief from all external examination and criticism."[62] Such unrestricted freedom permits religious individuals and groups to isolate themselves and avoid engaging with and negotiating with the societies in which they are situated. If active suppression of religious freedom causes faith communities to turn inward and isolate themselves as an expression of affirmative hostility and opposition to society, unrestricted religious freedom can have the same result due to the irrelevance of societal norms and values to religious practitioners.[63]

Isolationism born of pluralistic indifference to religion can result in religious extremism in much the same way as can draconian restrictions on religious freedom. If actively suppressing religious freedom causes faith communities to turn inward and isolate themselves as an expression of affirmative hostility and opposition to society, unrestricted religious freedom can have the same result due to the irrelevance of societal norms and values to religious practitioners that can do as they will within their own communities. When faith traditions are freed from the need to engage society, there is no way for either secular societies or religious communities to seriously examine and evaluate religious expressions, or to distinguish between positive and harmful constructions of religious values and practices. In extremely pluralistic environments, society cannot control or critique its own religious communities or cultures for fear of violating secular commitments to religious freedom. Likewise, religious communities themselves, thusly disengaged from dialectical tension with outside norms and values, lack any external yardstick or alternative sources of truths to help guide the development of religious expression. In such a neutral environment, religious practices and cultures that promote extreme, black-and-white visions of the world and human experience can develop easily and uncritically.[64] This is especially true in the contemporary online world where sensational extremism is popular currency, dangerous, anti-societal

62. Roger Trigg, *On Religious Freedom and Religious Extremism* (Sept. 9, 2011), The Religious Freedom Project, The Berkley Center for Religion, Peace, and World Affairs, https://berkleycenter.georgetown.edu/essays/roger-trigg-on-religious-freedom-and-religious-extremism.

63. *See* Gedicks, *supra* note 61, at 51–55; Ayelet Shachar, Multicultural Jurisdiction: Cultural Differences and Women's Rights 81–85 (2001).

64. For more on this from a Jewish view, see Aharon Lichtenstein. *Torah and General Culture: Confluence and Conflict*, *in* Judaism's Encounter with Other Cultures (Jacob J. Schacter ed., 1997). This work is not the place to review this extensive literature that has been amply shown to be true and has been the focus of much work by the eminent Dr. Martin Marty of the University of Chicago.

religious views and practices can be promoted, spread, and take hold with relative ease. If societies grant too much freedom and autonomy to religious individuals and communities to practice whatever faiths they see fit, these kinds of extreme religious views can take hold and thrive without internal or external checks.

In either case, religious isolationism has deleterious effects on society. When religions turn inward and become at best indifferent and at worst hostile to their host societies, the broader society must contend with constituent individuals and communities that actively oppose its norms, values, and way of life from within. In some cases, extreme and isolationist religious groups who see stark contradictions between societal standards and their own faith-based values may turn to violence in order to express outrage or bring about substantive change to societal norms.

In addition to its societal ills, isolationism of this kind is also bad for religion and for religious communities and individuals. In basic, materialistic terms, isolationist religious groups most often find themselves at the fringes of society, and this socioeconomic marginalization goes along with crime, poverty, and lack of advancement. Moreover, isolationist extremism is often harmful to more moderate segments of broader faith communities who are often unfairly identified with more puritan elements by concerned but poorly informed members of society at large. Perhaps most important, the kinds of religious extremism and isolationism that tend to result from either severe restriction on religious freedom or unmitigated pluralism have negative impacts on the integrity and viability of religious traditions themselves. To remain meaningful and persuasive, religions must offer their adherents convincing and helpful accounts of real world experiences and needs. Religious teachings must engage the world around them, and must appreciate the needs and experiences of their members, in order to remain vital. Faith traditions cannot do this, however, from positions of isolation and puritan dogmatism. When religious traditions engage the outside world, they are forced to self-examine, evolve, grow, and respond to real world contexts. These negative processes tend to produce more robust, more nuanced, and more sophisticated religious ideas that help faith traditions remain relevant while also preserving continuity with their origins.

If both extreme suppression of religious freedom and unmitigated multicultural pluralism tend to encourage religious groups to become more isolated and extreme, it appears that a more viable approach to dealing with religious minorities within a broader society should chart a middle path. Societies that seek integrated rather than isolationist religious minorities impose on faith communities some expectations of conformity without severely restricting the ability of religious individuals and groups to maintain their religious convictions and practices. In part, at least, this entails creating a societal environment in which religions have the opportunity and need to actively engage and negotiate with societal norms. Such interactions between the sacred and secular are a key ingredient to promoting the moderation and integration of faith traditions and communities into general society. Religious traditions that must engage with and confront external value systems and modes of living as meaningful and productive ways of experiencing the world must often negotiate tensions between abstract religious doctrines and lived experiences. This tends to produce more moderate and complexly nuanced modes of religious being that balance relations between various sources of truths about the world, society, norms, values, and the human condition.

Thus, instead of seeking to drive religion underground and out of society, society should create frameworks in which religion can exist, operate, and be practiced within society, albeit with some societal oversight. When society allows religion to function and gives religious communities limited authority over their own religious affairs, and the ability to rely on the coercive arm of the state to actualize that delegated authority, then religion will tend to moderate in order to work within that framework. This allows the state to exert some appropriate oversight and control over religion, and helps give an incentive for religious communities to not exert coercion on their own, which would be destabilizing to society and oppressive to individuals. A moderate approach to facilitating religion encourages religious practitioners and communities to make the tradeoff of interpretatively moderating their own practices in order to work within the framework established by secular society. This would not work if the tradeoff demanded is too great so as to expect religious communities to fundamentally change their religion, or do things that they would themselves regard as compromising on the overall integrity of the faith.

Legal frameworks providing for the practice and judicial enforcement of faith-based dispute resolution offer precisely this kind of environment. Religious arbitration gives religious individuals and communities an opportunity to sustain their religious commitments and practices in an effective way. Without a legally enforceable dispute resolution forum, individuals would be unable to rely on their co-religionists upholding their own religious obligations in cases of conflict arising from co-religionist commerce. Religious individuals and communities would then be compelled to abandon their traditions and instead abide by secular laws enforced by secular courts with enforcement powers. Instead of turning to the courts, however, some deeply committed adherents would simply turn inward to construct their own informally coercive religious communities beyond the reach of state oversight. By providing religious parties with the ability to resolve their disputes according to religious norms in ways that will be legally enforceable, societies provide religious communities with a powerful incentive to remain part of the general society on whose judicial enforcement powers any such religious arbitration scheme would rely.

Religious arbitration regimes do not give religious commentaries and faith-based dispute resolution tribunals full reign to do as they please. Secular arbitration law sets important procedural and substantive benchmarks that must be met if religious practitioners wish to have the courts respect and enforce religious arbitration decisions. These requirements enshrine many of the most important societal commitments to procedural justice, while also limiting the extent to which substantive religious norms can be actualized when those depart too sharply from prevailing secular policy commitments.

Most important, these requirements induce religious groups interested in developing legally enforceable faith-based arbitration to engage in a conversation with the demands set by societal norms and values. The examples of the Beth Din of America in the United States and the Muslim Arbitration Tribunal in the United Kingdom illustrate how religious communities can adapt and reinterpret their own traditions in order to comply with important societal demands. These Jewish and Muslim dispute resolution tribunals do not punish ritual offenses or use coercive methods, and generally afford parity to litigants and witnesses regardless of their gender or faith. Traditionally, Judaism and Islam imposed corporal and other penalties for religious offenses, policed the boundaries of the religious community, and distinguished between men and women, and between members of their own or other faiths in the courtroom. However, the BDA and MAT, as well as other religious arbitration organizations have subtly adapted their religious laws to comply with secular requirements. Arguably, it is precisely because secular societies have given religious communities the opportunity to benefit from judicially enforced arbitration, and because they have done this judiciously—imposing only the most necessary limits on religious practice where it conflicts with societal norms—that many faith traditions have been willing to adapt and integrate in order to take advantage of these legal benefits.

Ultimately, the prevailing legal scheme that permits religious arbitration within certain necessary limits helps encourage religious minorities to become more integrated into the general society, rather than more isolated. This is good for society, which avoids the problem of separatist religious groups with antagonistic attitudes toward society and the state. This is also good for religious communities, which are afforded the immediate benefit of being able to voluntarily practice their religious norms in a way that will be legally enforced. Religious communities also gain from their interactions with the norms and values of society, with which they must negotiate on religious terms in order to comply with societal demands and enjoy the benefit of judicial respect for their internal dispute resolution mechanisms.

E. SECULAR RECOGNITION OF RELIGIOUS ARBITRATION PROMOTES VALUE SHARING THAT ENRICHES PUBLIC POLICY AND DISCOURSE

The final section of this chapter suggests that religious arbitration is important because it helps faith traditions participate in important societal discussions on law, policy, ethics, and other normative concerns. Although engagement between religious and secular norms and values through a system of faith-based dispute resolution helps moderate religion by encouraging it to contend with outside norms and values, this engagement is a two-way street. Just as religion stands to learn and grow from its integration with society, secular society can benefit from its interactions with religion. In liberal, pluralistic societies it is important to have numerous voices and traditions as part of any deliberative public discourse.[65] Religious traditions, no more or less than various ideological, philosophical, cultural, ethnic, or political frames of reference, are important perspectives that ought to be included in such conversations.

Many scholars have noted the important role that religious beliefs and practices have historically played in shaping legal traditions broadly, as well as specific legal norms and principles. Harold Berman's seminal works, *Law and Revolution* and *Law and Revolution II*, traces such influences in the Western legal tradition from the papal revolution of Gregory VII in the late 1000s, through the Protestant reformation and accompanying upheavals of the sixteenth and seventeenth centuries. In both cases, religious teachings exerted substantial influence on how law was thought about and practiced.[66] Indeed, James Brundage has shown that the legal profession itself, and the formalization of secular legal practice, can be traced to the

65. *See* Michael A. Helfand, *Religious Arbitration and the New Multiculturalism: Negotiating Conflicting Legal Orders*, 86 N.Y.U. L. Rev. 1231, 1274–75 (2011).
66. *See* Harold J. Berman, Law and Revolution II: The Impact of the Protestant Reformations on the Western Legal Traditions (1983).

university-educated and trained judges and counsels of medieval canon law courts.[67]

These religious influences on the development of law are in many ways just another instance of the phenomenon that Alan Watson has described as "legal transplants."[68] Watson's central claim is that most changes in most legal systems occur through a process of transplantation or borrowing from existing concepts in other legal systems. The norms and principles of a legal system evolve and change, often slowly, in response to the real-world experiences of practitioners and actors within that system. Oftentimes, laws develop through a process of trial and error. Lawmakers pass laws, and judges and other officials interpret and apply laws in ways designed to achieve desired ends under changing social, economic, and political conditions. Sometimes these efforts work well, but other times they fail to attain the intended results. In the latter case, the law goes through continued development through legislative and judicial processes in order to find the correct normative formula for realizing political ends through legal means. During this process of legal change, rather than try to develop effective solutions to new problems from the ground up, legal officials often look, explicitly or implicitly, at analogous experiences of other societies and legal systems with using similar policies. Laws and doctrines that work well to address similar problems in other systems may be adapted and adopted to deal with contemporaneous concerns.

Secular legal systems do this with each other, to be sure. But secular law also borrows from religious legal traditions. This is especially the case in those areas of the law that most obviously touch on ethical and moral concerns such as medical ethics; the law of war, recently including treatment of prisoners and terror suspects; proper treatment of criminal defendants and issues related to criminal punishment; and assisted suicide.[69] Powerful streams of Western legal thought, especially in recent centuries, have sought to largely divorce legal jurisprudence from ethical or moral concerns.[70] Although there are obvious benefits to this, it does mean that conventional legal tools are often inadequate to deal with many of the knottier problems of contemporary life that we sense must be legally regulated, but

67. *See* JAMES A. BRUNDAGE, THE MEDIEVAL ORIGINS OF THE LEGAL PROFESSION: CANONISTS, CIVILIANS, AND COURTS (2008).

68. *See* ALAN WATSON, LEGAL TRANSPLANTS: AN APPROACH TO COMPARATIVE LAW (1974).

69. *See generally* BORIS I. BITTKER ET AL., RELIGION AND THE STATE IN AMERICAN LAW 111–48 (2015).

70. *See* Harry W. Jones, *Law and Morality in the Perspective of Legal Realism*, 61 COLUM. L. REV. 799 (1961).

which have serious moral and ethical dimensions. Lawmakers and scholars have therefore often drawn on religious traditions—especially religious traditions grounded firmly in religio-legal practice—for insights into how to reasonably address these issues in balanced ways. It is often erroneously thought that religious legal traditions view such issues in stark black-and-white terms unsuited to nuanced modern jurisprudence. However, this is largely untrue. Religions that do religious law in a serious way have been grappling with these kinds of questions for centuries, and it is precisely because they have dealt with them flexibly and pragmatically while also hewing closely to the demands of their ecumenical norms and values that these systems have lasted and retained the allegiance of their adherents for as long as they have.

A particularly fine, if mundane example of how secular law interactions with religious legal traditions can serve as vehicles for legal development is offered by Lynn Stout. Without drawing on specific religious doctrines, Professor Stout argues in part that law can and should be used as a means of encouraging law-abiding citizens to act with conscience.[71] This is an idea found in numerous nomos-centric faith traditions. In a forthcoming book, Chaim Saiman argues that many areas of traditional Jewish law exist in large part in order to teach and inculcate certain values and attitudes that Judaism values.[72] Likewise, important strains of Islamic legal theory maintain that although observing Islamic law is imperative, Muslims lose sight of the ultimate purposes of religious norms if they fail to use the performance of ritual imperatives to impact their characters, attitudes, and ways of interacting with others. Stout incorporates such ideas about using law to effect good human attitudes and actions into proposals for innovative approaches to tort and contracts, as well as criminal law and punishment.

Ultimately, reasonable people can differ on the propriety and advisability of using lessons gleaned from religious law traditions to further develop secular legal norms. However, from a liberal perspective, there is another important societal value in encouraging robust interactions between functioning religious law systems and secular jurisprudence. In short, societies work better, progress faster, and innovate more creatively when public discourses on important issues of law and policy are more diverse. This claim was famously made by Scott Paige in his 2008 book, *The Difference: How the Power of Diversity Creates Better Groups, Firms, Schools, and Societies*.[73]

71. *See* Lynn Stout, Cultivating Conscience: How Good Laws Make Good People (2011).

72. *See* Chaim Saiman, *Halakha*: The Rabbinic Idea of Law (forthcoming 2017).

73. *See* Scott E. Paige, The Difference: How the Power of Diversity Creates Better Groups, Firms, Schools, and Societies (2008).

Paige's arguments are important for two reasons. First, his methodology is empirical and quantitative; his argument is not that societies should be more diverse for moral or philosophical reasons, but that in fact groups that partake of diversity and reach decisions based on input from multiple perspectives are in fact more successful in the long run.[74] Second, and relatedly, Paige's claims are pragmatic. His study seeks to discover how organizations can be more productive and successful, and his research-based conclusion is that they can be so by including individuals and groups from very different perspectives.[75]

Based on this, it seems advisable for liberal societies to facilitate the kind of diversity that will enable numerous robust and active cultures, traditions, and points of view to put forward their own insights and ways of thinking about societal issues in public conversations. In particular, and based on the history of religious traditions contributing to the development of secular law, societies should enable faith-based communities to practice and develop their religious practices so that these groups can and will seek to weave themselves into a more diverse—and thus more productive—societal tapestry.

A robust secular law framework for the recognition and enforcement of religious arbitration processes helps promote these societal goods. By enabling religious communities to resolve co-religionist disputes through the application of traditional religious laws to contemporary problems, secular law can contribute to the construction of strong religious communities capable of participating in important public discourses. As discussed earlier, this model of dealing with religious minorities can encourage religious individuals and groups to integrate into society.[76] In this integration process, religion will pick up cultural norms and values from the general society, and will evolve and adapt in order to strike an acceptable balance between these standards and its own traditions. As religion picks up and synthesizes aspects of general culture, however, it also injects its own perspectives, teachings, and practices on important societal issues into the public discourse. As religion adapts and evolves in order to integrate into society, society also adapts and evolves to integrate with religion.

On a more micro level, a robust practice of faith-based arbitration encourages religious leaders and decision-makers to think hard about the best ways to resolve real-world problems using traditional religio-legal sources and methods. This not only helps religious traditions develop more

74. *Id.*
75. *Id.*
76. *See supra* Chapter Ten (D).

nuanced and complex doctrines and practices that are responsive to contemporary issues, but empowers religious groups to develop the kinds of creative and innovative ways of approaching these problems that can serve as instructive models for secular law and policy. Both of these positive outcomes would likely be retarded if religious communities were not given opportunities to resolve co-religionist disputes through faith-based arbitration. In that scenario, much of religion would remain highly abstract, dogmatic, and removed from providing practical answers to contemporary concerns. By providing a framework for religious groups to address complex problems through a religious lens, however, secular law can encourage faith communities to tackle developing issues head-on, thereby strengthening religious groups internally and providing a valuable repository of wisdom and experience upon which general society can draw as it works to address similar concerns through law and policy.

F. CONCLUSION

Precisely because as a society we can no longer agree on a single definition for what were once commonly held legal sacraments—and maybe in a federal system such as the United States, we never really had one—religious arbitration is a fundamental tool for allowing many different and competing parts of society to flourish. For example, if traditionalists and progressives are to reach a workable détente on divisive questions of marriage equality, it will not be because all agree with a single vision about who should marry, what a civil union looks like, or what equality in marriage means. Rather, it will be because the government will increasingly move to the contract model of unions, in which its secular model is merely the default model and people build their own model of marriage with prenuptial agreements.[77]

77. At least one province in Canada has gone in a different direction, prohibiting the private arbitration of all family law matters according to any substantive law other than that of the Canadian Province. A decade ago, Ontario considered the prospect of private arbitration by Islamic tribunals in accordance with religious law under general arbitration statutes. A report produced by the former attorney general recommended authorizing religious arbitration in family and inheritance law, subject to forty-six proposed "safeguards." *See* MARION BOYD, DISPUTE RESOLUTION IN FAMILY LAW: PROTECTING CHOICE, PROMOTING INCLUSION 133–42 (2004), available at http://www.attorneygeneral.jus.gov.on.ca/english/about/pubs/boyd/fullreport.pdf. The report generated significant political backlash; ultimately, Ontario's Arbitration Act, S.O. 1991, c. 17 (Can.), and Family Law Act, R.S.O. 1990, c. F.3 (Can.), were amended to require that family arbitration be "conducted exclusively in accordance with the law of Ontario or of another Canadian jurisdiction." Family Statute Law Amendment Act, S.O. 2006, c. 1 (Can.). "Family arbitration" was defined as "arbitration that . . . deals

What will faith-based communities do? They will write their own contracts of marriage, or even appeal to secular authorities to recognize that marriages performed by their own clergy have different rules and ought to have a different secular law.[78] One group's contracts will be different from another's, which will be different still from those of others. Indeed, within the Jewish tradition there might be more than one model of contract that people can choose to enter. That is the joy of contracts: they are almost endlessly customizable.

Furthermore, the "Rise of Contract" as a fundamental basis of liberty allows for the proliferation of a wide array of religious arbitration tribunals across the United States. Of course, there have to be limitations: operating within the context of a secular legal system means that arbitration panels that enforce religio-legal norms must accept that religious principles will not excuse religious parties from criminal and other forms of liability under the relevant secular legal system.[79] In order to garner the respect of the secular justice system by genuinely respecting secular law, arbitration institutions must educate their communities on the necessity of adhering to general legal norms.[80]

So too, religious arbitration cannot address matters that are not fundamentally contractual between the parties. Occasionally, such exclusive, binding authority is not limited to criminal matters; it is found in certain civil matters, such as bankruptcy law, as well. According to federal

with matters that could be dealt with in a marriage contract, separation agreement, cohabitation agreement or paternity agreement." *Id.* § 1(a).

78. This is exactly the history of the New York Jewish Divorce Law, where the state of New York enacted a special provision of the law regulating marriages done by clergy who have specific requirements for divorce. For more on this, see BROYDE, *supra* note 31, at 138.

79. *See* S.D. v. M.J.R., 2 A.3d 412, 422–23 (N.J. Super. Ct. App. Div. 2010), a New Jersey case that evoked nationwide criticism of Islamic law and the relationship between Muslim religious norms and the American justice system. This case illustrates the importance of Islamic arbitral courts' teaching their communities about the importance of following American law, even when it prohibits acts that may be permitted under religious law. It is worth noting that this case was affirmed on appeal.

80. Based on this, one suspects that communities such as the Christian Domestic Discipline community will ultimately be subject to significant legal sanction over the use of force. *See* Welcome to CDD, Christian Domestic Discipline, http://christiandomesticdiscipline.com/home.html (last visited Nov. 25, 2014). Indeed, these communities seem aware of this issue and seek to address it through general consent. See "Nonconsensual" Consent? A Guideline to Consent in CDD, Christian Domestic Discipline, http://christiandomesticdiscipline.com/nonconsensualconsent.html (last visited Nov. 25, 2014). But, there is ample legal precedent for the idea that the state-sanctioned monopoly on force—particularly in the area of domestic violence—will not be set aside without a much more particular and detailed consent by the woman being hit.

law, after a party has filed for bankruptcy, there is an automatic stay in place, and no one may interfere with or seek to collect a debt without the bankruptcy court's permission.[81] Private arbitration panels are bound by this limitation, and rulings that violate the automatic stay will simply be disregarded.[82]

But this will be the exception and not the rule. In most areas, the law should not grant unique and exclusive authority to the state. If anything, the trend is to move further and deeper into contract and less and less into fixed, sacramental models set by the government that one cannot opt-out of at all.

81. *See* 11 U.S.C. § 362 (2010).

82. *See* Michael A Helfand, *Fighting for the Debtor's Soul: Regulating Religious Commercial Conduct*, 19 GEO. MASON L. REV. 157, 187–88 (2011).

CHAPTER 11

Concluding Thoughts

As a general idea, this book is supportive of the idea of religious arbitration. Putting aside religious arbitration of matters that can never be adjudicated by a civil court, such as insular church doctrinal disputes (which are outside the framework of this book), secular society benefits in many ways from allowing religious communities and their members to contractually resolve their commercial and family law disputes. Such religious arbitration is more accurate within its cultural norms, more respectful of autonomy rights of individuals, and more sympathetic to the values of a multicultural society. Each of these values represents important American ideals. In addition, this is part of the religious freedom that is fundamental to American law and culture.

Of course, secular society must regulate such arbitration in three very important ways. First, it must make sure that people are voluntarily agreeing to such arbitration in a way that shows a true consent to religious arbitration. Second, society must make sure that such arbitrations are limited to monetary matters and do not tread on the unique police powers of the general society. Third, it must make sure that procedural due process is followed in arbitration hearings. Related to that is that religious arbitrators, to be successful, must integrate the norms of the secular society that intermingles with their own religious community.

As America transitions from a society in which there is a dominant religion—Christianity—and a dominant cultural norm—the Judeo-Christian ethic—to something else, the question is what should society do with those groups that still adhere to the old traditions? In a slightly different vein, one way to think about the problems in this book is whether the winner of the cultural wars in the twenty-first century should vanquish the losers (as winners of cultural wars have historically done), or should our America society seek a different peace to the most recent cultural war? If a different peace is found, maybe the winner-take-all cultural wars of the past will not have to be fought again?

This book contains the germ of an answer to this question. It argues that one of the basic ways the Founding Fathers crafted a barrier against imposing imperialism was through divided power, and this approach should be employed again to prevent cultural wars and values imposition. This insight is the idea of federated justice. America is almost unique worldwide in that power is very much decentralized. The federal government has three co-equal branches and even when it is united, the fifty states—each with its three branches—have independent power that cannot be usurped by the national government. Liberty in America is acquired by diffuse power. Religious arbitration continues this aspect of diffusion, which is common in America.

As this iteration of the culture war ends, what should our society do with people and religious groups that refuse to surrender? The answer to that question will set the tone for much societal discourse for the next many decades. This work proposes that allowing such communities—made up at this moment of Evangelical Christians, Orthodox Jews, newly immigrant Muslims, traditional Mormons, and many other smaller subgroups scattered nationwide—to form their own communities, where they use the limited tools of religious arbitration to adjudicate disputes between members of their community who consented to such adjudication, should be encouraged. Of course, as this book has noted many times, such arbitration should be confined to financial matters and maybe child custody. Secular society must maintain a monopoly on its police powers, and must take steps to ensure that religious adjudication is limited to people who genuinely consented.

Religious arbitration is an aspect of liberty. Like all sources of power in a balanced system, it has to be subject to checks and balances, but when reasonably checked, the central idea of this book is that robust religious arbitration is a valuable tool for ensuring democratic liberty, accurate adjudication, and moderate religions, each of which is needed to ensure a viable secular society. People of a common faith or idea are entitled to order their lives as they see fit by crafting a legally binding private religious adjudication process that serves to regulate many aspects of the law governing their family, commercial, and private lives.

Allowing this religious arbitration not only serves the best interest of the religious community, but of secular society as well. The United States will be better for it.

One final observation is worth noting. All of this need not be so: the law need not be this friendly to religious groups. Some secular legal regimes leave no breathing room for crafting private agreements that go against secular norms. One province in Canada has already legislatively prohibited private adjudication in family law matters[1] and France, following the principles of *laicite* (the secular legal norms in France) is throttling communal religious values.[2] It is worth recognizing that it is possible to suffocate communal religious liberty without denying personal religious freedom (which no democracy can do). When the substantive law is secular and the arbitration law resists the application of legal rules selected by the parties contractually in private law, religious communities can no longer function. Of course, France does not suffocate individual religious liberty but in insisting that every dispute between two or more people be resolved without reference to the religious rules that the parties wished to govern them, this religious community is vastly diminished.

Indeed, this approach is increasingly cited even within the American framework, not specifically about religious arbitration, but about arbitration generally, and it has the possibility of vastly curtailing religious arbitration also. Arbitration can—as Justice Cardozo noted a century ago—be prohibited (although that would require a repeal of the Federal Arbitration Act, and is unlikely). But even without repeal, arbitration can be drastically curtailed by limiting it to a forum selected by the parties and not allowing the selection of an alternative legal framework. For example, in August 2016, a panel of the United States Court of Appeals for the Ninth Circuit insisted simply that:

> The FAA does not mandate the enforcement of contract terms that waive substantive federal rights. Thus, when an arbitration contract professes the waiver of a substantive federal right, the FAA's saving clause prevents a conflict between the statutes by causing the FAA's enforcement mandate to yield.[3]

1. Family Statute Law Amendment Act, S.O. 2006, c. 1 (Can.).
2. *See generally* Knowledge Resources, Georgetown Univ.: Berkley Ctr. for Religion, Peace & World Affairs, http://berkleycenter.georgetown.edu/resources/countries/france (last visited Nov. 25, 2014).
3. Morris v. Ernst & Young, LLP (No. 13-16599) Filed Aug. 22, 2016 at https://cdn.ca9.uscourts.gov/datastore/opinions/2016/08/22/13-16599.pdf at page 18.

This statement—said only in the context of labor law, but easily understood as a general principle in future cases—argues that, although arbitration should be allowed, our nation should not allow vibrant choice-of-law provisions (as such Islamic, Jewish, or French law) when they curtail rights granted by the civil law. All selections of alternative legal systems do this: Jewish law curtails the right to adultery, French law curtails the right to a trial by jury, and so on. At a most basic level, every legal system is incompatible with every other legal system, if the law wants it to be, and bold statements such as this argue for the abolition of vibrant arbitration, and particularly religious arbitration with its very different laws and principles. It is easy to understand how states could follow this and limit arbitration so that all arbitrations have to follow state law as well, at least when the matter is subject to secular law. In this model, arbitration is merely an alternative procedural model of court, but cannot have alternative rules. Religious law will always violate such a framework for arbitration.

This could be the counter-revolution to the ideas found in this book: a rule that arbitrators must completely and directly follow the law of the United States in every jot and tittle would destroy religious arbitration by depriving people of the right to choose to be governed by their own religious law. Religious arbitration that is not allowed to reach substantively different results than that which secular courts would have reached is of little value in supporting religious community.

This does not abolish arbitration, but it certainly does abolish parts of religious arbitration, and is, in this writer's view, a very bad idea. It will limit the variety and depth of religious communal expression in the United States and diminish our republic.

America now has a wonderful status quo: it is a very secular state with very vibrant religious communities existing side by side in peace, so long as all parties respect the distinction between public and private law and allow contractual arbitration law to operate under any substantive legal rubric the parties agree to. New York State is an excellent example. New York is widely considered one of the most liberal states in the Union, and yet has the most vibrant Jewish, Islamic, and Catholic communities, with many different religious arbitration tribunals. Furthermore, New York uniquely accommodates Jewish and Islamic marriage law with special statutory provisions.[4] Liberal and secular Western democracy is compatible with

4. As noted in Michael J. Broyde, Marriage, Divorce, and the Abandoned Wife in Jewish law: A Conceptual Understanding of the Problems in America 161–62 (2001).

religious community. Arbitration contracts are an essential part of what makes for compatibility.

In sum, we in America live in a society in which religious traditions—Judeo-Christian or otherwise—have receded into the background of our legal culture. The legal norms that once reflected those values are being replaced by secular principles, the most fundamental of which seems to be contract law. What this means is that our law should be increasingly open to the idea that people can structure their relationships around a contract, rather than around sacrament. And the default model does not need to be the only model—customization can be allowed and even expected. Religious arbitration is a vital part of that multicultural salad.

INDEX OF CASES

INDEX

Printed in the USA/Agawam, MA
October 23, 2017

661037.002